SERGEI O. PROKOFIEFF, born in Moscow in 1954, studied painting and art history at the Moscow School of Art. He encountered anthroposophy in his youth, and soon made the decision to devote his life to it. He has been active as an author and lecturer since 1982, and in 1991 he co-founded the Anthroposophical Society in Russia. In Easter 2001 he became a member of the Executive Council of the General Anthroposophical Society in Dornach. *Anthroposophy and The Philosophy of Freedom* is his twenty-first book to appear in English translation.

CW01019710

By the same author:

Anthroposophy and
The Philosophy of Freedom

Anthroposophy and its Method of Cognition

The Christological and Cosmic-Human Dimension of
The Philosophy of Freedom

SERGEI O. PROKOFIEFF

TEMPLE LODGE

Translated from German by Maria St Goar

Temple Lodge Publishing
Hillside House, The Square
Forest Row, RH18 5ES

www.templelodge.com

Published by Temple Lodge 2009

Originally published in German under the title *Anthroposophie und 'Die Philosophie der Freiheit'* by Verlag am Goetheanum, Dornach, in 2006

A catalogue record for this book is available from the British Library

ISBN 978 1 906999 02 5

Cover by Andrew Morgan
Typeset by DP Photosetting, Neath, West Glamorgan
Printed and bound by Cromwell Press Limited, Trowbridge, Wiltshire

Contents

I asked Rudolf Steiner: 'What will remain of
your work thousands of years from now?'
He replied: 'Nothing but *The Philosophy of Freedom*.
But in it everything else is contained.
If one realizes the act of freedom described there,
one can discover the whole
content of anthroposophy.'

From the conversation between Rudolf
Steiner and Walter Johannes Stein
Den Haag, April 1922

'One who is willing can indeed find the basic principles
of anthroposophy in my *Philosophy of Freedom*.'

Rudolf Steiner, 11 June 1923

Translator's Note

In this book some of the quotations from the Bible are taken from the Revised Standard Version (RSV); those followed by the letters JM are from Jon Madsen's translation of the New Testament (published by Floris Books, Edinburgh).

Unless a quotation is followed by RSV or JM, my approach is as follows. I first read the German original, then compare it to the King James version or Martin Luther's classic German. I may then come up with my own composite of the quotation—whatever comes closest to what Sergei O. Prokofieff is trying to clarify in his text. (He sometimes uses the Russian Orthodox version, which on occasion is superior because it is closer to the original Hebrew or Greek.)

All emphases in the quotes, if not noted otherwise, are by Sergei O. Prokofieff.

Preface

The present work was originally begun as an extension and elaboration of the brochure *What is Anthroposophy?*, published recently at the Goetheanum Publishing House. In the process of working on it further the contents increased so much that something quite independent has come about in the end.

The attempt is being made to demonstrate how anthroposophy, the central stream of esoteric Christianity, is inseparably connected even from its roots of cognitions with what forms its very centre, namely the death and resurrection of Christ Jesus.

Anthroposophy is today essentially called upon to show mankind how fundamentally Christianity differs from all other world religions, for they are without exception religions of wisdom. Accordingly, at their core they contain a particular revelation of wisdom that in most instances was compiled into book form: the Vedas for the Indians; the *Bhagavadgita* for the followers of Krishna; the Buddha-discourses for Buddhists; the Old Testament and the Talmud for the Hebrews; the Koran for Muslims. For Christianity, on the other hand, the wisdom that does indwell it too is not its determining feature. Its fountainhead—as attested to by the Gospels—is above all the earthly life of Christ Jesus that culminates in a unique deed, the Mystery of Golgotha. Thus, Christianity is not a religion of wisdom but of a deed.

From the very beginning it was the Apostle Paul who emphasized this most emphatically: 'If Christ has not been raised, then our preaching is in vain and your faith is in vain' (1 Cor. 15:14). Here the word 'preaching' points to Christianity's content of wisdom and the word 'faith' to an inner relationship of the human being to Christ Jesus.

Rudolf Steiner likewise points in the following words to this principal feature of Christianity. 'What came into the world with Christianity should be viewed not only as a new theory but as something real, factual . . . For the most important thing is not what Christ Jesus taught but what he gave to humanity. His Resurrection is a birth-process of a new member of human nature; of an imperishable body . . . This is nothing less than the greatest sacrifice that could be brought by the Christ Entity to Earth evolution!' (GA 131, 11 October 1911.)

Through this deed by the Christ, the creation of the 'imperishable body' in His Resurrection and as a result of that the redemption of the human 'I', awareness of which is dependent on the form of the physical body, the Mystery of Golgotha has a direct link to every human being on earth inasmuch as they are 'I'-bearers. Through the deed on Golgotha the new future human nature was initiated; the whole of World evolution, from Ancient Saturn to Vulcan, was bound up in a higher unity. Moreover the foundation was laid for the Tenth Hierarchy of freedom and love that is to originate out of humanity. This is why Rudolf Steiner could say: 'While Christianity was a religion at its beginning, Christianity is greater than any religion! Christianity is even greater than the religious principle itself.' (GA 102, 24 March 1908.) This is because the Mystery of Golgotha gave Earth its higher meaning and with that the possibility of its entire future evolution. For according to Rudolf Steiner's spiritual-scientific research, Christ's death on the cross and His subsequent union with the earth became at the same time the birth of the new sun in the universe as seed of the future cosmos of love. And this event has decisive significance not only for human beings but for all the gods (hierarchies) as well.

It can also be said that just as Christianity differs from all other religions in the world because in its very nature it is not a religion in the traditional sense, so anthroposophy is completely different (connecting as it does today directly to the Mystery of Golgotha) from all world views of the present day. And the pivotal point of its divergence is its relationship to freedom. For man's true freedom, on which rests the future of every one of us, is embedded only in Christianity. All other religions possess freedom merely in limited form. In Judaism it is the Law that is all important; in Islam the 'Will of God' dominates; in the eastern religions it is mainly a matter of liberation from all earthly concerns rather than true freedom.

Now, freedom in its most radical form, as delineated by Rudolf Steiner in his early work, is the only way that bestows full meaning on love. Love then manifests as the highest creative power of the universe, a power out of which the new cosmic creation will eventually come into being through the free actions of human beings.

As had earlier been shown in the brochure *What is Anthroposophy?*, anthroposophy is not merely Christian because Rudolf Steiner communicated so much about the nature of the Christ, of the Mystery of Golgotha, about the Gospels and facts out of the life of Christ Jesus unknown until then, but because anthroposophy's methodology of cognition is itself Christian. This in turn signifies that this cognitive method is founded on and inseparable from the central Christian Mystery, the Mystery of the Resurrection.

Rudolf Steiner laid the foundations for this method of research in his book *The Philosophy of Freedom* (1894), where, in accordance with his own words, the 'seed' for the whole of the presently appearing anthroposophy can be found (GA 78, 3 September 1921). This is why any attempt to point out the Christian nature of the anthroposophical method of cognition must lead inevitably to a perusal of this work.

Only a thorough examination of the deeply Christian roots of this book can throw a new light not just on the spiritual sources of anthroposophy as a 'science of resurrection', but likewise on the whole importance of *The Philosophy of Freedom* for modern Christian esotericism. Not merely does the central position of this book in the spiritual history of the Occident become manifest but also its truly cosmic-human dimension.

A further reason that led to the origin of the present work was to show how the modern scientific method of research (anchored as it is in *The Philosophy of Freedom*), a method that Rudolf Steiner later extended to the contents of the whole spiritual world, can be understood as the direct presence and contemporary spiritual activity of the Christ Impulse within humanity's evolution. For in this book we deal with nothing less than the founding of a new consciousness that will be the consciousness of future mankind, a humanity that has attained the objective of earthly development. This new consciousness originates out of the living experience of the resurrection forces, first in the process of cognition itself and then in the free creative activity of man out of the power of love. This is why one can designate this new consciousness as the Christ consciousness in the truest sense of the word.

In conclusion it should be pointed out that the above-mentioned brochure is a suitable introduction to this work's content and can significantly aid the reader to better understand its content.

Sergei Prokofieff
Goetheanum, Easter 2005

1. Method of Cognition in Anthroposophy

In the first chapter of the book *The Stages of Higher Knowledge* (GA 12), Rudolf Steiner speaks about four stages of cognition in anthroposophy: material (or physical) cognition or knowledge, imaginative cognition, inspirative and intuitive cognition. Following this, he points out that, properly speaking, the first stage includes four more levels or four factors: '(1) the *object* that makes an impression on the senses; (2) the *picture* a person produces of this object; (3) the *concept* through which a person arrives at a mental grasp of an issue or a process; (4) the "*I*" which, based on the impression of the object, forms the picture and concept'. (Emphasis by Rudolf Steiner.)

Based on their further characterization, the first four stages of 'material cognition' can be brought into connection with the following basic concepts of *The Philosophy of Freedom* (GA 4), particularly if their further characterization is considered.

The first stage corresponds to 'perception' [Ger.: *Wahrnehmung*], for only by perceiving with the bodily senses does our first encounter with outward objects occur.

The second stage is the 'mental picture', also called by Rudolf Steiner 'individual concept (or idea)'. It always has a pictorial character. As a further elaboration, the faculty of the 'participative power of discernment' [Ger.: *anschauende Urteilskraft*] belongs here as well. With the aid of such power of discernment, we try in our thinking mentally to partake in nature which creates and works all around us. Goethe describes this discernment as the faculty with which, 'through the viewing of an ever-functioning nature, we become worthy of partaking spiritually in its productions'.[1] This signifies that such a 'participative discernment' unfolds in that region of the soul that lies between outer perception and pure thinking. Above all, here belongs the region of percepts (mental pictures).

The third stage therefore consists in pure thinking that can gradually be intensified to 'intuitive thinking'.[2]

The fourth stage, that of the 'I', corresponds to the 'exceptional state' as described in *The Philosophy of Freedom* in which, through the heightened activity of the 'I' (an activity that brings forth thinking creatively), perception of the 'I' itself can likewise take place. On this stage the 'I' is thus the entity that brings forth thinking and observes it.

From the standpoint of the modern path of initiation, these four stages can furthermore be characterized as follows. At the first stage, that of perception, the spirit disciple must above all intensify his attention in regard to all processes surrounding him.[3] The second stage, that of the picture or mental image (percept), leads him into the broad area of concentration exercises. Then, on the third stage, actual meditating begins for a student of the spirit, the goal of which is attainment of sense-free thinking. Aside from the exercises leading to the higher stages of knowledge, Rudolf Steiner has given many incentives and references in his books as well as in the material from the Esoteric School recently published concerning these three initial stages.

Only when the spirit-disciple has made his thinking sufficiently free of the body through regular meditative practice can he take the risk through further spiritual exercises of making the transition from meditation to actual contemplation of the spiritual world. The latter can happen as a result of the gradual transformation of body-free thinking into a new organ of perception that in time can reach to the experience of imaginations (on Diagram 1 on p. 6, the transition from point 3 through the 'I'-point [4] to point 5). With that the spirit disciple rises to the first stage of supersensible cognition to which, in man's further evolution, the inspirative and intuitive stages are connected.

In the earlier quoted book, *The Stages of Higher Knowledge* (GA 12), Rudolf Steiner describes a process that actually signifies the continuation and intensification of the 'exceptional state'. Here on the stage of imaginative cognition the student of the spirit experiences a variety of colour-shapes that he perceives spiritually, and by beholding them he simultaneously has the feeling that he lives in them and even has a share in their coming into being. This experience in the imaginative world is comparable to the activity of thinking in the exceptional state. In the latter, human beings observe their thinking as they normally do other perceptions, and at the same time they experience themselves completely within this thinking as its creator.

This experience becomes even more powerful in the advanced imaginative beholding that arrives at the border to Inspiration. Now one experiences one's own self with much more intensity than a person who simultaneously beholds *and* produces the imaginative forms and figures of the astral plane. Rudolf Steiner describes this supersensible activity in the following words: 'Yes, one feels the "I" as the sketcher and at the same time as material with which the sketching is being done' (GA 12). It becomes obvious from these words how, in genuine meditative exercise, one can find the path from the exceptional state in thinking into the spiritual world. What begins first in pure thinking continues on and is repeated in an elevated imaginative form already beyond the Threshold so

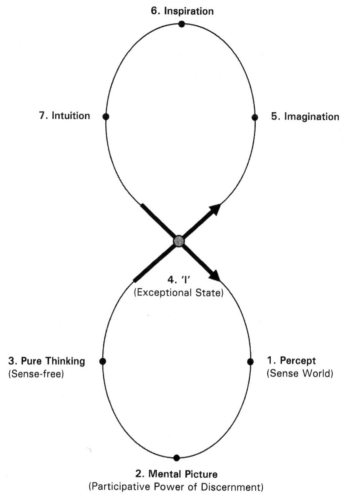

Diagram 1

that a firm bridge comes into being on which thinking consciousness can open itself to objective spiritual perceptions without losing any of its composure.

If one would wish to characterize the exceptional state more pictorially, one could also say: Ordinarily human thinking appears in the image of a spear or arrow that is always directed to the corresponding object of the sense perception. Rudolf Steiner describes this condition of thinking in the following words: 'While I think I do not observe my thinking that I myself produce but the object of thinking that I do not produce' (GA 4). When I direct my thought-activity to thinking itself, and in so doing consciously and willingly produce the exceptional state, my thought-activity is transformed into a chalice that originates out of the activation of will in thinking and then becomes capable of receiving imaginations out of the spiritual world. Cognition of these imaginations can then be experienced as a form of spiritual communion. While this is only the lowest stage of the latter (for full communion does not occur until Intuition is attained), here man already enters upon an inner path on which, through continuing spirit schooling, he arrives at what Rudolf Steiner points out in the last chapter of *Occult Science, an Outline* (GA 13) as follows: 'The path into the spiritual worlds, the first stages of which are described in this book, leads to the "science of the Grail".' The way in which the cognitive path (that begins with the exceptional state) of *The Philosophy of Freedom* leads directly into the essence of the modern Grail Mysteries will be shown in more detail at the end of this book.[4]

Summing up the described stages, they can be depicted as in Diagram 2.

7. Intuition	
6. Inspiration	
5. Imagination	

4. Exceptional State	–	4. Contemplation
3. Intuitive Thinking	–	3. Meditation
2. Percept	–	2. Concentration
1. Perception	–	1. Attentiveness

Diagram 2

Within the modern path of initiation, the four lower stages connect with the three higher ones in this manner and together form a *sevenfoldness*—the lower square and the higher triangle. As a unity on the other hand, the seven stages bear within themselves an important threshold. It is the threshold that on the modern path of initiation consists in rising from 'objective beholding or cognizing' (that represents the starting point of *The Philosophy of Freedom*) to 'cosmic cognizing' (GA 78, 3 September 1921). Rudolf Steiner points this out by saying: 'If we seek a cosmic cognition corresponding to this philosophy of freedom, we must take what we have done here on a more limited basis and expand it by developing the stages of cognition: objective cognizing, Imagination, Inspiration, Intuition' (ibid.).

One can penetrate still more deeply into the inner nature of this sevenfoldness if one brings it to expression in the form of a lemniscate (see Diagram 1, p. 6).

It becomes clear from this diagram how the so-called 'pre-anthroposophical' writings by Rudolf Steiner (above all *The Philosophy of Freedom*) are inseparably connected on the level of the path of cognition with his later anthroposophical works. The first three stages (1 to 3) relate to the insights that, according to Rudolf Steiner, are attainable '*prior* to entry into spiritual experience' (GA 4, emphasis by Rudolf Steiner). The three higher stages (5 to 7) are the main fount of modern spiritual research. In the middle (4) man's 'I-being' is located, which links the two spheres—the upper and lower one—with each other. (A similar linkage of seven elements—three and four—also formed the spiritual basis of the First Goetheanum's ground plan.[5])

The transition from intuitive thinking to conscious cognizing in imaginations (from 3 to 5) occurs through the intensified activity of the 'I' (4). Already in practising intuitive thinking the human being carries out an inner activity that is of a purely spiritual nature. That is why the transition to imaginative perception can take place most surely based on the further development of intuitive thinking. 'As soon as a human being experiences the spiritual world of perceptions, it cannot remain something unfamiliar to him, for already in intuitive thinking we have an experience of a purely spiritual character,' writes Rudolf Steiner in *The Philosophy of Freedom*. However, this experience does not lead by itself to the perceiving of entities and processes of the supersensible world. Initially, intuitive thinking must be re-shaped through inner work of the 'I' into a new organ of perception that can then consciously take hold of imaginations. This transformation comes to pass through the further development of the above-described exceptional state, in which the 'I' experiences itself more and more as an entity that is independent of the physical body and can therefore direct the thinking that has become body-free to the surrounding spiritual world to which it has belonged from the very beginning.

The inner process that occurs here can be traced archetypically in the scene of John's Gospel when Mary Magdalene encounters the resurrected Christ on Easter Sunday. This encounter has three stages. First Mary Magdalene stands weeping before the tomb since she cannot find Jesus. Then she sees the angels and asks them where he might be.[6] Following this—it is the second stage—'she turned' (20:14) and only then she sees the Resurrected One, who to her appears as the gardener and asks her the same question the angels posed to her ('Why are you weeping?'). At this stage the true nature of the Resurrected One still remains hidden to her. She can only perceive of him what corresponds to her own human nature. This is why she sees him as the 'gardener'. Following this comes the third stage. The Resurrected One calls her by name, and with that awakens the powers of her 'I'. Through this strengthening of her forces she can turn once more ('and again she turns', 20:16). Only now can she fully consciously recognize Him. Yet the Resurrected One does not allow her to touch Him.

If one looks from this event at the Turning Point of Time to its replica within a human being who is on the modern path of (inner) schooling, one can rediscover these three stages in that individual's soul. At first, the student finds the tomb of the brain empty because living thinking cannot be found there. Only dead intellectual thinking, itself a corpse, rests there. However, in order to progress further, man must turn his intuitive thinking ability around and 'look back', as it were. This is precisely the nature of the exceptional state, where thinking directs its attention upon itself so as to be able to observe its own activity. At this instant, in so doing, the bringing about of this exceptional state and its observation form a unity. This corresponds at the Turning Point of Time to the moment when Mary Magdalene does not yet recognize the Resurrected Christ but does see Him, even though at first only on her own 'purely human level', as the 'gardener'. The latter is a human being like herself. In this sense, they are equals. In other words, at this stage she can merely behold the human side of the God Man; and yet, although invisibly, Christ is present here. Then comes the third stage: the 'I' gives its thinking a thrust that causes it to turn around once again so as to become a new perceptual organ for the objective spiritual world.[7] In that way the Resurrected Christ in His divine form can be known and seen by the 'I' of man. (In Diagram 1 (on p. 6) the three stages just described correspond to points 3, 4 and 5.)

In the process described here, special significance must be attached to thinking's turning around twice, something that first leads to the exceptional state, and then to perception of the spiritual world. Here too the Gospel is extraordinarily precise. First the process of 'turning back' is mentioned, meaning to reach back to one's own activity, to something that one carries out on one's own and can now observe as well; and then the 'turning back' is referred to that demands a complete inner *transformation* of the human being, a transformation that is necessary for the conscious encounter with Christ.[8]

Today this twofold turning around of thinking leads above all to the experiencing of the Etheric Christ in the world of imaginations. The perception of Him must originate in our age out of transformed thinking. Rudolf Steiner calls it 'intellectual clairvoyance', something that is attained through the transition from intuitive thinking to cognizing in imaginations. Only in this way can the true spiritual world and above all the manifestation of the Christ in etheric form be experienced today. 'Progress then consists of the fact that human beings do not develop higher intellectuality only for themselves but bear it up into the astral world. Through such a process of becoming clairvoyant, the etherically visible Christ can and will appear more and more clearly in the course of the next three millennia to human beings who have advanced in this sense.' (GA 130, 18 November 1911.)

The further ascent into the spiritual world (referring to 6 and 7) takes place through the gradual liberation of feeling and willing from their original state of attachment to the physical body. With this the possibility opens up for the spirit disciple to utilize feeling and willing as new organs of perception in the spiritual world.[9] Just as the transformation of thinking leads to an organ of perception for experiencing the Etheric Christ on the astral plane, so in the same way the transformed feeling leads to perception of His Being as the Greater Guardian of the Threshold on the plane of Devachan. The transformed willing reaches up to the so-called Midnight Hour as the highest point the human soul can reach on its journey between two incarnations. On this highest level the Christ appears to the human soul as the origin of its true 'I' and as Lord of Karma.[10] Viewed cosmologically, this leads the thinking (which has become an organ of perception) into the Moon-sphere, the transformed feeling into the Sun-sphere, and the transformed willing into the starry sphere all the way to the Midnight Hour.

Rudolf Steiner also connects these three great stages of cognition with the possibility of cognizing the three groups of the spiritual hierarchies. Through imaginations reached based on body-free thinking, one recognizes the Third Hierarchy; through Inspiration that originates from body-free feeling, the Second Hierarchy is recognized; through Intuition that springs out of willing which has become body-free, the First Hierarchy is recognized. Only this highest hierarchy possesses the power to master earthly matter itself with its spirit impulses, which are derived from the heights of the Cosmic Midnight Hour, where with their cooperation the future earth lives of human beings are formed (GA 239, 25 May 1924). 'The most powerful First Hierarchy manifests as the force that is spiritually effective in the physical domain. It shapes the physical world into a cosmos. The Third and Second Hierarchy are the ministering beings in all this.' (GA 26.) In this way, their forces can carry out the transition from the highest spiritual sphere all the way to earthly matter, meaning to the world of sense perception (Diagram 3).

The capability to work out of the spirit even into physical matter so that

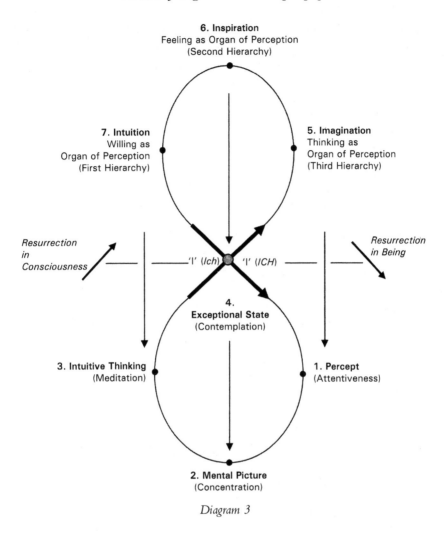

6. Inspiration
Feeling as Organ of Perception
(Second Hierarchy)

7. Intuition
Willing as
Organ of Perception
(First Hierarchy)

5. Imagination
Thinking as
Organ of Perception
(Third Hierarchy)

*Resurrection
in
Consciousness*

'I' (*Ich*)   'I' (*ICH*)

*Resurrection
in Being*

**4.
Exceptional State**
(Contemplation)

3. Intuitive Thinking
(Meditation)

1. Percept
(Attentiveness)

2. Mental Picture
(Concentration)

Diagram 3

matter might serve the spirit allows the First Hierarchy to shape the whole karma of humanity and to imprint it into the physical world in such a manner that man on earth encounters the consequences of his past deeds as a kind of necessity of nature that confronts him.

The last transition that closes the lemniscate points this out: out of the realm of intuitions with which the First Hierarchy rules over matter, it leads into the outer world of perception (from 7 to 1). Such a taking hold of matter, however, does not occur from this but from the other side of world existence (not from the midday-side but from that of midnight) and thus from the direction where the Christ reigns today as Lord of Karma. Since the Christ in His karma-transforming and karma-ordering activity constantly bridges the abyss between the Cosmic Midnight (the highest sphere of Intuition) and the physical world (the sphere of physical cognition), He in this way also creates the possibility for us as human beings to consciously participate in this process.[11]

The event that guarantees for human beings this bridging between the highest spiritual sphere and the earthly world is the Mystery of Golgotha, and its innermost centre is the Resurrection of the Christ. Only this freest deed of His divine 'I' brings about the direct connection between the sphere of Intuition—wherein live the forces of the cosmic will—and the physical world, where they find their outer manifestation. And here this occurs not as is the case with the beings of the First Hierarchy from above to below, but for the first time in the whole of the world development from below to above. For the event of the Resurrection that was preceded by the so-called descent into hell by the Christ takes place out of the depths of the tomb (the inner layers of the earth) and leads back to the highest regions of the spirit manifested in the ascent to heaven as the continuation of the Mystery of Golgotha.

Now in order better to comprehend the connection between the nature of the Resurrection-body and the above-characterized sevenfold path, we must recall that as to its substance the Resurrection-body or Phantom consists of pure will—the will that was sacrificed on Ancient Saturn by the Thrones for the creation of the physical body of man. In the so-called Fall through Lucifer and later even more strongly through Ahriman, this cosmic will-substance was subsequently corrupted. Then, in the Resurrection, it reappeared in its full original radiance. (GA 131, 10 October 1911.)

As we have seen, the human will by its very nature is related to Intuition, for the latter arises in man when his will turns into a new organ of perception through spiritual development. One can therefore say: In the process of the Resurrection, out of the pure force of cosmic Intuition that originates from the heights of the World Midnight Hour, the Christ with His Cosmic 'I' has taken hold of the inner will-substance of His physical body all the way into its material content in order completely to transform this part of the perceptual world out of the spirit (transition from 7 to 1). With that, for the first time in human evolution, a part of the perceptual world has originated (the Resurrection-body) that is both physical and at the same time purely spiritual, meaning where the contrast between spirit and matter or 'I' and world no longer exists. Thus, this fully spiritualized part of the perceptual world could become a seed for the gradual spiritualization of man and all of nature.

What signifies the exceptional state in human cognition (on the microcosmic level) as transition from thought-intuitions to imaginative perception of the spiritual world, to that (as an archetype) corresponds macrocosmically the absolutely exceptional state of the Death and Resurrection of the Christ on the Place of the Skull on earth. After all, never before has an entity of the divine-spiritual worlds passed through death in the earthly body so as to bring the message of its overcoming to the gods.

What was said could be formulated moreover as follows. The highest *concept*, as defined by Plato, the highest idea that encompasses and generates all the other ideas (for Plato they were spiritual entities) is the Logos. It unites at the Turning Point of Time with a human body that is the loftiest object of *perception* in the physical-sensory world. For it bears in itself as microcosm all the forces of the universe.[12] This essential living union of the highest concept with the most perfect perception then takes place at the Turning Point of Time as a 'mystical fact', quite in accordance with Aristotle's 'mental pictures', so that in Christ Jesus the divine (the highest idea or—using Aristotelian verbal practice—the form) submerges into matter and becomes inseparable from it: 'And the Word became flesh' (John 1:14). In this unique world event the Logos Itself inhabited and took hold of the physical body all the way into its material components, in order then to lead it to resurrection.

Just as on the cognitive path of *The Philosophy of Freedom* a new reality comes into being on the microcosmic level through the union of the percept with the corresponding concept, not merely something formal, so in the Resurrection a new cosmic reality was created on the macrocosmic level as a foundation for the origination of a future cosmos.[13]

Rudolf Steiner points to this connection in the lecture of 8 May 1910 in which he designates the cognitive theory of *The Philosophy of Freedom* as being one that has arisen 'in the sense of Paul' or 'on the Pauline basis' (GA 116). For prior to uniting percept and concept in the process of cognition, the world appears to man merely as a divided, imperfect half-reality, a kind of double illusion or maya. Out of this, through its own activity, the soul must now create a new reality that transforms world-maya into higher truth.

The fact that in our time this process of creating a new reality became possible for the human being is the direct consequence of the presence of the Christ Impulse in Earth evolution since the Mystery of Golgotha. This is why every person can tell himself: 'What you yourself have turned into maya you must make right again within you. And you can do this by receiving into your being the Christ forces that show you the outer world in its reality!' (GA 116, 8 May 1910.) Furthermore, in accordance with

Paul, Rudolf Steiner shows that the fact on the basis of which the outer world appears to man as an illusion is the consequence of what the Bible describes as the 'Fall'. Through the latter, and through man's expulsion from Paradise (spiritual world), the original reality splits apart for human beings into the two domains of thinking and perceiving through which the whole world turns into illusion for us. On the other hand, in the deed of the Christ the consequences of the Fall were cancelled. With that, the path of true cognition and moral action became possible: the path that for our age is described in the two parts of *The Philosophy of Freedom*.[14]

Naturally, human beings who in pre-Christian times sought for cognition could likewise bring that about on the basis of uniting percept and concept. Then however the result, to the extent that it related to the physical sense world, was of a kind that either, in the sense of an orientally coloured philosophy (which in Europe reached as far as Plato), the outer world was experienced as maya (for Plato, only the spiritual ideas possessed full reality) or—as was the case with Aristotle who was the first to recognize the significance of the sense world—that the spiritual settings of the ideas increasingly moved into the background and thus indwelled his philosophy only as memories of the ancient Mystery contents and no longer as direct visions. (GA 109/111, 12 June 1909.)[14a]

Thus (until Plato), the world of outer perceptions was in fact only maya in the East. In the West (beginning with Aristotle) the world of concepts became more and more distant from the spirit.[14b] This is why their union did convey an insight, but by no means one of which, in accord with Rudolf Steiner, one could say 'that truth is not the ideal reflection of something real but a *free* product of the human spirit that does not exist anywhere if we were not producing it ourselves'. (GA 3, Preface; emphasis by Rudolf Steiner.) One could moreover say 'that without this activity ... the world-happenings could not be imagined as a totality complete within themselves'. (Ibid.)

Neither Plato nor Aristotle could utter such words but only the human being of the present who has already begun consciously and in freedom 'to become an *active* co-creator of the world-process'. (Ibid.)

Diagram 3 on p. 11 makes it clear how the vertical connections come about on this sevenfold path. Such a link exists between intuitive thinking and Intuition as a higher stage of spiritual cognition. The latter works as an invisible will-like basis in every activity of the thought-intuition (7–3) situated below it. On the other hand, in order to take hold of this source fully consciously and having gone through the portal of the exceptional state, one has to pass through the three stages from Imagination via Inspiration up to Intuition (from 3 through 4, 5, 6 to 7). Likewise in every perception (or percept), deeply concealed lives the element of Imagination (from 5 to 1). Now, to become conscious of it one must similarly traverse the path that leads from sense observation past percept to intuitive thinking, and from there once again through the portal of the exceptional state to the conscious perceptions in the spiritual world (from 1 through 2, 3, 4 to 5). For in the sense of *The Philosophy of Freedom* 'the "percept" is here taken to be everything that approaches man through the senses *and through the spirit*' (GA 4, Chap. VII; emphasis by Rudolf Steiner). The first form in which spirit approaches man as *percept* is Imagination. One can moreover discover a link between Inspiration and intuiting power of discernment. In the latter, the hidden inspiration is always active as its inherent discernment-forming impulse (from 6 to 2).

In connection with the secret of resurrection, two transitions in particular are of decisive significance: from intuitive thinking to Imagination (3 to 5) and from Intuition back to perception in the physical sensory world (7 to 1). This is why resurrection can also be characterized as follows. In the first transition, it is a matter of experiencing the resurrection forces in human thinking which thereby attain the new faculty consciously to perceive true imaginations in the spiritual world in order, among them, sooner or later to encounter the imagination of the Etheric Christ. In this way, man can experience resurrection in his consciousness. For thinking works here in an absolutely body-free and sense-free manner. This in turn means his consciousness has verily arisen from the tomb of the body (the brain) and can consciously perceive the spiritual world all around.

In the second transition, it is a matter of the Resurrection that occurred not on the level of human *consciousness* but on the all-encompassing level of *existence* only once at the Turning Point of Time. During this unique event, the forces of the Cosmic Will that constitute the physical body from the spiritual side and can be fully taken hold of and mastered only in Intuition, became directly effective and visible in the earthly sense world or world of perceptions. In other words, here the loftiest fact of the spiritual world became at the same time a perceptible fact of the physical sensory world. In accord with the apostle Paul, one could say: In the maya into which the world has developed through the Fall of Man, something appeared for the first time that represents a completely physical and simultaneously spiritual reality—the Resurrection-body. And in this consists the central secret of the Resurrection: it has the same significance in both worlds and connects them forever with each other, but in such a way that the human 'I' can consciously participate any time in this Deed of the Christ.

Initially this participation takes place in pure thinking which represents the firm starting point of modern initiation, then in transformed feeling and willing which gradually turn into new organs of perception for the spiritual world, and finally this participation culminates in the highest sphere, that of Intuition, after the whole path of seven stages has been completed. Only now, through the intuitive attainment of the forces of the Midnight Hour, can the initiate consciously take the last step back into the perceptual world in order to partake microcosmically in the macrocosmic Resurrection of the Christ to the full extent through the connection with His Resurrection-body. For the actual connection with this body is only possible if the supersensible forces of Intuition begin to take hold of the perceptual world all the way even into matter. See Diagram 4 below.

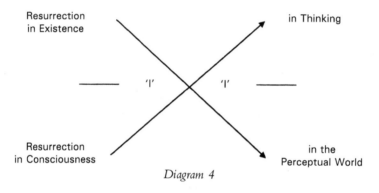

Diagram 4

The most important result that comes from the methodical starting point of cognition in anthroposophy, as Diagram 3 symbolizes, consists in the central importance of the 'I' for the whole of human and Earth evolution (point 4). This is located in the centre of the lemniscate and links its lower and upper segment, the physical-sensory and the spiritual world, in an inseparable unity. Likewise the two directions, defined in the drawing by two arrows, pass through the 'I' as their centre and therefore cannot be entered upon outside of the 'I'. The first direction arises from intuitive thinking to the fully conscious and thought-pervaded perceptions of the spiritual world and thus to the experiencing and unfolding of the resurrection forces in human consciousness, first on the imaginative and then the succeeding stages. The second direction moves from the highest realm of Intuition directly back into the earthly world of perceptions during this transition, in order to exercise the forces of resurrection as fount of the spiritualization of all physical existence.[15]

From what has been pointed out it becomes clear that the central task of anthroposophy, and the path of cognition presented by it, is the ever-increasing awareness of the 'I' as a purely spiritual entity, as well as its continuous evolution. The goal of Earth evolution lies in this unceasing unfolding of the 'I' that leads all the way to man's ascent (culminating in the Tenth Hierarchy). This goal can only be attained through the conscious union of man with the Christ Being as World-'I' and loftiest archetype of every human 'I', as well as with His deed in the Mystery of Golgotha—a deed that encompasses the whole cosmic future.

The 'I' of man belongs among the greatest secrets of the human being and likewise of anthroposophy. Rudolf Steiner considered it in his works from so many varying aspects that an overview, not to mention a conclusive summary, is not easily achievable.[16] The small but extraordinarily valuable booklet by Rudolf Steiner *The Threshold of the Spiritual World* (GA 17) offers an important introduction to this theme. In it, he describes the nature of the human 'I' as being threefold. First there is the ordinary 'I' which in accordance with Chapter IX of *The Philosophy of Freedom* can also be designated as 'ego-consciousness' conditioned upon the physical body. This ego is what a person experiences as 'I' under normal circumstances and indeed calls it that in everyday life. In his other works, Rudolf Steiner also describes it as the lower 'I' in man.[17]

In the above book, the second or individual 'I' in the human being is called 'the other self' by Rudolf Steiner. Of it he says that it progresses from one incarnation to the next and in this way represents the actual nature of man. In other writings, Rudolf Steiner also designates it as the higher 'I' or self which at man's birth really does not descend into his physical body at all, but remains throughout in the spiritual world.[18] It shines from there down into the corporeal sheaths of man. Normally he thus considers its reflection in the body to be his own 'I' (first 'I').

Rudolf Steiner speaks frequently and in detail about this second or actual [Ger.: *eigentliche*] 'I' of man, above all in his early lectures. It originated at the beginning of Earth evolution through the sacrifice of the Spirits of Form, who moreover appear in the Bible as the creators of man under the name Elohim. At that time these exalted spirits forfeited a part of their own being as 'I'-substance to the human being, something whereby this being could start on its own autonomous evolution. In *The Philosophy of Freedom* this 'I' is called the 'actual I' that can only be experienced independently of the body in pure thinking (GA 4, Chap. IX). That is why this 'I' is the one most familiar to readers of anthroposophical literature. The transition from the ordinary or lower to the higher 'I' forms an important stage on the anthroposophical path of inner schooling. Rudolf Steiner describes it a number of times, not only in many of his lectures but above all in his basic works.[19]

In his booklet *The Threshold of the Spiritual World*, Rudolf Steiner introduces yet another, a third form of the 'I', which he designates as the true 'I' of man. This third 'I' lives like an 'I' in the 'I' and forms the actual essence of the human being. In the booklet itself, Rudolf Steiner mentions its origin nowhere. He only states that, in contrast to the 'other self' (higher 'I') which emerges out of the spiritual world, the true 'I' stems from the 'supra-spiritual [Ger.: *übergeistige*] world'. If the spiritual world (in the sense of the human soul's life between two incarnations) can be designated as 'spirit-land' or in more theosophical terminology as 'Devachan', then what the book *Theosophy* describes as the third world (after the physical and soul-world) corresponds to a still higher world-sphere. Rudolf Steiner designates this as the plane of Buddhi or Providence. From there descend the divine archetypes, according to which everything in the three lower worlds is fashioned and created[20] (GA 10).

Even though Rudolf Steiner does not convey anything definite about the origin of the true 'I', this question can be answered quite precisely from other passages of his work. Since this was described and substantiated in detail by the author elsewhere, it need not be repeated here. Suffice it to say that, as to its substance, man's true 'I' is equivalent in being to the Word of Worlds, therefore to the Logos who at the Turning Point of Time had became man on earth.[21] This is why the path for grasping the true 'I' of man proceeds solely through the conscious encounter with Christ in intuition and the cognition of the mystery of his Resurrection connected with it.[22] For in the Resurrection, as will be shown in the next chapter, the divine 'I' of the Christ has totally transformed the nature of its body with the highest spiritual forces (only recognizable in intuition) all the way into physical matter.

The origins of the threefold human 'I' can best be retraced on Diagram 3, p. 11. Here, the lower part of the lemniscate corresponds to the unfolding of the ordinary 'I' of man. It slowly liberates itself from any dependence on the body and can perform a first contact with its higher 'I' in intuitive thinking. This is the reason why the transition from 3 to 5 through the point of intersection 4 signifies the conscious rise from the lower to the higher 'I'. In the drawing, the actual sphere of development of the latter is located in the upper part of the lemniscate. It consists in the step-by-step transformation of the soul forces of thinking, feeling and willing on the modern path of inner schooling into the spiritual organs of perception of the higher 'I'. With these the human being can independently research wider and wider realms of the supersensible world. The stages of higher cognition originating from them are correspondingly designated by Rudolf Steiner as those of the imaginative, inspirative, and intuitive levels.

Only after having reached the stage of Intuition on the path of his initiation can the spirit disciple recognize the nature of the Christ as the divine origin of his 'true 'I' and in this way take conscious hold of this 'I'. Thus the innermost nature of the Mystery of Golgotha becomes manifest to the spirit disciple, who at this stage turns into a modern Christian initiate, namely the creation of the Resurrection-body out of the forces of the macrocosmic intuition, forces that work in the will of the Christ and in this way take full hold of and spiritualize the spirit disciple's physical sheath.

On the microcosmic path of modern initiation, this central deed of the Christ corresponds to the transition from the higher to the true 'I' of man (in the diagram from point 7 to point 1). Man thereby comes into possession of his true 'I' (point of intersection 'I' [Ger.: *ICH*]) which makes the cognition of the transforming activity of the spirit in the world of matter itself (world of perception) accessible to him.[23]

In the above-mentioned drawing, we find the summary of the whole development of the lower and the higher 'I' as well as the transition from the first to the second one[24] whose further unfolding is crowned by attainment of the true 'I'. This is something through which man can experience his kinship of being with Christ as the Cosmic 'I' and as a result can attain conscious access to the nature of the Mystery of Golgotha, and in that way to the resurrection forces.[25] They are then in a position to bring about a complete metamorphosis of the whole human being, a metamorphosis, however, that in our time has to start with the transformation of human thinking which thereby turns into what Rudolf Steiner designates as Christ-consciousness. What this signifies in actual human life will be dealt with comprehensively further on in this book.

2. *The Philosophy of Freedom* and the Mystery of the Resurrection

From the standpoint of *The Philosophy of Freedom*, the statements of the previous chapter can be understood in yet another way. In so doing, the following words by Rudolf Steiner come to mind most of all: 'In this book the endeavour is made to justify cognition of the spirit-realm *prior* to entry into spiritual experience' (GA 4; emphasis by Rudolf Steiner). If the Diagrams 1 and 2 therefore describe the perceptions in the spirit-realm even *after* entry into spiritual experience, the following drawing remains purely within the boundaries that Rudolf Steiner himself gave in these remarks (Diagram 5).

Regarding this drawing an additional explanation must be given. If a human being wishes to act in the world in the sense of the principle of freedom as one who is not initiated, this has to take place as follows. Using his thinking, he must first obtain a certain moral intuition out of the all-encompassing world of ideas, and with the aid of his moral imagination turn it into a *picture* of what he correspondingly desires to carry out afterwards with the help of moral technique as a free deed. If, however, he has entered upon the inner path of modern schooling, and in this way has begun the process of grasping the origin of his free actions from the spiritual side, then the sequence of the stages differs. First the spirit disciple must recognize the nature of moral imagination and *only following that* the nature of moral intuition. For on the path of schooling, through the 'exceptional state' in meditation, the first stage consists in bringing about the transition from intuitive thinking to consciously cognized imaginations. And these on the other hand form the spiritual background of moral imagination. This is why Rudolf Steiner states that 'spiritual-scientifically' one can also designate moral imagination as '*imaginative* impulses of morality' (GA 193, 12 June 1919).

Not until the spirit disciple has penetrated to these spiritual back-grounds of moral imagination can he take the next step so as to attain to the spiritual backgrounds of moral intuition in a similar manner. Both stages are accessible only through meditative efforts—meaning by actively penetrating one's thinking with the will. Then the other sequence is likewise justified for the spirit disciple (the sequence that is portrayed on the next page).

Rudolf Steiner describes this process as follows: 'The very fact that we

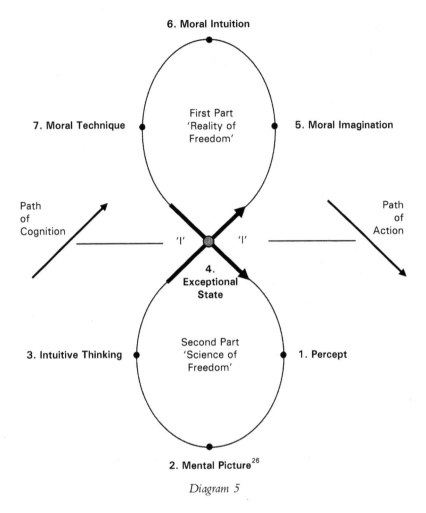

Diagram 5

strengthen the will in our thinking more and more prepares us for what I called in *The Philosophy of Freedom* moral imagination, which is something, *however, that arises* to moral intuitions and then irradiates and penetrates our will—the will that has turned into thought or our thought that has turned into will' (GA 202, 19 December 1920).[26a]

If the spirit disciple has risen so far on the modern path of initiation that he has reached the stage of Inspiration, the spiritual backgrounds of moral intuition likewise are revealed to him. These consist of the cosmic *inspirations* that the human being (otherwise unconsciously) receives out of the life prior to birth. By contrast, the spiritual backgrounds of moral imagination that the spirit disciple recognizes on the previous stage in the (otherwise unconscious) imaginations are linked to his after-death life.

'One only learns to cognize freedom if one knows that the unconscious imagination [unconscious so long as we have not entered upon the modern path of inner schooling] that prepares our life after death works together with the unconscious inspiration that resonates up from the life prior to birth as strength in our soul.'[27]

A still higher stage of spirit-discipleship is required for cognition of the spiritual backgrounds of *moral technique*. For here our intuitively grasped moral ideas that turned into pictures of our actions become directly involved in the world of perceptions. In that way this perceptual world is changed (including even its physical components) so that new karma can originate in it. In order fully to comprehend such processes spiritually, according to Rudolf Steiner one must have reached the highest stage of spirit-cognition, that of Intuition. For only this faculty can trace the karma-shaping activity of the spirit all the way to the deepest forces of matter and gradually learn to master them.

In conclusion, it can also be said that the first sequence results when one follows the path from *The Philosophy of Freedom* to anthroposophy and the second one when we seek a transition in the opposite direction, from anthroposophy back to *The Philosophy of Freedom* (see more on this in the Epilogue).

★

Based on the previous descriptions, Diagram 5 can be considered an explanation of a fundamental result of research by Rudolf Steiner regarding his *Philosophy of Freedom* that he himself denoted as 'remarkable' (GA 78, 5 September 1921). It consists in the spiritual-scientific deter-mination that not only are the body's organic activities repressed during beginning thought-activity (something that Rudolf Steiner pointed out early on in *The Philosophy of Freedom*), but during further unfolding of thinking a spiritual-physical process takes place in the human being that leads to total disintegration, i.e. to *destruction* of matter in man's organism.[28] 'To the same degree that the material processes are obliter-ated, there can expand in us what now replaces the obliteration of the material process, namely, thinking, imagining'. (Ibid.)

A truly epochal discovery by Rudolf Steiner is that a second process occurs ceaselessly in the human being that runs parallel to the (above) process of destruction of matter. What is destroyed by thinking is con-stantly regenerated anew from the domain of the will, and not in the way it was before but in a completely transformed way, as a sort of '*new for-mation* in a quite material sense'. (Ibid.) In other words: what thinking requires as its basis from the death-forces in order to facilitate the experience of freedom for the human being[29] is time after time built up out of a different domain, or else the human being would physically die as a result of the activity of his thinking. The domain where this new creation takes place all the way into the material sphere is moreover the one where, out of his moral intuition, man forms ethical ideals so as to cause them to become effective in his actions, extending even into the world of sense perceptions. Through this up-building activity of ethical (or moral) ideas, including even the materiality of the physical body, human morality acquires the character of reality; it becomes 'world-forming'. (Ibid.)

Rudolf Steiner brings this process into connection with his *Philosophy of Freedom* so that the first half of the process, the destruction of matter for the sake of human freedom, corresponds to the first part of the book; and the second half, the newly built-up (that is to say the new creation that originates in the human body), corresponds to the book's second part.

Due to the importance of all this, Rudolf Steiner's own words must be quoted here in full: 'Inasmuch as we attain in our moral motivations (in the sense of my *Philosophy of Freedom*) truly to free moral intuitions, we live a life as humans that in a will-like way places transformed matter out of its (bodily) organization into that area where matter has been destroyed. Man becomes inwardly creative; inwardly regenerative. In other words: Within the cosmos we see the "Nothing" in the human organization filled with "new formation in a quite material sense". This implies none other than this: To the extent that one follows the path of anthroposophical cognition consistently, one reaches the point where, within the human being, *purely moral ideals arise that work in a world-forming manner even down into materiality*. With that we have discovered, as it were, where the moral world [of man] becomes creative; where something originates that out of human morality bears witness to its own reality because it carries it within itself—creates it within itself.' (Ibid.)

At this point Rudolf Steiner indicates a twofold process in man's inner being that can only be designated as a microcosmic death, and following it, the microcosmic resurrection. Such a resurrection is the direct result of the Christ Impulse's actual working in every human being since the Mystery of Golgotha. For only this presence of the Christ in man gives him the new faculty—following the destruction of matter in his body[30] that is required so that his 'I'-consciousness can come about—to create new matter, and with that the basis of the foundation of the new moral cosmos out of his free ethical deeds that spring from moral intuition. The special point here is that even though the Christ bestows this new faculty of moral creating on every human being through His Resurrection, man can carry out the realization of this possibility only out of complete freedom through activating his intuitive thinking and moral imagination.

In pre-Christian times too, human beings could attain morality and be active based on their ethical ideas in the outer world. Socrates was even of the opinion that genuine morality is teachable. Yet this acting out of morality could never lead as far as the creation of new matter, meaning that it could become cosmically creative in the sense of building up the future cosmos, and with that the creating of a new reality as such. What kind of new cosmic-earthly reality is referred to here? In another lecture Rudolf Steiner replies quite clearly to this question: 'Where substance fades away in the human being, turns into semblance and new substance comes into being, there we have the possibility for freedom, for love. Freedom and love belong together, as I indicated earlier in my *Philosophy of Freedom*' (GA 202, 19 December 1920). In this sense freedom belongs to the first part of the book; doing that can only be moral in so far as it is carried out based on pure love of the deed, to the book's second part.

Both the faculties, freedom and love, belong to the fundamental nature of humankind inasmuch as they will be the future Tenth Hierarchy, and the cosmos that will originate out of free human morality is the new Cosmos of Love, the origin of which Rudolf Steiner described at the end of his book *Occult Science, an Outline*, and John the Evangelist depicted it at the end of the Apocalypse in the vision of the heavenly Jerusalem.

We find the highest prototype for such creative acts out of freedom and love in the sacrificial deed of the Christ on the hill of Golgotha. This deed was actualized by Him out of highest divine freedom and deepest godly love. For Christ is the only 'god who carried out the deed [on the hill of Golgotha] out of free will—which means out of love—so that earth and humanity might attain their goal' (GA 131, 14 October 1911).

This prototype in no way infringes on the freedom of individual man and his actions, the motives of which he gleans out of intuitive thinking from the overall world of ideas. For in Christ as the creative Logos all cosmic ideas take on being from the very beginning, and in Christ as the Son of God we find the ultimate fountainhead of all possible moral intuitions, intuitions which as light (cognition) and warmth (love) penetrate the world.

Rudolf Steiner subsequently summarizes this central position of the deed by the Christ concerning human freedom in the following words: 'We owe the fact that we can be free beings to a divine deed of love. As human entities, we may thus feel ourselves to be free beings, but we must never forget that we owe this freedom to the God's act of love. Human beings should not be able to grasp the thought of freedom without grasping the thought of salvation by the Christ.' (Ibid.)

If today on occasion the opinion arises that such words by the spirit researcher might contradict the basic trend of *The Philosophy of Freedom*, this is possible only because one has not yet overcome the merely philosophical-philological path into this book of life. If, on the other hand, one approaches this book with true anthroposophical comprehension there is no contradiction here. Its contents will appear to the reader as if woven out of the very purest Christian substance. That is why the path of *The Philosophy of Freedom*—if only trodden by human beings intensively and far enough—leads to a personal experience of the Mystery of Golgotha, and with that to the final solution of the question concerning the nature of human freedom 'without which the thought of salvation by the Christ' cannot be attained. Those who still cannot understand this 'should'—according to Rudolf Steiner—at least 'recognize that human opinions mean nothing as compared to cosmic facts; that in due course they will be quite pleased to acknowledge that they have acquired their freedom from the Christ.' (Ibid.)

Rudolf Steiner characterized the above-described process of the 'new forming' or 'new creation' once more from the viewpoint of our earth becoming a sun in the lecture of 18 December 1920. First, he speaks about how in the ancient Mysteries the initiates viewed the origin of all morality in the central spiritual Being that (for them) dwelled in the sun and later on appeared as Christ on earth. 'First of all they pictured the Sun as a spirit being. The initiated individuals thought of this spirit being as the source of all that is moral.' Directly following these words, Rudolf Steiner starts to speak in the same vein about his *Philosophy of Freedom,* saying that the moral intuitions referred to in this book spring from the same source, meaning from the Christ Being itself. 'What I therefore referred to in my *Philosophy of Freedom,* namely that the moral intuitions are obtained *from this source,* is moreover obtained here on earth' (GA 202). There lies the main difference between the ancient pre-Christian Mysteries, which did not acquire their moral impulses from the earth but out of the cosmos and, put more precisely, out of the sun. Only since the Mystery of Golgotha has it become possible to find the moral impulses on earth as well, meaning *in man himself.* Their highest fount, however, remains the same: the being of the Christ, but now as the new spirit of the earth and archetype of every human 'I'.

If man finds the fount of moral principles in himself and carries them out in his free actions, something can radiate out of the human being into the whole cosmos like a 'new creation'. 'From out of human beings they [the moral intuitions] shine forth, from what can dwell in human beings as moral enthusiasm.' Then from another—a cosmic—side, Rudolf Steiner points to the same process of a 'new creation'. It is a new creation that, as a result of man's inner enthusiasm for this new free morality (as it is based on *The Philosophy of Freedom*), can bring the earth to the point of shining forth 'sunlike' in the universe; meaning, to bring it to the point of actually becoming a sun. This implies a truly cosmic responsibility that we as human beings have in regard to the realization of what is ingrained in *The Philosophy of Freedom*. 'Just imagine how our responsibility increases when we know that if nobody were here on earth whose soul could glow with enthusiasm for true genuine morality (or spiritual ideals in general) we would not contribute to a continuation of our world, to a *new creation*— only to a dying of our world.' (Ibid.) The latter could happen if human beings on earth would not find conscious access to the resurrection forces of the Christ. People would therefore be forced to move towards a future signifying death without resurrection. Yet even if only a few people on earth would find it in themselves to reach up to actual moral enthusiasm based on the Christ force in themselves, and that way make their presence felt 'with bright moral-spiritual enthusiasm, then the earth would nevertheless begin to shine forth in spiritual sunlike form' (ibid.) and would thus arrive at the process of becoming a sun.[31]

Summing this up it can be said that through the unfolding of freedom and love precisely at the point in man's nature where matter is destroyed and built up again through moral deeds we humans begin in the most direct way to participate microcosmically in the macrocosmic process of the Resurrection of the Christ, and with that in our earth's becoming a sun. For the new matter originates in the human body out of man's moral will-activity, which is akin in its nature to the will-like foundations of the physical body where the Resurrection has taken place at the Turning Point of Time as an effect of the free moral will of the Logos. And out of the force of inner enthusiasm for the participation in this 'new creation', our earth can shine forth in the cosmos in a 'spiritual sunlike' way.

The relationship between the gradual build-up of the new corporeality in man through his moral deeds in the sense of the second part of *The Philosophy of Freedom* and the nature of the Resurrection-body consists in the following. When in the above-described manner the new matter is created in man's physical body, it can receive into itself the forces of the Resurrection-body all the way even into the material foundations of the human organism. With that begins a process in man microcosmically that is similar to the one that occurred once macrocosmically in the Mystery of Golgotha on the stage of world history.

Rudolf Steiner calls this process the 'incorporation' of the Resurrection-body all the way into the bodily organization (GA 131, 11 October 1911). Now, the Resurrection-body can only connect with those parts of the body's substances that are created by man himself through his moral actions in the world.

When in the future this creation-process will have advanced far enough in the human body, it can moreover traverse to outer nature, because man as the microcosm bears within himself all the kingdoms of nature. In this way the forces of resurrection will gradually begin—proceeding with man—to take hold of the earth and to transform (spiritualize) it. Consequently, man will approach 'the highest ideal of human development ... imaginable', formulated concisely by Rudolf Steiner as: ' ... the spiritualization man attains through his own labour' (GA 13). In the inner enthusiasm for the moral ideals, produced in the sense of *The Philosophy of Freedom* by our own efforts (and therefore inseparably linked with the human soul), this process manifests outwardly already today in the above-described lighting up of our earth.

What was said above can be brought to expression in still another form. The faculty to cause creation of new matter in the human body by way of moral deeds originated through the Mystery of Golgotha. Still, this faculty alone cannot lead as yet to the complete fulfilment of the aforementioned 'highest ideal'. A direct connection is required for this with the resurrection forces. The aforementioned faculty can, however, bring it about for such a connection to be produced by an individual through free efforts. It is the reason why one can attain the 'highest ideal' 'through one's own labour', meaning in full accord with the basic theme of *The Philosophy of Freedom*. In other words, since the Mystery of Golgotha, the objective basis is given; but attaining this goal is up to each individual person himself. Through the Mystery of Golgotha, the pure sun forces flowed out into the human being and Earth evolution. But the possibility of their further activity that is meant to lead to the ultimate transformation of the Earth into a new sun rests solely with man and depends on his or her pure and conscious cooperation in this process of self- and world-spiritualization.

★

For the inner development of human beings, the path described here has still another significance that is not only connected to a distant future but likewise to the immediate present. The instant a person begins to imbue himself with the resurrection forces and build up his new sun-corporeality with their help, these forces can ensure for him not only his immortality as an individuality but also the personality existing here on earth,[32] thus giving him an unshakeable guarantee for the eternal continuance of his 'I'.

Rudolf Steiner refers to this decisive step made in Christianity in contrast to the whole pre-Christian development in the words that Christ 'has the secret not only of lifting the spirits away from the earth but to redeem the bodies from it as well; to spiritualize them after they have passed through all the numerous incarnations. The owner of the secret of love is the Sun Spirit whom we call the Christ. And because He is not only interested in the individuality but directly in each earthly personality, we call Him the great sacrifice of the earth, or the "Mystical Lamb".' (GA 102, 24 March 1908.)

Spiritualization of the physical body will be possible only when the human being finds direct access to the Christ Being and discovers how Christ is active since His mighty sacrifice, the Mystery of Golgotha in Earth evolution. With that, man moreover finds access to the forces of Christ's Resurrection-body—the Phantom. 'It is possible to bring about that relationship to the Christ through which earthly man fits this Phantom that has risen out of the tomb on Golgotha into his otherwise corroding physical body [above all through the activity of his 'I'-consciousness]' (GA 131, 11 October 1911).

Through the above-mentioned creation of new matter in the human bodily organization as the result of the free moral deeds (as described in the second part of *The Philosophy of Freedom*), this process deepens and intensifies to such a degree that it can lead to the actual 'incorporation' of the Phantom of Golgotha. The consequence of this will be that man experiences a never before imagined enlightenment and widening of his 'I'-consciousness (as was the case during the initiation of Rudolf Steiner), a widening that will extend beyond all boundaries of birth and death as well as all incarnations of the human being. For it is from this source that Rudolf Steiner obtains his faculties as a modern researcher of the spirit— faculties that appear almost superhuman.[33]

As always, Rudolf Steiner affirms this in a completely objective manner with the following words: 'Inasmuch as he [the human being] incorporates this incorruptible body into his being, he increasingly comes to the point where he causes his "I"-consciousness to become brighter and brighter. He will ever more recognize in his nature that which moves from incarnation to incarnation.' (Ibid.)

In this consists the central secret of the human personality that originates purely on earth out of the working together of the individual 'I' with the form of the physical corporeality. This is why the human personality can attain eternal life only when the physical body that is connected with it overcomes the boundaries of matter, and following the Resurrection-body of the Christ can itself enter into the spiritual world as the supersensible sheath of the individual 'I'. This is why Rudolf Steiner writes, 'It is precisely this advance that is made by Christianity, namely that the personality is taken along into eternity.[34] The Christian belief is therefore correct: You will arise in your *transfigured* body.' (GA 264; emphasis by Rudolf Steiner.)

Until this highest goal of humanity's development on earth can be fully attained, the Christ will work in such a way that man (through his conscious relationship with Him) will increasingly be in a position to penetrate his eternal individuality with the forces of the purified earthly personality. In so doing, he is able to take his 'I'-consciousness into the spiritual world to the full extent. 'The Christ became the central point [of Earth evolution] in so far as the individual personalities of human beings were to be sanctified and purified. Everything that man can bring as fruit out of the single personality into the individuality he achieves by having a connection with the Christ Being.' (GA 102, 24 March 1908.)

What Rudolf Steiner said makes it comprehensible why from the very beginning *The Philosophy of Freedom* was structured (indeed had to be structured) on an intense individualism. Even though to this day this individualism is often misunderstood in the outer world (last but not least by Christians as well), it is just this particularly personal element that links the content of the book with the Mystery of Golgotha. For only in individual man (in his/her personality) is moral imagination even possible. 'The result [of the fact that through the Mystery of Golgotha the Christ united himself with the earth] is that on the one side man has the possibility to place as much as possible on the scale of freedom and to move truly to the ultimate consequences of individualism, for moral imagination is found only in the individual human being. This is really, why some have called my *Philosophy of Freedom* the philosophy of individualism in the most extreme sense. Indeed it had to be that, for on the other side it is the most Christian of all philosophies.' (GA 212, 7 May 1922.) A little later in the same lecture, Rudolf Steiner characterizes the inseparable homogeneousness of these two sides of his philosophy of freedom by pointing out that in the contemporary human soul there must be alive 'on the one side a powerful impulse of freedom and on the other side ... a strong impulse to inwardly live through the Mystery of Golgotha.' (Ibid.)

Now, 'inwardly to live through the Mystery of Golgotha' signifies nothing less than the conscious and individual participation of man in the process of Resurrection through receiving and utilizing the resurrection forces all the way even into the substance of his/her physical body. And although this process has taken place following the Mystery of Golgotha bit by bit unconsciously in all human beings, still (by means of pursuing the path of *The Philosophy of Freedom*) this path can be taken up into 'I'-consciousness so that one can become a conscious co-worker of the Christ in the process of spiritualization of mankind and the earth.

This way the extreme individualism—one could even say 'personalism'—of *The Philosophy of Freedom* connects directly with the central essence of the Christian Mystery. Moreover it is not a merely theoretical but a practical concern over this work by Rudolf Steiner that leads one inwardly to experience the full reality of the Resurrection, and with that 'to having stood' in the spirit 'before the Mystery of Golgotha in innermost earnest celebration of knowledge', as Rudolf Steiner experienced it himself at the end of the nineteenth century. (GA 28, Chap. XXVI.)

★

Going back to Diagram 5 at the beginning of this chapter, it becomes even more understandable how the path of cognition (the basis of which is intuitive thinking) and the path of action (of deeds)—they correspond to the two parts of *The Philosophy of Freedom*—link up through the Mystery of Golgotha into a new, inseparable unity out of the fount of moral intuition. Likewise, the key word of the whole *Philosophy of Freedom*—'ethical individualism'—indicates a similar connection of this book's two parts. For true individualism is to be unfolded solely on the basis of intuitive thinking and realized in ethical actions based on true love for a deed.

We must not find it contradictory right away that in both Diagram 1 (p. 6) and Diagram 3 (p. 11) the word 'Intuition' appears in position 7, whereas in Diagram 5 as 'moral intuition' it is in position 6. Spiritual connections are complicated and various forces often work into each other. This is why Rudolf Steiner says in another context, after having definitively brought the nature of will into connection with Intuition, that will is not only linked with this highest stage of cognition but already with the preceding one. Thus, he writes in the first chapter of his book *The Stages of Higher Knowledge* about the second inspirative stage, 'Inspirative cognition that can likewise be called the "will-like" one' (GA 12). For on the level of Inspiration, man's will forces, which originate in his astral body, unfold only as far as his etheric body (in Imagination they remain completely in the astral body). Not until the stage of Intuition do they take hold of the whole physical body all the way into its material substance, whereby human action become possible in which the spirit, working as it does even into the earthly world, is taken into account fully consciously by the one involved in action. This is why, in the terminology of *The Philosophy of Freedom*, the initiation-stage of Intuition not only corresponds to moral intuitions but in an even more appropriate sense to their being carried out through moral technique.

In regard to what was just stated, it is of special importance how Rudolf Steiner himself makes characterizations between moral intuitions in the second part of *The Philosophy of Freedom* and the Intuition-stage of the modern path of initiation. In order to ensure the transition here, one has to take what occurs initially as human intuition only within man and extend it over the whole cosmos into a kind of 'cosmic Intuition'. 'When this is cultivated for the whole cosmos through such a philosophy of freedom for the basis of human action [as moral intuition], one finds Intuition actualized over the whole cosmos' (GA 78, 3 September 1921). Then this higher Intuition in the cosmos corresponds to what otherwise is moral intuition in the human being. (Ibid.)

If however one considers the above-mentioned extension of soul forces in their relationship to the stages of modern initiation and to the contents of the first part of *The Philosophy of Freedom*, this can also be depicted as in Diagram 6 below:

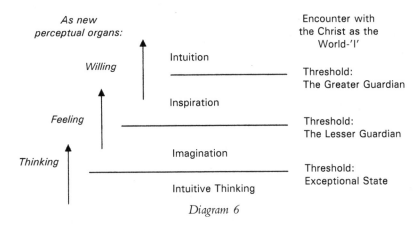

Diagram 6

Here intuitive thinking leads through the first threshold of the exceptional state directly into the world of Imagination, or what amounts to the same thing, to 'intellectual clairvoyance'. The feeling, having turned into the new organ of perception, brings about the transition from Imagination to Inspiration across the second threshold where the Lesser Guardian stands. Then the awakened will makes possible the step from Inspiration to Intuition across a still higher third threshold where the Greater Guardian of the Threshold appears. Ultimately, during the further development of Intuition on the path of modern initiation, one attains to the conscious encounter with the Christ as World-'I' and with that to the spiritual communion with His Cosmic 'I'-Being. As a result of this, the true insight and whole significance of the Mystery of Golgotha dawns on the initiate (see GA 13), something that on this stage of initiation also connotes the conscious connection with the forces of the Resurrection-body.

From what has here been described, one can infer how consistent and resolute the path was on which Rudolf Steiner moved from his early philosophical work to anthroposophy. It led from experiencing intuitive thinking as a purely spiritual activity independent of the physical body across the threshold of the exceptional state into the objective spiritual world—a world that manifested itself to Rudolf Steiner as the world of supersensible perceptions.[35] Rudolf Steiner himself points this out in his Appendix added to the 1918 edition of *The Philosophy of Freedom*: 'But a living comprehension of what is meant in this book by intuitive thinking will lead quite naturally to a living entry into the world of spiritual perception.'

Above all it becomes obvious from the following remark in his auto-biography, *The Story of My Life,* that Rudolf Steiner himself pursued this path from his earliest youth. Already at age 19/20 (around his first moon-node), after he had become a student at the *Technische Hochschule* in Vienna and had begun his decade-long confrontation with modern natural science, it was not long before he arrived at the following decisive conviction: 'My exertions for natural-scientific concepts had finally brought me to see in the activity of the human "I" the one and only starting point for true knowledge. When the "I" is active and perceives this activity, one has something spiritual that is directly present in one's consciousness—so I told myself.' (GA 28, Chapter III.)

The primal activity of the 'I' consists above all in the production of thinking. When this is observed by the 'I' itself, then we have exactly the condition of the exceptional state that Rudolf Steiner later on described in his *Philosophy of Freedom*. This exceptional state can only be brought about in pure thinking in which it is possible to come to terms with the true nature of the 'I', and following this the conscious transition into the spiritual world becomes feasible.[36] After all, 'with the exception of the "I" that is experienced in pure thinking, ordinary consciousness ignores anthroposophy for the purposes of its research' (GA 35, 17 August 1908).

In Chapter III of *The Philosophy of Freedom*, Rudolf Steiner points out in regard to the exceptional state that one can never produce thinking and its observation simultaneously, only one after the other, and for the following reason: 'I would have to split into two personalities, one that thinks and another that watches itself in this thinking if I were to observe my present thinking. This I cannot do.' This is a quite obvious description of the situation on this side of the threshold to the spiritual world. For on this side of the threshold, the above-mentioned split into two personalities can only be pathological. After crossing the threshold however, this splitting occurs almost immediately and belongs among the first supersensible experiences that in modern spiritual schooling is 'typical' and 'the same for everybody'. (GA 113, 24 August 1909.) Rudolf Steiner describes it as follows: 'The first experience that . . . occurs as an effect of meditation, concentration, and so on, could be expressed . . . as an experience that, if trying to describe it, could best be termed a *fully conscious* split of our whole personality that occurs within itself. You tell yourself at this moment when you experience this: Now you actually have become something like two personalities.' (Ibid.; emphasis by Rudolf Steiner.) The exceptional state is brought about through 'meditation, concentration, and so on', and is moreover extended from this side of the threshold to its other side through the *healthy* split of the personality—healthy because it is carried out through mental exercises and thus controlled. In this way one can produce thinking and simultaneously observe it. Along these lines, one can break through to the spiritual origin of thinking and with that enter the spiritual world fully conscious, something that is necessary for genuine spiritual research.

This is why Rudolf Steiner could write in his autobiography—still referring to the same time in his life—just a few lines after the above-quoted words: 'For me there existed a world of spirit beings. It was a matter of direct perception for me that the "I", which itself is spirit, lives in a world of spirits.' Later Rudolf Steiner made this experience the very basis of his *Philosophy of Freedom*. While it is not explicitly mentioned there, as to its contents it is immanently present.[37] Thus in 1923 he summarized the essence of this book as follows: 'These two aspects—first that a spiritual kingdom exists; and secondly that man is connected with the innermost "I" of his being to this spiritual kingdom—are in fact the fundamental points of *The Philosophy of Freedom*' (GA 258, 11 June 1923).

This path led him further through the ascending stages of Imagination, Inspiration and Intuition, through the encounters with the Lesser and afterwards the Greater Guardian of the Threshold on up to his purely spiritual 'having stood before the Mystery of Golgotha' at the summit of Intuition. In this manner, Rudolf Steiner moved from the experience of resurrection first in his thinking all the way to his union with the forces of the Resurrection-body during the renewed entrance of his Intuition from the spiritual heights back into the world of perceptions. With this, his path of cognition was complete inasmuch as he was able to experience the primal source of the resurrection forces on the hill of Golgotha in his consciousness through an objective spiritual experience. Now, on this unshakeable foundation, he could then erect his whole anthroposophy at the beginning of the new century.[38]

One could also say: Rudolf Steiner's initiation path began already in his youth with the experience of the pure communion of thought, which he proclaims in truly epochal words: '*Becoming aware of the idea in reality is the true communion of man*' (GA 1; emphasis by Rudolf Steiner). On Diagram 1 (p. 6), this corresponds to the transition from stage 3 to stage 5, brought about by the strengthened activity of the 'I' in pure thinking (stage 4). This path then reaches its culmination in the lofty domain of Intuition during the transition from stage 7 back to stage 1 in the form of the purely spiritual communion.[39] It is the human 'I' here that forms the transition and fully actualizes in itself the words of Paul 'Not I but the Christ in me' (Gal. 2:20) and in so doing receives into itself the forces of the World-'I' of the Christ.[40]

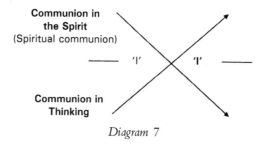

Diagram 7

The following perspective results moreover from the viewpoint of the threefold 'I'-being of man as was depicted at the end of the first chapter. Based on the clairvoyant gift available to Rudolf Steiner from childhood on (a gift he had developed through his occupation with modern natural science up to precise research in the spiritual world), he could already in his youth perform the transition from his ordinary to his higher 'I'. It is only of this second 'I' that one can say that it is 'spirit itself' and 'lives in a world of spirits', as he reports in his autobiography. Yet, from this stage it was still a long way to the fully taking hold of the 'true I', something that around the turn of the century occurred in the encounter with the Being of Christ in Intuition. By means of this, Rudolf Steiner directly entered the sphere of the Resurrected One, a sphere out of which he could then establish anthroposophy as the free accomplishment of his 'true I'.[41]

★

The relationship of *The Philosophy of Freedom* to the resurrection impulse of the Mystery of Golgotha as characterized in this chapter can also be summarized as follows. The first conscious encounter with the resurrection forces takes place on the path of *The Philosophy of Freedom* in the domain of human thinking. These forces bring about the experience of true freedom in the human soul. For this freedom consists above all in the full independence of man's 'I'-consciousness from material processes of his body, hence from the forces of death at work in him. Still, this stage corresponds merely to the beginning of the path towards the attainment of freedom. For the goal of this path lies not only in earthly freedom, which is reachable through the transformation of human consciousness, but in the attainment of cosmic freedom. The latter freedom consists of man being able, out of the power of his 'I', fully to control and transform the whole world of sense perceptions in the service of the Spirit, who then—through the 'I' and in it—makes Its appearance creatively.

This stage of cosmic freedom can only be reached through the conscious participation by man in the Resurrection of the Christ, not merely on the level of consciousness but—even if only microcosmically—on the level of cosmic existence. For higher freedom is rooted in the cosmic-telluric reality of resurrection. Only drawing out of this wellspring can the human being realize his freedom all the way even into its cosmic dimension and thus attain full independence from matter, an independence he requires for his free actions. However, this refers in no way to a flight from matter, only to its total transformation (spiritualization) and submission through the power of the human spirit. This is the higher freedom that leads man as the Tenth Hierarchy in the future to the faculty, out of freedom and love, independently to create the new cosmos as well as the new 'I'-beings who will then inhabit this cosmos. (See GA 110, 14 April 1909–11.)

With that, the human being rises to the stage of cosmic evolution on which, as the micro-logos, he can himself become creative in the universal all. This future activity of man as micro-logos was for the first time in Earth evolution described and elucidated in *The Philosophy of Freedom*. What appears in this book still on a purely human level will at the end of the whole evolution be actualized by man as a new hierarchical being on the cosmic level.

At the Turning Point of Time the consciousness of the Apostles awakened through the Whitsun-event in the sphere of Resurrection, and hence in the sphere of freedom. This is why Rudolf Steiner designated this event as 'the festival of the free individuality' (GA 118, 15 May 1910), the celebration that points to the future process of becoming free on the part of all human beings. Rudolf Steiner describes this inner liberation (in consequence of the Whitsun Spirit) as follows: 'Man can become free only in spirit. So long as he is dependent on what his spirit indwells as its corporeality, so long does he remain a slave of this corporeality.'[42] He can only become free when he rediscovers himself in spirit, and out of the spirit becomes master over what is within him. 'Becoming free pre-supposes finding oneself as spirit within oneself. The true spirit in which we can find ourselves is the general human spirit[43] that we recognize as the force of the Holy Spirit which, Whitsun-like, moves into us. It is a spirit that we must bring to birth, to manifestation, within us.' (Ibid.) This birth of the spirit in the human 'I' begins already with the first actuation of intuitive thinking that conveys a fundamental experience of the super-sensible world on the human being, namely to be a spirit among spirits.

The words quoted here by Rudolf Steiner (completely in accordance with the first part of *The Philosophy of Freedom*) can attain their full sig-nificance only if the other aspect of the Whitsun event is included as well. That aspect has a similar relationship to the second part. There the point is that as a free being, man (guided by his own moral imagination) can carry out his actions out of pure *love* for the deed. Rudolf Steiner thus describes in the lectures dealing with *The Fifth Gospel* that the souls of the Apostles experienced 'fructification with the all-reigning Cosmic Love' on Whitsun day in their innermost being (GA 148, 2 October 1913). This celebration of the Spirit thus became a prophetic indication of future humanity as the Tenth Hierarchy, which ultimately will be creative in the cosmos out of freedom and love. The highest synthesis of the individual and social principle will be realized in that hierarchy, the synthesis of unlimited individual freedom with infinite love as basis of a new social community. Germinally these two elements are already present in *The Philosophy of Freedom*. In the first part the path is shown that leads to experiencing true freedom in intuitive thinking; in the second part, the origin of the future community of 'free spirits' is shown, which is based on the individual activation of moral imagination which in turn leads to actual deeds of love.

From what has been said it now becomes evident that we have in *The Philosophy of Freedom* the book that inwardly builds on the resurrection-impulse, and thus in seed-form bears within itself the whole future of man and the cosmos. Now we can moreover understand the words by Rudolf Steiner[44] who replied to the question 'What will remain of your work in thousands of years?' by saying, 'Nothing except *The Philosophy of Freedom*,' and then he added: 'But all else is contained in it. If one realizes the act of freedom described there, one finds the whole content of anthroposophy. Then one recognizes this philosophy in its true essence as the modern science of resurrection.'[45]

3. *The Philosophy of Freedom* and the Working of the Hierarchies

Comprehension of the whole significance of *The Philosophy of Freedom* can be deepened fundamentally when we try (on the basis of Diagram 5, p. 21) to place this unique book in the cosmic-hierarchical perspective that it deserves. In the lecture on 19 December 1914, Rudolf Steiner describes by means of the sources of his spirit-research how, inasmuch as human beings on earth perceive, have mental pictures and think, they produce a sort of spiritual light in that world without initially being aware of it in which the entities of the highest, the First Hierarchy, show great interest. 'The Cherubim come and gather this light and use it for the evolving cosmic order. Inasmuch as we *think, perceive and have mental pictures*, we are the lights of the Cherubim in the order of the cosmos. Inasmuch as we live here, we see how these lights of the physical world shine. Thus we are the light-givers of the spiritual worlds for the Cherubim.' (GA 156, 19 December 1914.)[46]

From what has been stated it follows that particularly in actualizing the first part of *The Philosophy of Freedom* that deals with work on perceptions, mental pictures and thinking (stages 1, 2, 3 in Diagram 5), we continuously bestow light on the Cherubim in the cosmos. In accordance with the second part, when we carry out truly ethical deeds through moral imagination out of our will impulses that are en-fired and guided by our moral imagination, it is the Seraphim who receive the inner warmth of our will which is immersed in love. 'Not only do actions occur outwardly through us in the world, but in so far as they are *moral actions* they are gathered by the Seraphim. These moral actions are the fountainhead of warmth for the whole cosmic order.' (Ibid.)

In the above quoted lecture, Rudolf Steiner points out that this even takes place through ordinary thinking and actions. It is that much more the case when, in the sense of the first part of the *Philosophy of Freedom*, thinking arises to intuitions of thought and, in accordance with the second part, actions are carried out by means of moral imagination. Then man shines light into the cosmos for the Cherubim and becomes a source of warmth for the Seraphim in a manner that hardly ever occurs elsewhere in the universe. Rudolf Steiner sums this up in the following words: 'You see, the world-view that spiritual science gives us becomes very real. Spiritual science makes us aware that when you think you are the enkindled light of the Cherubim. When you act, do something, when you unfold your will, you are the source of warmth—the source of fire—for the Seraphim.' (Ibid.)

Now one can better understand why the third category of the entities of the First Hierarchy, the Thrones or Spirits of Will, gave man the predisposition for the future physical body as early as on Ancient Saturn. They did this in order that, later on earth through the physical body, we could attain to individual 'I'-consciousness and thus (through our individual cognition and personal action) we could become light-sources for the Cherubim and warmth-sources for the Seraphim, a fact that in turn enables them to spread light and warmth throughout the whole cosmos.

Now this possibility to radiate and warm the world of the First Hierarchy from the earth (out of the fully conscious 'I') is given to all human beings through the Mystery of Golgotha. And if, through *The Philosophy of Freedom* and the other 'pre-anthroposophical writings' by Rudolf Steiner, we can be effective all the way into the domain of the Seraphim and Cherubim, then anthroposophy leads us in its direct continuation even into the sphere of the Word of Worlds. This is the Logos that became 'flesh' at the Turning Point of Time, and took on the human corporeality in order (through Its complete spiritualization in the Resurrection) to enable all human beings to tread the path of man's becoming a logos.

The Word of Worlds first had to become man once so that in future time every human being can become a microcosmic logos so as to live fully conscious both on earth and in the spiritual world simultaneously as an eternal persona or immortal 'I'. That is why anthroposophy can likewise be depicted as follows. As a science of resurrection, it is at the same time the path on which man can ascend (through the conscious connection with the resurrection forces) to the micro-logos that is related in its essence with the World Logos, the Christ. This path corresponds anthropologically to the transition from the human 'I', a gift of the Exusiai at the start of Earth evolution (higher 'I'), to its true 'I' in the sense of the saying, 'Not I but the Christ in me'.[47]

★

On the basis of Diagram 1 (p. 6), we can now discover a relationship between the initiation path of seven stages pictured there and the great planetary development that likewise runs its course through seven (here) cosmic stages. (The connection between these two will be established in the next chapter.)

Each of the seven planetary stages of our Earth's evolution has one hierarchy as its regent. Thus, for Ancient Saturn the Thrones have this function; for the Old Sun, the Kyriotetes; for the Old Moon, the Dynamis. For our Earth, it is the Exusiai (or in biblical terms, the Elohim) who endowed man with his 'I'. This development continues in a similar manner into the future. Today's Archai will be the regents of the future Jupiter; the Archangels will be the leaders of the future Venus, and the Angels the leaders on Vulcan.

Only after that will the central creator-function in our cosmos be passed on to human beings as the Tenth Hierarchy so that they can create the new solar system out of freedom and love. According to Rudolf Steiner, this will come about as follows.[48] At the conclusion of its evolution the old solar system will draw together (contract) into a sun (on Diagram 8 the transition from 7 to 8), then turn inside out (in the centre of the world-lemniscate) and become a periphery in the form of a new zodiac. In its centre, this zodiac will then create a new sense-perceptible world (the further path from 8 to 1). The prototype and inner foundation for this grand metamorphosis, which represents the great cosmic sacrifice on the part of the beings bringing it about, will be the Mystery of Golgotha for them. This is why, according to Rudolf Steiner, this lofty stage of development is the 'great cosmic offering-service' in the universe.[49]

Man will attain this stage only at the end of the Vulcan time. Rudolf Steiner describes it in the following words: 'When will has attained a stage where it is in a position to carry out what is called the great offering [or sacrifice], it creates a universe, large or small, and this universe is a mirror-image that receives its task through the being of the Creator itself. By means of this we have characterized what the creative will is in the divine entity.' (GA 96, 28 January 1907.) The reference to the will in this process also links what has been said with the Vulcan condition, which on a much higher level will repeat Ancient Saturn, which originated out of the substance of will. Man himself will then possess such a creative will. (Diagram 8.)

This drawing makes it evident that in the entire development just described the two transitions or points of intersection are, above all, of special significance (points 4 and 8). After the Spirits of Form had given man the 'I' at the beginning of Earth evolution (point 4), there took place in the middle of its two halves of Mars and Mercury the Mystery of Golgotha, which represents the centre of the world-lemniscate. With the Mystery of Golgotha, evolution in its entirety was given its actual meaning. As a result, the path into the future of our World evolution likewise became feasible, the first step of which is the transition to Jupiter

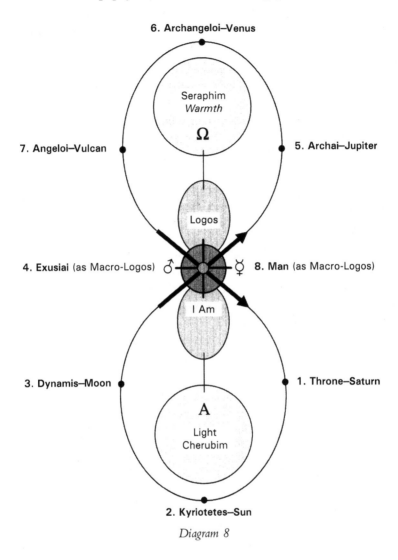

Diagram 8

(point 5) which John depicted in the Apocalypse as the imagination of the Heavenly Jerusalem.

One can likewise say that through the Mystery of Golgotha the 'I' of man received the strength to fulfil its actual mission at the end of our World evolution. This mission (or task) is that the human being, having come to resemble the Logos, will in the future reach the point of creating a new solar system. This process of the cosmic new creation, which will take place as the result of the union of man's 'I' with the 'I am' of the Christ, corresponds in Diagram 8 to the transition from point 7 to the new point 1. In the centre of this transition as its spiritual source of strength stands the second intersection-point of the whole development (point 8), the moment in which humanity as Tenth Hierarchy will rise towards the level of creating a new cosmos. Of this new cosmos of 'freedom and love', man will be the creator and regent just as were the seven preceding hierarchies on the earlier evolutionary levels.

In regard to the two highest hierarchies, those of the Cherubim and Seraphim, they are so exalted that they do not directly participate in the whole above-described development. (They work into it more through the lower hierarchies ministering to them.)[50] Still, as explained before in this chapter, they too receive something back from man, namely the light of individual cognition and the warmth of free deeds of love. Moreover, because these exalted entities stand out from the boundaries of the sevenfold evolution they can therefore principally guard and represent this evolution's beginning and end.

The Bible pointed this out early on by relating that after humankind's expulsion from Paradise a cherub with a fiery sword was placed at its threshold as its guardian (Gen. 3:24). Thus the Cherubim (as spirits of the highest harmony) are furthermore the cosmic guardians of the primordial, universal wisdom's[51] spiritual light, or the Spirits of the *Beginning*. Rudolf Steiner too describes how they were present in the environs of Ancient Saturn[52] as those spirits who primarily had to ensure the transition from the pre-Saturnian cosmos to the coming about of our solar system.

In comparison to them, the Seraphim are the guardians of the objective of that cosmic evolution which consists in the coming about of that hierarchy which, based on its own responsibility (without any higher guidance) freely acts out of love as the highest world-creative power, and shall create the new cosmos. With that, the Seraphim as the Spirits of the *End* are moreover the guardians of the Heavenly Jerusalem, which, according to Rudolf Steiner, will come into being in future time out of the white magic of love. (See GA 104, 29 June 1908.) For 'inasmuch as the moral ideas are gleaned out of the spiritual world through moral imagination, they express themselves in its [the moral imagination's] power, becoming the power of *spiritual love*' (GA 74, 24 May 1920). Out of these deeds of spiritual love, the Heavenly Jerusalem will ultimately be constructed. And the Seraphim will remain guardians of the *End* up until future Vulcan and beyond. (Diagram 9.)

The Cherubim and Seraphim are in addition the regents of the entire process that is described at the end of *Occult Science, an Outline* as the transition from the Cosmos of Wisdom to the Cosmos of Love. The secrets of the first cosmos are guarded by the Cherubim, those of the

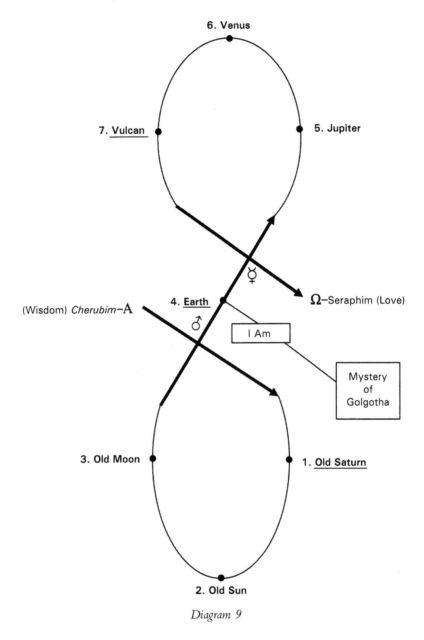

Diagram 9

second by the Seraphim. The change from the first to the second cosmos can only occur through the actions of man's free 'I' which has received the forces of the Christ-'I' into itself and with that has become a micrologos.

One might also say that the activity of the Word of Worlds through the

Cherubim and Seraphim encompasses the whole of cosmic evolution from beginning to end, from the World Alpha to the World Omega. With that, Diagram 9[53] is merely the clarification of the words from the Apocalypse: 'I am the Alpha and the Omega, the beginning and the end, says the Lord God, who is and who was and who is to come, the Almighty' (Rev. 1:8).

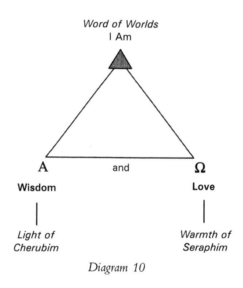

Diagram 10

The other hierarchies also do not remain detached from the activity of the Word of Worlds, particularly when, one after the other, they reach the culmination in their creative activity, become regents of the cosmic development and create a new category of 'I'-beings. It is then that the Logos works directly through them. Thus, He worked through the Thrones on Ancient Saturn when they endowed the Archai with the 'I', through the Kyriotetes who (on the Old Sun) created the Archangeloi as 'I'-beings and through the Dynamis (on the Old Moon) during the creation of the Angeloi.

In the same way the Logos worked through the Exusiai during the Earth-aeon (especially through the seven Sun Elohim) when, at the beginning of Earth evolution, they created man. Rudolf Steiner points out this secret particularly in the cycle dealing with the Gospel of John where he mentions the Logos, meaning the Christ, in direct connection with the seven Sun Elohim prior to His descent to earth. (GA 103, 20 May 1908.)

This process will also be continued in the coming conditions of our cosmos. On Jupiter, the Word of Worlds will work through the Archai of today, who thereby will ascend to the rank of regents of the cosmic evolution and its creators. On Venus, the Word of Worlds will work through today's Archangels and on Vulcan through today's Angels. Concluding this whole development, the Word of Worlds will manifest through the Hierarchy of Humans as the fount out of which these humans will not only create the new Sun system as the Macro-Logos, but will moreover endow the new kind of beings with the 'I' in this new solar system.[54]

★

In conclusion, another developmental aspect can be pointed out—a development that becomes discernible from Diagram 5 (p. 21) and relates particularly to our present age. In various lectures Rudolf Steiner alludes to the fact that the handing over of the management of the thought-content of our cosmos from the Exusiai to the Archai (and with that from the domain of the Second to the Third Hierarchy) belongs among the most important events of the spiritual world that have occurred since the Mystery of Golgotha.[55] This occurrence has immeasurable consequences for the whole spiritual development of mankind on earth. For the spirits of the Second Hierarchy do not descend into the inner being of man. They work from outside through the processes of nature, or like higher revelations that man can simply follow. Conversely, the spirits of the Third Hierarchy unite directly with the soul of man[56] and produce in it the faculty of individual forming of thoughts. This is why the leading spirits of the Third Hierarchy are named Spirits of *Personality* in spiritual science. The result of this is that man can develop his thoughts today out of his own inner activity in order to experience freedom in this way, and on this basis to attain to free moral intuitions as primary motives of his actions.

Rudolf Steiner himself brings this cosmic happening into a direct connection with *The Philosophy of Freedom*. Having described the whole process of handing the cosmic thoughts over from the Spirits of Form to the Spirits of Personality with all its consequences, he comments on the content of this book: 'As you can find out from my *Philosophy of Freedom,* the fundamental condition for man's freedom is that human beings develop their thoughts themselves through inner activity, and that out of these self-developed thoughts that I called "pure thoughts" in my *Philosophy of Freedom* they can moreover glean the moral impulses.' (GA 222, 18 March 1923.)

This signifies that it is not until after the handing over of the cosmic thoughts from the Exusiai to the Spirits of Personality (in Diagram 8,

p. 41, the transition from Mars to Mercury within Earth evolution) that the actual epoch of freedom began. What is more, a book such as *The Philosophy of Freedom* could only be written after this transition of thought-guidance in the cosmos. In the book itself, one can see a terrestrial replica of this hierarchical-cosmic happening.

When we place this transition into a greater cosmic correlation, we find that the process described above has taken place in earlier times twice before *within* the Second Hierarchy—during the handing over by the Dynamis of the content of cosmic thoughts to the Exusiai (from 3 to 4), and before that by the Kyriotetes to the Dynamis (from 2 to 3).

Still, this process is in no way concluded with the handing over of the cosmic thought-content to the Archai. It will continue. That means a similar handing over will occur in the future by the Archai to the Archangeloi (from 5 to 6) and later by them to the Angeloi (from 6 to 7). Not until after that will something quite special occur in cosmic evolution. The cosmic thought-content will leave the domain of the Third Hierarchy and descend to the realm of mankind to be freely available to human beings (transition from 7 to 8). Thus, the concluding stage of the octave will have been reached in this development and with that a foundation laid for humankind's whole future creative activity of human beings, a stage on which the latter's whole, free unfolding will be possible. For in order to be creative out of love, not only on earth but likewise in the cosmos, one must possess freedom, not merely on the earthly but likewise on the cosmic level. Just as we can become free in human thinking on earth only when attaining to intuitive thinking, so we can become free in the cosmos only when we have its thought-content at our disposal in the same way as we do our earthly thoughts today. In our age, human beings can attain this cosmic freedom only through modern initiation on the stage of Intuition.

It follows from what has been stated in the characterized development that two transitions are of overriding importance: the one from the Exusiai to the Archai and the other from the Angeloi to Man—both proceeding from the central 'I'-point (Diagram 8, p. 41). With that, a reference is made at the same time to their connection with each other and their relationship to the Mystery of Golgotha. Moreover, in both cases the transition takes place not only within *one* hierarchy, but the cosmic thought-content in each instance leaves a large cosmic sphere, once out of the Second to the Third Hierarchy and then from the Third to the emerging hierarchy of humans. Through the first handing over beginning in our time, the goals that the Mystery of Golgotha has posed to human beings can for the first time truly be comprehended, as made possible today through anthroposophy, out of which the first steps can likewise be taken towards their realization. After the second future handing over, this activity of humans will attain a hierarchical–cosmic dimension.

★

The contents of this chapter can add as well to a deeper comprehension of what Rudolf Steiner stated in The Hague to Walter Johannes Stein.[57] To the question of the latter, 'When you wrote the *Philosophy of Freedom*, were you already aware of the hierarchies that you describe in *Occult Science, an Outline* and other sources?' Rudolf Steiner replied, 'They were, but the language that I then spoke offered as yet no possibility of formulation. That came later. However, through the *Philosophy of Freedom*, one rises up to the perception of man as a purely spiritual being. Furthermore, even though *The Philosophy of Freedom* describes only this, it is nevertheless true that one who struggles through to the experience of freedom then finds the hierarchies in the environs of spiritual man whom he then perceives ... This is why they are not formulated in *The Philosophy of Freedom* there, but are contained in it nevertheless.'

4. Aspects of the Study of Man in
The Philosophy of Freedom

The seven stages of the inner path of anthroposophy described in the first chapter of the book *The Stages of Higher Knowledge* (see Diagram 1 on p. 6) have a direct connection to the sevenfold structure of the human being (as depicted in *Theosophy*, GA 9) and consequently to the whole of our World evolution. Thus the first stage, perception, is linked with the physical body, which was created on Ancient Saturn. Even the organs of perception were already predisposed in this body then. For the development of his mental images, the human being required the cooperation of its etheric body, which originated on the Old Sun. The etheric body is the powerful source of all that bears a pictorial nature in the human soul. By contrast the thinking in man is primarily connected with the astral body. The latter was fitted into the human being on the Old Moon. This is why one must seek for the roots of thinking on the Old Moon. (See GA 121, 11 June 1910.) On the Earth the 'I' is added. With it, the human being becomes an individuality that is enclosed within itself.

The three higher members are borne within man today only in rudimentary form. They will reach complete fruition and be in our possession during the three future evolutionary stages of the cosmos: the Spirit Self on Jupiter, the Life Spirit on Venus, and Spirit Man on Vulcan. As early as now, the initiate can recognize the three spiritual members and partially develop them through the activity of his 'I'. For that he must, however, have attained the higher stages of spiritual cognition (or knowledge). On the stage of Imagination, he links himself with the forces of the Spirit Self, on that of Inspiration with the forces of the Life Spirit, and through Intuition he reaches the forces of Spirit Man.

Based on what has been said, we can add the sevenfold structure of man as well as the sevenfold evolution of the cosmos to our drawing (Diagram 11). Here the lower half of the lemniscate depicts the world of the past, and in the upper half the new future world that will originate in due course through the activity of the free 'I' out of the old one (transition from 3 to 5 through the decisive 'I'-point [4]). This also corresponds to the transformation of the Cosmos of Wisdom into the future Cosmos of Love on the path of individual 'I'-development.

The other transition (from 7 through the great cosmic 'I'-point to the new one [1]) points to the Mystery of the Resurrection. For on this path

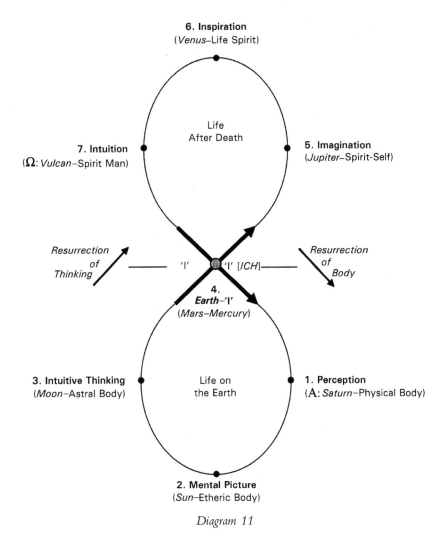

6. Inspiration
(*Venus*–Life Spirit)

Life
After Death

7. Intuition
(**Ω**: *Vulcan*–Spirit Man)

5. Imagination
(*Jupiter*–Spirit-Self)

*Resurrection
of
Thinking*

'I' — 'I' [*ICH*]

*Resurrection
of
Body*

**4.
Earth–'I'**
(*Mars–Mercury*)

3. Intuitive Thinking
(*Moon*–Astral Body)

Life on
the Earth

1. Perception
(**A**: *Saturn*–Physical Body)

2. Mental Picture
(*Sun*–Etheric Body)

Diagram 11

the fully developed Spirit Man of the Christ as the supersensible form of His divine 'I' penetrates the physical body of Jesus of Nazareth.[58] Rudolf Steiner mentions this when he says of the Christ Being: 'There we have the being as god, a being that man as man will be at the end of the Vulcan development' (GA 346, 7 September 1924). With this, Christ connects the beginning of our cosmic evolution (the creation of the physical body on Ancient Saturn) with its end (the genesis of Spirit Man on Vulcan), and can therefore say in the Apocalypse: 'I am the Alpha and the Omega, the beginning and the end ... who is and who was and who is to come ...' (Rev. 1:8.)[59]

In this penetration of the physical body (A–Alpha) with Spirit Man (Ω–Omega), the whole evolution of humankind and the world reaches its culmination and thus closes the lemniscate which, from its highest stage (7), returns to the starting point (1). Yet this does not take place as a sort of return to what was in the past; rather it is a mighty breakthrough into the future.[60] For through the Resurrection of the Christ the foundation was created for the new cosmos of love, at the origin of which the human being who has received the Christ Impulse into himself will participate freely and consciously.

The path that has been outlined in Diagram 11 encompasses the totality of the anthroposophical study of man (the sevenfold human being) and shows how in its centre stand the two inseparably linked, most important factors of all of Earth evolution, a macro- and a microcosmic one: the Resurrection of the Christ and the development of the individual human 'I', which initially can trace this deed of the Christ in its spiritualized thinking.

If one comprehends the lemniscate depicted here as a Möbius strip in which the exterior of its one half forms the interior of the other half and the other way round, one can arrive at an apt symbol for how, through the Mystery of Golgotha, the two worlds—the physical and the spiritual (or earthly and after-death) worlds—were linked with each other in a completely new way. And if today the 'I' of the human being inwardly links up with the Mystery of Golgotha, it can continually be active fully consciously in both worlds as was demonstrated in exemplary manner by Rudolf Steiner in his life and work.

★

Everything in evolution that will appear to the full extent later must be prepared earlier as a kind of presentiment. How this can occur today is shown in Diagram 5 (p. 21), which relates to *The Philosophy of Freedom*.

In accordance with this drawing, one can say that the most important task of our fifth post-Atlantean epoch is for the largest number of people to develop *intuitive thinking* (point 3) in themselves so that through the intensified activity of the 'I' (point 4) they will arrive at the possibility of becoming active through moral imagination. Just as in our time a decisive role is ascribed to the development of thinking and the individualism based on it, an equally important role will be ascribed to *moral imagination* in the sixth cultural epoch. And just as today everything aims towards the development of individuality, so everything will then be directed towards the unfolding of the social element. This is why social questions can never be solved purely through human thinking, but only through the aid of pictorial (imaginative) mental images that lead to the faculty of free moral imagination. Consequently, the sixth cultural period, which will receive the forces of the Spirit Self into itself, will likewise be the time of the greatest unfolding of moral imagination in the human being as well as in the social life of mankind.

A similar significance as is attributed in the sixth period (that of the Spirit Self) to moral imagination will be attributed in the seventh cultural period (in which man attains to the first contact with the Life Spirit) to a yet higher faculty of the human soul, namely that of *moral intuition*. Outwardly, this will be the horrible time of the War of All against All. To endure as a human being in that chaos, and to fulfil one's task on earth despite it all, one will above all need moral intuitions. Only thereby will we be in a position to follow the good freely and uphold it in the realm of evil, which will then surround us on all sides.

Ultimately, in the first period of the great Sixth Epoch which then begins following the War of All against All, man will more than anything else require the faculty of *moral technique* in the devastated world he will then confront, moral technique to assure the construction of a new lofty spiritual culture over the whole of earth. This will moreover be the time when humanity's first contact with the forces of Spirit Man will take place, forces out of which alone people can bear the spiritual impulses all the way into the physical world in order there to be able to become creatively active.

In summation it can be said that in the above-mentioned three evolutionary stages as described in the second part of *The Philosophy of Freedom* lie the very beginnings for the faculties that even today prepare man's future connection with the forces of the Spirit Self, the Life Spirit and Spirit Man, and along with that the future cultural periods. The conscious development of these faculties will, however, only be possible if—at least incipiently—man actualizes the goals of the first part of *The Philosophy of Freedom* and arrives at the experience of freedom in thinking. (Diagram 12.)

In the domain of thinking, a process takes place on a higher level in the human being that resembles the one in our brain and nervous system. In the latter, death forces are uninterruptedly active during man's conscious life, forces that must constantly be evened out through the remaining organism. The thinking that is tied to the brain likewise possesses this dead character. And only because this is so is human freedom possible at all.

Considered from the viewpoint of spiritual science, brain thinking is merely a shadow, a corpse of the entity-possessing living thinking that every human being had in the spiritual world prior to birth. 'If you wish

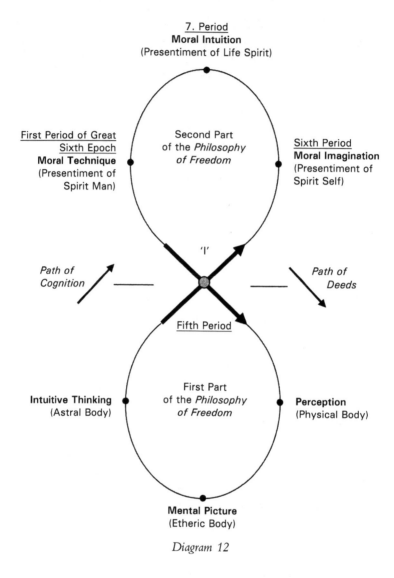

Diagram 12

to understand ordinary thinking, you have to tell yourself that it is dead, that it is a soul–corpse and that its living element existed in pre–earthly life. There the soul lived without the body in the aliveness of this thinking.' (GA 257, 6 February 1923.) Today, man must come in a new way through the portal of the 'exceptional state' to this being-like living thinking that originates in the world of Imaginations. Then this thinking will serve man as a supersensible organ of perception for consciously cognizing the spiritual Imaginations. As if out of the dark tomb of the physical brain, the new thinking radiantly appears here in order to penetrate through the whole world, and with that to make it visible for hierarchical consciousness.

In this process of enlivening the thoughts that appear initially as if dead in man there lies the first rudiment of individually experienced resurrection. Thinking thereby enters the spiritual world and receives—as does everything in the spiritual world—an entity-possessing, moral character. Here, a profoundly Christian Mystery takes place on the level of thoughts. And because this path of enlivening thinking is described and well-founded, above all in *The Philosophy of Freedom*, Rudolf Steiner can say of this book: 'This *Philosophy of Freedom* is actually a view of morality that tries to give direction on how to enliven the dead thoughts as moral impulses, to bring them to the point of *resurrection*. In so far as this is the case, in such a philosophy on freedom, Christianity is indeed inwardly present. (GA 211, 2 April 1922.) In this way the resurrection of thinking takes place in the domain of imaginations with which we can behold the life prior to birth and directly following death.

Now if somebody who is a spirit disciple advances further on the anthroposophical path of cognition, he arrives with his enlivened thinking in the realm of Inspirations. In this way, life in the spiritual world between two incarnations can be perceived and consciously traced. This only becomes possible if the resurrection process that has been individually experienced in thinking is now extended into feeling. Yet it is not until the ascent into the dimension of Intuitions that man at the same time recognizes his earlier incarnations. This occurs when he expands the resurrection process that began in thinking into the will. Now he can consciously experience the Midnight Hour in intuitive cognition and at the same time the activity of the First Hierarchy, which imprints the karma of the earlier Earth incarnations into the present life. This experiencing of the First Hierarchy's karmic world-working is the main condition of the truthful research of a man's earlier incarnations.

With these highest spiritual forces that are in a position to take hold of and transform even physical matter in order then to place it in the service of the spirit (of karma), the resurrection of the Christ at the Turning Point of Time is directly connected.[61] Likewise, His present activity as Lord of Karma comes about based on the forces of the Cosmic Midnight Hour through the mediation of the spirits of the First Hierarchy as a direct result of the Mystery of Golgotha.[62]

For this reason Rudolf Steiner could say, 'the proper comprehension of the idea of destiny and the tracing of this idea all the way up into the spiritual worlds not only establishes a philosophy of determination but a true philosophy of freedom' (GA 215, 15 September, 1922). For in the light of the Christ's activity as Lord of Karma, the idea of destiny (karma) is rooted in the Mystery of Golgotha itself, which means in the deed of highest freedom and love. In turn, through this deed the inner space was created in every human being for the realization of freedom and love. This is why, according to Rudolf Steiner, the right usage of freedom that finds fulfilment in creative deeds of love and the unique deed of the Christ on the hill of Golgotha are inseparably connected. He says that only in the sphere of resurrection and only through the connection with its forces is human freedom even possible. This is why the highest form of this freedom consists in the individual and objective 'co-experiencing' of the Resurrection itself as well as in its realization in one's own soul through the inner activity of the 'I' in thinking, feeling and willing.

In this way, Rudolf Steiner's whole path of accomplishments comes together in a wondrous unity. He starts on it with the establishment of a philosophy of freedom and concludes it with the mighty karma revelations in the lectures of 1924 (GA 235–240). The reason why these two domains (which initially seem so far removed from each other that they appear contradictory) are united in harmonious consequentialness is their inner relationship to the Mystery of Golgotha, and its effects to this very day.

In the chapter about initiation in *Occult Science, an Outline*, Rudolf Steiner writes about two deeply connected paths into the spiritual world. He characterizes them in the following way. One is 'the way that leads through the communications of spiritual science into sense-free thinking; a path that is absolutely safe'. Of the other he says, 'Now there is still another path that is safer and most of all more accurate, but for many people it is more difficult. It is depicted in my books *Goethe the Scientist* and *The Philosophy of Freedom*'.[63]

These two paths with their different stages are symbolized in Diagram 3 (the first path), on p. 11 and Diagram 5 (the second path), on p. 21. With each of them, although in a slightly different manner, a profound Christian secret is still connected in the light of the preceding deliberations. For the two most important decisive transitions (from 3 to 5 and from 7 to the new 1), which belong to each of the paths, point at the same time to the two most important events in the spiritual world, events that are connected with the contemporary activity of the Christ Being involving humanity. The first event is the Christ's appearance on the astral plane in etheric form, meaning in imaginative form. Every human being who takes a further step today on the path of modern initiation from sense-free (intuitive) thinking to the development of 'intellectual clairvoyance' (in order consciously to enter the world of Imaginations) will sooner or later encounter the imaginative figure of the Etheric Christ there.

His etheric appearance, according to Rudolf Steiner, is the result of the second supersensible Mystery of Golgotha, which consisted in the extinction of the Christ-consciousness in an angelic being during the second half of the nineteenth century and the lighting up of that same Christ-consciousness—one level deeper—in the souls of earthly human beings starting from the twentieth century. (See GA 152, 2 May 1913.) This new imaginative consciousness can lead present-day human beings, beginning from the second third of the twentieth century, to the perception of the Etheric Christ.

The second transition, which leads directly out of the highest spiritual realm (that of Intuition or the Cosmic Midnight Hour) into the world of sense perceptions, is a direct consequence of the Mystery of Golgotha on the physical plane. This is moreover the way on which the karma of humankind reaches just fulfilment on earth. For this reason, the Christ has been connected with this process since the Turning Point of Time. For already then His present-day karma-activity was preconceived. The words of John the Baptist give testimony to this: 'See, the Lamb of God who takes the sin of the world upon himself' (John 1:29 JM). The Christ, however, has assumed this position of judge as Lord of Karma only in most recent times in full measure, namely at the end of the twentieth century (see GA 131, 7 October 1911), meaning approximately one hundred years after the second supersensible Mystery of Golgotha.

Man can moreover approach this event as well through modern initiation when he attains the stage of Intuition and from there, based on full insight into karmic relationships, begins to be active on earth. By means of this he can gradually become a fully conscious co-worker of the Christ as Lord of Karma.

Summing this up one can say that the spiritual founts of today's karma-activity on the part of the Christ are rooted in the Mystery of Golgotha at the Turning Point of Time, just as the spiritual sources of His appearance in etheric form originate from the second supersensible Mystery of Golgotha (see Diagram 13 next page). These two experiences, the encounter with the Etheric Christ and cooperating with His present karma-working, can be attained not merely on the first path[64] but, although in another form, likewise on the second, the path of *The Philosophy of Freedom*. Thus, the actualization[65] of the first part of *The Philosophy of Freedom* leads to the perception of the Christ in the etheric realm through the metamorphosis of thinking that gradually turns into a

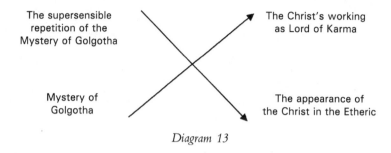

The supersensible repetition of the Mystery of Golgotha

The Christ's working as Lord of Karma

Mystery of Golgotha

The appearance of the Christ in the Etheric

Diagram 13

new organ of perception for Imaginations. The actualization of the book's second part leads the individual through the corresponding metamorphosis of the will—which thereby becomes capable only of deeds of love—to the free cooperation with the Christ as Lord of Karma.[66]

Here the path of *The Philosophy of Freedom* (Diagram 5 on p. 21) and its further development and continuation in modern initiation (Diagram 1 on p. 6) pass in like manner through the crossing point of the *human 'I'* (point 4 in both diagrams). With that, reference has not only been made to the central significance of man's ego-development in Earth evolution, but also to the fact that the two relationships to Christ (in his etheric revelation and in his karma-ordering activity) can only be attained by the fully conscious and completely free 'I' out of pure cognition and love.

★

With this we have characterized the modern path of the human soul to Christ in the sense of spiritual science and *The Philosophy of Freedom*. The consequences of this path are, however, not only of decisive importance for the individual human being but equally for human social life. In this, both paths ultimately flow together and appear in their inseparable unity as the great future ideal of a new Pentecost community.

Just as the cognitional inception of *The Philosophy of Freedom* leads to the comprehension of the resurrection forces in thinking, so their social inception (which culminates in the forming of a community of 'free spirits') brings about the future perspective of the origination of a new Pentecost community on earth. For the miracle of Whitsun always follows the inwardly experienced Mystery of the Resurrection.

This is why Rudolf Steiner says about the Pentecostal spirit: 'In this way, the Holy Spirit is for us humans the Spirit of evolution towards the free man, the free human soul in regard to our future development ... So, the symbol of Whitsun is transformed for us into our mightiest ideal of the free development of the human soul towards a free individuality complete within itself.' This, 'our mightiest ideal', is indeed the highest ideal of the first part of *The Philosophy of Freedom*, to which is then added the second mighty ideal of a future community of 'free individualities complete within themselves'. (GA 118, 15 May 1910.)

For even though all the Apostles received 'the individualized Holy Spirit' (ibid.) during the Whitsun-event, meaning each of them received his own *individual* tongue of fire,[67] they were all filled and permeated by *one* Holy Spirit (Acts 2:4). This corresponds exactly to what Rudolf Steiner in his *Philosophy of Freedom* characterized as the social 'fundamental maxim' of free human beings, a maxim that alone can guarantee their working together: 'A moral misunderstanding—a clash—is impossible between people who are morally *free* ... To *live* in love towards our actions and to *let live* in the understanding of the other person's will is the fundamental maxim of *free men*.' (GA 4, Chap. IX; emphasis by Rudolf Steiner.) This 'fundamental maxim' is at the same time the central element of the future Pentecostal community of humanity, meaning of all people who on earth '*are* of one spirit' (ibid.). This encounter with the other person in the same intentions is only possible when, in both persons these intentions spring from the same fount of the Holy Spirit, in which all human beings are connected with each other.

This Spirit who unites the free and (due to that) highly individualized human beings in a new brotherhood of free spirits is moreover called by Rudolf Steiner in reference to the Gospel of John the 'spirit of truth'[68] (GA 97, 17 March, 1907). Then he continues: 'Two human beings who know the spirit of truth will on their own feel attracted to one another.' This means that when two or more people have truly realized the lofty ideal of freedom, they will in a quite independent manner link up with each other. Only in this way will a free union of human beings eventually result among mankind, whose prototype and example will be the Pentecostal community at the Turning Point of Time. For, 'this has come to expression in such a wondrous way in the miracle at Whitsun, where the Apostles expanded their brotherly union to a union of humanity and spoke in a language that everyone understood. This must come to expression more and more, namely alongside the highest development of the individuality. And all are united by the Spirit of Truth.'(GA 96, 25 March 1907.) While not in so many words but out of the whole nature of inwardly recognized and experienced freedom in his *Philosophy of Freedom*, Rudolf Steiner likewise points to this Whitsun Spirit of Truth, which unites all free human beings.

5. The Three Sciences

In the lecture where Rudolf Steiner refers for the second time in detail to the 'Pauline spirit' of *The Philosophy of Freedom*,[69] we come across the following passage: 'Starting with this philosophy it is possible to find the bridge across to the Christ Spirit, just as the bridge can be found from natural science to the Father Spirit' (GA 176, 4 September 1917).

The connection of today's natural science with the domain of the Father is made possible through Goetheanism. For based on its own resources, today's science offers only the basis for a radical atheism due to its materialistic form, and thus disavows any actual relationship to the Father. Goetheanism, on the other hand, not only links human beings anew with the domain of the Father but bears within itself the seeds for the next stage. Rudolf Steiner indicates this in the words: 'Goetheanism is at the same time a mood of expectation for a new conception of the Mystery of Golgotha' (GA 188, 11 January 1919). This is why Goethe's theory of knowledge forms a bridge from his science to *The Philosophy of Freedom*.

But only the philosophy of freedom leads directly to the Son, or put more precisely the science of freedom as it was established in *The Philosophy of Freedom*, and is grounded in the latter's two parts like two supporting pillars, as freedom and love.

Ultimately to these two sciences a third one is added, the science of the spirit or anthroposophy. Thus we have a total of three sciences:

Natural Science	— Science of the Father
Science of Freedom	— Science of the Son
Spiritual Science	— Science of the Holy Spirit.[70]

As the 'most Christian of all philosophies' (GA 212, 7 May 1922), *The Philosophy of Freedom* contains the Christ Impulse within itself through its *ethical individualism*. As yet the latter does not enter man's whole consciousness, remaining instead as if in the background, for in this book 'cognition *stops short* of entry into spiritual experience'. (GA 4; emphasis by Rudolf Steiner.) Yet as we have seen, this path of *The Philosophy of Freedom* leads ultimately to 'having stood before the Mystery of Golgotha' and with that to the spiritual experience in which the Resurrection forces work directly. For, 'ethical individualism actually relies on the Christ Impulse in man, even though this is not brought up in my *Philosophy of Freedom*.'[71] (GA 74, 24 May 1920.)

Along with anthroposophy, Christ Himself enters human consciousness. This takes place, however, through the mediation of the Holy Spirit,
for otherwise no human being could consciously tolerate the presence of
Christ's cosmic being.[72] Thus, the new Christ-consciousness originates in
man that consists in the working of the Christ through the Holy Spirit in
the human soul. This is the true birth of the science of the spirit out of the
science of freedom. And at the moment when Rudolf Steiner on his
initiation-path had reached this Christ-consciousness, he could establish
anthroposophy in the world.

The three afore-mentioned sciences can also be characterized as follows. Once the first science has overcome its materialism, and with the
help of Goetheanism will arise to the stage where 'the laboratory
worktable is lifted to the level of an altar' (GA 130, 4 November 1911), it
will contribute more to the general sacramentalization of human life. By
then the encounter between two people will be a sort of sacrament that
will lead gradually to a new foundation for true brotherliness. This new
sacramentalism will be the only way for bringing about the union of
humanity and will form a basis on which true art and true religion can
stand unshakeably. Here at this point, relating to Schelling, one can also
designate this development as that of *Peter*.[73]

The second science (the one of freedom) is developed by Rudolf
Steiner out of the spirit of *Paul*. In this spirit lives the possibility today of
attaining to the beholding of Christ in the etheric realm through the
transformation of thinking. The path of cognition based on it is the
modern metamorphosis of the inner path of Paul that led him to
Damascus. Taking hold of the Resurrection forces in thinking and with
that rising to the experience of true human freedom forms two inseparable facets of the same process. This is why Rudolf Steiner brings the
whole development of human freedom on earth into a direct connection
with this fundamental experience of Paul: 'On the one hand one can
therefore be totally inclined to what is necessary for freedom, but on the
other ... one can find the way to the Pauline words: Not I but the Christ
in me.' (GA 212, 7 May 1922.) Thus there has to live in the soul 'on the
one side a strong impulse towards freedom, and on the other side there
must live in the soul a strong impulse to inwardly live through the
Mystery of Golgotha' (ibid.). Only then can such a 'contemporary soul
place itself in the right way ... into World evolution' (ibid.).

We moreover find in Paul the greatest acknowledgement and strongest
emphasis of individual freedom. According to Paul, this follows directly
from the Christ's Deed on Golgotha and liberates the human being from
the inner slavery of sin and the outer law on which the human being, who

is 'called to freedom' (Gal. 5:13), can stand self-evidently and unshakeably. 'So stand firm in the freedom into which the Christ has freed us; do not let yourselves be harnessed again in the yolk of servitude' (5:1). These words of Paul correspond exactly to those that in a certain connection represent the culmination of the central Christological cycle by Rudolf Steiner, *From Jesus to Christ*: 'Human beings should not be able to grasp the thought of freedom without the thought of the Redemption on the part of the Christ. For only then is the thought of freedom a justified one.' (GA 131, 14 November 1911.) This fundamental result of Rudolf Steiner's research, which was likewise Paul's firm conviction, is in no way contradictory to the content of *The Philosophy of Freedom*, but a direct continuation of its inner path. But what was for Paul at the Turning Point of Time the unexpected and grace-filled revelation from above (the Damascus event), became for Rudolf Steiner a result of the modern, strictly scientific path of cognition, which alone corresponds to the present era of the consciousness soul.

The third science in which the whole profundity of the Christ Mystery makes its appearance represents the path of John or the actual path of esoteric Christianity. For this chosen Apostle did not experience the Whitsun event (as did all the other Apostles) 50 days after Easter, but already at the eve of the day of Resurrection. This is why it is only in his Gospel that this pure Easter spirit-outpouring is found that emanates from the Christ Himself (John 20:22).[74] With that, as the first of all human beings, John was in a position to receive into himself the forces of the World-'I' of the Christ through the mediation of the Holy Spirit,[75] and this means that he was the first to develop the Christ-consciousness on earth. On this foundation, he could then write the most profound gospel (the Gospel of Sophia) and the Apocalypse in which the primal fount of the Christian as well as the Christian-Rosicrucian initiation is to be found.[76] With this John, at the Turning Point of Time, became the prophetic representative of the later science of the spirit.

All above-mentioned qualities—the new sacramentalism, which encompasses human life (even including ordinary matters); the impulse of freedom, which in human relationships relies on absolute freedom of thought and mutual recognition; and pneumatology or modern spiritual science, which conveys the actual insights concerning the spiritual world—these are supersensible images that the angels develop today in the astral bodies of human beings. Rudolf Steiner describes this in the lecture *What Does the Angel Do in Our Astral Body?* where he describes this activity of the angels as follows: 'Spiritual science for the spirit, religious freedom for the soul, brotherliness for the bodies. This resounds like cosmic music through the work of the angels in the human astral bodies' (GA 182, 9 October 1918).

This 'angelic' music—which resounds inaudibly to outward hearing in every human being in regard to body, soul, and spirit, filling our whole nature—finds its earthly expression and its concrete forms of appearance in the three characterized sciences:

Natural Science   —   for the body
Science of Freedom   —   for the soul[77]
Spiritual Science   —   for the spirit

Thus the circle closes, and with the help of anthroposophy the human being can even today begin to do conscious work together with the beings of the spiritual world, and with that take the first step on the path to the Tenth Hierarchy.

In our time, Michael plays a decisive role in this conscious teamwork between the human being with the entities of the higher hierarchies that begin with the angels. 'For the point here is that the paths of gods and men come together in our present age'. And 'Michael will become the great mediator between the paths of the gods and the paths of men'. (GA 346, 22 September 1924.) Proceeding from these words, we shall now speak about the significance of Michael for the main subject of this book.

6. Michael and *The Philosophy of Freedom*

An attentive reader may have noted that in this work nothing has been said as yet about the relationship of *The Philosophy of Freedom* to the Time Spirit, Michael, a relationship that Rudolf Steiner referred to with great emphasis particularly at the end of his life in the so-called 'Michael Letters' (GA 26). The reason for this is that I have dealt with this subject already in detail elsewhere, for instance in Chapter 7, '*The Philosophy of Freedom* and the Christmas Conference', in my book *May Human Beings Hear It! The Mystery of the Christmas Conference*, and considered more from the viewpoint of Rudolf Steiner's biography in Chapter 1, 'Rudolf Steiner's Course of Life in the Light of the Christmas Conference'.

The goal of the work presented here is above all to focus on the Christological foundations of *The Philosophy of Freedom*. By doing that we moreover touch upon the present-day activity of Michael, for he has the task today to bring mankind the new light of cognition that leads to the true comprehension of the Christ Being and the Mystery of Golgotha. 'Michael can give us new spiritual light'—says Rudolf Steiner—'that we can view as a transformation of the light that (through him) was given at the time of the Mystery of Golgotha, a light under which human beings in our time are allowed to place themselves.' (GA 152, 2 May 1913.) This Michaelic light penetrates the whole content of *The Philosophy of Freedom* and continues on into anthroposophy where the contemporary Michael-revelation becomes accessible to all human beings of good will.

Here we shall now deal with one aspect of the theme that I had not yet touched upon. In a variation of the 'Golden Legend', Rudolf Steiner describes how, after Adam's exclusion from Paradise, the two trees (the one of knowledge and the one of life) became entwined with each other. And in front of them (these two trees that had become one) Michael was placed as their new guardian. (GA 96, 17 December 1906.) Seth, Adam's third son, who had attained an initiation and therefore was allowed to re-enter Paradise for a brief time, took three seeds from this entwined tree (Michael permitted this) and placed them into Adam's mouth after his death. The three seeds are the germinal beginnings for the higher spirit-nature of the human being, Spirit Self, Life Spirit and Spirit Man, which thereby were fitted into humanity's evolution. Since then they indwell this evolution as the gifts of the entwined tree of Paradise and promise of humanity's future.

If looking at the two trees to begin with in their separate condition, one can determine that while the first tree gives humankind the insights that lead to the awakening of individual consciousness they cause death at the same time in man. What has been consumed from this tree awakens earthly ego-consciousness, which is mortal due to its bond with the physical body. The second tree does bestow eternal life (immortality) on man but it is of a kind in which an individual consciousness cannot survive. In the separate trees we thus have the whole tragedy of the alternative: either ego-consciousness that is mortal or immortality of the soul without ego-consciousness.[78] In the union of the two trees, on the other hand, there exists a prophetic preview of the solution of this alternative through the Mystery of Golgotha. For it was through it that the individual ego of man was saved and the portals of immortality were opened wide for the 'I'-consciousness. The future development of the three spiritual members of the human being also became possible as a result, and with it the attainment of the ultimate goal of all evolution.

This process which took place macrocosmically on the level of existence at the Turning Point of Time continued on microcosmically on the level of human consciousness in *The Philosophy of Freedom*. Thus, in the first part of this book a path is outlined on which dead thinking as the original bearer of ego-consciousness, freeing itself from its dependence on the body, can ascend to the pure or *living* thinking. In this way, the possibility arises for the human being to eat of the Tree of Knowledge without succumbing to Lucifer or death respectively. This is brought about inasmuch as human beings fill their thinking with will and strengthen it so much thereby that, without supporting itself with the brain, thinking can endure outside the body as intuitive thinking.

In the second part of the book, an additional path is outlined on which man learns to unfold the faculty of moral imagination with the aid of what had previously been attained through the transformation of thinking. Working based on this, one will then be able to perform actions out of pure love for the deed. With this we are going to be in a position *consciously* to take hold of our 'I' in the otherwise unconsciously working will, in order thereby to act freely and to create the good in the world. In this activity man can eat of the Tree of Life without forfeiting his 'I'-consciousness and subsequently falling prey to Ahriman or evil respectively. This happens due to the fact that one penetrates one's will with the light of intuitive thinking and out of this fount can carry out moral deeds or acts of love.[79]

On the firm foundation of these two entwined trees, all human beings today have the opportunity to attain to the stage of *ethical individualism* in their inner development. For, as Rudolf Steiner states, we 'build on what man strives for in the way of freedom, inasmuch as we transform ordinary thinking into what I called *pure thinking* in my *Philosophy of Freedom,* [a thinking] that rises into the spiritual world and then out of it brings to birth the motivations for moral actions . . . through *moral imagination.*' (GA 74, 24 May 1920.)

The two paths are connected as an inseparable unity in *The Philosophy of Freedom,* for their two parts, 'Science of Freedom' and 'The Reality of Freedom', blend into one another organically and show how the modern human being can achieve freedom in order then to be able to implement it in concrete human actions. In fitting these two parts together, one can behold an earthly replica today of the inseparably connected trees in the spiritual world whose connection in human life is expressed in individual cognition and the subsequent following free actions.

Likewise, a reference to the two linked trees is contained in the twofold concept of 'ethical individualism', for the final consequence of eating from the Tree of Knowledge is man's ultimate development towards acquiring individuality. The eating from the Tree of Life corresponds to the free human deeds that emanate from moral imaginations, and therefore bear an ethical character from the very beginning. It can thus be said that we have a kind of archetype of ethical individualism in the two entwined trees, something like its celestial idea that Michael himself guards in the spiritual world.

This heavenly primal idea of ethical individualism could, however, only be actualized on earth after the Mystery of Golgotha. For through this unique sacrificial deed by the Christ, a deed that in a new way linked heaven and earth, human beings were given the possibility for free actualization of this highest ideal of humanness. Already during the epoch of the consciousness soul, human beings will have brought their 'I' to the corresponding maturity and independence so that 15 years after the start of the present Michael age Rudolf Steiner could write *The Philosophy of Freedom* out of his direct connection to the Time Spirit (1879–94).[80]

The fact that Michael guards the two joined trees in the spiritual world even today is of great significance, for he works there as the 'spiritual champion of freedom' (GA 233a, 13 January 1924) who moreover 'cosmically establishes' human freedom just as *The Philosophy of Freedom* does for human beings. (See GA 28.) One could also say that Michael would like to guide human beings in our age through the inner actualization of *The Philosophy of Freedom* in the sense of the words by the Christ, 'I am the way, the truth, and the life' (John 14:6), in so far as one can comprehend these words in a somewhat modified form: 'I am the path to truth and to life'. Here the 'I Am' is the esoteric name of the Christ[81] out of the fount of which Michael opens up the path for human beings 'to truth and to life', meaning to the entwined trees of knowledge and of life in the spiritual world, so that every person on earth can actualize the ideal of ethical individualism.

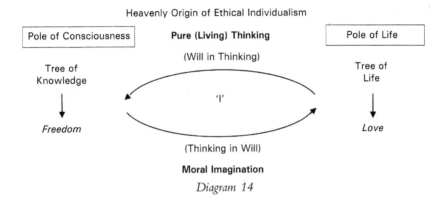

Diagram 14

On this path, these two trees likewise go through a fundamental transformation in man. The Tree of Knowledge does not only allow the human being to recognize the highest truth, but in the sense of *The Philosophy of Freedom* to co-create the truth. In strengthening his thinking through the will man experiences true freedom, and in this way transforms the Tree of Knowledge into the *Tree of Freedom*. And man changes the Tree of Life in such a way that, through permeation of the will with the light-force of thoughts, this tree turns into the *Tree of Love*. 'Just as we come to freedom through irradiation of the thought-life with will, so we come to love through permeation of will's life with thoughts.' (GA 202, 19 December 1920.)

In the spiritual world Michael is the guardian of this highest ideal of humanity as the Tenth Hierarchy, to the fulfilment of which the path leads solely through the portal of ethical individualism.

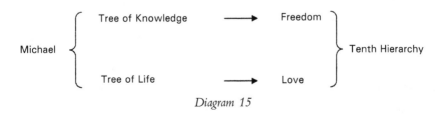

Diagram 15

★

The most important result of an inwardly lived and experienced first part[Tr.1] of *The Philosophy of Freedom* is that the 'I' of the human being recognizes itself through the experience of intuitive thinking as a spirit being among spiritual beings, and can thereby recognize the *truth* about its own self and the world. And through the inwardly lived and experienced second part, the human being finds out in a contemporary form what in earlier times was designated by the word *Grace*. For according to Rudolf Steiner, the modern definition of the concept of grace 'is the faculty of soul to do the Good based on its inner being [meaning based on its own initiative]'. (GA 103, 22 May 1908.) This is the goal of the second part of the book, namely that human beings can do good in the world based on their moral imagination.

We find these two qualities, truth and grace, in two important passages of the prologue of the Gospel of John. First in the words: 'The Law was given through Moses; grace and truth have come into being through Jesus Christ' (1:17 JM). This transition from the rule of iron law in human life to truth and grace, and with that from conditionality to freedom, can be carried out on the level of consciousness by individual man in the actualization of *The Philosophy of Freedom*. In the spiritual world, this process in our age is reflected in the karma-administering office of Moses being shifted to the Christ. Thereby the working of karma in human life is increasingly recognized clairvoyantly as a direct truth; and the possibility to compensate for it in a free manner in the spirit of Christ, meaning for the sake of the greatest benefit for all mankind,[82] is experienced as grace.

Then these two concepts appear one more time in the central proclamation of the prologue dealing with the incarnation of the Christ: 'And the Word became flesh and lived among us full of grace and truth' (1:14). In his translation of this passage, in place of the word 'grace', Rudolf Steiner uses the term 'devotion' [Ger.: *Hingabe*],[83] which he then interprets in connection with the second part of the *Philosophy of Freedom* as follows: 'Devotion to the outer word that penetrates us ... is nothing else but *love*' (GA 202, 19 December 1920'; emphasis by Rudolf Steiner).

Only when developing such devotion in one's mind is one in a position to function in the world out of pure love. Now if this love is taken hold of and strengthened by moral imagination, it can gradually turn into spiritual fire that blazes as true revelation of the *power* of spiritual love in the human soul.[84] This glows as inner fire through all the free actions of the human being and fills one with the grace of being able to work creatively in the universe.

The two most important consequences of the truly experienced and lived *Philosophy of Freedom* consist of what has been said above. One recognizes oneself (one's 'I') as spirit among spirits and feels oneself enfilled by the creative fire of love. Taken all together that is the inner condition in man that the Christ described as the baptism with the Holy Spirit and fire (Matthew 3:11).

The above-mentioned allows us to comprehend more deeply the fact that it was Michael himself who inspired John to write his prologue. Rudolf Steiner calls the prologue the first Michael-revelation that culminated in the Word becoming flesh, meaning in what occurred at the Baptism in the Jordan. Now today we live in the age of the second Michael-revelation, which proclaims the beginning of a new epoch in which man gradually can become the micro-logos (see Chapter 2 of this book) in order to be able consciously to dwell in the kingdom of the Word.[85] And just as at the Turning Point of Time, so this epoch too has a baptism in its centre. No longer was it carried out with water however, but with fire and spirit. To lead human beings to this spiritual baptism, that is Michael's task and the aim of *The Philosophy of Freedom*.[86]

The secret of the inner fire that develops in the soul from studying *The Philosophy of Freedom* and subsequently anthroposophy is frequently characterized by Rudolf Steiner. He even calls it 'the anthroposophical fire'. He says for instance: 'The anthroposophical fire that can be enkindled in us is simply an effect of the universal cosmic fire that spiritually streams forth from beginning to end' (GA 152, 1 May 1913). The beginning and end mentioned here, or in Greek the alpha (A) and omega (Ω) point on their part to the presence of the Cosmic Christ in the whole above described process (see Rev. 1:8). This is why, at the conclusion of this chapter, the additional words by Rudolf Steiner must be mentioned that throw light on the mystery of this 'cosmic fire'. 'You will not only comprehend the Christ [through spiritual science] who passed through death, but you will moreover understand the triumphant one, the Christ of the Apocalypse who has risen into the *spiritual fire*, [the Christ] who has been pre-proclaimed.' (GA 109, 11 April 1909.)

It is of *this* risen apocalyptic Christ who manifests as a purely spiritual being that Michael is the spiritual countenance of today. He would like to guide humankind *to Him* by way of *The Philosophy of Freedom*, the path that finds its direct continuation in anthroposophy. In turn, actual access to this apocalyptic reality of the Resurrection opens up to human beings through the inner baptism with spirit and fire.

★

At the end of this chapter, one concrete example—the number of which could be multiplied—can demonstrate how the contemporary guiding impulse of Michael is directly present in *The Philosophy of Freedom*.

In the ninth chapter, Rudolf Steiner defines a noble action of a person as follows: 'I acknowledge no external principle for my action, because I have found in myself the basis for my action, namely my love of the action. I do not work out by way of reason whether my action is good or bad; I carry it out because I *love* it. My action will be "good" if my intuition, steeped in love, stands within the intuitively to be experienced world-relationship. It will be "bad" if this is not the case.' (GA 4; emphasis by Rudolf Steiner.)

In this quote almost every word relates to the various characteristics of Michael that Rudolf Steiner himself could observe around that time in the spiritual world.[87] First, as is the case in the whole of *The Philosophy of Freedom*, we are dealing here with the human being who 'seeks freedom' because freedom is the main impulse of our present epoch, which is led by Michael in such a way that he himself turns more and more into a 'spiritual hero of freedom' (GA 233a, 13 January 1924) in order to accompany human beings on their path to freedom as their cosmic prototype. On this path man gradually learns to overcome his egoism in order to be able to carry out his earthly actions based on pure love for a deed. By doing so, man can increasingly draw closer to Michael, the current Time Spirit. '*When a person seeks freedom* without leanings towards egoism—when freedom turns into pure love for the action about to be performed—then the possibility arises to draw closer to Michael' (GA 26). Such selfless deeds are moreover not judged by abstract intellect as to whether they may be good or bad, for Michael himself has no interest in abstract intellectuality.[88] Not the 'intellectual' consideration but 'the intuition immersed in love' is required by Michael. For one can approach him when one has liberated one's cognitive forces completely from the bodily organization, something that is not possible before the stage of intuitive thinking is reached. Such thinking must then submerge completely in love so that the human being can act *freely*, meaning purely 'out of love for the object' (GA 4), or what amounts to the same thing, out of love for the external world.

If one has reached this level of action, one can experience a mighty cosmic example for that in Michael: 'With all the seriousness of his nature, his demeanour, his actions, Michael passes through the world in love. He who follows him *nurtures love in his relationship to the outer world* ("love of the objects").' (GA 26, p. 118; emphasis by Rudolf Steiner.) Here, this 'following him' means moreover to know quite concretely what

Michael's activity consists of in the spiritual world, and how based on such insight one can link up with it. For only such free deeds out of 'love for the objects' can be received by Michael into his kingdom, where they will continue to be effective not as human but as cosmic deeds.[89] Only this way can there be attained what Rudolf Steiner designates in the above-mentioned quote as 'intuitively to be experienced world-relationship'. Now, this 'world-relationship' is by no means something abstract in the spiritual world. It is represented there in living form through the presently ruling Time Spirit himself. In other words, it is Michael himself who reveals 'world-relationship' as cosmic intellectuality. 'Michael, however, has never appropriated intellectuality for *himself*. He administers it as a divine-spiritual force inasmuch as he feels connected with the divine-spiritual powers' (GA 26). But because this 'world-relationship' that is administered by Michael is of an intellectual character, it can only be grasped by us humans *intuitively* (through the body-free intuitive thinking). In so doing we connect *that part* of the cosmic intelligence that has become our property[90] with the intelligence that continues to belong to Michael, and in this way enter consciously into the spiritual world. Now since this connection can only be attained through the permeation of thinking with the will, one might also say that in this way we unite in a quite free manner through our own will with Michael's cosmic will, and consequently also with the whole 'world-relationship' that is rooted in that (Michaelic) cosmic will.

As a free being, one can approach Michael in the sense of the *Philosophy of Freedom* and only in *that way* would he, as the Time Spirit of the epoch of freedom, like to receive the human being in order to make the contemporary path to Christ—whom he himself serves—accessible to man. 'One who adheres to Michael practises love in his relationship to the outer world and thereby finds *the* relationship to the inner world of his soul that brings him together with Christ' (GA 26; emphasis by Rudolf Steiner). See Diagram 16 on next page.

The three stages in that diagram signify the following. First there takes place the transition from grasping the concept of the *free human being* in intuitive thinking in the sense of the first part of *The Philosophy of Freedom* as a kind of culmination of human self-cognition. Then follows the gradual actualization of this ideal in so far, by inner work on oneself, one adds the corresponding perception to the concept of one's own self. With that one is in the position to act as a free individual in one's life, as is described in the second part of *The Philosophy of Freedom*. This path of self-actualization of man as a free being then leads one to Michael, because this activity contains the main task of our epoch which Michael administers as

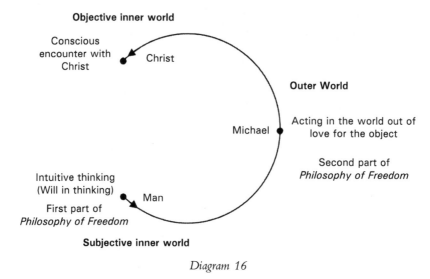

Diagram 16

Time Spirit. From Michael the path continues on to the conscious experiencing of the Christ, for in our age 'the Michael-path ... finds its continuation in the Christ-path'. (GA 194, 23 November 1919.)

On this path Rudolf Steiner himself found the transition from Michael to Christ, and with that from *The Philosophy of Freedom* to anthroposophy.[91] And this same path then led him further to his sacrificial deed during the Christmas Conference, where the highest good (in the sense of *The Philosophy of Freedom*) was reached through his 'intuition that was immersed in love', an intuition that stands fully in the 'intuitively to be experienced world-relationship' of the whole Mystery evolution of humanity.

Out of consciously having stood before Michael-Christ, Rudolf Steiner accomplished this freest deed in which *Intuition* as the source of cognition attested to the complete freedom of him who was doing the deed: the sacrificial *love* brought about the connection with Christ, and experiencing the *world-relationship* guaranteed the connection with Michael. Thus Rudolf Steiner demonstrated during his life to an exemplary degree what it signifies actually to stand on the foundation of *The Philosophy of Freedom*, and to act concretely out of its impulse.

The path from Michael to Christ, which is becoming visible from this, can also be explained as follows. Even prior to the revelation of the Michael Mystery in the karma lectures and articles from the year 1924 (consisting of the descent into human souls of the cosmic intelligence that had been administered by Michael), Rudolf Steiner already pointed out in his lecture of 30 January 1923 (GA 257) that human intellectuality and the human freedom connected with it have moved from the spiritual world into humanity. He described this process as 'a heavenly gift'. Although Michael's name is not mentioned in the above lecture, it becomes obvious in the light of the later Michael articles that we are dealing here with the same process concerning the appearance of this intelligence on earth that had until then been administrated by Michael himself. That this is so is shown by the term 'intellectuality' used by Rudolf Steiner alongside the concept 'intelligence' in the article of 19 October 1924: 'To administer the cosmic intellectuality is his [Michael's] task' (GA 26). In the same article he moreover points to the connection of the experience of freedom of today's human being with the cosmic Michael-mission. 'In my *Philosophy of Freedom*, you find the "freedom" of man in the present world epoch verified as the content of consciousness. In the depictions of the Michael-mission that are given here you find the "evolution of this freedom" cosmically verified.' (GA 26, Leading Thought, No. 111.) In other passages too, Rudolf Steiner likewise remarks that Michael in particular takes man's freedom into account, and for that reason represents it most ardently in the spiritual world. (See GA 233a, 13 January 1924.)

This participation by Michael in the development of intellectuality and freedom on earth has still another side. Along with the gradual ascent of humanity to individual freedom on the path of intellectuality, the necessity is connected at the same time with gaining a new and conscious relationship to the spiritual world and its entities so that humanity may not fall prey to Ahriman. 'Inasmuch as these heavenly elements (intellectuality and freedom) have entered into earthly life, another form of looking up to divinity has become necessary for mankind than was the case earlier on. And this different looking up to the divinity has become possible for humanity through the Mystery of Golgotha.' (GA 257, 30 January 1923.) For it is only because Christ thereby connected himself with humanity that the fully conscious (intellectuality-filled) and free relationship to the divine-spiritual world has become possible on earth.

That this is the case was confirmed first and foremost through Rudolf Steiner's own development, which moved logically from *The Philosophy of Freedom* to anthroposophy and on to the modern science of the spirit. That is why he could furthermore say, 'If the contemporary soul wishes to place itself in the right way into Earth evolution, there has to live in it on the one side a strong impulse of freedom, and on the other a strong impulse inwardly to live through the Mystery of Golgotha.' (GA 212, 7 May 1922.) These two sides of modern world development can moreover be characterized in the following words: Intellectuality and the impulse of freedom as well as the faculty to be able to live in pure concepts come from Michael out of the spiritual world. Christ on the other hand adds the possibility of being able, with them, to enter into a new and fully conscious relationship to the spiritual world and its entities.

Here begins the fulfilment of the lofty ideal of which Christ spoke in His last address to His disciples. 'No longer can I call you servants, for the servant does not know what his master is doing, but I call you friends because I have made known to you all that I have heard from my Father' (John 15:15, JM). But what distinguishes the servant of God from his friend and therefore likewise from his co-worker is the *spiritual cognition* that can be acquired in the contemporary Michael epoch in a new and completely free manner by human beings through anthroposophy.

So that this ideal may some day become actuality on earth, the human being prior to birth encounters the light of Michael and the love of the Christ. Michael shows man where his earthly individuality comes from, and Christ makes manifest what is supposed to happen to it in the sense of Earth evolution. For we live in a time where people must gradually come to the insight 'What is the most holy within us in this age must be pervaded by the Christ Impulse, namely the faculty of grasping pure concepts and the faculty of freedom' (GA 257, 30 January 1923).

It was out of the Michael spirit that Rudolf Steiner established these two faculties in his *Philosophy of Freedom*. This is why their development leads in man to the Christ. Thus the path of *The Philosophy of Freedom* belongs to what Rudolf Steiner calls the 'Michael-path that finds its continuation in the Christ-path'. (GA 194, 23 November 1919.) In this manner through the unfolding of the impulse of freedom in man's nature based on Michaelic intellectuality, there results the transition from *The Philosophy of Freedom* to anthroposophy, and with that also to the Christ who today would like to appear in His etheric form to the faculties of the consciousness soul that are in the process of becoming clairvoyant.

This is why Rudolf Steiner said concerning the only fitting approach of man to the Christ in our present age: 'People are indeed becoming more liberated, and inasmuch as they are becoming spiritually freer and freer, their association with the Christ will become increasingly more immediate' (GA 155, 16 July 1914). And today Michael would like to lead human beings to such an 'immediate association' with the Christ, an association that is coming about based on the full unfolding of human freedom.

7. *The Philosophy of Freedom* in the Light of *The Fifth Gospel*

The communications from the spiritual world that Rudolf Steiner summarized in lectures of 1913 and 1914 under the title *The Fifth Gospel* (GA 148) form the very centre of anthroposophical Christology. For the first time he spoke of this subject in a direct way during the foundation stone laying of the First Goetheanum in Dornach on 20 September 1913. Yet, according to his statements, a number of communications in this area of spiritual research can be found in earlier lecture cycles as well.

In his various accounts, Rudolf Steiner also called the Fifth Gospel 'the anthroposophical gospel' (GA 148, 3 October 1913) and points out that it was initially taught in esoteric Rosicrucian schools. (See GA 118, 18 April 1910.)

At the core of the communications from the Fifth Gospel stands the secret of the two Jesus boys. In 1909, Rudolf Steiner spoke of it for the first time in the cycle on the Gospel of Luke given in Basel. On that occasion, he primarily revealed the secret of a very special entity who in the Jesus of Luke was incarnated on earth for the first time. Concerning the other, the Solomon-Jesus in whom dwelt the individuality of Zarathustra, Rudolf Steiner had spoken already earlier in several lectures.

During the characterization of these two Jesus boys, whose births are described correspondingly in the Gospels of Matthew and Luke, Rudolf Steiner refers particularly to the absolute polarity of their beings. The individuality of Zarathustra belongs among the oldest of humanity. In many incarnations on earth and varied initiations, Zarathustra gathered the richest earthly experiences and most profound wisdom. By contrast, not until the Turning Point of Time did the mysterious entity of the Jesus in Luke's Gospel enter for the first time into a human incarnation on earth. Until then this being was protected by the hierarchies in the spiritual world, where in the lofty Sun-sphere it was the guardian of the original form of man dating back to the era prior to the Fall (into sin). Whereas Zarathustra represented the highest evolved human ego—which along with the remainder of mankind had, however, participated in the Fall— the most significant aspect of the being that Rudolf Steiner designated as 'the Mother Soul of humanity' (GA 114, 18 September 1909) or 'this Sister Soul' of Adam' (GA 142, 1 January 1913) was that it was shielded from Adam's Fall, and for that matter from the Fall of all humanity.

In the Bible, these completely diverging paths of humankind are indicated in the picture of the two trees in Paradise. We are familiar with how Adam eats of the Tree of Knowledge and thus succumbs to the Fall. Through him, all of mankind subsequently descends down to the physical earth. The journey through earthly incarnations begins. This journey is the consequence of partaking of the fruit from the Tree of Knowledge. In regard to the other tree, the Tree of Life, it says in the Bible that, at the behest of the gods, man may not eat of it. According to Rudolf Steiner, we have in this imagination an indication of the fact that the entity that incarnated at the Turning Point of Time for the first time was even then already separated from the rest of humanity and thus protected from the Fall, being therefore guarded in the spiritual world. (See GA 114, 18 September 1909.) This entity therefore bears within itself the eternal archetype of the human being as it had originally been created by the gods. Zarathustra on the other hand represents that earthly individuality who had overcome the consequences of the Fall to the furthest degree (to the extent that this was even possible prior to the Mystery of Golgotha) through his own inner efforts.

Aside from these two trees, that of knowledge and that of life, there is in the Bible yet another pair of concepts, which in a somewhat different form point to the same secret. In the first chapter of Genesis we find the following words in connection with the creation of man: 'Let us make man in our image, after our likeness' (Gen. 1:26 RSV)[92] In regard to this passage there exists above all in eastern Christendom a rich theological tradition that implies that during the Fall only the likeness of man fell. His divine image on the other hand was protected from the Fall and was held back in the spiritual world.[93]

This Bible passage, as well as the various directions taken by image and likeness, can be truly understood only through anthroposophy and with the aid of what Rudolf Steiner has communicated concerning the two Jesus boys. For it was the celestial sister-soul of Adam (the Jesus in Luke) who was retained in the spiritual world as the image of God. On earth (to the extent that this was possible in pre-Christian times), the individuality of Zarathustra (the Solomonic Jesus) demonstrated the highest level of development of the fallen likeness in the direction of its restoration.

At the Turning Point of Time when these two individualities appeared simultaneously on earth, the two original principles of creation, 'image and likeness', were present, the image coming out of the spiritual world and the likeness in utmost earthly unfolding. When Zarathustra departed from the corporeality of the Solomonic youth, when both Jesus boys had reached the age of twelve and passed over into the boy of the Luke Gospel (scene of the twelve-year-old Jesus in the temple), image and likeness of man were thereby connected in humanity's history in the way it had previously been possible only in Paradise prior to the Fall.

The words of the Gospel of Luke that follow directly after the temple scene, 'And Jesus progressed in wisdom, in maturity, and in grace in the sight of God and men' (2:52), point to the union of the two entities in the one earthly being, Jesus of Nazareth. Here 'wisdom' indicates the likeness developed by Zarathustra, 'grace' points to the image brought along by the other entity, and finally 'age' to the growing up of the corporeality in which henceforth the two individualities as image and likeness were united. Even the further words of the quote, 'in the sight of God and men', refers to the two individualities. Thus, the genealogy of Luke's Jesus goes back to God (Luke 3:38), meaning to the time before the Fall, and the genealogy of the other Jesus only to Abraham (Matt. 1:1), meaning that it remains in the domain of humanity's development.

Beginning with this temple scene, there existed on earth a new entity that contained in itself the best fruits of both developments. From Zarathustra this entity had the greatest earthly wisdom that dwelt in his 'I' in the form of a living treasure of thoughts, which had been taken along with the transition into the other Jesus. From the Jesus in Luke's Gospel, that new entity had the instantaneous relationship to the world that man originally had around himself prior to the Fall—the reflection that every child possesses to this day as a pure perception before its individual thinking awakens. In contrast to the ordinary human being, however, the Jesus of Luke's Gospel retained this original faculty of perception beyond his childhood until the age of 30. This determined his whole special relationship to the outer world, a relationship that was not guided by knowledge but by a perception filled with purest love and compassion.

In Jesus of Nazareth, there united into this *essential living* form—above all in his thinking and perception—the wisdom of the likeness and the love of the image. And when after 18 years the ego of Zarathustra left the sheaths of Jesus of Nazareth directly prior to the Baptism in the Jordan, his whole wisdom remained united with him.

An important reason why this aid by Zarathustra was necessary consists in the following. In many lectures that likewise belong directly to the content of the Fifth Gospel, Rudolf Steiner describes the three so-called pre-stages of the Mystery of Golgotha that occurred in the spiritual world in the Lemurian and Atlantean time, and through which humankind was saved three times on the Earth.[94]

This salvation occurred because, three times, the later Jesus mentioned in the Luke Gospel became 'ensouled' through the Christ in the spiritual world. Seen from the spiritual viewpoint, this only became possible because in that Jesus the image of man had been preserved untainted and to the full extent. For only through this image could the Christ Being send His influences out of the spiritual world to the earth. Yet for His earthly incarnation this did not suffice. For a complete union with the physical world, not only were the heavenly forces of the image required but moreover the forces of the likeness developed on the earth itself; and these were forces that could only be presented by the highest initiate. That is why, for 18 years, Zarathustra had to permeate the being of the Luke-Jesus with his Sun-wisdom. This process reached its culmination in the conversation of Jesus with his mother shortly before the Baptism in the Jordan. Rudolf Steiner described it in the following words: 'He did not know for certain that he bore the Zarathustra-soul within himself, but the ancient Zarathustra-teaching, the Zarathustra-wisdom, the ancient Zarathustra-impulse arose in him during the conversation. Together with his mother, he experienced this mighty Zarathustra-impulse; all the beauty and greatness of the ancient Sun-teaching arose in his soul.' (GA 148, 6 October 1913.) Only after the Zarathustra-'I' had ultimately surrendered its whole cosmic wisdom to Jesus in this conversation was it allowed to leave the being of Jesus and cross over into the spiritual world adjacent to the earth. (GA 264, 22 October 1906.)

The entity who now walked towards the Jordan for the baptism was no longer an initiate; it was man as such or primal man. 'What the Christ-bearer was *is truly man*, not an initiate' states Rudolf Steiner in this regard (GA 131, 7 October 1911), a 'true human being', who for the first time since the Fall united in himself both image and likeness so that into the human vessel thus formed the most high of all worlds, the Christ Being, could be received.[95] For with His incarnation and the subsequent Mystery of Golgotha, Christ does not lead man's evolution back into the past to the original paradisaical condition of man but into the apocalyptic future of the whole ensuing evolution, all the way to Vulcan.

In this regard, it is amazing how precise some formulations by Rudolf Steiner are if viewed in the light of the events of the Fifth Gospel. As early as in the book *A Theory of Knowledge Based on Goethe's World Conception* (GA 2), we come across the following passage: 'Science instils perceived reality with the concepts that have been grasped and worked through by our thinking. It supplements and deepens what has been passively received by us through what our spirit lifted by its very own activity out of the darkness of mere possibility into the light of reality. This presupposes that perception requires supplementation through the spirit and [in itself] is in no way something final, ultimate, and complete.'

The whole secret of the working together by the two Jesus boys and the 18-year-long mission of the Zarathustra-'I' in the soul of Jesus of Nazareth is accurately described in the above words. Only the Jesus of the Luke Gospel had the direct possibility of perception through the physical body. But what he thereby experienced had, to begin with, a 'passive', merely 'receiving' character. Yet in this manner he received into himself all the suffering of the world that surrounded him with greatest intensity. And this had to be 'supplemented and deepened' absolutely through the wisdom (the treasure-trove of thoughts) of the Zarathustra-'I'. For without this supplementary activity, Jesus of Nazareth lacked the experiences of earthly incarnations as well as the possibility to gather corresponding experiences in this, his first, incarnation. For only based on such experiences could he become a 'final, ultimate, and complete' being on earth

What Jesus of Nazareth lacked (in order to become such a being) could be given him only by a highly developed individuality such as the one Zarathustra possessed. Due to his 'spirit' and 'through his activity', he alone was in a position, along with the 'concepts grasped and worked through' by him, to lift the world-encompassing insights out of 'mere possibility into the light of reality'—insights needed by Jesus of Nazareth for the fulfilment of his world-mission.[96]

In other segments of the above-mentioned book, one can likewise discover in the formulations that describe the nature of modern cognition characteristics that throw light on the nature of the two Jesus beings: *'Pure experience is the form of reality in which this [reality] appears to us when, completely divested of our self, we approach it.'* (GA 2; emphasis by Rudolf Steiner.) Here the relationship of the Luke-Jesus to his environment is characterized most accurately. For in facing the world around him he lived *'completely divested'* of his self. Filled purely with love and compassion, his soul manifested as one that had brought along the highest force of sacrificial selflessness from the prenatal domain.

The following words characterize Zarathustra's nature in a similarly accurate way: 'There really exists *only one* thought content, and our individual thinking should be but a working into this *thought-centre* of the universe on the part of our self, our individual personality' (ibid.; emphasis by Rudolf Steiner). In this way the individuality of Zarathustra, who in pre-Christian times had brought his 'I' (self) or its 'individual personality' to the highest evolutionary level attainable then, experienced in the Sun-region (or put more precisely through the Sun-god Ahura Mazda himself) that 'thought centre' out of which he gleaned the whole content of his Sun-teaching.

When Rudolf Steiner writes further that '*our thinking is the translator that interprets the gestures of experience*' (ibid.; emphasis by Rudolf Steiner), Zarathustra's significant task regarding the Luke-Jesus can be discerned. He who bore in his being the richest earth experiences from previous incarnations had to make this completely new world comprehensible— even in a cognitive way—by means of his thoughts for the other, who for the first time entered upon earth's ground. This literally means that Zarathustra had to translate his perceptions into earthly forms of cognition through the addition of the corresponding concepts.

The quote mentioned earlier (p. 77) by Rudolf Steiner (GA 2), introduces the part of his book that is entitled 'Science'. This makes it clear that the 'theory of knowledge' described in the book leads to a new and Christian science. In this sense it is significant that in the introductory lecture of the first cycle concerning the Fifth Gospel Rudolf Steiner accentuates the Christian sources of occidental science in detail and with great emphasis. (See GA 148, 1 October 1913.) If western science is presented differently today, in most cases (and this often even appears anti-Christian) this is merely a result of the Arabian influence.[97] That is why the controversy between Goethe and Newton regarding the teaching of colour is a world-historical symptom of the confrontation between Christian and Arabian science.

Based on what was said in Chapter 5, one can designate the former as the science which on the path of Goetheanism seeks the transition to the world of the Son from nature (the world of the Father) and thereby establishes the freedom and dignity of man in the midst of the knowledge of nature.

Outer science harshly opposes this development and maintains its standpoint that God can have no Son, from which follows that, forfeiting his freedom, man is supposed to stay put as a small, insignificant cog in the great mechanism of the universe. As has become clear from the previous descriptions, the roots of a Christian science, by contrast, must be sought for in the Fifth Gospel. For this gospel describes the path from Jesus to Christ and therefore contains on the level of consciousness the archetype of the path from the Jesus-consciousness to the Christ-consciousness in the domain of cognition, and thus of science.

★

In summary one can say: What occurred at the Turning Point of Time as a world-historical fact in humanity's evolution on the level of *existence* is repeated in making use of the anthroposophical method of cognition in all details on the level of human consciousness.[98] In his book *The*

Philosophy of Freedom, Rudolf Steiner describes how, through the uni-fication of concept and perception, man creates a new reality in his cognition. And when we seek for a world-historical archetype of this process of cognition and consciousness, we discover it at the Turning Point of Time in Jesus of Nazareth at the moment when—after Zar-athustra's 'I' has left him—he walks to the River Jordan as the pure *Son of Man* to receive the *Son of God* there.

In *The Philosophy of Freedom,* Rudolf Steiner furthermore writes that separation of perception and thought does not exist objectively in the world, only in the human being conditioned by his earthly organization (GA 4, Chap. V). Since the latter, the physical body, was exposed the most to the consequences of the Fall, it is quite obvious to seek the reason for its imperfection in this. Rudolf Steiner also mentions that man, during his descent into matter, has himself recast outer reality into illusion. Then he continues, 'Call it, biblically speaking, the Fall into Sin or whatever causes the outer world to appear as illusion to man' (GA 116, 8 May 1910). Nobody was more aware of the consequences arising from this for man's domain of cognition than the apostle Paul, who developed from them the foundations for his 'theory of knowledge'. Rudolf Steiner summarizes them in unequivocal words: 'What you yourself have turned into maya, you must make right again in your self. And you can only do that if you accept the Christ-power into yourself that shows the outer world to you in its reality!' (ibid.). Following these words, Rudolf Steiner speaks of the fact that in his *Philosophy of Freedom* he has placed his whole theory of cognition (theory of knowledge) on this 'Pauline base'.[99]

In this regard, Rudolf Steiner expresses himself even more directly in another lecture where he points out that 'true science ... [is] the replacement of illusion with full reality' (GA 176, 4 September 1917), something that is brought about when in his cognitive activity man adds a corresponding concept to outer perception. 'Starting out from this idea that the world in its initial form (as it presents itself to the senses) appears unreal to us because of us—not because of itself—and that this form of the world (which through us is an unreal one) is made through subjective effort into reality, that is what allows me to call this thought the Pauline thought in the domain of the theory of cognition. For it is nothing other than the Pauline theory of cognition (transposed to the philosophical domain of knowledge) that due to the way man has entered the world through the first Adam he encounters this world in an inferior manner [split up into perception and concept]; and only experiences it [the world] in its true form through what he becomes through the Christ [as the second Adam].' (Ibid.)[100]

From what was said, it follows that at the Turning Point of Time the foundation was laid for modern cognition, and with that the possibility for true science to overcome the consequences of the Fall in the process of cognition and thus attain a conscious discovering of the spiritual world.

What happens here on the level of consciousness was actualized for the first time on earth at the Turning Point of Time through the union of the two Jesus boys, and consequently in a human form of image and likeness. With that a completely new entity originated in humanity's evolution as prototype for any true cognition. That is why Rudolf Steiner says that 'true human self-knowledge must harbour the Jesus-seed'. (GA 183, 19 August 1918.)

When this Jesus-principle is fully developed in the above-described way on the level of consciousness in the process of cognition (meaning that it is brought all the way to the stage of the Son of Man), it is then capable of receiving the Christ as the Son of God into itself. Thus, if pursued consistently, the path of knowledge (or cognition) of *The Philosophy of Freedom* leads from the Jesus-consciousness to the Christ-consciousness. A logical transition originates this way in the sense of an uninterrupted inner development from Rudolf Steiner's whole early philosophical work to his later establishment of anthroposophy.

8. The Fifth Gospel and Rudolf Steiner's Path of Initiation

The path, described in the last chapter, to the modern Christ experience can also be traced in detail through Rudolf Steiner's life. Proceeding from his work on Goethe's natural-scientific writings, he creates a scientific foundation for the union of 'image' and 'likeness' on the level of modern cognition in his next three works:

- *The Theory of Knowledge Implicit in Goethe's World Conception* (1886)
- *Truth and Science* (1892)
- *The Philosophy of Freedom* (1894)

A scientific path for the attainment of the Jesus-consciousness as an inevitable prerequisite for attaining the Christ consciousness is substantiated and opened up for the contemporary human being. With these three works, first in the domain of cognition, nothing less occurs than a final overcoming of the chasm between science and religion, between this world and the world beyond, between humans and their divine-spiritual origin.

At this point, a brief aside must follow concerning the largely deprecatory attitude that Rudolf Steiner maintained concerning this question towards institutionalized Christianity. For what was said above makes it comprehensible why he protested so radically against Kant without compromise, and above all why he protested against the doctrine of the official Christian Churches regarding the inaccessibility of the world beyond to man's cognitive forces.[101] To continue to speak of a 'beyond' after Christ had brought the highest creative power (the creative power of the Word of Worlds) out of the womb of the Divine Father to earth and subsequently had united it through the Mystery of Golgotha with humanity's evolution—this means pure and simply to deny the nature of the Resurrection. Its denial, however, makes Christianity unchristian in the most eminent sense and with that turns it into the greatest obstacle on the paths to the goals of mankind, goals to which *The Philosophy of Freedom* would like to guide us. For the opposite path signifies the establishment of a Christianity without Christ, something that in a most excellent manner was depicted by F. Dostoevsky in his book *The Brothers Karamasov*, in the legend of the Great Inquisitor.

The apostle Paul on his part referred in particular to this decisive question, for as was shown before, his conception of Christianity is closest to *The Philosophy of Freedom*. This is why he expressed the following essential words of true Christianity in the First Letter to the Corinthians: 'If Christ has not been raised, then our preaching is in vain and your faith is in vain' (15:14). But if Christ has in fact risen, then there no longer exists an inaccessible world beyond for the cognitive forces of man; on the contrary through this deed of the Christ, all the world beyond [*Jenseits*] was to the fullest extent made part of the world on this side [*Diesseits*].

Viewed in a more spiritual-scientific sense, one can say: In his defence of logical consistent monism against any dualistic view of life, Rudolf Steiner at the same time opposed all pre-Christian elements in Christianity that (without having undergone the complete metamorphosis in the Christ Impulse) no longer occupied a justifiable place within Christianity in the old form. This likewise applies especially to one-sided Platonism,[102] which reached its high point in western philosophy in the Kantian dualism.

With this, Rudolf Steiner already prepared the ground in his youth for the later spiritual-scientific comprehension of the Mystery of Golgotha as the central message of anthroposophy. This is why at the end of his life, looking back on the 21 years of anthroposophy's development on earth, he would be able to say with full justification: 'But the impulse—even for everything anthroposophy can bring about—is contained in the Mystery of Golgotha' (GA 239, 31 January 1924).

Now this Mystery cannot, however, be understood only with earthly means of cognition, for it is 'the only action on earth . . . that is completely supersensible' (GA 142, 17 December 1912). Precisely here lies the main difference between Rudolf Steiner and Nietzsche, who as yet could not arrive at a purely spiritual grasp of Christianity. He too sought in vain (as did the young Rudolf Steiner) for the Christ in traditional Christianity or rather in the religious denominations representing it. In actual fact, he only denounced the unchristian element in Christianity in his vehement criticism of the churches. But without having come to the real effectively working supersensible Christ, Nietzsche in the end had to determine that in the historical Christianity of his time Christ was not to be found at all.

This is also how Rudolf Steiner experienced it. Looking back on this later, he wrote in his autobiography: 'The Christianity I had to look for I found nowhere in the denominations' (GA 28, Chap. XXVI). Following from these critical remarks, also calling to mind Nietzsche, he said in this regard, 'Earlier I always pointed to a Christian content that lived in the then existing denominations. Well, Nietzsche did that too.' (Ibid.)

One can moreover say that in his soul Nietzsche experienced particularly strongly the words of the angel by the tomb of Jesus of Nazareth: 'I know that you seek Jesus who was crucified. *He is not here . . .*' (Matt. 28:5–6) Nietzsche sought him with all the forces of his deranged soul but found him nowhere in existing denominational Christendom.[103] But where the living Christ has remained connected with the whole of Earth evolution (since His resurrection), there Nietzsche could not reach. For in this incarnation Nietzsche was unable consciously to rise up into the spiritual world in which alone the Resurrected One is to be found. Shortly before Nietzsche finally left the earthly world, however, this was realized by Rudolf Steiner. At the turn of the century, through his own inner strength, he penetrated to the spiritual essence of Christianity in order to experience there the encounter with the living Christ in intuitive cognition. 'After the time of trials had exposed me to hard struggles of soul, I had to submerge myself into Christianity, namely in that world where the spiritual speaks about it.' (Ibid.)

On this path the full cosmic-telluric significance of the Mystery of Golgotha, and with that the whole perspective of mankind's evolution (as outlined in the last chapter), manifested itself to Rudolf Steiner. This is why there actually exists no disparity between the earlier and the later statements by Rudolf Steiner regarding Christianity. For the one kind of (critical) statements were connected, as in Nietzsche's case, to the Church-related denominations with their unchristian teachings of an unreachable world beyond; the other (positive) ones refer to the spiritual-scientific insight concerning the Christ Himself.

In order to arrive at this spiritual-scientific knowledge of the Christ, Rudolf Steiner first had to overcome a main obstacle in the domain of cognition. It was the unchristian faith in a world beyond, and he did this thoroughly in his early work. In that way the conscious transition from Jesus to Christ became possible for him.

If one now tries to trace the cognitive path from Jesus to Christ in Rudolf Steiner's biography further, one must not forget that he was on this path not before but *after* the Mystery of Golgotha. For the Mystery of Golgotha brought a decisive metamorphosis into the nature and further working together of 'image' and 'likeness' in the earthly human being. For an understanding of this secret one must consider the following.

Human beings, who at the Turning Point of Time had an awareness of the simultaneous appearance of 'image' and 'likeness' in human form on earth, were the Shepherds and Kings. In the spiritual revelation that the Shepherds in the field received during the night of Christmas (Luke 2:14) the revelation of the heavenly image of man was contained as well, an image that in the Jesus of Luke had found its way to earth in one single incarnation. In the simplicity and privation of their hearts, the Shepherds could receive this message directly.[104]

The evolutionary path of the Kings appears completely different. In the Gospels they are called Magi (or Magicians) as well. This indicates that in the Orient they were initiated into the Mysteries that had been inaugurated by Zarathustra in his incarnation in the seventh pre-Christian century. Rudolf Steiner refers to these three Magi as the reincarnated disciples of Zarathustra who came to Palestine to pay homage to the earthly birth of their master.[105] They on their part had passed through a long path filled with trials in the Persian Mysteries, a path in the centre of which stood the inner work of lifting up the fallen 'likeness'. The greatest example of this work was for them the individuality of Zarathustra.

Thus, prior to the Mystery of Golgotha, the Shepherds represented the revelation of the 'image' and the Kings represented the work (rooted in the Mysteries) on the 'likeness'. After the Mystery of Golgotha (and as its direct continuation), both paths passed through a decisive metamorphosis. Rudolf Steiner describes this in the Christmas lectures of 1920. By means of the fact that the Shepherds and the Kings had absorbed forces of the Mystery of Golgotha into themselves, they also received the impulse to develop the opposite quality in themselves, and to lead it to a higher synthesis in the sense of the principle of polarity and intensification. In other words, the Shepherds acquired an inner tendency to become Kings and the Kings to become Shepherds. (See GA 202, 23 December 1920.) For it was the power of the Mystery of Golgotha that made possible a completely new relationship of human beings to the 'image' and 'likeness', and with that brought about the above-described metamorphosis of the Shepherds and Kings. We must now look at this more closely.

As a result of the working by the Christ Impulse in Earth evolution, every person today can not only become aware in reverence of the original image of man (in the sense of a retrospection to the cosmic past), but out of his own 'I'-force create in his soul the new image, an image that eventually, when it is fully actualized, will be the foundation for the Tenth Hierarchy of freedom and love.[106] That is the beginning of the new creation that is founded on the power of the Mystery of Golgotha. In this way every *idea* (out of the domain of the likeness) can be lifted up to the *ideal* (image) indicative of the future. At the same time it is the new path from the Kings to the Shepherds.

The second path can likewise be traversed today out of the Christ Impulse, the path from the Shepherds to the Kings. In the domain where formerly only the revelations of the image held sway, an individual development in the sense of the new likeness has thereby become possible. This means that man can not only grasp the new ideals that point to the future, but change himself in such a way that he can fully correspond to his own ideal as a new percept.

These two paths, which in reality are not to be separated from each other, are described by Rudolf Steiner in precise scientific form in *The Philosophy of Freedom*. In the book's first part he develops the concept of freedom and formulates the highest ideal of Earth evolution, namely the ideal of the free human being. With that, in the midst of inner cognitive work (the original domain of the 'likeness') the ideal of freedom is generated as the new 'image' of man. In the second part, the actual means and ways are shown of how, proceeding from the original domain of the 'likeness', one can bring the perception of self through self-education and self-transformation in the sense of a discipline (or 'work') on the 'likeness' to actualization of free man. This becomes possible for man as a result of his deeds, actions in which only selfless love for them holds sway as a motivation.

In *The Philosophy of Freedom* the first path is formulated as follows: 'We cannot, however, think out the concept of man completely without coming upon the *free spirit* as the purest expression of human nature' (GA 4, Chap. IX; emphasis by Rudolf Steiner). The second path is formulated as follows: 'His [the human being's] true concept as a *moral* being [free spirit] is not objectively united from the start with the percept-picture 'man' needing only to be confirmed by knowledge afterwards' (ibid.; emphasis by Rudolf Steiner). And then Rudolf Steiner indicates the union of these two paths: 'Man must unite his concept with the percept of man by his own activity. Concept and percept coincide in this case only *if man makes them coincide*. This he can do only if he has found the concept of the free spirit, that is if he has found the concept of his own self.' (Ibid.)

Through such a finding of the 'concept of the free spirit' there originates for man his new 'image'. And the realization of the new 'likeness' is connected with the fact that 'in the perceptual object "Man" the possibility is given to change oneself', for 'only man *himself* can turn himself into a *free* being'. (Ibid.; emphasis by Rudolf Steiner.) In this way 'intellectual life' ... overcomes 'the dual nature [of the human being] through cognition; the moral [life] through the factual actualization of the free spirit' (ibid.). In the sense of what was said before, the first signifies the realization of the new 'image' in the domain of the 'likeness', and the second the development of the new 'likeness' in the original domain of the 'image'. By these means, in the process of the fulfilment of *The Philosophy of Freedom,* the Kings can become Shepherds and the Shepherds

Kings today in *every* human being. And with that the direct effectiveness of the Mystery of Golgotha can be experienced in the soul.

In a certain regard the words quoted above represent the culmination of the whole book and comprise its two parts. For in the spiritual-practical sense one grasps the nature of freedom through the 'exceptional state' of consciousness (first part) that is brought about by oneself and its realization occurs through the stages of moral intuition, moral imagination and moral technique (second part). Thus, for the first time in humankind's history, the nature of freedom is worked out and the paths to its realization are made evident. With that *The Philosophy of Freedom* points to man's self-creation. Here we are dealing with nothing less than the creation of the *new human being*.

Out of this source a new faculty will gradually come about in human souls. Just as is the case with other faculties in humanity's development—following a stern spiritual law—here too the foundation for it has to be laid by *one* human being, so that his individual primal deed [Ger.: *Ur-Tat*] can subsequently become a 'reachable goal' [Ger.: *Erreichnis*].

Rudolf Steiner illustrates the above-mentioned cosmic law by the example of two great individualities in the past. The reason why everyone can pursue the Eightfold Path of Buddhism (which principally is connected with the development of the 16-petalled lotus flower), even if on the whole that person has as yet quite modest spiritual abilities, is due to the unique deed of the historical Gautama Buddha who because of his illumination under the bo tree made this new faculty accessible to all human beings. The second even more significant example that Rudolf Steiner mentions in the same lecture directly following the one of Gautama Buddha is that of Aristotle. The fact that everyone today possesses the faculty of logical thinking is the result of the world-historical deed by Aristotle. He was the first on earth to discover and formulate the laws of logical thinking, and through untiring implementation of this new faculty created for all human beings the foundation to it. (See GA 114, 17 September 1909.)

The epochal deed by Rudolf Steiner must be comprehended in the same way. He was the first to create the new 'image' of free man in the domain of cognition and then also actualized it in his life in the sense of the new 'likeness'. This means that he brought it to outward perception in his own human personality. 'He is free'; these words with which Rudolf Steiner concluded the first edition of *The Philosophy of Freedom* in 1894 relate all-inclusively to himself (GA 4). He became in his life the freest man on earth. Since this achievement (*Erreichnis*), the predisposition to this new faculty is objectively present in humanity, and *The Philosophy of Freedom* is the main teaching-manual and guide-book to its actualization.

Yet as has been said before, the first breakthrough to such a faculty is something quite different from the later development of it through countless human beings. This is why in Rudolf Steiner's biography this path is established quite differently than in all those who have already pursued this path since he did, are on it, and will yet pursue it. What for all other human beings is the establishment of the science of freedom (see Chapter 5), of the fruits of which they are able to avail themselves for their inner development, was for Rudolf Steiner a conscious journey through the greatest and most dangerous crisis of his life. For his path to the deepest and ultimate roots of freedom (out of which alone it could be established) was likewise the path into the abyss of death. Rudolf Steiner describes this 'journey into Hades' in detail in his autobiography in Chapter XXVI (GA 28).

Why does the quest for the origin of human freedom lead into the realm where the forces of death hold sway? The reason for this is that contemporary man can attain to full freedom only in the mineral kingdom, which is lifeless, for there the spiritual hierarchies are no longer present and man is completely on his own.[107] This is why on his journey to the spiritual unearthing of human freedom Rudolf Steiner had to descend fully consciously with his clairvoyant forces into that domain of the spiritual world which is inhabited by ahrimanic spirits who are the spirits of death. With this on his path of initiation, he encountered the decisive question of life (discussed elsewhere in more detail[108]). The question is: in this domain of death where everything has to die, how can one not succumb to dying in regard to one's mind and even body, instead maintaining one's self by struggling through to one's individual freedom and grounding one's self on the pure 'I' impulse?

This was possible for Rudolf Steiner only by establishing (based on his own strength) the fully conscious connection to the Mystery of Golgotha, meaning to the sphere of resurrection in this kingdom of death. With this he moreover created the bridge from the Jesus-consciousness, on which all his early works were founded, to the Christ-consciousness, on which he subsequently based anthroposophy at the beginning of the twentieth century. What is more, the transition was made from the science of freedom in his *Philosophy of Freedom* to the science of the spirit, or anthroposophy.

What was hereby attained for the whole of humanity can be depicted as follows. If to start with an individual arrives in the sense of *The Philosophy of Freedom* at an inner experience of the ideal (of the concept) of free man (first part), and then through the work on himself creates a perception corresponding to this ideal of his own being, then through bringing the two into correlation in his consciousness he reaches the stage of Jesus who can then receive the Christ Impulse into himself. On the level of consciousness, this self-transformation of the human being corresponds to the world-historical move by Jesus of Nazareth to the Baptism in the Jordan (see Addendum I, pp. 238–9); but what in the life of Jesus was a kind of cosmic necessity was achieved by Rudolf Steiner based on a free decision.

Rudolf Steiner himself moved on this inner path in an exemplary manner. During the period between publication of *The Philosophy of Freedom* (1894) and the end of the century (1899), he was able through intensive work on himself to add to the ideal formulated in his book (the concept of 'free man') the corresponding percept (realization of free manhood). In doing so he united 'image' and 'likeness' in his 'I'-nature in the above-described changed form and reached the stage of the Son of Man on the level of consciousness. This led accordingly to his spiritual encounter with the Son of God, or in his own words to the 'spiritually having stood before the Mystery of Golgotha in innermost earnest celebration of knowledge'. (GA 28, Chap. XXXVI.)

Only after this cognitive event, which represents the culmination of Rudolf Steiner's initiation, could the founding of anthroposophy become possible out of the newly acquired Christ-consciousness. For him, the path opened up for ever-increasing creative activity based on freedom and love, as well as out of the sacrifice that is the basis of all creation.[109]

When we comprehend the life of Rudolf Steiner from 1894 to 1899 as a path from Jesus-consciousness to Christ-consciousness, meaning as a *spiritual* path to the Jordan, then this throws new light on the subsequent occurrences of his biography during this period.

According to the content of the Fifth Gospel, Jesus of Nazareth had three encounters on this path, namely with two Essenes, with a desperate person, and a leper. What happened here world-historically was repeated in Rudolf Steiner's life in a completely different way, but was brought about here too by three actual encounters. The first was his initial contact with the Theosophical Society which made such a negative impression on him that he expressed himself quite sharply in his article 'Theosophy' (1897) published in the 'Magazine for Literature'. At that time he saw in this society merely an unworldly, unrealistic movement: a group of people who, like the Essenes, pursued merely their own special interests. Then his meeting with ailing Nietzsche occurred (1896), who was a genuinely desperate person during the last period of his life. He too searched in his own manner—in contrast to Rudolf Steiner, however, mostly unconsciously—for 'the path to the Jordan' (it was not for nothing that he signed his last letters with 'the crucified one'). He could not find the path and mentally broke apart at the abyss of freedom because the spiritual world on yonder shore remained unattainable to him. Finally Rudolf Steiner encountered Ernst Haeckel in 1894 on the occasion of his sixtieth birthday. Haeckel was one of the most outstanding representatives of materialistic science in his age.[110] The parallel to the Turning Point of Time is obvious here too. What leprosy was at that time in the way of experiencing the death forces on one's own still alive body turned into a soul-problem for western humanity, along with the dawn of materialistic science. For viewed spiritually, materialism (which inevitably gives rise to total atheism) is a form of inner disease in man. (See GA 182, 16 October 1918.)[111]

Thus on his inner path to the Jordan, Rudolf Steiner took along these three impulses in order, out of the Christ-consciousness he had attained, to redeem and transform them into something for the future. This is why his first *anthroposophical* book was called *Theosophy*, a work in which he laid a foundation—in accordance with the modern scientific age—for the Christianization and transformation of ancient theosophy. For subsequent to the Mystery of Golgotha and the union of the Christ with mankind's evolution, the divine was no longer outside the human being in spiritual heights but was to be found within man himself. Consequently the correct name for spiritual science was no longer 'theosophy' but 'anthroposophy', a name coined by Rudolf Steiner even prior to his connection with the Theosophical Society.[112]

The element that was missing in Nietzsche's inner development and led to his tragic fate was described by Rudolf Steiner in his second basic anthroposophical book, *Knowledge of the Higher Worlds and Its Attainment*, which is the path of modern man into the spiritual world, where at the abyss of existence he experiences the encounter with the Christ (as the Greater Guardian of the Threshold). Only entry into and the pursuit of *this* path could have spared Nietzsche from his tragic fate.

Finally, through Rudolf Steiner's occupying himself with Haeckel's natural science still prior to the turn of the century, this led to his third work, *Occult Science, an Outline* (1910). Its main part is taken up with World evolution whose magnificent imaginations arose from the spiritual metamorphosis of Haeckel's teaching. How this occurred is described by Rudolf Steiner as follows: 'Having been touched by the Rosicrucian initiation-principle referred to here, study Haeckelism today with all its materialism, study it and allow yourself to be penetrated with the cognitive methods as depicted in *Knowledge of the Higher Worlds and Its Attainment*. What you learn in Haeckel's anthropogenesis concerning the human ancestors in a way that perhaps repulses you ... and then bear this up to the gods, you are given what is narrated in my book *Occult Science, an Outline.*' (GA 233a, 13 January 1924.)

What has been described here in regard to Rudolf Steiner's biography can in conclusion be summed up in Diagram 17:

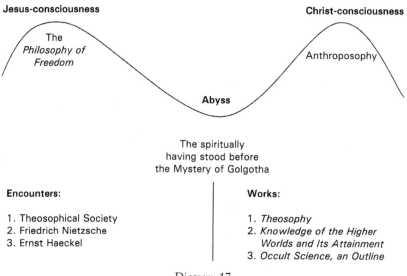

Diagram 17

Rudolf Steiner's further path after attainment of this new Christ-consciousness can only be understood in the sense of an Imitation of Christ that is undertaken in modern initiation out of complete freedom and love.[113] This is why this Imitation led Rudolf Steiner from the heights of his initiation at the Turning Point of Time to the depths of humanity when at the Christmas Conference of 1923 he united in a self-sacrificing manner with the Anthroposophical Society, including even his own karma.[114] Just as Christ on His macrocosmic path has taken upon Himself mankind's karma, thus, in the light of the present activity of the Etheric Christ as Lord of Karma, Rudolf Steiner took upon himself the karma of the Anthroposophical Society. In so doing he reaches a culmination on his path of the Imitation of Christ and reveals his earthly mission to be that of a lofty master of esoteric Christianity.

Looking back from this pinnacle of his life, it does not surprise us any more how accurately the content of the Fifth Gospel appears reflected in Rudolf Steiner's life. The only difference is that since the Mystery of Golgotha the Baptism in the Jordan no longer takes place outwardly with water but inwardly with fire and spirit (see Chapter 6) as a total metamorphosis of human consciousness in the way Rudolf Steiner had exemplified this to all of humanity at the end of the nineteenth century. All this took place at the time when, starting in 1879, the new Michaelic age had begun, so that one has to consider Rudolf Steiner's above-described initiation experiences and the spiritual activity of the Time Spirit as processes that are deeply connected with one another.

In addition in the three seven-year periods of anthroposophy's development (1902 until 1923), one can see a microcosmic reflection of what macrocosmically took place in the three years of the Christ-life on the earth. The forces, which in the latter led to the spiritualization of the three systems of Jesus of Nazareth's physical body, continued to work on the soul-level within the Anthroposophical Movement in the three main stages of its development up until the Christmas Conference. Thus, first thinking, then feeling, and finally the willing of human beings was taken hold of by the transformation-impulse of anthroposophy in the way it was then—as if summarized—manifested in the Foundation Stone Meditation. In this regard it is moreover significant that Rudolf Steiner has secreted the central events of the Fifth Gospel into the *eurythmic* representation of the Foundation Stone Meditation on the occasion of Easter 1924, something that elsewhere has already been depicted in detail.[115]

Through the Saturn rhythm that Rudolf Steiner mentions on the last day of the Christmas Conference (1 January 1924), still another event is connected with this. Moving back 30 years from 1924, we arrive at 1894, the year in which *The Philosophy of Freedom* was published. As shown before, in its centre stands the attainment of the Jesus-consciousness which through the spiritual baptism with fire and spirit leads to the Christ-consciousness. And in the Foundation Stone Meditation, which forms the spiritual centre of the Christmas Conference, we have the same process but described from the standpoint of the Christ-consciousness. In the three microcosmic segments of the first three parts of the meditation it is the Jesus-consciousness that is primarily characterized, in the three macrocosmic segments of the same, the Christ-consciousness. Both are then united in the light of the 'Christ-Sun' which is mentioned in the fourth part where all main themes of the Fifth Gospel emerge in a new way.[116] In Rudolf Steiner's biography this fourth part of the meditation corresponds to his 'having stood before the Mystery of Golgotha' and the experiencing of how the spiritual sun rises out of this Mystery.[117]

In this way Rudolf Steiner's course of life and spirit-path are rounded out in a unique, consistent unity and barely imagined beauty of an archetype whose nature opens up only with the key to the Fifth Gospel. As the one who in his own biography spiritually exemplified the Fifth

Gospel, Rudolf Steiner was allowed to be the first to communicate its truths to humanity. And those whose fortune it was to be present at these communications, if only they were sufficiently awake, bear witness to what it means to speak about the Christ in the presence of the Christ.[118]

★

A special secret is connected with the lighting up of Christ-consciousness on the path of Christian initiation, the understanding of which can lead us even deeper into the nature of the Fifth Gospel in its relationship to Rudolf Steiner's course of development. He speaks about that once in the lecture of 30 July 1922 (GA 214). It deals with the following. As the Son of God, Christ is such a world-encompassing entity that during His entry into a human being no human 'I' could remain in its position in the body by the side of the Christ-'I'. That is why the 'I' of Zarathustra had to leave the sheaths of Jesus of Nazareth already prior to the baptism by John. With that the decisive question was posed for the future development of mankind: How can Christ live in a human being without the 'I'-consciousness of the latter being extinguished thereby? Rudolf Steiner states in this regard: 'He [the Divine Son] wanted to indwell humanity but did not wish to dampen down the dawning 'I'-consciousness of human beings. He had done that once in the Jesus being in whom, in place of the 'I'-consciousness, He dwelled in the Son-consciousness. But this was not to occur in human beings in future times. In humans of future ages, the 'I' was supposed to be able to arise in full awareness, and the Christ nevertheless was to be in a position to indwell these human beings.'[119]

This main problem of the future presence of the Christ in human beings was however solved by Him through the pouring out of the Holy Spirit on Whitsun Sunday: 'Thus the Holy Spirit is really what was supposed to be sent out by the Christ so that a person can maintain his or her 'I'-consciousness while the Christ indwells the human being unconsciously.' (Ibid.)

Such a presence of the Christ in every human being—initially still an 'unconscious' presence after the Mystery of Golgotha—could be lifted, through the connection with the Holy Spirit, into consciousness on the path of modern Christian initiation without the individual 'I' being thereby in the least dimmed or disturbed. Moreover, as the result of this presence of the Christ in the human 'I' through the mediation of the Holy Spirit, the spiritual forces of this 'I' could be increased immeasurably.[120]

The first human beings who in the manner just described experienced the shining forth of the Christ-consciousness were the Apostles during the Whitsun miracle. For this reason, Rudolf Steiner begins the communications from the Fifth Gospel in his first and most significant cycle in Christiania with the description of the Whitsun event. (See GA 148, 2 October 1913.) With this he points out that it is only through the link with the Holy Spirit, in those days as well as today, that the Christian initiate might attain Christ-consciousness to the full extent without any harm being done thereby to his 'I'.

In addition, such a union with the Holy Spirit can even enable a human being in our age—the generally prevailing intellectual culture notwith-standing—to comprehend spiritual matters out of this very culture, which in fact means the comprehension of the results of modern spiritual research. 'Inasmuch as the Christ sent humanity the Holy Spirit, He enabled them to rise out of the intellectual element itself to compre-hension of the spirit' (GA 214, 30 July 1922).

Here too, what has been said relates initially to ordinary human beings of the present who thereby can understand spiritual-scientific commu-nications about the higher worlds with their thinking. For the initiate on the other hand, the conscious link with the Holy Spirit signifies the possibility of being able to research the spiritual worlds as accurately and precisely as do scientists in regard to the phenomena of nature.

All this allows us to understand in what way, following his descent into the realms of death, Rudolf Steiner himself could attain to the point of 'spiritually having stood before the Mystery of Golgotha out of this abyss'. In the lecture of 16 October 1918 titled 'How do I find the Christ?' (GA 182) he describes how today's human being can begin to approach the conscious experience of the Mystery of Golgotha. When we proceed from the assumption that Rudolf Steiner here too—as he always emphasized—speaks from his own spiritual experience, then the fol-lowing experiences also refer to him, albeit on a much higher level.

Rudolf Steiner points out that the contemporary way for man to share in the experience of the Mystery of Golgotha consists of two basic elements. The first is the feeling of overwhelming 'powerlessness ... to raise oneself to the Divine at any point of time in one's life'. This 'point of time' arose most forcefully in Rudolf Steiner's life when, as was pointed out above, he had descended into the domain of the ahrimanic death-forces. For in this realm one not only can experience how the physical body is doomed to gradual death, but in the present cycle of humanity's evolution the soul and with it the 'I'-consciousness of man as well. For this inner feeling of overwhelming powerlessness is a direct result of the fact that 'in our soul we ... have become akin to death' (ibid.). For only at the moment when everything appears to reach ultimate annihilation, a total 'turnaround', something like a complete transformation of soul, can take place as if through a miracle, when all moral and cognitive forces of the human being are stretched and activated to the utmost. This reversal is based on the fact that 'we can have the possibility to rediscover our soul and connect it to the spirit' (ibid.). For since the Mystery of Golgotha, every human being carries within himself this 'possibility' of the soul's salvation, even in the realm of death.

In our age, the modern approach to the Christ Being consists of a twofold experience: '... that of experiencing death in the soul through the body [because this body bears in itself the dead mineral substances,[121]] and that of resurrection of the soul through the spirit' (ibid.). Only a person who has gone through this twofold inner experience 'is on the supersensible path to the Mystery of Golgotha. He finds in himself forces that stimulate in turn certain supersensible forces that lead him to the Mystery of Golgotha.' (Ibid.)

Now the same process that *starts* the ordinary person (who reaches this experience 'of powerlessness and the resurrection out of it' (ibid.) with still fragile soul forces) *on the path* leading to the supersensible experience of the Mystery of Golgotha brings about in another person who consciously experiences the initiation path the 'spiritually having stood before the Mystery of Golgotha'. For during such an experience of powerlessness and its inner overcoming, such a modern initiate on the level of consciousness recapitulates the stages of the Mystery of Golgotha through which the Christ Himself passed in Gethsemane, albeit in world-historical form. It was not for nothing that here Rudolf Steiner uses the words '*resurrection* out of powerlessness', for this microcosmic resurrection is experienced by the human being as the result of conscious union with the spirit that is truly the Holy Spirit: *Per Spiritum Sanctum reviviscimus*. For only it is in a position to bring about the inner resurrection of the soul and with that moreover the shining forth of 'I'-consciousness in the spiritual world that leads to experiencing the Christ and his deed, the Mystery of Golgotha.[122]

From what has been said, it becomes understandable why Rudolf Steiner does not speak in his autobiography about a Christ encounter but the living experience of the Mystery of Golgotha, meaning about what actually took place in his life. For with this, a mighty breakthrough of his 'I' was connected for him to the Spirit and through the Spirit to the new Christ-consciousness.

The spiritual standing under the Cross on Golgotha had yet another consequence for Rudolf Steiner that can allow us to comprehend still better how out of this archetypical experience of his initiation at the beginning of the twentieth century he established anthroposophy on earth. For this establishing too had its archetype at the Turning Point of Time. Then two human beings were present as his direct witnesses under the Cross on Golgotha. They were the Mother of Jesus, through whom for the first time on earth the lofty entity of the heavenly Sophia manifested fully—the heavenly Sophia who was still linked with Christ as the Son of God, meaning the true Theosophia—and the disciple whom the Lord loved, John, the first human being initiated by Christ himself, the genuine Anthropos.

John relates about what happened under the Cross in the following words: 'When Jesus saw his mother and the disciple whom he loved standing near, he said to his mother: 'Woman, behold, your son!' Then he said to the disciple: 'Behold, your mother!' And from that hour the disciple took her to his own home.' (John 19:26–27.) Rudolf Steiner interpreted this passage based on his spirit research as follows: 'He [Christ Jesus] Himself transferred the Sophia that had been in Him onto John. He turned him into the son of the Sophia.' (GA 97, 2 December 1906.)

Here, as a world-historical fact, Christ Jesus Himself entrusted *Theosophia* to the earthly human being, whereby she became *Anthroposophia*. For the Being Sophia, who earlier was the heavenly 'mother' of the Christ,[123] and subsequently had become the earthly mother of Jesus, was now in the actual living sense of being united with the earthly man John, so that he could then hand her over through the writing of his Gospel to all human beings. 'The spiritualized mother of Jesus is itself the Gospel. She is the wisdom that leads human beings upwards to the highest insights. The disciple has given us the mother Sophia, meaning he has written the Gospel for us. (GA 100, 25 November 1907.)

Primarily in Revelations, which was received from the same spiritual source, the Sophia herself appears in the twelfth chapter as the Heavenly Virgin, who for the earth gives birth to the Child—the higher 'I' of the human being—the 'I' that still must wait for a long time until human beings, through the transformation of their consciousness (a consciousness that under the Cross was established through the union of the mother of Jesus with John), enter into new manhood.

What occurred at the Turning Point of Time as 'mystical fact' world-historically on one occasion must come newly alive today in the soul of man and there become a higher reality so that these world events can in him become facts of his changed consciousness. This happened for the first time in Rudolf Steiner's consciousness during his 'spiritually having stood' under the Golgotha-cross, when he received the nature of the *Sophia* into his soul and thereby, as a human being, could generate *anthroposophy* out of his 'I'. In this way the Sophia appeared twice on earth: once in presence [*Dasein*, usually translated as 'existence'] at the Turning Point of Time as Mary-Sophia, and then in *one* human *consciousness* at the threshold to the twentieth century.

The first predisposition for a future human species was created through the union of John and Sophia under the Cross. Through the creation of anthroposophy in the twentieth century this future generation received the new spiritual consciousness, with the unfolding of which every human being can live and find his/her way into this new species of mankind. And just as in his day John handed over the Sophia entrusted to him to all human beings in the form of his Gospel and the Apocalypse, so did Rudolf Steiner with his anthroposophy. He entrusted it to all people of good will, so that it would lead them to the birth of the spiritual child in their souls, the child who in the spiritual world waits for every individual in the form of his/her higher 'I', with which alone human beings can reach the goal of Earth evolution.

9. Metaphysical Foundations for Unconditionality in *The Philosophy of Freedom*

'I said: You are gods.'

(John 10:34)

'Man bears the predisposition for
divinity irrefutably in his personality.'
Friedrich Schiller, *On the Aesthetic
Education of Man* (Eleventh Letter)

The chief trend of *The Philosophy of Freedom's* theory of cognition is its unconditionality. Rudolf Steiner describes and establishes this principally in his book *Truth and Science*, which he designated as the 'prologue to a 'philosophy of freedom''. Through this trend the aforementioned theory of cognition can examine the nature of cognizing itself and with that becomes the precondition of all remaining sciences and in a deepened sense even of spiritual science. (GA 3, Chap. I.)

In the above-mentioned book, Rudolf Steiner initially intends to determine the 'absolute very first', the 'first' that still lies '*outside* cognizing' and therefore is to be sought directly prior to cognizing'. (GA 3, Chap. IV; emphasis by Rudolf Steiner.) He characterizes this 'absolute first' that precedes any cognition in the following words: 'Such a beginning can, however, be made only with the *directly given world-view*; that is with that world-view that presents itself to man before he has subjected it in any way whatsoever to the process of cognition, hence before he has made even the least statement about it, before he has undertaken to make any thought-out determination concerning it.' (Ibid.) We are dealing here with a world image that to begin with one cannot define at all, for any definition already implies a first cognitive act. The only fact that can be considered (not in the sense of a cognitive definition but merely as an indication of the encountered situation of what has been determined as the very first beginning) is what Rudolf Steiner describes as the 'directly given'.

In order to begin this process of cognition on this basis, Rudolf Steiner seeks in this world image a part that belongs to the given world and yet is created by man at the same time; meaning is added only through his own participation to the generally given. 'For true cognizing, everything depends on our finding somewhere in the given an aspect where our cognizing activity not merely *presupposes* a given, but stands actively in the

very midst of the given. In other words: it is in the very act of holding fast
to the merely given that we realize that not everything is such a given.'
(Ibid.) What in our world-view are both the given and at the same time
something produced by an act of cognition are our 'concepts and ideas',
which 'always enter only in the act of cognition through the act of
cognition, and through it into the sphere of the directly given'. This is
'why we must first produce them if we wish to experience them' (ibid.),
for they are only given to us as experience through our inner cognitive
activity.

In the sixth chapter Rudolf Steiner summarizes the cognitive process
depicted before, and at the same time amplifies it in the following form:
'Outer and inner cognition and its own existence are directly given to the
"I" as central point of consciousness. The "I" feels the urge to find more
in this—the given—than is *directly* given. In the face of the given world,
the second world, that of thinking, dawns in the "I" and links the two by
making real out of a free decision what we have determined as "idea" of
cognition.' (Ibid., Chap. VI; emphasis by Rudolf Steiner.) In what has
been said, three stages or three elements of cognition are clearly to be
distinguished from one another:

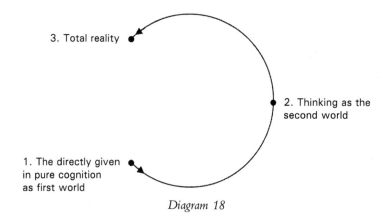

Diagram 18

1. Cognition given to the 'I' as central point of consciousness, which
   contains all that is external and internal as well as its own existence.
2. The urge of the 'I' as expressed in the creative activity of thinking to
   extend beyond the directly given through creating a 'second world'.
3. To link up anew the arisen thinking (second world) with what has
   been cognized (first world), i.e. the concept with the directly given
   out of a 'free decision', and with that to create for cognition a
   'whole reality' (third world).

With this the path of an unconditional cognition is precisely described in strictly scientific form.

If one then asks where to find—but now not on the microcosmic level of human cognition but on the highest level of world-existence (meaning at the very first creation of the world)—a macrocosmic process that corresponds to the same unconditionality, one arrives at the following.

When one seeks the absolute unconditionality in the creation of the universe, one has to go back to the 'Ground of the World' that precedes everything and has been described in the religions of antiquity as that which is 'the Absolute'. Only this absolute Godhead, namely *before* its appearance as Trinity, finds itself in that condition that neither is nor can be preceded by anything. This, its primal condition, is at the same time absolute unconditionality. One can also say that in this condition the Godhead is only preceded by itself in all eternity. In the esoteric Christianity of Dionysius the Areopagite, one ascribed to this primal condition of the Godhead only negating qualities, namely what it is *not* (apostatical theology), because all direct definitions must by necessity become silent here so that it can only be honoured by silence.

To this absolute Godhead is attributed above all its own boundless creative potency which, in the very first act of a purely spiritual creation, consists in the indescribable and unfathomable transition from the state of oneness into a triune condition. Thereby there manifests out of the Primal Ground, which the Gnostics describe as 'Primal Depths' or 'Silence', the Neoplatonists as the 'Inexpressible' and the Cabbalists as the indescribable 'Ain-Zof' ('En Zof—the Nothing of the Infinite), the threefoldness of the Trinity as Father, Son and Holy Spirit. This transformation of the one primal principle into the three, which on their part are linked with each other 'purely [unblended] and inseparably', takes place in three stages which can be quite accurately described in the terminology of the book *Truth and Science*.

First there manifests out of the 'Primal Ground' in the process representing a kind of self-observation the Divine Father who in all that He observes is only He himself. On this first level the inexpressible Primal Godhead becomes the manifest Father of Worlds, who is to be considered as the highest *personage*, meaning as the 'I'-Being who potentially bears all and everything within Himself. One can therefore say: On this first level, aside from this 'I' of God, nothing exists. And the inner life of this all-encompassing 'I' consists first of all only in self-observation, or self-perception respectively. On an abstract philosophical level, Johann Gottlieb Fichte with his doctrine of the absolute 'I' had an inkling of this primal state.

This transition from the indescribable primal state of the absolute Godhead to its very first inner movement within itself in which it turns into the Divine Father of later creation is a process which in its human reflected splendour is familiar to true mysticism as its primal origin. Rudolf Steiner characterizes this primal mystical experience in the following words: 'If I do not light up to myself in my self-perception, I am not existent to myself. If I do light up to myself, I then *have* myself likewise in my perception in my primordial very own being. No remnant remains of me outside my perception... Perception of one's self is therefore at the same time awakening of one's self.' (GA 7; emphasis by Rudolf Steiner.)

Only after this appearance of the Father God out of the indescribable absoluteness can the next step, the birthing of the Son out of the womb of the Father, take place. For what is the very element of the Divine 'I' of the Father as the infinite creative potentiation strives for manifestation, namely from the potential to the actual. And the first power that would like to come into being here is the potential of love. For love requires an opposite, another being. This is why God the Father had to give birth in all eternity to the Son, so that love could even come about in the universe. 'A being can only love another—another from whom it is separated (GA 155, 12 July 1914). In other words, a second individuality is always required for love. Rudolf Steiner demonstrates this using the following example: 'Imagine that we would pass through the portal of death in such a way that we would lose our human individuality, that we would unite with an overall divinity. Then we would be within this divinity, we would belong to it. We could not love the deity any longer; we would be within it. Love would have no meaning if we were within the god.' (Ibid.) Thus there originates in the womb of the Father the Divine Son as the first opposite, and the Father would now like to share His highest creative potentiality with it out of love for His Son. This implies that on this level '[the Father Godhead] feels the urge to find more in this opposite [the given] than what is directly given' (GA 3). This inner urge leads it to a kind of birth or procreation process, out of which the divine son emerges as the first equivalent oppositeness [Ger.: *Gegenüber*] of the father, or as a newborn 'second world' still completely within the original Godhead. This birth of the son can most appropriately be compared with the expressing of the Creator Word. That is why the nature of the Son is like the word or Logos, which bears within itself the whole *meaning* of future creation, and to whom the Father bestows His highest creative potentiality. One could also say that the Son as Logos receives from the Father the whole future creation as a thought-form with the charge to actualize these divine thoughts through His own creative activity in the creation of the universal all. He subsequently carries out this deed in complete freedom out of the power He receives from the Father, a power that in its nature is love as the highest creative force.

On the third level, the divine Son turns back to the Father and in so doing resolves the oppositeness [Ger.: *Gegenüber*] in a new unity: 'I and the Father are one' (John 10:30). This new connection occurs now out of the nature of the Holy Spirit, thus circumventing the Son's fusing completely with the Father, and thereby ceasing to be an independent person ('I'). One can even say that this new connection between the two is itself the Holy Spirit who adds to the principle of disparity-of-being (incompatibility) the principle of connectedness-of-being (inseparableness). With this the Holy Spirit can lead the formerly arisen duality to a new higher community between Father and Son and out of full freedom at that so that the inner unity of the Trinity endures. This free reunion of the Son with the Father out of the Holy Spirit's freedom is the third and concluding step (for the time being) in the process of the origination of the Trinity itself.

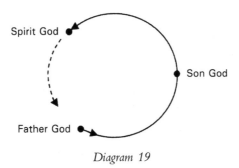

Diagram 19

Out of the absolute unconditionality of the Divine Primal One, there arises the 'total reality' of the Holy Trinity as the first and only precondition for the whole world (cosmos) about to come into being. This latter is then created in the sense of the prologue of the Gospel of John by the eternal Logos in the form of an evolutionary process out of which, one after the other, all nine hierarchies emerge. This comes about inasmuch as each of the hierarchies in their very being represent (reflect) a certain characteristic of the Deity: love, harmony, will or courage, wisdom, all-pervasive motion, the formative force that shapes all, and so on. This is why Dionysius the Areopagite points out that the designation 'Angelos' (messenger) is applicable as a collective concept to all nine hierarchies.

It follows from what has been said that the hierarchies are above all implementing spirits who move the impulses of the Trinity through the mediation of the Logos into reality (actuality). Of the nine or three orders of hierarchies respectively, only the first or highest one enjoys direct view of the Deity. 'Now what is it that the Seraphim, Cherubim and Thrones have that is an advantage over all other beings in the universe? They have what in antiquity was called the direct view of the Deity [the Trinity].' (GA 110, 18 April 1909–II.) This is why they consider themselves 'purely as executors of the Divine Will, the Divine Wisdom. That is how it is with the loftiest hierarchy'. (Ibid.) It is similar in the case of the Second Hierarchy. While they no longer enjoy the direct view of the Deity, they can directly receive their revelations. The Third Hierarchy is still further away from the central divine source, but it too receives the impulses of the Trinity through the mediation of the higher spirits and the power of the Logos penetrating all the hierarchies respectively.

Despite the fact that all these hierarchies have merely a ministering or executing function in regard to the Holy Trinity and cannot refuse the impulses they have received from it, they do possess—although in a different sense from human beings (that will be considered later)—a sort of freedom that extends above all to their 'will', 'wisdom', that is to say their intelligence. These 'divine-spiritual beings with whom man was originally connected ... are presently purely spiritual powers who bear in themselves perfect free intelligence and perfect free will'. (GA 26.)

These words are not contradictory with the just described activity of the hierarchies in regard to the execution of the impulses received from the Holy Trinity. Although it is said that 'the Seraphim have the task to receive out of the Trinity the highest ideas, the objectives of a cosmic (planetary) system, freedom is in no way excluded in other domains of their cosmic creating. For what they then do with the thus received impulses, how they prepare them for the next lower hierarchy and convey them to this hierarchy—in this is contained the freedom of these beings. The Cherubim, too, who prepare these impulses for their further execution (realization) as well as the Thrones who then actualize them are free in carrying out this activity. (See GA 110, 14 April 1909–II.)

As compared to this hierarchical freedom, human freedom is of another kind. That is why Rudolf Steiner emphasizes so very much that, with the exception of the Angels, *all* the hierarchies can do something that runs counter to World evolution only by 'permission' of the highest Deity. This means that for this different kind of activity they are 'ordered away' from above (18 April 1909–II). This is why the hierarchies on their own do not under any condition decide for evil. Evil, and with it the new quality of freedom, arises for the first time only among that segment of the Angels who on the Old Moon fell away from regular development. 'Led astray' by higher spirits, they voluntarily pursued the path of evil. (Ibid.) Although their freedom already resembled human freedom, it remained limited to a large extent. The above-stated is summed up by Rudolf Steiner like this: 'In the midst of the ranks of Angels the possibility of freedom begins; but it is only in the human being that freedom is developed in the correct manner' (ibid.).

The difference can be clearly pictured by the following. The Angels absolved their human stage on Old Moon, where the material substance that constituted their bodies had condensed only so far as the watery element, meaning the material substance resembled plants. Now everything plantlike is permeated by etheric forces in which cosmic and spiritual impulses are constantly active. This is why Angels could never reach a death-experience in their bodies and as a result could not attain to materialism, much less to any form of atheism or spirit-negation. In other words, in the phase of their 'I'-development their separation from the divine-spiritual world never reached such an ultimate form as in man. (The Fallen Angels, for example Mephistopheles, therefore know about God and the spiritual world, but insinuate the opposite to human beings for the very reason that they are moreover the Spirits of the Lie.)

The most absolute and highest form of freedom can only be achieved on earth by the human being. This becomes possible only because we have descended much deeper into matter than the Angels—so deeply that with our body we belong to the dead mineral world in which the divine-spiritual powers are no longer active. This is the reason why only man can deny God and the Spirit (be an atheist and materialist), something that is impossible for any of the hierarchies.[124] This is the dark, the abysmal aspect of man's divine calling to absolute freedom, the freedom out of which the most sublime in the cosmos will emerge eventually.

This highest aspect, distinguishing man from all the hierarchies that ultimately will in future time place him above them all, can be imagined as follows. The source of the creative power of *all* the hierarchies lies in the Holy Trinity and is mediated through the Divine Word or Logos. Only humans will in due course find this source in their own individual nature and be capable of working out of it. This means that humans as the Tenth Hierarchy will be the first-born of all creation who will bear the primal quality of the highest Deity (its creative potency) not as if inspired by it from outside but autonomously and completely within themselves. With that, when at the end of Vulcan man will have ascended to the highest creative activity out of freedom and love, he will glean the motivations for this not out of the Holy Trinity but out of himself. Thus, at the end of their evolution, humans will become godlike to a degree never yet reached until then by any of the nine hierarchies. One could also say that man will in himself bear the full power of the Logos, not receiving it from above as do all the other hierarchies. As the micro-logos, man will carry out his new creation in the world-all at his own risk and his own responsibility.

In order that man might reach this new stage of World evolution, a few hierarchical beings were 'ordered away' and placed as spirits of obstruction into human evolution. 'So we see that in a certain regard it was only through the fact that the Powers [Spirits of Movement] were 'ordered away' that human beings were given the possibility *on their own to reach the goal that even the loftiest Seraphim cannot attain on their own*. That is the main point.' (GA 110, 18 April 1909–II) This is why the apostle Paul, well aware of this secret, says: 'Do you not know that we are to judge angels?' (1 Cor. 6:3 RSV). And in the same lecture Rudolf Steiner refers to this one more time in the following words: 'He [the human being] can tell himself when he looks towards the future: I am called upon to view on my own out of my innermost being all that gives me the impulses of actions—not based on beholding the Deity as do the Seraphim, but out of my innermost being.' (Ibid.)

In order to reach this elevated goal that will place the human being above the Seraphim,[125] man at one point of his evolution had to become instilled in the innermost depths of his being with this highest faculty of resemblance to God, hence the possibility to become creative himself as the micro-logos. The Primal Deity's highest creative potency that initially was possessed purely by that Primal Deity—and as the Divine Father only shared it with the Divine Son for the purpose of creating the cosmos— was meant to be implanted eventually into man to the full extent. With it, something was given man that all the hierarchies do not possess in this direct form. Only after such a transformation could the human being become the true crown of the spiritual cosmos, and with that 'the ideal and aim of the gods' (GA 26) or the 'gods' religion' as Rudolf Steiner described this set of circumstances in an earlier lecture. (GA 153, 10 April 1914.)

From what has been said it follows that the process of cognition that man actualizes on earth is in its unconditionality itself a microcosmic replica of the origin of the Trinity out of the Primal Deity or the 'Absolute'.[126] And just as the Trinity's origin is the only necessary con- ditionality for the then following creation of the world (cosmos), so in man's case too in the unconditional theory of cognition is found the only conditionality for his own conscious creating that comes to expression in his individual actions (the transition from the first to the second part of *The Philosophy of Freedom*). Now, this original process of cognition may not—if man eventually is to reach the goal of his evolution—remain in its further continuation and unfolding merely on the level of man's consciousness (his cognition). It must reach the level of existence along with the new faculty, not only to cognize the highest, but moreover to *create* the highest out of cognition as well.

Such a faculty could only be implanted into man *directly* out of the womb of the highest Deity, circumventing all the hierarchies who do not possess such a faculty, and therefore have to live and work outside the Deity in the created world (cosmos). This transmission was moreover to occur not just on the level of cognition ('as a matter of consciousness' so to speak), but out of *living being (wesenhaft)*, meaning through a concrete entity who does not stem from the world of the hierarchies but out of the womb of the Godhead itself.

A Being who in its nature is identical to the highest Deity was supposed to come to earth into the human kingdom in order to bring to all men the highest faculty that otherwise is to be found only in the womb of the Deity. This occurred through the appearance of the Christ on earth when, at the Turning Point of Time, the Divine Word had become flesh and had dwelt among humans (John 1:14). For this reason, John could say in the prologue of his Gospel about Christ: 'No human being has ever seen the divine Ground of the World with eyes; the only Son who was in the bosom of the Father, he has become the guide in such seeing' (John 1:18 JM). For only He who comes directly out of the Father's womb could show human beings the Father's nature and with that His highest creative power and then mediate this as well in the Mystery of Golgotha.

So the Christ, who originates from the womb of the Father and as the Divine Word represents the highest power of the former (the Father), has united Himself with evolution of humanity so as to bring the possibility to earth that every human being can henceforth develop this highest divine power within him/herself. But this is only possible when people decide, based on their freedom and love, to unite themselves with the Christ and the essence of the Mystery of Golgotha. For this central deed of the Christ, through which He made this highest faculty accessible to every human being, is of such a nature that from then on everyone, if only he or she is willing, can receive it from the Christ in full freedom. 'This deed [the Mystery of Golgotha] is of such a kind that it works on no human being unless that person on his own allows it to work on himself, meaning if it is compatible with the absolutely free nature of his individual "I" ...

and the "I" must freely decide to accept the Christ' (GA 110, 18 April 1909–II) and along with that the creative Power of the Logos in the Christ. Only on this basis will 'a hierarchy gradually mature ... in man *that carries out its own tasks*. Through the Jupiter, Venus and Vulcan evolution the human being will mature to become the executor of his/her own impulses.' (Ibid.) Along with this, man will learn not only to cognize unconditionally but likewise to create in the cosmos unconditionally. This boundless and godlike freedom to which man will have risen is then moreover linked with the full responsibility for his new creation.

This is why Christ can proclaim to human beings: 'Yes, I say to you: Whoever takes me into himself will also be able to do the deeds that I do, and greater deeds he will do, because I go to the Father' (John 14:12).[127] Christ connects this 'going to the Father' in this passage with the promise of the Holy Spirit. For the creating that we deal with here is the *new* creating which in Christian esotericism is also called the 'Creation out of Nothing'. In accordance with the book *Truth and Science*, only this kind of creating can be designated as unconditional.

Asking once more about the spiritual origin of this 'new creating', we find it in the above-described beginning of the Trinity which emerged from the womb of the original Godhead. This is the first Creation out of Nothing that proceeds out of the Father God. The second step in this sequence proceeds from the Son and His deed in the Mystery of Golgotha. In this regard Rudolf Steiner says that it was the only deed on earth not carried out due to past karma; moreover it did not produce any karma. From the very beginning this deed was therefore karma-free, hence unconditional. 'This means, speaking anthroposophically, that this Spirit [Christ] had no earthly karma ... He had to go through earth experiences lasting three years without any karma burdening Him. (GA 148, 3 October 1913.) These words are found in Rudolf Steiner's lectures on the Fifth Gospel, the gospel he then termed an 'anthroposophical gospel', thus bringing this whole set of facts into a direct relationship with anthroposophy. 'The Fifth Gospel is the anthroposophical gospel and shows us that the three-year-long life of Christ is the only life in a human body that was lived without karma; a life to which the concept of karma is not applicable in the human sense.' (Ibid.) And in another lecture Rudolf Steiner points in the same direction, saying that the Mystery of Golgotha 'has no archetype in the higher worlds' (GA 132, 5 December 1911). This likewise confirms that one is dealing here with the purest Creation out of Nothing.

What has been stated can once more be summarized in the following way. The Father God as Creator of the World, as a God of Love (1 John

4:16), would like to share everything He possesses with His creation. On man, on the other hand, He wishes to bestow His innermost faculty which rests in His 'womb'—namely the creative power to create everything out of freedom and love unconditionally.[128]

Out of his womb, God then had to convey this highest faculty directly to man so that ultimately, at the end of his evolution, the human being might attain absolute resemblance to God (image) on the path of God-likeness, so that out of his own resources and completely at his own risk he can create the new cosmos. In order to bestow on human beings this faculty, God the Father had sacrificed to them His only begotten Son who sojourned in His womb. 'For God so loved the world [in E. Bock's German translation: 'human beings'] that He gave [them] His only begotten Son' (John 3:16). For this to happen, Christ came to earth in order to carry out His highest deed, the Mystery of Golgotha, as a pure sacrifice out of freedom and love.

Thus the Divine Father fulfils the first unconditional creation or Creation out of Nothing, and the Son carries out the second Creation out of Nothing in the Mystery of Golgotha that likewise was completely unconditional, and by comparison with the first creation bore divine *and* human character simultaneously. 'For whatever He does, that the Son does likewise' (John 5:19).

One could moreover say: Out of the womb of the Father, Christ brought us His 'only begotten-ness' [Ger: *Erstgeborenheit*] and shared it with us. He thus became the spiritual brother of all human beings. He bestowed on humans the innermost nature of God Himself, a nature that none of the nine hierarchies can fully fathom, much less possess. Even the highest among them, the Seraphim, who stand closest to the 'Throne of God' cannot look directly into the inner nature of the Deity. Instead, they must receive from the Godhead the plans and directives 'as if from outside'. (See GA 110, 14 April 1909–II.) In the whole universe it is only human beings who, through their conscious connection with Christ, can partake in this state of being 'only-begotten' out of the Deity.

In the lecture 'Evolution, Involution and Creation out of Nothing', Rudolf Steiner points out that the faculty of creating the absolutely new out of nothing was embedded in humanity through the deed of Christ on Golgotha, and can be brought into being only through the conscious connection of man with that deed. 'The human being is now capable of fitting into this Creation out of Nothing [out of his/her freedom]. We will be capable of this, however, only by striving upward to this freedom of self-creating through the freest deed which can become our example. What is this freest deed? The freest deed is that the creative wise Word

[Logos] of our solar system determined on its own to enter into a human body and to participate in Earth evolution through a deed that was not part of any previous karma. When the Christ decided to enter a human body, He was not forced through any earlier karma. Rather, He did this as a free deed that was merely founded on the advance view of humanity's future evolution that had never before existed and first originated in Him as a thought out of the Nothing.' (GA 107, 17 June 1909.)

In this manner through the Mystery of Golgotha, the principle of Creation out of Nothing enters into humanity's evolution. It is transmitted to man by the Christ directly out of the womb of the Divine Father, bypassing all nine hierarchies. Rudolf Steiner also depicts what the consequence of this will be as follows: 'Thus, to evolution and involution is added the Creation out of Nothing right in the middle of our development. After [Ancient] Saturn, Sun and Moon have gone by, the Christ appears on the earth as the mighty element of enrichment that brings it about that on Vulcan *something completely new* will be present, something that did not yet exist on Saturn.' (Ibid.)

This completely new factor consists of the voluntary acceptance of the above-described divine faculty on the part of human beings. This in turn signifies nothing less than accepting the Christ Himself (who as the Word of Worlds *is* in actual fact this faculty) into one's own 'I'. As described in Chapter 5, such an acceptance of Christ can only occur through the mediation of the Holy Spirit who had been sent into the human 'I' ahead of time by the Christ as the necessary prerequisite for His entry into man's 'I'.

As a result, through the penetration with the Holy Spirit, man himself can gradually become creative out of nothing. 'The Holy Spirit beatifies man when he is in a position to create the Right or the True, the Beautiful and the Good out of nothing. But so that one has reached the point of being in the position to create in accordance with the Holy Spirit, one first had to have been given the foundation as is the case with all creating out of nothing. This foundation has been given to us humans through the Christ's entry into our evolution. Inasmuch as human beings on earth could experience the Christ Event, they became capable of developing upwards to the creating in the Holy Spirit.' (GA 107, 17 June 1909.)

If we try in this way to trace the primal sources and future perspectives of unconditional creating, we arrive at the following stages: the original creation of the Father at the beginning of the universe; the new creation by the Son in the Mystery of Golgotha; then the primary creative activity of man himself out of his state of being permeated with the Holy Spirit. In the development of Christendom this third stage begins with the Whitsun event, but to start with remains restricted to a few human beings especially blessed from above. This stage becomes accessible to all other persons only in the New Mysteries that incline towards the transition to the fourth stage. This stage consists of the actualization of what Rudolf Steiner calls the second Michael revelation. It stands in a mirror-like position to Michael's first revelation which initiated the transition from the stage of the Father to that of the Son, and culminates in the fundamental proclamation of the prologue to the Gospel of John: 'And the Word became flesh and dwelt among us' (John 1:14). This first Michael revelation was given to humans out of his last guidance of mankind which directly preceded the Mystery of Golgotha. Today, beginning from 1879, we live in the new period of Michael's guidance inasmuch as we receive his second revelation and are able to take the first steps towards its actualization. It involves the fact that henceforth 'the flesh once again ... [must] be permeated with spirit so that it becomes capable of dwelling in the kingdom of the Word, of beholding the divine secrets' (GA 194, 22 November 1919). In other words, at the Turning Point of Time the Logos itself had to become man so that, at the end of World evolution, man on his part will become a micro-logos creating out of his own initiative, or as designated by the ancient Rosicrucians the 'eternal persona'. With this begins the fourth stage of the above-described development today. It is a development that in the distant future will lead to the origin of the Tenth Hierarchy in which the ideal of the absolutely autonomous personality (persona) will have become reality, the personality that out of its own being will produce its creative impulses.

The spiritual genealogy of unconditional cognition can thus be depicted as follows in Diagram 20:

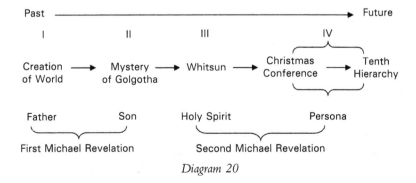

Diagram 20

In the Foundation Stone Meditation, we can find a similar sequence. From the first three segments it follows that the First Hierarchy receives its guiding impulses above all from the realm of the Father; the Second from the realm of the Son; the Third from the realm of the Holy Spirit. Only when man has accepted the Christ Sun into his being in accordance with the fourth segment and, based on its power, has reached the level of the Tenth Hierarchy (or the eternal persona) will he as a godlike being out of his own self, meaning unconditionally and without the influence of former karma, be creative out of 'nothing'.

What has been stated here can be related to the Foundation Stone Meditation in still another way. For its first three segments correspondingly reflect the nature of Christmas, Easter and Whitsun, which are all linked with the Mystery of Golgotha at the Turning Point of Time. In the Christmas events, this mystery is prepared and at Whitsun its first effect in humanity occurs. The fourth segment of the meditation on the other hand is connected with the Michaelic half of the year and thus likewise with the supersensible Mystery of Golgotha that took place in the second half of the nineteenth century in the spiritual world adjacent to the earth.

Along with this second Mystery of Golgotha, the foundation was laid for the transformation and spiritualization of human consciousness, the result of which will be conscious perception of the Etheric Christ. Rudolf Steiner points in this regard primarily to the participation of the Archangel Michael in this second Mystery of Golgotha. (See GA 152, 2 May 1913.) This occurred during the assumption of his current guidance of humanity as its new Time Spirit. The beginning of Michael's second great revelation is likewise connected with this, as a result of which, starting in our time, man can enter upon the path that will lead him to becoming logos-like. Moreover, with this path that represents the microcosmic mirror-image of the Christ's path towards becoming human, the Luke-Jesus (the Nathan-soul) is connected in a special way, for he is the entity who was shielded in the spiritual world by Michael from the Fall at the beginning of Earth evolution.[129] At the Turning Point of Time this entity likewise became the bearer for the likeness and image of God, and after that the example for the true Christophorus or Christ-bearer to whom, through the development of the new Christ-consciousness, every human being will evolve in the future.

The two main qualities of the immortal persona of man are connected with the realization of this future ideal, namely freedom and love. This is why Rudolf Steiner says in the lecture of 11 June 1910 (GA 121) that on Old Saturn will was preconceived, feeling on the old Sun, and on Old Moon the thinking of man, to which love was only added on the earth.

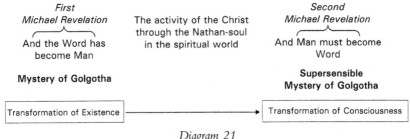

Diagram 21

This secret is likewise indicated in Goethe's 'Fairy Tale' where the Green Snake (by its decision to sacrifice itself) can communicate to the Old Man the fourth secret, namely that of love, love with which the actual meaning of earth is connected. Only through the revelation of this secret can the Prince enter the temple of the higher 'I' so as to receive the initiation through the Three Kings. Now he can unite with the Beautiful Lily and thus attain to the stage of freedom and love (or the immortal persona).[130]

Only out of the attainment of freedom will spiritual love eventually emerge as the highest creative power of the human being. This is why the path to *such* a love leads through *The Philosophy of Freedom*. Likewise the goal of all of Earth evolution—the transformation of the previous cosmos of wisdom into the future cosmos of love (see GA 13)—is only possible through the creative activity of the 'I' that will have reached the stage of a free spirit, a spirit who, as the only motive of its actions, will have reached pure love.

In its development, such a human being then moves microcosmically along the same path followed by the Trinity in its origination: from the first shining forth of the 'I' to the ideal of freedom and love, and from these to the activity of creating new existence, an activity that is the adequate expression of its consciously achieved eternal persona.

★

What has been said in this chapter can throw new light on some statements by Rudolf Steiner that can easily be misunderstood and/or wrongly interpreted. In his introduction to Goethe's natural-scientific writings he notes down: 'The most exalted idea of God, however, is certainly the one which assumes that after the creation of man He withdrew completely and left the latter completely to its fate (GA 1). In writing about 'Nature and Our Ideals' we discover an even more radical statement in this regard: 'We should finally admit that the God who a humanity of the past pictured as living in the clouds dwells in our heart, in our spirit. In full self-renunciation He poured himself out completely into mankind. As to His own will He chose to retain nothing, for He willed to have descendants that govern freely over themselves. He has been absorbed in the world. Human will is His will; the goals of humans are His goals.' (GA 30.) And then—brought to the actual point—'He has ceased to be for the sake of humankind's freedom and the world's divinity. *We have taken into ourselves the highest potency of existence.* This is why no external power, only our own creations can give us satisfaction.' (Ibid.)

It is obvious that these words could easily be understood in the sense of Nietzsche's determination of 'God is dead'. In the light of what was described before, however, they do not lead to the rejection of God in Rudolf Steiner's life but to *The Philosophy of Freedom* and from it to the modern Christ encounter founded on freedom and love. For the way to the fount of this 'highest potency of existence' which human beings have absorbed into themselves leads directly to the cognition of the Mystery of Golgotha and out of it to the conscious experience of the Christ in His eternal presence.

For God the Father has in fact withdrawn from the world so as to make possible human freedom. But at the same time He sent humanity His only begotten Son in order, through the *free* connection with Him (the Son), to actualize all that has been outlined in these considerations. That is why Christ says in the Gospel of John: 'No one finds the way to the Father but through me.' (14:6 JM.) And at the end of World evolution the portion of humanity that is united with Christ will have attained a *new* relationship with the Father God unlike the one that all the hierarchies have, but one resembling that relationship which the Divine Son alone has to him since the primal beginning.

On this path, Rudolf Steiner reached the highest point for our time and thereby became the greatest example for mankind. This was made evident particularly at the Christmas Conference, when out of the forces of the Trinity itself he created the supersensible Foundation Stone in the spiritual world adjacent to the earth.[131] It was a creative deed in which, for the first time, a human being carried out an action out of the realm of the future Tenth Hierarchy, a deed whose foundations were individual freedom and the new creation of love (Foundation Stone of Love).

As was described in detail in another passage, this deed by Rudolf Steiner that crowned the path of his whole life and initiation was the actual fulfilment of *The Philosophy of Freedom*.[132] For his decision to convene the Christmas Conference was an act out of pure moral intuition, and because of that a *first decision* as such (see GA 4), the beginning of a new creation (Foundation Stone) proceeding from the free human being. Furthermore, the fact that Rudolf Steiner in his sacrifice-filled union with the Anthroposophical Society initially did not know the consequences of his action and received the full affirmation on the part of the spiritual world only later corresponds to the second basic rule of man's free actions, namely 'that in our moral actions we ourselves create the facts that we recognize afterwards' (GA 4). And at the same time it was Rudolf Steiner himself who at the Christmas Conference gave his free actions the esoteric content (GA 4), for this act of his was in the most direct sense of the word a creation out of nothing.

With this he demonstrated quite concretely what it means to carry out actions on the basis of an unconditional theory of knowledge (or cognition), actions in which the human being can make evident his or her new resemblance to the deity. This, however, is only possible if (as did Rudolf Steiner) one actually takes hold of and makes use of the faculty that Christ brought out of the womb of the Father into our world, and with this brings to expression man's divine cosmic predestination as well as the truly Christian direction of his future evolution. Now, this evolution consists of the fact that man, through his free connection with Christ, can overcome Lucifer's original temptation (see GA 110, 18 April 1909–II) and the words of the seducer, 'You will be like God' (Gen. 1:3, 5), and instead actualizes Christ's words: 'I said, you are gods' (John 10:34). At the end of human evolution, man will not be *like* the gods, that is to say all the other hierarchies. Rather, we consciously have to take hold of the divine nature we have received into ourselves through Christ and bring it to complete fulfilment. On our own we must become gods.

10. *The Philosophy of Freedom* and the Being Anthroposophia

What was stated at the end of the previous chapter can furthermore be understood in the time-perspective of humanity's evolution in yet another way. When we consider the most important era in this evolution, it is comprised of the three post-Atlantean periods, the fourth, fifth and sixth. Based on Rudolf Steiner's spirit research they have the following tasks.

The encounter of humanity with death had to occur first and foremost in the fourth cultural period. For this reason, the Mystery of Golgotha could only take place on earth during that time. As the result of this encounter with death, human beings can experience and exercise freedom in our fifth cultural period. At the same time mankind will increasingly face the encounter with evil during this time,[133] which in the sixth cultural period will as a consequence call forth the attribute of love as a new socially formative force.[134] Armed with freedom and love, human beings will then moreover be prepared in the sixth cultural period to lay the groundwork for the transition to the Great Sixth Epoch of Earth evolution. Following the 'War of All Against All', the Sixth Epoch will begin at the end of the seventh cultural period, and during the immediately following era lead to the actual spiritualization of man and earth.

We find the starting point of this whole development in *The Philosophy of Freedom*. In its first part the path is depicted that leads to the experience of inner *freedom* in intuitive thinking; in its second part the actions are described that can be carried out based on this freedom out of the power of *love*. What is therefore preconceived in this book was practised permanently by Rudolf Steiner himself since the founding of anthroposophy at the start of the twentieth century. All true spiritual research, in which what has been envisioned in the spirit is initially grasped with human thoughts and then becomes transformed into human language, inwardly contains a process of dying and becoming and, along with that, the essential element of a new creation, something that is to be equated with a creation out of nothing.

This activity by Rudolf Steiner finds its culmination in the creation of the supersensible Foundation Stone during the Christmas Conference. In its esoteric essence, this Stone represents a pure creation out of nothing, a creation that was carried out by Rudolf Steiner out of freedom and love.

This is why, reflecting on this conference, Rudolf Steiner stated several times that he had not known the consequences of his own action beforehand. Their unconditionality came to expression inasmuch as Rudolf Steiner took upon himself the karma of the Anthroposophical Society. By doing this he microcosmically carried out a deed resembling the one that Christ carried out macrocosmically through the Mystery of Golgotha. For through his sacrificial deed, Christ assumed the karma of all of humanity, something that came to expression subsequently in the words of John the Baptist: 'See, the Lamb of God who takes the sin of the world upon himself' (John 1:29 JM).

A deed such as that by Rudolf Steiner has the attribute of not arising out of old karma, which always has to be offset; it represents a new or Sun-karma. To take upon oneself the karma of others is always a new beginning in the domain of karma. This is the case with Christ in regard to humanity. It is the case with Rudolf Steiner in regard to the Anthroposophical Society. Such a deed of sacrifice can only be carried out based on complete freedom and on what became possible for human beings following the Mystery of Golgotha. Rudolf Steiner calls it love for karma or *amor fati* (see Addendum II).

This process in which a human being assumes the karma of another person or a human community was already designated by the apostle Paul in his premonition as 'the law of Christ' which in a future time will be actualized by all human beings: 'Bear one another's burdens, and so fulfil the law of Christ' (Gal. 6:2). It is quite clear that Paul does not refer to external burdens but to the karma of others. And the deed of Christ stands here as the supreme example. This is why Rudolf Steiner says in this regard: 'When a mighty individuality like Christ Jesus comes to the aid of all mankind, then it is His sacrificial death that works into the karma of all humanity' (GA 96, 12 April 1907). This can be repeated by the modern initiate in microcosmic form. 'Thus, instead of one single person, one can likewise help a whole group of people. By doing so one fits oneself into the karma of these people inasmuch as one helps them' (ibid.). The latter is exactly what Rudolf Steiner did at the Christmas Conference through his total link with the Anthroposophical Society, which at that time faced almost complete failure.

This individual and free action on the part of Rudolf Steiner was therefore not only unconditional but moreover signified, as he himself avowed, a complete break with all earlier existing laws in esotericism. For this deed of the Christmas Conference, which was carried out purely out of freedom and love, represents such a decisive, unheard-of new fact in the history of esotericism that even to this day, more than 80 years later, anthroposophists find it extraordinarily difficult to understand this deed correctly, much less link up with it in the esoteric sense. For in its spiritual effectiveness, this deed is of an importance that encompasses not centuries but millennia of humanity's evolution.

With this an essential step was taken for solving the main problem of our time, a solution that alone can guarantee the proper transition from the fifth to the sixth cultural period. For the fifth cultural period is entirely oriented towards the unfolding of the free human individuality, and due to that reason has central significance for the whole of Earth evolution. By contrast, the sixth cultural period will primarily make evident the social forces in a human community as the necessary prerequisite for the Great Sixth Epoch.

This motif of the transition from the individual to the social element pervades the whole Christmas Conference and finds its mantric expression in the Foundation Stone. This meditation begins with the call to the individual human being, 'Soul of Man!', and ends with the call to the human community, 'May human beings hear it!' The powerful 'we' then makes itself felt once again at the end of the fourth part as a result of the individually experienced Christ Sun: 'That good may become, what we . . .' This motif can moreover be discerned in regard to the Foundation Stone created at the Christmas Conference. Only through a completely individual decision can this stone be implanted in the ground of the human heart, but subsequently it works there as a foundation stone for the Anthroposophical Society, which means for an actual earthly community of human beings.

The traces of this fundamental motif of the Christmas Conference can already be found in *The Philosophy of Freedom* in the transition from its first to the second part. In the first part the most extreme individualism is established as an indispensable prerequisite for the attainment of freedom. In the second part, on the other hand, the question is posed how a new community of free spirits can develop out of this radical individualism. For this future relationship of human beings, Rudolf Steiner offers in his book as a guideline the 'fundamental maxim' mentioned earlier of free human beings (see Chapter 4). And after that Rudolf Steiner puts into concrete terms the spiritual conditions under which such a community of free spirits can even arise and exist: 'A free human being lives with the confidence that the other free individual together with him or her belongs to *one spiritual world*' (ibid.). This 'one spiritual world', which Rudolf Steiner also designates as the 'world of ideas common' to all men (ibid.), is the one out of which the free person can gather his individual thoughts and moral intuitions (for his cognition and actions). And such a spiritual world that is *common* to all free spirits and encompasses all imaginable ideas and concepts, meaning the totality of world-wisdom, has always been designated in Christian esotericism as *Sophia*.

In this sense Rudolf Steiner describes this future human community—preconceived as it is in *The Philosophy of Freedom*—which up until the sixth cultural period must come into being as a community of free spirits on earth: 'It will be a time when human beings will possess common wisdom (Sophia) to a far greater degree than now; they will be immersed in a common wisdom, so to speak [which also means being immersed in a common spiritual world]. A sensation of sorts will begin to make itself felt that one's most innate core being is at the same time the most universal one ... Then the truth found in one soul fits in exactly with the truth in the other soul; one no longer quarrels with the other ["a moral misunderstanding, a clash of minds is impossible among morally free human beings" (GA 4)]. That is the guarantee of true peace and true brotherhood, for there is only *one* truth, and this truth really has something to do with the *spiritual Sun*.' (GA 103, 30 May 1908–I; emphasis by Rudolf Steiner.) This spiritual sun is none other than the 'Christ Sun' which is mentioned in the fourth part of the Foundation Stone Meditation, in the light of which the individual element is no longer impaired by the social element nor does the individual element destroy the social. Both together form a higher synthesis constantly fructifying both, a synthesis out of which alone a community of free spirits can emerge.

The forming of such a social community based on a spiritual impulse (in the Christmas Conference its basis is the supersensible Foundation Stone) was always understood to refer in Rosicrucian tradition to the building of a spiritual temple. In accordance with *The Philosophy of Freedom*, on the other hand, this 'construction' must take place out of full human freedom as the basis of such joint activity. 'The old [temple] is the covenant of the creative god where the deity works on the temple of man. The new [temple] is the one where the human being on his own enwraps the deity with the temple of wisdom; where one reconstructs this temple so that this human "I" has a refuge on this earth when, liberated, it resurrects itself out of matter.' (GA 93, 22 May 1905.) Rudolf Steiner describes this as the work 'on the great temple of mankind' (ibid.), which is at the same time the social temple of the Sophia—the mighty ideal of true Rosicrucians, the Templars and, in the present-day period of freedom, anthroposophy. In establishing a new human community, it is therefore in the esoteric sense a matter of the building of the social temple for the being of the *Sophia*. And as we have seen, this process has its starting point in the full unfolding of the free human individuality, meaning in what represents the nature of the *Anthropos* on earth. Thus, the solution of the problem of the individual element and the social one belongs to the primal tasks of *Anthroposophy*.

This too is already fully set up in *The Philosophy of Freedom*. Rudolf Steiner writes, for instance, about the nature of man or the Anthropos: 'Now, we cannot exhaustively think through the concept of man without arriving at the *free* spirit as the purest expression of human nature' (GA 4; emphasis by Rudolf Steiner). In order to move from this cognitive fact to the activity in the world, and hence to the forming of a community of free spirits, human beings must have the experience that they all belong to '*one* spiritual world', out of which they gather their intuitions. As we have seen, this joint world of wisdom is that of the Sophia, but a world with which contemporary man (Anthropos) can only unite as a free spirit.

In this manner, the whole of anthroposophy is already set up in *The Philosophy of Freedom*: the individual development of the Anthropos on the basis of cognition, and the moral actions consequently following from this basis which lead to a forming of the community out of the nature of the Sophia. This state of being rooted in the early works by Rudolf Steiner on the part of the entity Anthropos-Sophia was possible due to a fact that we have already described elsewhere.[135] It was a matter of a process that Rudolf Steiner described as the passage of the Sophia-being through the consciousness soul of humanity (see lecture of 3 February 1913 in *Das Wesen der Anthroposophie* [The nature of anthroposophy], separate edition, Dornach 1998). During this passage of the Sophia through the soul of modern human beings, there arose out of her the spiritual Anthropos-Sophia who subsequently was brought into being on earth by Rudolf Steiner. Prior to the turn of the century, however, when her passage through humanity was not yet completed, Rudolf Steiner was the only one on earth who experienced this process fully set up in *his* own consciousness soul, and from it created all his early work.

Thus this early work is the direct results of the Sophia's passage through humankind and with that her transformation into the Anthroposophia. Now she could objectively reveal herself to human beings as that entity who would like to reveal itself out of the spiritual world as that being who would like to guide mankind from the individual element to the social one, hence from the fifth to the sixth cultural period. (Ibid.) And the result of this, her revelation, was the founding of anthroposophy at the beginning of the twentieth century.

From what has been mentioned, one can truly understand why Rudolf Steiner could say with full justification that, as far as the spiritual consistency and consequence in his perceptions and actions were concerned, he never experienced any interruption in the course of his development or contradiction between various periods in his life. Rather, he inwardly followed only the objective metamorphosis of the entity Anthroposophia in its passage through his consciousness soul (earlier works) up until its appearance in the spiritual world out of the sphere of the Spirit Self.

Likewise the whole direction of his autobiography, *The Course of My Life*, attests to this unbroken consistency: 'I did not move forward in contradictions, as many believe. If that were the case I would gladly admit it. However it would not be the reality in the way my life progressed. I moved forward in such wise that I added new dimensions to what dwelled within my soul.' (GA 28, Chap. XXX.) This statement is in complete accord with the supersensible course of development by Anthroposophia and mirrors its most important stages that led to her revelation on earth. In this regard, Rudolf Steiner's biography is the human reflection of the heavenly-earthly evolution of the Sophia herself.

As described earlier elsewhere, Rudolf Steiner calls this being in two important passages by its celestial name (not Anthroposophy but Anthroposophia), first in the afore-mentioned lecture where mention is made of its passage through humanity, and then during the Christmas Conference. In both cases it is a matter of founding a human community: in 1913 an anthroposophical society independent of the Theosophical Society; in 1923 during the Christmas Conference, the new founding of the Anthroposophical Society as such. During the latter on the day of the Foundation Stone laying, this being is twice addressed directly by its name Anthroposophia, namely first in relation with an individual task and then a social one. Initially we are dealing with 'the enlivening of the human heart with Anthroposophia' (GA 260, 25 December 1923), something that represents a purely individual and intimate process, then with the establishment of a 'true association of human beings for Anthroposophia' (ibid.) as the essential task of a new human community that in this direction must learn to work with the beings of the spiritual world consciously and freely.

The motif of temple-building is likewise present at the Christmas Conference. On the last day of this conference, Rudolf Steiner speaks of a spiritual structure that must be freely built out of all our actions within the Society and outside in the world on the Foundation Stone of love. 'We have laid the Foundation Stone here. Upon this Foundation Stone the *structure* will be erected, the individual stones of which will be the work that in all our groups will be accomplished by individual people the world over'. (Ibid.) Although Rudolf Steiner does not explicitly mention the spiritual temple, his earlier expositions make it quite clear what is meant here. For example, during the founding in Neuchatel of the Christian Rosenkreutz Branch, he says in the name of Christian Rosenkreutz: 'So may the branch be one of the building stones for the temple that we want to build up.' (GA 130, 28 September 1911.)

In this way, the Anthroposophical Society was set up during the Christmas Conference as the freest society in the world, a society in which freedom in cognition and love in social action can be exercised by human beings who in the sense of *The Philosophy of Freedom* wish to work together with the Being Anthroposophia for the future of humanity.

11. The Rosicrucian and Michaelic Impulses in *The Philosophy of Freedom*

The origination of *The Philosophy of Freedom* has its preconditions in the history of esoteric Christianity as well as in Rudolf Steiner's biography. This does not contradict the fact that the epistemology at the basis of this book is unconditional as such. In this chapter the streams must be characterized that prepared its origination.

As was outlined elsewhere,[136] anthroposophy originated on the basis of the union of two spiritual streams: the main stream of esoteric Christianity (the Rosicrucian stream), and the stream of cosmic or Michaelic Christendom. In both one can find the impulses that led to the origin of *The Philosophy of Freedom*. Rudolf Steiner describes that work on it was done above all in the Rosicrucian brotherhood under the direct leadership of Christian Rosenkreutz. 'Christian Rosenkreutz and his seven disciples created the origin for the cognition of the law of morality so that this law would not re-echo in human beings through what is given by religions, but so that this law, recognized as such, might awaken in every human being to individual life' (GA 264). These words point out that already among the first Rosicrucians one finds indications that allude to the later *Philosophy of Freedom*, indications in which it is established how human beings can generate moral laws, that is to say moral motivations, for their actions not from without but cognitively out of themselves. 'Now, the moral laws are indeed first created by us' is what Rudolf Steiner will be writing later on in his *Philosophy of Freedom*.

Likewise the fundamental rejection of any dogmatism and principle of authority in true Rosicrucianism[137] points out how man's modern-day freedom was prepared there, a freedom which finds its highest expression in *The Philosophy of Freedom*. Ultimately, the martyrdom of Christian Rosenkreutz, which begins in our age, will be caused most of all by rejection of individual freedom and the responsibility connected with it in regard to man's own development. (See GA 133, 20 June 1912.) From what has been stated one recognizes the central significance ascribed to human freedom within the Rosicrucian stream from the very beginning. After all, in this important stream of esoteric Christianity, the full inner autonomy of human beings, destined as it was to appear along with the start of the consciousness soul era, was prepared many centuries ago.[138]

In another form, but no less fundamentally, human freedom—and with that the whole impulse of the *Philosophy of Freedom*—was prepared in the Michaelic stream, now not on earth but in the supersensible world. For among the seven Archangels, leading humanity one after the other, Michael is the only spirit who unequivocally accepts and supports human freedom. This is why Rudolf Steiner describes him as 'the spiritual champion of freedom'. (GA 233a, 13 January 1924.) This signifies that human beings—following the cosmic law that kin only strives for kin—can only find Michael in the spiritual world if they themselves strive for true freedom, i.e. when we seek to actualize in our age what is written in *The Philosophy of Freedom*. Rudolf Steiner states in this regard: '*When man seeks freedom* without a trace of egotism, when freedom becomes for him unadulterated love for the impending act, he arrives at the possibility of approaching Michael' (GA 26; emphasis by Rudolf Steiner). The formulation of these words corresponds exactly to what is indicated in the second part of *The Philosophy of Freedom* as the main condition for man's free actions. Then man encounters Michael in the spiritual world as 'the *freely* active paragon' (GA 26; emphasis by Rudolf Steiner) through which he can find that entity whom Michael himself serves as his Sun-countenance. While fully maintaining his individual freedom, man in this way can find the conscious path to Christ in order thereby to achieve the objective of earth's and humanity's evolution.

In this way the conditions for two different events are quite similar: for the individual actions out of freedom, and for the spiritual relationship with Michael as Time Spirit. 'A free action can only be one where no natural event in or outside the human being exerts an influence,' writes Rudolf Steiner in the 'Michael Letters' (GA 26). In the sense of *The Philosophy of Freedom*, this fundamental condition is guaranteed in the exceptional state where we free ourselves of any dependence on our physical sensory organization and (beyond that) in every true moral intuition. This applies equally to Michael who, in the process of carrying out his earthly mission, 'in no way wants his being to come in contact with the physical presence of earth life', something which, as far as he is concerned, he can 'only view as a contamination of his nature' (GA 26). It follows from this that man today can only link up with Michael through those of his actions that are derived from sense-free insight.[139] But if the latter occurs in freedom and out of pure 'love of the object', then such a 'linking up with Michael' is of a kind that man can 'thereby find the way to Christ' (GA 26). This Michaelic path to Christ is the only one today that corresponds completely to the nature of *The Philosophy of Freedom*, hence also to the nature of the spirit of the times out of which this book was written.

In summation, one can determine that the present-day path to Christ is comprised of three stages. First the preparatory (initial) stage in accordance with the fundamental traits of modern Rosicrucianism, which introduces today's period of freedom and in this sense would like to be active further. This is why this Rosicrucian path leads as a consequence into the vicinity of Michael (second stage) and from him, through his free example, to Christ (third stage).

In an exemplary way, all three stages can be discovered in Rudolf Steiner's life. First his destiny led him to the Rosicrucian Master in Vienna who has remained unnamed. This encounter took place around 1879, when Michael assumed the guidance of humankind in the spiritual world adjacent to the earth. This brought it about that the Rosicrucian path of initiation, which Rudolf Steiner pursued from then on, had to bring him inevitably into Michael's surroundings.

From the beginning, true Rosicrucianism worked in the direction of trying to prepare Michael's guidance begun in 1879 in the current period of freedom. 'True Rosicrucianism is certainly in line with the activity of the Michael-mission. It helped Michael on the earth in preparing what he wished to prepare as his spirit-work for a later era (the "later era" refers to today's Michael period).' (GA 26.) In this working together with Michael, even the 'most enlightened spirits [minds]' could not encounter Michael fully consciously in the spiritual world. For prior to the beginning of the current Michael period this was not possible due to objective reasons having to do with the evolution of humanity and the world. 'The activity of Rosicrucianism is characterized by the fact that its most enlightened spirits had a powerful longing to encounter Michael. They could do so only as if in a dream. Since the end of the last third of the nineteenth century human beings can encounter Michael in the spirit in a conscious way.' (GA 233a, 13 January 1924.) With this, the direct path from Rosicrucianism to Michael was outlined for Rudolf Steiner. And he was the *first* who was allowed to encounter Michael *consciously* in the spiritual world following the beginning of the Archangel's epoch. Only through this experience could Rudolf Steiner later on unite these two streams inseparably in his life's work for the whole of humanity's future.[140]

As already described above, Rudolf Steiner was able to arrive at the insights of World evolution because he conveyed Haeckel's natural science in changed form up into the spiritual world by means of the Rosicrucian schooling (in accordance with the free modern path of inner discipline). In turn, he received it back from the gods who primarily are united with Michael as the contents of *Occult Science, an Outline*. From this transaction we can still more deeply comprehend his supersensible encounters with Michael just at the time when he worked on his *Philosophy of Freedom* in Weimar. For the book's crowning point is the pivotal concept of ethical individualism which Rudolf Steiner portrays as the culmination of the whole of natural development. 'Ethical individualism is therefore the crowning point of the edifice that Darwin and Haeckel envisioned for natural science. It is the spiritualized teaching of evolution transferred to the moral life.' (GA 4, Chap. 12.)

It follows from this that when the bearing up into the spiritual world of the transformed contents of Darwinism and Haeckelianism is met by the gods in the environs of Michael, then Rudolf Steiner could encounter Michael as the cosmic hero of freedom when he likewise bore ethical individualism as the highest achievement of earthly mankind up into the spiritual world. For ethical individualism that has been realized on earth represents the power that brings man in the spiritual world into Michael's vicinity.

From Rudolf Steiner's communications concerning the relationship of the Rosicrucians to Michael in the article of 6 December 1924 (GA 26), one can gather that the main condition for the spiritual encounter with Michael was the absolute purification of the human soul from all sense impressions. The same thing that the Rosicrucians accomplished with their souls then is to take place today in regard to the forces of cognition for a person who wishes to encounter Michael in the spiritual world. These must be cleansed in a similar way of all sense impressions of a sensuous nature, meaning, become sense free as is described in *The Philosophy of Freedom* in reference to intuitive thinking. This book thus represents a direct continuation of true Rosicrucianism in its relationship to Michael and, in the sense of the modern consciousness soul development, to a conscious encounter with him in the spiritual world adjacent to earth.

In Rudolf Steiner's life such a supersensible encounter occurred with the Time Spirit in the period when he himself worked on his *Philosophy of Freedom* in Weimar, a period in which the results of this experience likewise found their expression. This is why he could write at the end of his life: 'One can however say that *The Philosophy of Freedom* prepares one to recognize concerning freedom what then can be experienced in the spiritual coming together with Michael.' (GA 26.) The first part of this sentence relates to the readers of the book, and the second to the author himself who could only write it down owing to the above-mentioned 'spiritual coming together with Michael'.[141]

What is stated above makes it comprehensible how the continuation of this spiritual path in the tracks of Michael could lead Rudolf Steiner to the experience of the Christ in Intuition, and as a result to the 'spiritually having stood before the Mystery of Golgotha'. This path however led him first into the Ahriman-sphere of death out of which, through the image of Michael who perpetually holds fast the dragon under his feet, he could struggle through to the encounter with Christ.

In Chapter XXVI of his autobiography, *The Course of My Life*, Rudolf Steiner describes his descent into the sphere of the ahrimanic spirits at the end of the nineteenth century. Yet he likely passed through this most difficult initiation-trial after he had already had the inner encounter with Michael, and subsequently could have this lofty spirit constantly before him as his paragon in order then to follow him in full freedom. Later in the 'Michael Letters', he would be describing this path to Christ out of the depths of the Ahriman-sphere as follows: 'Such people [who behold the supersensible world most closely adjacent to the visible world] see how the human being is meant to be guided *in freedom* by Michael's image in the Ahriman-sphere away from Ahriman to Christ' (GA 26, 19 October 1924). In such perfect inner freedom, Rudolf Steiner could find his way to Christ at the turn of the century so as to erect the totality of anthroposophy on this basis.

The above-mentioned three stages that led Rudolf Steiner from his encounter with the Rosicrucian Master to the one with Michael, and then on to the meeting with Christ, correspond on the modern path of schooling to the progression from Imagination to Inspiration, and finally to Intuition.[142] When we understand this path as the ascent from the level of an initiated person to the encounter with the representative of the spiritual hierarchies and from there to the encounter with the Son of God himself, this path is a mirror image of what one can find in the three macrocosmic parts of the Foundation Stone Verse as the descent of the divine Trinity through all nine hierarchies to the Rosicrucian stream (the three Rosicrucian lines), further on to the elemental spirits of nature and ultimately to earth's human beings.[143] With this, the macrocosmic parts of the Foundation Stone Verse encompass the whole perimeter of anthroposophical spirit-research. Their microcosmic parts, on the other hand, describe the path of inner development that Rudolf Steiner himself pursued and whose stages found their exoteric replica in his pre-anthroposophical early work.

If in this sense one takes the microcosmic segments of the three first parts of the Foundation Stone Meditation as the esoteric foundation for the early work, and its macrocosmic segments as a revelation of anthroposophy's totality, one can bring its fourth part into connection with Rudolf Steiner's Christ-encounter at the turn of the century. This encounter represented the crowning of his initiation-path and at the same time made possible the spiritual transition from his early work to anthroposophy. The whole of this corresponds to the main rhythm of the Christmas Conference in which Rudolf Steiner read the Foundation Stone Meditation for the first time during the laying of the Foundation Stone of the Anthroposophical Society on 25 December.[144]

★

The way in which the just described connection of the young Rudolf Steiner to the Rosicrucian and Michaelic stream could lead him to the encounter with Christ can also be characterized in the following manner.

According to Rudolf Steiner's spiritual research, there exist two streams of time in the universe. The first flows from the past to the future and thus brings about the whole earthly history of humanity and its evolution. The other, opposite stream flows out of the future. All the spiritual hierarchies work and create in it. It is not difficult to determine that the whole development of Rosicrucianism—to the extent that it is part of humanity's general history and from the esoteric direction prepares the contemporary epoch of freedom—is anchored principally in the first stream of time. In contrast, everything that is connected with Michael's supersensible activity belongs to the second stream in which the whole future of the earth in its supersensible form is already set up. One can also say that, working within the first stream, the genuine Rosicrucians tried through their methods of initiation to enter the second stream, the one of the spiritual world, in order there to encounter Michael. While the first stream originates by means of the time element being added to the three dimensions in space, we arrive at the number four which is also the basis of the form of the cross. Now the second stream can be brought to expression through the seven roses. For the spiritual world of the etheric, which is closest to the earthly world, manifests through the living rhythms of the sevenfold metamorphosis. Thus the Rosicrucians sought above all for the transition from the cross to the roses.

In the case of Michael, on the other hand, who from the beginning worked out of the other stream of time, it was a matter of the opposite transition—from the roses to the cross, from his cosmic activity to his new presence in the hearts of earthly human beings. In this sense, Michael wishes—albeit in purely supersensible form—to follow after the Christ, who through his Resurrection added the roses for all future times to the cross; or if one wishes to express it in another way, who out of the Sun-sphere brought the new spiritual time into the world of space. (See GA 236, 4 June 1924.)

Moreover, the central question of humanity's development, how can man remain an 'I'-being without dying in this process,[145] is to be answered on the basis of the union of the two time-streams. For in the first or exoteric stream of time, the free 'I' of man unfolds within Earth evolution, but remaining solely in this stream it can never attain its immortality. By contrast, the esoteric stream of time originates in the sphere where no death can come to exist and persist. But in this sphere of original immortality, man can neither find nor further unfold his individual 'I'. For that he needs above all to come in touch with the forces of death which are only operative on earth in the physical sense world.

One can likewise say that the hierarchies, who live in time only in the esoteric sense, are in fact immortal and therefore know neither death nor earthly 'I'-consciousness. Consequently, they are spiritual individualities but not in the sense of the human personality. Earth-humans, on the other hand, who with their ordinary consciousness live only in the exoteric stream of time, are in possession of 'I'-consciousness but do not know of immortality on earth. They are personalities during their earthly incarnations, but to start with live without a conscious connection to their eternal individuality that moves from incarnation to incarnation.[146]

The union of the two streams and with that the answer to the above-mentioned central question of humanity's evolution was given in the Mystery of Golgotha. It is the only—in its nature supersensible—event that took place in the physical-sensory world on the open stage of Earth history. This is why the Mystery of Golgotha belongs on the one hand to the exoteric stream of time, occurring at a certain point in time of outer history—an occasion that dates back almost two thousand years. At the same time the Mystery of Golgotha changed the whole spiritual configuration of the hierarchical cosmos. Rudolf Steiner called it an event that was of decisive importance, not only for human beings but likewise for all the gods (hierarchies).[147] In this regard it belongs to the esoteric stream of time.

Even the physical body of Christ Jesus originates on the one side from the primordial stream of heredity that is described above all in the Gospel of Luke. After His Resurrection however, it belongs in an all-embracing way to the supersensible world. In this way, connected with both worlds, the Resurrection Body as a sensible-supersensible form is the only guarantor for the immortality of our personality and consequently also of the human 'I'. This is why Rudolf Steiner speaks in connection with Christ's Resurrection of the saving of the human 'I' for the whole future of Earth evolution. (See GA 131, 11 October 1911.) For man's 'I' awakens and experiences its immortality only at the crossing point of the two streams of time, the point out of which blossom the seven eternal roses, in order, from this union, to fulfil its task on earth.[148]

In the sense of *The Philosophy of Freedom*, these two streams of time can also be characterized as follows. The first that runs the course of the whole of humanity's evolution, and from epoch to epoch shapes earthly history, contains as its driving force man's longing for full freedom and personal autonomy. For our material world originates out of this stream and only in it can human beings attain freedom.[149] By contrast the hierarchies, working as they are in the esoteric stream of time, unfold love as their highest creative power. This is why one can consider the union of the two streams in the Mystery of Golgotha as the founding of the new humanity as Tenth Hierarchy, a hierarchy that, ultimately uniting freedom and love in the human 'I', will create the new cosmos based on its own responsibility. That new cosmos will then originate as a pure 'creation out of nothing' (see Chapter 9 on this), the greatest example of which was given in the Mystery of Golgotha. It follows from this that the human being as the precondition for this new creation must unite the above-mentioned streams of time in his/her 'I'. For it is only on this basis that a creation out of nothing is even possible.

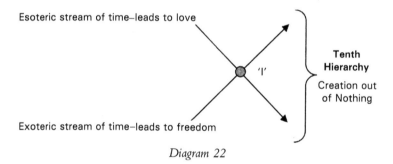

Esoteric stream of time–leads to love

'I'

Tenth Hierarchy

Creation out of Nothing

Exoteric stream of time–leads to freedom

Diagram 22

As we have seen already, the path of cognition to freedom is established in the first part of *The Philosophy of Freedom*; the path of deeds for acting out of love represents the basic motive of this book's second part.

Now, just as in the primal macrocosmic form the two streams of time were united on the Place of the Skull on earth in the World-'I' of Christ, from that moment on every human being who today endeavours towards modern initiation can unite these two streams in his or her 'I'. According to Rudolf Steiner, we create with that a firm foundation for the new fully conscious and 'I'-born exploration of the supersensible world, and thus for what Rudolf Steiner designates as spiritual science. For ordinary scientific cognition unfolds to begin with in the exoteric stream of time;

spirit, on the other hand, enters into such knowledge out of the esoteric stream of time. This is why it is only through the linkup of both that a modern *science of the spirit* can come into being which finds its culmination in a creation out of nothing, as was carried out by Rudolf Steiner at the Christmas Conference.

In other words, through the free and conscious connection of the human 'I' with the Mystery of Golgotha and thus with the forces of the Resurrection-body—something that is only possible on earth—can the above-described ideal of the immortal personality or 'persona' be attained. This persona, working in both streams of time, can then belong likewise to both the physical and the supersensible world. On this basis a modern form of historical research becomes possible that moves with the same sovereignty in the physical as well as in the super-physical world. In the domain of cognition it thus represents the beginning of realizing the lofty ideal of Christendom, namely the attainment of the eternal *persona* as guarantor for the immortality of the human 'I'.

This ideal was preconceived already by Rudolf Steiner in *The Philosophy of Freedom* with its theory of knowledge that is valid for both worlds, the physical and the supersensible, which presupposes that its author attained control of both streams on his inner path and could write his book in the first place only based on this experience.

This process can moreover be described as follows based on the spiritual-scientific perspective of modern-day humanity's development. In his book *The Spiritual Guidance of Man and Mankind*, Rudolf Steiner depicts how modern science proceeded out of the sources of 'more recent esotericism': 'Through the inspiration of more recent esotericism, the same impulse then worked in such a way that great minds like Nikolaus Cusanus, Copernicus, Galileo . . . Giordano Bruno could be inspired' (GA 15, Chap. III). That we are dealing here with true Rosicrucian esotericism follows unmistakeably from the subsequent words: 'Such a *new* inspiration is necessary, the inspiration that the great esotericists of the Middle Ages prepared beginning from the thirteenth century, an inspiration that from now on must penetrate more and more into the public domain' (ibid.; emphasis by Rudolf Steiner). In these words, the reference to the thirteenth century when the initiation of Christian Rosenkreutz took place and, with it, the starting point for the Rosicrucian stream was generated (see GA 130, 27 September 1911) points particularly in this direction. Moreover these words, as well as the depictions subsequently connecting with them by Rudolf Steiner, confirm that in our time these Rosicrucian inspirations are beginning to flow through anthroposophy into the general cultural life of mankind.

From what was stated, a clear picture arises of how on the one side modern science was being prepared by Rosicrucianism but moreover how this science would be led over into the new spirituality of anthroposophy. In other words, it was a matter here of the union of scientific intellectualism that is no longer oriented by sense impressions (see GA 15, Chap. III) with the new spirituality, or the transition from natural science to spiritual science.

The same process was likewise prepared in the Michael stream. Thus, prophetically pointing to the coming Michael age, Alanus ab Insulis taught in the school of Chartres how the still living science of the Middle Ages had to arrive at the intellectual abstractions of the later Copernicus and others so that subsequently Michael, taking the newest development of science merely as a direction for his activity, might be able to fulfil the same task, but from out of the spiritual world. 'For there will be one in the spiritual world'—so said Alanus ab Insulis in the circle of his most intimate disciples—'who will take this signpost [of modern science] which for the renewal of the world will have nothing more than the direction, so that together with intellectualism he can establish the new spirituality ... But that will be', said Alanus ab Insulis, 'Saint Michael'. (GA 240.) Elsewhere, too, Rudolf Steiner spoke unequivocally of the fact that it is the contemporary task of Michael to penetrate scientific intellectuality with the new spirituality and with that to carry out the transition from natural science to spiritual science.

Thus this main task of the Occident was prepared from two sides through the 'new esotericism' of the Rosicrucians, and in the spiritual world through the supersensible Michael school. Its union, however, as well as the above-mentioned transition, was accomplished at the beginning of the twentieth century by Rudolf Steiner in anthroposophy. With that he fulfilled the most important endeavours of the genuine Rosicrucians as well as those of Michael. How he accomplished this is described by Rudolf Steiner in detail in his lecture of 13 January 1924. There he points out how to begin with he himself had to study materialistic science and then moved forward on the path of modern Rosicrucian initiation (in the sense of the book *Knowledge of Higher Worlds and Its Attainment*) so as to transform the indications of natural science in his own soul in this manner. In this changed form, he then carried them towards the gods in order, out of them, to receive the contents of spiritual world development in the sense of *Occult Science, an Outline*. With that, out of the Rosicrucian sources, the transition from natural science to spiritual science was guaranteed. Furthermore, because this was also a task of Michael's, Rudolf Steiner could in this way encounter Michael himself (ibid.).

The possibility to carry out this transition and with it to connect Rosicrucianism with the Michael impulse was, however, already created along with *The Philosophy of Freedom*. For in it Rudolf Steiner validates a theory of cognition that applies equally to natural science as well as to spiritual science. This is why it was only on this basis that the connection between intellectuality and spirituality in anthroposophy could become possible.

Like no other work that in our age originated through a human hand, *The Philosophy of Freedom* is in this way connected with the world's goals in the light of the entities who were mentioned in this chapter. This is why this book should in no way remain merely an object of study for its readers, but become a genuine *book of life* for all those whose heart's concern is the full realization of mankind's true destiny.

★

In this chapter, one more domain of spiritual-historical cooperation between the Michaelic and the Rosicrucian stream needs to be pointed out. As described earlier in Chapter 6, the human faculties, which at the end of the nineteenth century facilitated the origin of *The Philosophy of Freedom* (intellectuality and freedom), initially moved like 'a heavenly gift' (GA 257, 30 January 1923) out of the spiritual world into the general consciousness of humanity. That the location from which they moved down to earth was the Michael- .or Sun-sphere is made clear, above all from the so-called 'Michael Letters' by Rudolf Steiner. There he writes in this regard: 'In my *Philosophy of Freedom* one finds the *freedom* of the human being ascertained as the content of consciousness; in the depictions of the Michael-mission which are given here one finds the "development of this freedom cosmically proven".' (GA 26, Leading Thought 111.)

To this cosmic course of freedom's development belongs its simultaneous descent out of the spiritual world, together with intellectuality, into the earth's realm of human beings. Knowledge concerning this results only from direct connection with Michael, out of which Rudolf Steiner conceived the so-called 'Michael Letters' at the end of his life, letters that lead into the cosmic mission of Michael in which the nature of freedom is described based on this Archangel's Sun-viewpoint.

As already shown, those occidental esotericists were the true Rosicrucians who knew something about the above and for that reason were from the beginning oriented towards Michael in their inner work in order to prepare for his impending period of guiding humanity, which was to begin in 1879. 'Thereby, *for Michael*, the genuine Rosicrucian will formed the path—situated on earth—for *his* impending earth mission.' (GA 26;

emphasis by Rudolf Steiner.) And because these Rosicrucians not only prepared the contemporary Michael period but also sought for a direct encounter with him in the spiritual world (see GA 233a, 13 January 1924), the following has become possible at the morning of the dawning epoch of freedom among humanity.

In the earlier quoted lecture of 30 January 1923 (GA 257), Rudolf Steiner gives a more exact date concerning when intellectuality and freedom appeared on earth. It took place in the first third of the fifteenth century, coinciding with the beginning of the consciousness soul period (1413). Shortly afterwards, in the 'second' half of the same century, something unique occurred in the then leading Rosicrucian circles, indeed something remarkable. 'In turn it was in one of those modest dwelling places of the Rosicrucians where, in the most solemn form ... during the second half of the fifteenth century, the sacrifice of the star-knowledge was offered up during a cultic act which had been planned for this very purpose.' (GA 233a, 6 January 1924.)

This renunciation of the ancient supersensible cognition took place due to the awareness that, along with the so-called 'Fall', humanity had forfeited its position as the future Tenth Hierarchy.[150] In order nevertheless to reach this goal of its evolution, humanity was supposed to pass through a time of complete separation from the ancient wisdom so that, out of full freedom, it could subsequently struggle through to a totally new relationship with the spiritual world and the hierarchies. 'That is why,' so these Rosicrucians told themselves, 'the higher cognition may be offered up for a certain time so that humanity can return once more to its rank of the Fourth Hierarchy and discover in *the free will* what the gods earlier attempted to do for and with human beings.' (Ibid.) Then Rudolf Steiner describes how 'certain entities of the spiritual world who are not of humankind' then receive this free offering, something whereby human freedom became possible in the first place on earth. '*In turn, the impulse for freedom* [as an answer to this offering] became possible for human beings out of the spiritual world'(ibid.).

Due to the fact that in the last lecture of the same cycle Rudolf Steiner spoke in detail about the relationship of the Rosicrucians to Michael and their constant attempts to encounter him in the spiritual world (and also depicted Michael himself as the spiritual herald of freedom), one can conclude from this that the spiritual beings who accepted the above-described offering were the hierarchies serving Michael.

In this way, the appearance of freedom on earth at the beginning of the consciousness soul period was prepared from two sides: from the Sun-region of Michael in the spiritual world and from the act of sacrifice of the

true Rosicrucians on earth. This is why Rudolf Steiner could later conclude: 'For "freedom" is directly given as a fact to every human being
who understands himself [as living] in the present segment of humanity's
evolution.' (GA 26, Leading Thought 110.)[151]

Here we have an example of the marvellous collaboration by the
Rosicrucians with Michael and the spirits who serve him for bringing
about humanity's freedom on earth. This means the creation of all those
conditions that later on made possible the origin of *The Philosophy of
Freedom*. That is why all these spiritual-terrestrial events belong to the
esoteric 'biography' of this book.

At this point another weighty question arises. How was the characterized development of mankind supposed to continue in the epoch of
freedom? The answer results from the fact that the streams working
together here—the Michaelic and Rosicrucian stream—were in the
deepest sense permeated with the Christ Impulse and on this foundation
could attain the new connection of humanity with the spiritual world.
'Inasmuch as this heavenly element, intellectuality and freedom, moved
into earthly life, a different way for looking up to the divinity became
necessary for mankind than was the case earlier.' This refers to something
different than was practised before, leaving behind the ancient star-
wisdom. 'And this different way of looking up to the Divinity has become
possible for humankind through the Mystery of Golgotha' (GA 257, 30
January 1923). Still, humanity had to wait until the dawn of the new
Michaelic age, and anthroposophy, which was to be established in it,
when all preconditions for that to happen could be fulfilled. 'The Christ
Impulse first had to permeate what is most holy in this age, namely the
faculty for grasping pure concepts and the faculty of freedom' (ibid.). In
other words, in order to ensure a new relationship, one that alone befits
our age of the consciousness soul, 'the human being [must] ... learn pure
thinking with Christ; to be a free being with Christ' (ibid.).

The Philosophy of Freedom in its two parts leads to the first goal, to think
purely and to be a free being. Anthroposophy, on the other hand,
founded as it is on this book, leads to the second goal, and that is the
penetration of these abilities with the Christ Impulse. If modern man goes
in this direction, he likewise experiences how, with this penetration, the
two most important Christ Mysteries of our time are insolubly connected.

When pure thinking becomes imbued with the Christ Impulse, its
further development leads to the new clairvoyance and, because it proceeds from thinking, Rudolf Steiner on occasion called it 'intellectual
clairvoyance'. This intellectual clairvoyance brings about the experience
of (or 'living through') the first Christ Mystery, namely His appearance in

etheric form. (GA 130, 18 November 1911.) And the further development of human freedom—when it becomes imbued with the Christ Impulse—leads to the recognition of the second Christ Mystery of the present age, namely his activity as Lord of Karma. This activity, starting in our time, brings it about that karma is gradually transformed from the law of iron necessity into an effect of grace so that it no longer contradicts freedom but turns into its most important instrument on the journey of human beings to their spiritual destination. For the fulfilment of karma in accordance with the Christ so that it can serve the whole evolution of humanity is Grace.

Likewise, the mighty transformations of the two main streams of esoteric Christianity, the Rosicrucian and the Michaelic one, come to pass in the light of this twofold Christ Mystery of the present. In the first stream the decisive metamorphosis through the creation of the Foundation Stone of Love at the Christmas Conference occurred, which signified the world-historical transition from the Stone of Wisdom to the Stone of Love.[152] With this, anthroposophy has assumed guidance of this stream for our time.

The remarkable karma-revelations that followed the Christmas Conference as a continuation of its esoteric impulse also demonstrate the nature of reincarnation and karma completely in the Christian sense, and thus to be entirely compatible with human freedom. What was formerly reserved exclusively for the highest stages of initiation and therefore kept strictly secret[153] becomes accessible to all human beings in anthroposophy.

Parallel to this transition from Rosicrucianism to anthroposophy, during which time the first obviously neither ceased to exist nor to work esoterically (merely relinquishing to anthroposophy some of its tasks that relate particularly to our age), we have as in a cosmic correspondence to this something comparable in the supersensible Michael stream. Just as the nature of the Foundation Stone (and with that the transformed Rosicrucian stream) has an esoteric correlation to the innermost essence of *The Philosophy of Freedom* (see Chapters 15 and 16 of this book), so the second Michaelic metamorphosis that occurred in the spiritual world is likewise deeply connected to this philosophy.

This second metamorphosis or transition that took place in the kingdom of Michael consists of the fact that the leading Time Spirit passed on some of his tasks to another hierarchical entity connected with him so that these tasks can be further pursued and led by that entity when Michael himself will withdraw from the guidance of mankind in three hundred years time. This being who in the hierarchical order of the cosmos can be viewed as Michael's successor is the Archangel Vidar.[154]

According to the spirit-research by Rudolf Steiner, he plays a central part in the etheric return of the Christ. For it is Vidar's cosmic task to form an etheric sheath for the Christ in the spiritual world in which he can work among human beings in the next three thousand years. (See GA 121, 17 June 1910.) As the servant of the Etheric Christ, Vidar will moreover accompany and protect him during that whole time.

Through his intimate connection with Michael, Vidar likewise has a direct relationship to the content (or 'being') of *The Philosophy of Freedom*. For the path of cognition depicted in this book represents an indispensable foundation for the development of the new clairvoyance that is 'illuminated by reason and science' and is represented in the spiritual world by Vidar. (GA 121, 17 June 1910.) This is why Rudolf Steiner frequently recommended the above book for meticulous study to people with an inclination towards ancient atavistic clairvoyance, as a definite means to surmount such vision. This process in the human being corresponds to Vidar's great victory over the wolf Fenris in the cosmos—the being that appears there as the demonic inspirer of a no longer timely chaotic clairvoyance (ibid.). From this it follows that Vidar will be above all the great leader of human beings towards the new clairvoyance that has its roots in *The Philosophy of Freedom*, and as its goal the conscious beholding of the Christ in the Etheric.

The unfolding of karmic clairvoyance[155] connected to his Second Coming likewise stands in a connection to Vidar's cosmic activity. For in this area too, it will be of decisive importance whether such karma-visions will spread among human beings in the correct manner—meaning for our age that they will be penetrated by 'reason and science'—or in a disorderly, chaotic manner that is distorted by the counter-forces.[156]

This is why Rudolf Steiner persistently emphasized the sternly scientific character of anthroposophy and method of its spiritual research, as well as the deep roots they have in his early works, particularly in *The Philosophy of Freedom*. Although not explicitly mentioned, behind this correctly deduced relationship that links his epistemological and spiritual-scientific works stands not only the Michaelic Time Spirit but likewise the Archangel Vidar. For this silent, mysterious Norse god ['Åse' in the German edition] has been designated by the Christ Himself in the coming three thousand years of His return to see to it that humanity will be able freely and independently, that is in the sense of *The Philosophy of Freedom*, to find its way to Him.

★

In conclusion it must still be pointed out that in most descriptions of the modern Christian-Rosicrucian path that begins with the stage of studying spiritual-scientific communications, Rudolf Steiner again and again mentions two of his early works, *Truth and Science* and *The Philosophy of Freedom*, which above all are indispensable in modern spiritual discipline for the necessary development of logical thinking. In one lecture, Rudolf Steiner even spoke of 'gymnastics for the soul and spirit' to which a person submits who thoroughly studies these two books. (GA 96, 20 October 1906.) For they are the great teaching tools in the acquisition of purified, disciplined and, above all, consequential and sternly logical thinking that a human being absolutely requires subsequently on all further stages of present-day initiation. Rudolf Steiner stated in this regard: 'But there exists something that, right through all the worlds up to Devachan, remains the same and does not change. That is logically trained thinking.' (Ibid.) It means that this thinking is suitable for the three worlds depicted in the book *Theosophy*. That is why the whole anthroposophical path of schooling is based on it: 'This [thinking] gives them [the three worlds] the foundation on which the [spiritual-scientific] Rosicrucian study is based.' (Ibid.) And more, only in this way does the Rosicrucian path become compatible with today's period of the consciousness soul.[157]

When, however, in accord with *The Philosophy of Freedom*, the thus acquired logical thinking rises still higher by one level and turns into pure thinking, that is, sense-free thinking, then the Michaelic intelligence can in this way be spiritualized and returned to Michael in the spiritual world through further spirit-schooling. With this, a solid basis is laid for the central Michaelic task of our age, which consists in the liberation of his intelligence which has descended down to the earth.

In this way the two most important early works by Rudolf Steiner play an important part in the modern Rosicrucian schooling as well as in the contemporary relationship of human beings to Michael.

12. *The Philosophy of Freedom* and Life between Death and Rebirth

One of the many surprises one can come across in regard to *The Philosophy of Freedom* and its inner relationship to anthroposophy is that in its ninth chapter one can discover the whole journey of the human soul between death and a new birth. Although no results of spiritual-scientific research are directly expressed in this chapter, the life of the human soul between two incarnations is depicted quite accurately, and broadly depicted like a mirror image of its soul-spiritual development.

At this point it must be explicitly stated that, beginning from his childhood, Rudolf Steiner discovered in himself the ability to follow the destinies of departed individuals, an ability which at the age of 21 he controlled consciously. By the time he was working on his *Philosophy of Freedom* in Weimar, he had developed it to a certain point of perfection in himself.[158]

At the beginning of Chapter IX, 'The Idea of Freedom', which in a certain sense represents the culmination of the whole book, Rudolf Steiner points to the experience of man's 'actual I' as distinguished from his 'I'-consciousness, for man's 'actual I' is a supersensible being that 'lies within thinking's very own being'. It is independent of the bodily organization, and as to its nature belongs solely to the spiritual world. This distinguishes the 'actual I' from the 'I'-consciousness, the origin of which is only determined by the bodily organization.

This distinction attests to the fact that, with the 'I' Rudolf Steiner is referring to here, he means the actual spiritual entity that is rooted equally in the domain prior to birth as well as the one following death. The connection of the two makes up the complete cycle of man's soul pilgrimage through the spiritual world between two incarnations.

Viewed spiritual-scientifically, it is in fact true that one cannot ever really grasp the actual being of the 'I' without the spiritual world that belongs to it. This was why, nearly 30 years after the first publication of *The Philosophy of Freedom,* Rudolf Steiner pointed out that this book leads back to two 'fundamental points': the existence of the spiritual world and the connection of the human 'I' with it. (GA 258, 11 June 1923) This is why one can only have the greatest admiration for the renunciation Rudolf Steiner made in creating his whole early work, and above all *The Philosophy of Freedom.* For, while already at that time standing fully consciously in the spiritual world, he did not allow any of this insight to flow in direct form into his book. In writing it all down, however, he placed himself 'strictly *before* entry into spiritual experience' (GA 4; emphasis by Rudolf Steiner).

Following the introductory part of the chapter, Rudolf Steiner describes two interconnected paths for the attainment of freedom. While they have completely different starting points, in the end they unite in a perfect synthesis. They consist of four levels and their union occurs on the highest, fourth level. In the case of both it is a matter, above all, of the step-by-step liberation of the human will. The original impulsion on the first path lies in the realm of human instincts, on the second path in the realm of motivations.

Let us consider them first in the sequence in which they are depicted in the chapter itself. The first path has its foundation in what Rudolf Steiner describes as the 'characterological inclination'. This consists of a sum of preconditions that the human soul discovers as given in earthly life. A human being can alter these preconditions to a degree, rooted as they are in the depths of his character, but they are basically brought along from prenatal existence in the spiritual world. Therefore, the possibility of changing a characterological predisposition in earthly life is not the same for all human beings and to a large extent is predestined out of the prenatal life. While the four stages that Rudolf Steiner describes in this regard refer primarily to the earthly life of man, at the same time they represent a replica of what he has experienced supersensibly during his descent from the heights of the spiritual world to earthly birth.

Generally, Rudolf Steiner separates the spiritual world which the human being passes through between two incarnations into four segments: the soul world, experienced directly after death where man spends approximately a third of the time spent during life on earth; then the spirit-land which consists of two stages which Rudolf Steiner designated as lower and upper spirit realm (Devachan) particularly in his earlier texts; finally follows the so-called Cosmic Midnight Hour, the high point between two incarnations.[159] These four levels are undergone by the soul, however, in reverse order when in the second half of its journey between two incarnations the soul descends from the heights of the Midnight Hour to earthly birth. In the ensuing depiction we will follow the direction that Rudolf Steiner indicates in the ninth chapter.

He characterizes the first, lowest stage as that of perception (cognizing). Here the characterological disposition of the human being produces merely the lowest animalistic urges. As examples, hunger, sexual drive, etc. are mentioned that become the driving force for action here. If one asks from where human beings, who stand on this lowest level of development, bring along such a characterological disposition, the spiritual-scientific reply is that prior to their birth they were above all influenced by the lowest regions of the soul world (Kamaloka).[160] These to begin with 'purely animalistic needs' can, however, appear on this first stage in altered form which already here belong to the general level of civilized humanity. Rudolf Steiner calls such higher driving forces of action 'tact or moral taste'. A human being who brings along these faculties of his characterological disposition into earth-life was connected prior to birth above all with the upper regions of the soul world. Such faculties are called by Rudolf Steiner soul-light, active soul-force, and soul-life. (GA 9.)

The second stage is that of feeling. Here Rudolf Steiner refers to quite diverse human feelings of which a few still belong to the lower regions of the soul world (for example, revenge), others to the higher ones (shame, sense of honour, duty, remorse). On the other hand, the loftier feelings of the human being (humility, compassion, gratitude, piety and love) already belong to the lower Devachan or spirit-land. It follows from this that the human being who in his characterological disposition brings along into life a natural tendency for these higher feelings acquired these faculties primarily in the lower Devachan on his path to incarnation on earth.

The third stage is that of thinking and mental picturing. Here, there originates the 'practical experience' that passes over 'into purely tactful action'[161] out of man's characterological disposition as the driving force of his willing. On this level are found human beings with the faculty of gathering the greatest possible life-experiences out of which, filled with wisdom, they then shape their lives and actions. One arrives at such a capacity if the soul on the way to the new birth was able to develop a special kinship to the region of the upper Devachan. On that level, there also exists for the human being the possibility of surveying his or her former incarnations as well as first overviews into future destinies. It is these experiences in particular that are mirrored on earth in the faculty not only of gathering rich life-experiences but especially of transforming them into profound wisdom of life.

Rudolf Steiner describes the concluding fourth stage as follows: 'The highest stage of individual life is conceptual thinking without regard for any definite content of perception. [Here, thinking has ultimately been liberated from the corporeality.] We determine the content of a concept through pure intuition out of the sphere of ideas ... When we act out of the influence of intuitions, the driving force of our action is *pure thinking*.' (Emphasis by Rudolf Steiner) The here described faculty is designated by

Rudolf Steiner as 'practical reason' or 'practical a priori'. It becomes the driving force when the impulse for action flows only out of human intuitions. The decisive factor here is that the human being on this final stage at last overcomes his original characterological disposition which derives from the previous stations of supersensible life, because here he experiences the Midnight Hour of his spiritual existence between incarnations consciously—the Cosmic Midnight Hour during which he is liberated from everything that determined him out of the past.[162]

In the earthly replica, this experiencing of the Midnight Hour appears as a complete transformation of man including even his character. Rudolf Steiner writes in regard to this: 'It is clear that such an impulse can no longer be counted among the characterological dispositions in the strictest sense of the word. For what is effective here as the driving force is no longer something merely individual in me, it is the ideal and consequently general content of my intuition.' If one recalls at this point that on the path of modern initiation the Cosmic Midnight Hour is reached fully consciously only in intuitive cognition (see Chapter 1 of this book), we can understand even better what a lofty domain of the spiritual world man's conceptual intuition is linked with, and whose earthly replica it represents.

What has been said here affirms how concretely Rudolf Steiner's following words must be taken, words with which he himself characterized his *Philosophy of Freedom* as a path into the spiritual world, meaning into that world where the soul of man dwells between two incarnations. 'It is therefore not possible in the sense of *The Philosophy of Freedom* to stop at the sense world but to go on to a spiritual kingdom founded on itself' (GA 258, 11 June 1923).

The four stages of the second path look completely different. On it the driving forces that stem from the characterological disposition, which from the beginning remains unconscious, are no longer in the lead but rather the conscious impulses that Rudolf Steiner designates as motives. In contrast to the characterological disposition, what man accomplishes in this area comes no longer out of prenatal life but belongs to the sphere of his earthly deeds that will have their consequences above all in his life after death.[163] In this sense it is justified to view the four stages of this second path as a replica of the human soul's pilgrimage after death through the same four regions of the spiritual world up to the Cosmic Midnight Hour.

On the first stage, only the lowest motivations of human action prevail and they can be described as 'pure egotism'. Here man merely pursues his own well-being at the expense of others. One who shapes his life solely according to this lowest principle sets himself up in the after-life for a most difficult time in Kamaloka. For everything that is egotistical connects the human being in particular with the lowest regions of the soul world.

The somewhat higher development of egotism consists of clever or shrewd morality. Although egotism remains effective as the main motivation, the consequences of such actions can under certain circumstances be of benefit to other people, something which then brings about a linkage to the higher regions of the soul world. Nevertheless, an individual who is only led by such motivations will have to remain a very long while in the soul world, because he or she brings along too little of what is akin to the higher spiritual realms.

On the second stage, 'purely conceptual content' comes into question most of all as the chief motivation. Such a person carries out actions that always follow specific 'moral principals' which 'in the form of abstract concepts guide moral life'. In so doing such a person is hardly concerned with the origin of such moral concepts but accepts them as commandments determining his life that derive from a 'moral authority' situated outside his own self. Here too Rudolf Steiner lists a whole 'hierarchy' of such authorities. Through obeying the commands of the 'head of the family, the state or social custom' and so on, the human soul is connected after death chiefly to the upper realms of the soul world. By contrast, the authority of 'divine revelation', which can moreover bring about a deepened religious life, already leads to the lower Devachan. Yet the soul becomes truly related to this region of spirit-land as a result of moral autonomy acquired on the earth—an autonomy that makes itself felt mainly as the inner voice of the conscience. For through it, the human being belongs fully to the lower Devachan.

In the upper Devachan, man unites with the goals and the higher development of humanity. Here, all segregating elements between human beings fall aside. What still existed on the lower Devachan as differences between nations, religions, cultures, and so on is at last overcome. Man lives in the upper regions of the spirit-realm as a pure representative of humanity and unselfish promoter of its development. This is why the motives that make the human being akin to this lofty spiritual realm are of a kind that leads to action, not through an authority but 'out of ethical insight'. On this stage of morality man allows the needs of his moral life to be determined through his insight. Here Rudolf Steiner mentions the two main needs that can move a person to inwardly motivated action: '(1) the greatest possible welfare of the whole of mankind purely for the sake of this welfare; (2) cultural progress or the moral *development* of humanity towards ever greater perfection'. (GA 4; emphasis by Rudolf Steiner.) The earthly deeds derived from these two fundamental motives link man above all with the upper regions of spirit-land where he spends the longest period of life between two incarnations.

The highest stage on this path encompasses the actions in which a human being only actualizes his 'purely individually grasped personal moral goals'. According to Rudolf Steiner, 'this is the highest imaginable moral principle', which from the first has no association to sensory perceptions 'but springs from the fount of pure intuition and only after the fact seeks the association to perception, to life'. Motivations like these that derive out of 'purely conceptual intuition' lead the human being after death to conscious experience of the Cosmic Midnight Hour, this highest point between two incarnations, where the future ideal of man's own evolution lights up before him. On earth the full implementation of individual human freedom corresponds to this experience, freedom that manifests during concrete action based on the pure love of it. 'Only when I follow my love for the object is it I myself who acts ... I acknowledge no external principle for my action for I have found in myself the reason for the action, the love for the action ... I carry it out because I love it' (GA 4; emphasis by Rudolf Steiner).

Thus on this level of freedom, conceptual *intuition* and *love* for the action inseparably flow together. With that, already still on earth, the essential connection between intuition and love is recognized and moreover practised. On the path of modern initiation, the stage of intuition, on which alone the conscious experience of the Cosmic Midnight Hour is possible, corresponds to this experience of *The Philosophy of Freedom*. This higher stage of cognition is, however, attained through the further strengthening and development of the human capacity to love. 'What manifests in intuition can only be attained through the highest development and spiritualization of the capacity to love. It must become possible for the human being to turn the capacity to love into a force of cognition.' (GA 227, 20 August 1923.)[164]

The full revelation of this connection between intuition and love is granted to the human soul after death in the Cosmic Midnight Hour, inasmuch as from this highest level it can behold the creative deeds of the hierarchies during the cosmic shaping of its own future destiny, deeds with which, out of love and intuitions, these beings bear the spiritual impulses even into physical matter.[165]

In that way, the two paths which the soul goes through between two incarnations (the prenatal path and the one after death) meet in this Midnight Hour. Rudolf Steiner also calls them the paths of 'unbornness' and 'immortality'. Only through the connection between both can human beings grasp the nature of eternity, and with that the 'truly eternal' within themselves. 'And when it is understood once again that eternity has these two sides, immortality and unbornness, only then will it be possible cognitively to penetrate into the enduring, the truly eternal, in the human being' (GA 227, 19 August 1923).

During the Midnight Hour this 'truly eternal' in man is not only recognized but completely taken hold of and experienced. An earthly replica of this experience appears in the union of the two paths in Chapter IX of *The Philosophy of Freedom*: the path of the driving force and that of the motive. Rudolf Steiner refers to this secret in the following words: 'Careful consideration of this soon makes evident that on this [highest] level of morality, driving force and motive coincide. This means that neither a previously determined characterological predisposition nor an external normatively assumed moral principle affect our action.' This signifies that here any dependence on the physical body on the part of the inner human being, on the characterological predisposition, and any sort of authoritarian principle, is completely overcome. This applies, however, only to actions that 'as to predisposition ... have the faculty of moral intuitions' and are carried out based 'on love for the object'. Viewed spiritual-scientifically, we are dealing here with deeds that are independent of past karma and therefore can establish new karma in the process of creating out of nothing.[166] Such creative deeds correspond in the existence after death to the condition of the soul in the Cosmic Midnight Hour, where it irreversibly overcomes all dependence on the earthly, and in so doing can link up totally with divine existence.

In summation it is possible to say: On earth, man works freely only when he acts based on his quintessential eternal being. The basis for this is that he pursues the two paths (described as they are in the ninth chapter of *The Philosophy of Freedom*) to the very end, and then connects them on the fourth stage with each other. Then the spiritual forces that originate equally from the after-death dimension and the prenatal one are effective together in each of his free deeds. Out of the realm after death, the unconscious imaginations appear as spiritual foundation of the 'moral imagination', and out of the prenatal realm the unconscious inspirations flow as spiritual basis for the 'conceptual intuition'. Only through the union of the two streams can the 'supersensible personality' or 'eternal persona' awaken and become active in man. It is then this 'persona' who carries out the *free* deeds. Rudolf Steiner states in this regard: 'One learns to recognize freedom only when one knows that unconscious imagination, which prepares our life after death, works together with unconscious inspiration, which resounds as a force out of the life before birth into our soul. Inasmuch as we instinctively carry out such actions that our immortal [eternal] human being performs, we carry out free actions. And the fact that we are aware of free actions is like the reflection, the *fata Morgana*, of what rests deep down in the *supersensible personality* as our immortal or eternal essence'.[167]

In other words, here it is a matter of the supersensible, that is to say immortal, *eternal personality* (persona) of man. It fully manifests only in the Cosmic Midnight Hour, meaning where the two paths (the pre-natal and the one after death) come to their full revelation, and their reflection on earth is human freedom. In this manner there is a direct connection between the Midnight Hour, in which the primal fount of man's eternal centre of being manifests, and the experience of freedom on earth. The fact that Rudolf Steiner already knew of this mystery during his work on *The Philosophy of Freedom* is affirmed by his words in Chapter IX: 'Yet in each of us dwells a deeper being in which the free man finds expression.'

In the sense of what was depicted in the last chapter, it can be said that in the Cosmic Midnight Hour man is shown the highest eternal idea of his own being in the way it was once generated by the highest Deity. Man, who in contrast to all nine hierarchies, will at the end of his evolution appear as a being that out of itself and based on its own responsibility (without referring back to the Deity) will create the new Cosmos of Freedom and Love.

We can learn from Rudolf Steiner's results of spiritual research how man's encounter with the divine idea of his own being, or his eternal personality (persona), occurs on the pinnacle between two incarnations, something Rudolf Steiner describes in the cycle *The Inner Being of Man and Life between Death and Rebirth*. There one can read how, through the connection with the Christ Impulse on earth, the human being can take this impulse along into after-death life. The consequence of this is that our 'I' is so strengthened in the spiritual world by the Christ Impulse that 'I'-consciousness is maintained up to the Cosmic Midnight Hour. When we now arrive on this summit of our spiritual journey with full 'I'-consciousness, we then experience the manifestation from above of the Holy Spirit who creates around us 'a new cosmic light', 'spreading above our own entity a radiance through which we grasp ourselves anew in cosmic existence, through which we awaken anew in cosmic existence . . . Through the Holy Spirit we are thus newly awakened during the Cosmic Midnight Hour. *Per Spiritum Sanctum reviviscimus*'. (GA 153, 13 April 1914.) This 'cosmic light of the Spirit' now illuminates the 'highest ideal' of the human being, the vision of which we need for forming our coming earth life out of the spiritual cosmos while on the way to our new incarnation. For the whole meaning of our earthly incarnations consists in the gradual actualization of this eternal archetype on the earth.

In the same cycle, Rudolf Steiner also speaks of this ideal of man as the highest religion of the gods (hierarchies). 'Thus hovers as the goal, as the highest ideal, as the gods' religion, an image of humanity before the gods. And as if on the distant shore of the gods' existence, there stands before the gods the temple, which as the greatest artistic achievement of the gods represents the replica of divine existence in the image of man.' (GA 153, 10 April 1914.) It is not difficult to recognize that with this description of the highest ideal of the gods' religion, reference is made to the immortal persona of man, which through the light of the Holy Spirit is revealed to him during the Cosmic Midnight Hour.

The possibility brought about by the Christ Impulse of receiving the Holy Spirit into oneself so as to envision the highest ideal of man with this Spirit's light has still another consequence for the human being, which is described by Rudolf Steiner at the end of that cycle: 'Thus must the Christ Impulse be present. Up until the Midnight Hour of Existence, it [the Christ Impulse] retains for us the possibility not to forget our "I". Then the [Holy] Spirit draws close to us during the Midnight Hour. Now, we have preserved the memory of our "I". When we bear this memory as far as into the Midnight Hour of Existence all the way to where the Holy Spirit approaches us ... then the Spirit can guide us henceforth to our reincarnation which we bring about inasmuch as we *form* our *primal image* in the spiritual world.' (GA 153, 14 April 1914.) Now, during our descent to the earth, we can properly form this primal image for the approaching earth incarnation only as the consequence of beholding the eternal essence of the human being (its persona) during the Cosmic Midnight Hour. But the Christ Impulse likewise continues to work in man on this descending journey so that 'the impulse of the Spirit' will be strengthened through 'the impulse of the Christ'. As a result the Spirit Impulse does not cease at birth but extends its activity in this strengthened form over the whole life on earth, and in this way lights up within the physical incarnation. According to Rudolf Steiner, when this occurs, human beings can attain to the beholding of the Etheric Christ during their life.

The further consequence of such activity on the part of the Holy Spirit in life on earth is the possibility of man's free deeds. For the Holy Spirit appears and manifests in man where the two streams, 'unbornness' and immortality, flow into each other and accordingly bring about the manifestation of the *eternal persona* which has to be actualized by man on the earth. This actualization has its beginning inasmuch as man moves on the two paths (referred to in Chapter IX of *The Philosophy of Freedom*) all the way to their union and on this foundation, based on his free moral intuitions, begins to carry out free deeds of love. Then such a person works out of the nature of the Holy Spirit, the Spirit that on earth is the true Spirit of Freedom. In his 'I', such a human being is then filled with the Holy Spirit and thus capable of producing the new Creation out of Nothing.

What has been said up to now is summarized in Diagram 23, p. 147.

This diagram can illustrate that man's experience of freedom on earth—at the *noon hour* of world existence—is a replica of his experiences in the heights of the spiritual world between two incarnations, meaning at the *Midnight Hour* of world existence. There he beholds his eternal persona as the future ideal of mankind and the gods in order then, having returned to earth, to actualize this ideal in cognition and in the free deeds resulting from it.

When we consider at this point that the human being comes in touch with eternity in the Midnight Hour between two incarnations so as to receive from eternity the impulses for his or her next earth life, we shall comprehend the great ideal of human freedom as described by Rudolf Steiner at the end of his book *Theosophy* in a quite different way. There it is a matter of 'the will for freedom', which in every human being has its origin in the experience of the Cosmic Midnight Hour. 'This acting out of the inner being can only be an ideal towards which one strives. The attainment of this goal is far away in the distance. But one who is beginning to know must have the will to see the way [towards it] clearly. This is one's *will for freedom*. For, freedom means acting out of one's own self. And only one who gathers the incentives out of the eternal may act out of his or her self.' (GA 9; emphasis by Rudolf Steiner.)

It was already mentioned above how, during the Midnight Hour and the overshadowing by the Holy Spirit, the human being experiences the cosmic '*Per Spiritum Sanctum reviviscimus*'. This is only possible through the prophetic connection of man with his highest ideal, the eternal persona, which he will fully actualize only at the end of his evolution on earth.

The third part of the Foundation Stone Meditation likewise points out how experiencing the '*Per Spiritum Sanctum Reviviscimus*' (macrocosmic part) is linked with the attainment of freedom on earth (microcosmic part). It is striking that the words 'free will' occur only in this part in regard to the 'I'—the 'I' to which the gods bestow their 'eternal aims' (referring also to the ideal of the creative persona) through the 'World Being's Light' of the Holy Spirit in the heights of the Cosmic Midnight Hour. For as was stated already, the 'manifestation of the Holy Spirit' in the Mid-

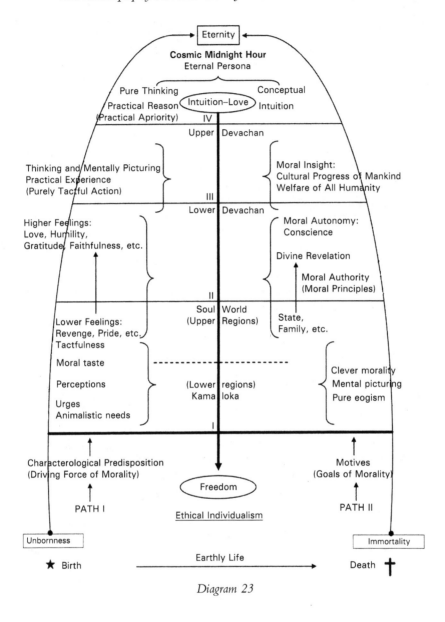

Diagram 23

night Hour corresponds to the full experiencing of human freedom on earth.

The vertical arrow in the middle, which on the diagram directly connects the Cosmic Midnight Hour with the earthly world, likewise indicates the path on which the Christ—as was explained in another book in detail earlier[168]—brought the forces of the Cosmic Midnight Hour to the earth in order to accomplish His corporeal resurrection with them. Through the creation of the Resurrection-body (Phantom), the eternal persona was for the first time made actual *on the earth*. With that, the ideal of the human being was conceived as a being working out of itself based on its own responsibility (see Chapter 9 of this book). Since then the possibility exists on earth for every human being freely and out his/her own strength to achieve this ideal described in *The Philosophy of Freedom*. For the Resurrection-body is the sensory-supersensible form of body that alone guarantees eternity for the personal 'I'-consciousness of human individuals so that while still sojourning in the body they can extend it out into the Midnight Hour (just as Rudolf Steiner could do it during his spirit-research).

The two arrows that move upward, which in the diagram (on the right and left) lead into the spiritual world to their union at the heights of the Cosmic Midnight Hour, in each case through the portal of birth (unbornness) and death (immortality), also represent the two main paths of initiation that were practised in the ancient pre-Christian Mysteries. One led into the spiritual world through immersion into the inner human being all the way to supersensible foundations of the physical body (path 1), and the other through the connection with the spirit of outer nature to the union with the spiritual cosmos (path 2). At the Turning Point of Time the two paths were represented by the Shepherds and the Kings, and their highest initiates were correspondingly the Gautama Buddha and Zarathustra.

According to Rudolf Steiner, these two great initiates of mankind launched the paths of the human soul to God, but in polar directions. Gautama Buddha sought the connection to the divine in the strictly backwards direction, meaning through the portal of birth in the way it is executed in exemplary fashion in the genealogy of the Luke Gospel which goes back to the creation of the first human being, Adam, and ends with the reference to God. In contrast Zarathustra sought the connection with the divine in the future. This path led into the spiritual world through the portal of death. This is why he became the great preparer of the Christ's appearance on earth and the Mystery of Golgotha. By means of this, the new union of human beings with the divine-spiritual world has become possible, a union that will extend to the apocalyptic con-clusion of Earth evolution. 'This is the difference between the teaching of the Buddha and that of Zarathustra ... Buddha says: Step backwards; Zarathustra says: In stepping forwards the soul will find the god. Whether one seeks the god in the Alpha or in the Omega, one finds him. Whether one moves backwards or forwards, one comes to God! ... The particular forces required to find the god in the Alpha are the primal forces of man. On the other hand, man must attain on his own here on earth the forces required to find the god of the Omega.' (GA 109, 25 May 1909.)

Both these paths are also present in *The Philosophy of Freedom*, although in hidden form (see Diagram 23, p. 147). On one hand we have the 'characterological predisposition' that points to the past and/or the pre-natal dimension, on the ennoblement of which Gautama Buddha and his disciples were principally at work in the one stream. On the other there are the 'motives' out of which human beings on earth consciously carry out their actions, the consequences of which humans take along into the world after death. Zarathustra and his disciples work above all on the ennoblement of the motives. Only through the appearance of the Christ at the Turning Point of Time could the two paths be united in a higher synthesis. This is why Christ could moreover say of Himself: 'I am the Alpha and the Omega, the beginning and the end' (Rev. 1:8). In this context it means this: 'I unite the initiation paths of Gautama Buddha and Zarathustra and lead them on further through the portals of birth (baptism in the Jordan) and death (Mystery of Golgotha) all the way to that place in the spiritual world where they ultimately flow together, where Alpha and Omega represent a unity, and this place is the Cosmic Midnight Hour.' Christ then brings its forces back to earth and unites them in His resurrection with the evolution of humanity. It was solely on this spiritual basis—even if Rudolf Steiner arrived at the paths' full cognition only after his spiritual encounter with the Christ—that in the sphere of *intuitive thinking* he could unite the two paths in *The Philosophy of Freedom*.

Still from another side, we can find traces of these two paths in *The Philosophy of Freedom*. In the lecture of 19 December 1910 (GA 124), Rudolf Steiner points out that on the two paths (which in pre-Christian times were connected with the southern and northern Mysteries and could therefore only be pursued in a strictly separate manner) those who were to be initiated on the first path encountered the Lesser Guardian at the threshold to the spiritual world. Those on the second path met the Greater Guardian at the threshold. Rudolf Steiner describes these two encounters in the most detail in his book *Knowledge of the Higher Worlds and Its Attainment* (GA 10). It states there among other things about the Lesser Guardian that his shape represents merely the spirit-disciple's 'own character', namely 'the effect of one's own past life', which at the threshold to the spiritual world 'was awakened to independent life'.

Here the reference to the 'character' of the human being proves that this passage can be brought into connection with the 'characterological predisposition' described in *The Philosophy of Freedom*, for in the encounter with the Lesser Guardian of the Threshold there appears before the spirit disciple his own 'characterological predisposition' in the form of a spiritual being independent of him which from then on he must consciously purify. Especially secret urges and unconscious dispositions to evil emerge here, as well as all manner of possible negative feelings that have infiltrated the most remote corners of the soul. It is common to all of them that they demonstrate the dependence of man on his physical body and therefore his lack of freedom, although in different ways. 'The degree of man's entanglement with the physical-sensory nature becomes visible to the human being through the [Lesser] "Guardian of the Threshold".' (GA 10.) Over against this, we have to place our higher feelings, practical life-experiences, and most of all our sense-free or 'pure' thinking that we have developed. For only in the sphere of this pure thinking can any dependency of man from his 'characterological predisposition' or the physical body (including the urges, passions, instincts, and so on that arise out of it) be overcome.

The trial that is imposed on man during the encounter with the Greater Guardian of the Threshold is completely different. Here it is a matter of overcoming all forms of egoism to which one still inclines in the depths of one's soul, egoism that often unconsciously still affects the motives for one's actions. If the spirit disciple succumbs at the threshold of the spiritual world to the seduction of egoism, which now makes its appearance to the full extent, he or she enters upon the so-called black path of occultism. 'For everything that *egoism* demands is by no means foregone on the black path. On the contrary, the fruits of this path are indeed the most complete fulfilment of egoism.' (GA 10.) By contrast, in *The Philosophy of Freedom* the path of transformation from any sort of egoism is identified. This path does not lead to egoism's elimination but to its augmentation towards 'the welfare of all mankind' as well as its overall 'cultural progress', which man then considers as his or her innermost interests. This, however, is not the final step on this path because on this level extraordinarily subtle residues of egoism can still remain attached. The complete liberation from it only takes place along with taking hold of the 'conceptual intuition'. For an ultimate overcoming of egoism is only found through the 'actualization of purely intuitively grasped individual goals of morality'. (GA 4.) While man on this level acts totally on an individual basis, he does however attain the motives for his actions out of pure thought-imbued intuition, which is objectively spiritual and therefore cannot contain anything egoistical *per definitionem* within itself.[169] This is moreover the most important quality that one requires for the encounter with the Greater Guardian of the Threshold. For in order even to bear up under it, one has to have overcome all selfish tendencies in oneself to the extent that this is otherwise the case only in true conceptual intuition.

If man has not carried out this purification of his motives to a sufficient degree, then the Greater Guardian of the Threshold blocks the further path for him. The spirit disciple hears only the following stern words from him: 'I block your entry into the *highest* [emphasis by SP] regions of the supersensible world as long as you have not devoted *all* your acquired forces to the redemption of the [whole] world around you.' (GA 10; emphasis by Rudolf Steiner.) The 'highest regions of the supersensible world' are those of the upper Devachan and above all the region of the Cosmic Midnight Hour in which the intuitive (essential living) union with the Greater Guardian of the Threshold will eventually become possible for the spirit disciple in the future.[170] Conscious access into this highest realm is opened up to him when he makes the decision, a decision at which he can only arrive in an absolutely free manner (meaning out of the momentary thought-intuition), to continue work on the 'redemption of the world' around him. Such work begins even where a human being carries out actions based on moral imagination on earth whose only motive is pure love of the action. For 'we gain nothing for our egoism by deeds of love, *but the world gains that much more*' (GA 143, 17 December 1912).

One can therefore say that the purification of the forces of cognition that are described in the first part of *The Philosophy of Freedom*, and which then appear in their most perfect form as thought-imbued intuitions that bear within themselves nothing any more of the subjective qualities of the characterological predisposition of man, can lead him to the conscious encounter with the Lesser Guardian of the Threshold. And the purification of the human motives, depicted in the second part, which following the overcoming of all egoistical tendencies turn into pure deeds out of love for the object, guides the human being to the conscious encounter with the Greater Guardian of the Threshold. In this hidden manner the most important elements of the modern path of spiritual training are present immanently in the two parts of *The Philosophy of Freedom*.

In taking issue with Kant and his duty-imperative (see more on this in the next chapter) which excludes any real freedom, Rudolf Steiner characterizes these kind of actions in *The Philosophy of Freedom* as follows: 'Why should my action benefit the general welfare any less because I have done it out of love rather than if I had done it *only* out of a sense of duty to serve overall welfare?' (GA 4; emphasis by Rudolf Steiner.) This open-ended formulation unmistakably points out that we are dealing here with actions that truly benefit 'general welfare' and with that can contribute to the 'redemption of the world around us'. These are deeds that are carried out based on pure love and therefore are solely actions based on freedom.

In *Occult Science, an Outline*, Rudolf Steiner writes that 'moreover, everything the human being accomplishes out of true understanding of evolution is a *sowing* that must ripen as *love*', a seeding out of which, based on the work of human beings, the new Cosmos of Love will originate in the future. (GA 13; emphasis by Rudolf Steiner.) In this passage, too, the 'true understanding' can be comprehended in the sense of the first part of *The Philosophy of Freedom*[171] and a 'seeding' of love that ripens in the free human deeds in the sense of the second part of the book.

Based on what has been said, the words in which Rudolf Steiner characterizes the main result of the spirit disciple's encounter with the Greater Guardian of the Threshold can be comprehended in a new way: 'He (the spirit disciple) offers up his gifts at the sacrificial altar of mankind' (GA 10). The greatest gifts man can ever attain are those that he himself is able to produce out of his thought-intuitions. Only these are truly *his own* and therefore *only* he can actually offer *them* up. (Everything that does not absolutely belong to him is not a pure offering.) But that he would like to offer the gifts up voluntarily to humanity or the world around him attests to the fact that he has actually taken the step from the first to the second part of *The Philosophy of Freedom* and now wishes only to act out of love for the object.

In his Introduction to Goethe's natural-scientific writings, Rudolf Steiner states that 'it can ... only be selfless devotion to the object to which one dedicates one's activity, *it can only be love*' (GA 1; emphasis by Rudolf Steiner). Love reaches its highest creative force when it can wholly sacrifice the best it possesses. The more love offers up, the greater and more creative does it become.[172] In these words the reference to 'selfless devotion' allows one to comprehend better why all masters of esoteric Christianity who have experienced the encounter with the Greater Guardian of the Threshold emphatically place '*selfless devotion* and willingness to make self-sacrifices ahead of all other faculties' (GA 10). In this manner the path of the *Philosophy of Freedom* and anthroposophy's inner path fit together seamlessly.[173]

It follows from what has been said that in Chapter IX of *The Philosophy of Freedom* the first path corresponds more to man's self-transformation (Buddha-path), and the second to the redemption of the surrounding world (Zarathustra-path). The union of these two paths or Mystery streams has become possible, however, only through the appearance of the Christ on earth and the Mystery of Golgotha. Since then both

Mystery streams can be followed not only separately as was the case earlier, meaning in two different incarnations, but simultaneously within the *one* modern path of initiation. Such a new Christian initiation path for all human beings, a path that encompasses *both* earlier Mystery streams, was founded by Rudolf Steiner at the beginning of the twentieth century. That is why we find at the end of his book *Knowledge of the Higher Worlds and Its Attainment*, as well as in the corresponding chapter in *Occult Science, an Outline*, the sequential description of the two encounters with the Lesser as well as the Greater Guardian of the Threshold.

Rudolf Steiner could unite the two ancient Mystery paths only because he had risen in his own initiation to consciously experiencing the Cosmic Midnight Hour where the two paths, from Alpha and Omega as the prenatal and after-death path, unite (see Diagram 23, p. 147), and where the encounter takes place with Christ in Intuition—Intuition that reveals the nature of the Mystery of Golgotha. In this way Rudolf Steiner moved on the microcosmic dimension of *consciousness* on the same path as did the Christ at the Turning Point of Time on the macrocosmic dimension of *existence*. (This path, which includes the two others, is then defined by the vertical arrow that represents the central axis of the diagram.)

In the book *Occult Science, an Outline,* at the end of the chapter on initiation, Rudolf Steiner brings out that only the encounter with Christ in the realm of Intuition reveals the Mystery of Golgotha in its full significance to the initiate. This is why he can affirm that 'the fact of the Mystery of Golgotha ... belongs among the most exalted experiences within the spiritual world' (GA 143, 17 December 1912). As a Christian initiate, Rudolf Steiner was able to attain to the height of the Cosmic Midnight Hour from the earth only because Christ Himself, the Cosmic Word, had earlier come down from this sphere to the earth.

What Rudolf Steiner made generally available in the above-mentioned anthroposophical books as the union of the two Mystery streams in modern initiation (all the way to the encounter with *both* Guardians of the Threshold) was already germinally present in his *Philosophy of Freedom*. In Chapter IX these two paths are described in philosophical terms, and it is pointed out that they flow together in the sphere of intuitive thought so as to form the basis of human freedom and moral action on earth.

From this it can be better understood what Rudolf Steiner means when in the book *Knowledge of the Higher Worlds and Its Attainment* he writes: 'But this once supersensible world *needed* the passage through the sensory world. Its further development would not have been possible without this passage. Only when beings will have developed within the sensory kingdom with corresponding *faculties* [emphasis by SP] can the supersensible world continue again with its progress. And these beings are the human beings.' (GA 10; emphasis by Rudolf Steiner.) It is a matter here of those faculties that the spiritual world (hierarchies) itself originally does not possess but absolutely requires for its further development. And these new faculties, which *only man can develop on the earth*, are at the very centre of *The Philosophy of Freedom* as freedom and love. Thus in the book's first part the experience of *freedom* is described and in the second part its practical implementation in the deeds of *love*. The coming together of both will come to pass in the future transformation of humanity into the Tenth Hierarchy. For true love as the central creative force of the universe out of which alone the new cosmos will one day originate is not imaginable without freedom in the sense it can be developed only by earthly human beings (meaning in the sense of *The Philosophy of Freedom*). It is therefore 'the great mission of man on earth that he is to bring freedom into the world and only along with freedom ... what is called love. For without freedom love is impossible ... That is why the earth is the Cosmos of Love and Freedom.' (GA 110, 18 April, 1909–II.)

The archetype of this future development of world and humanity was given in the Mystery of Golgotha in which 'a god ... accomplished the deed out of free will—meaning out of love—so that the earth and mankind can arrive at their goal' (GA 31, 14 October 1911).[174]

★

When in 1894 *The Philosophy of Freedom* had been published in book form, it evoked actual fear in some readers due to the radical manner in which the freedom of man was dealt with there. It was thought that such a freedom would allow human beings to live out their bodily instincts and pure egoism unconstrained. In reality, the path to freedom as described in *The Philosophy of Freedom* demands the strongest confrontation with the powers that from opposite sides do not want to let man attain to true freedom. In his later writings, Rudolf Steiner designates these opposing powers as the luciferic and ahrimanic forces. The former wish to seduce man into living out of pure egotism, and the ahrimanic ones want to chain him to his corporeality, i.e. to the instincts and urges linked to the body.

On the other hand, the twofold path outlined in the ninth chapter of *The Philosophy of Freedom* leads methodically and consequentially to the overcoming of both opposing powers in the human soul. It does not lead to the arrogant, egotistic contention of personal freedom as occurred at the beginning of World evolution through Lucifer, which brought about his downfall; likewise it does not lead to the ahrimanic temptation of unrestrained expression of instincts, passion and urges arising out of the corporeality, but to something completely different. For at the end of the first path the human being frees himself, as already shown, from any dependency on his characterological predisposition and with that from his corporeality in general; and on the second path the same takes place in regard to human egoism.

Speaking esoterically one can say: On the first path the ahrimanic temptation is primarily overcome and on the second the luciferic one. And when this has happened, the two paths can then unite in their advanced stages in order to prepare a new basis for the Christ-insight that culminates in the spiritual Christ-encounter. In their union they are then the philosophical expression of the sculptural group that originated later out of anthroposophy, which depicts the Representative of Mankind who vanquishes the two opposing powers, Lucifer and Ahriman, and endows every human being who struggles for individual freedom with this faculty.

In this sense the fulfilment of *The Philosophy of Freedom* leads to the free Imitation of Christ that culminated in Rudolf Steiner's greatest sacrifice at the Christmas Conference, but at the same time brought about a new creation that represents the crowning point of anthroposophy on earth.

★

A further aspect of what has been stated in this chapter consists in the following. The origin of earthly 'I'-consciousness is prepared in human life from two sides that are connected with each other. A newborn child is initially merely endowed with the faculty of *perception* through its sense organs. Only gradually does inner life in the human sense develop in it. This inner life develops at first in pictures, which to begin with have, however, a direct link to what is being perceived by the senses and therefore have the characteristics of dependent pictorial *conceptions*. Only later, the soul life's inward development evolves to the point where actual *thinking* can gradually awaken as the basis for the earthly appearance of the 'I'. We thus have three stages of development that precede the birth (or appearance) of the individual 'I' in earth-life:

Perception—Conception—Thinking—Appearance of the 'I'.[175]

Rudolf Steiner describes this process from still another side. It is also a matter of three stages or faculties that precede the earthly 'I'-appearance: walking (standing erect), speaking, and thinking. Both lines of development unite in the awakening of thinking, and in their phases are the terrestrial reflection of man's *prenatal* path through the spheres of the upper and lower Devachan and the soul world.

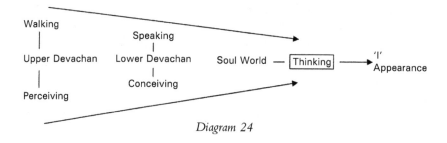

Diagram 24

With the first lighting up of 'I'-consciousness (the first manifestation of the 'I' in the earthly world), the possibility of cognition comes along that consists in the faculty of connecting perceptions with the corresponding concepts. When Rudolf Steiner states that the appearance of the 'I' in the human being occurs at the moment of our earliest memory in life (this goes back approximately to age three), then this moment is likewise the one starting from which—even though still quite incipiently—the corresponding concepts can link up to external perceptions. For the most innate activity of the awakened 'I' does indeed consist in the process of cognizing. This is why the 'I' brings along this faculty already during its very first appearance. In his early works, Rudolf Steiner brought this feature of the 'I' to expression in the pregnant sentence: '*The "I"sets up cognizing.*' (GA 3; emphasis by Rudolf Steiner.) This refers to the ability to add corresponding concepts to percepts (or mental images). This cognitive faculty of the 'I' reaches its full unfolding around the age of 21 in the human being. Viewed spiritual-scientifically, this can be designated as the actual moment of the birth of the 'I' on earth. From then on, the second process begins to work increasingly in human life. Now the 'I' can learn to act out of the insights gained in the world. And when, in the sense of the first part of *The Philosophy of Freedom*, it has struggled through to experiencing freedom in intuitive thinking, then earthly deeds resulting from such thinking will likewise be free ones. 'The *free spirit* [the free 'I' of the human being] acts according to its impulses and they are the intuitions that are selected out of the totality of its world of ideas by thinking.' (GA 4; emphasis by Rudolf Steiner.)

In *The Philosophy of Freedom*, Rudolf Steiner draws up three elements of such free deeds that consist of moral imagination, moral intuition and moral technique. And even as the three above-mentioned faculties are given to man out of the prenatal sphere without his participation (because that occurs before the appearance of the 'I'), his free deeds bear their fruits during existence after death. Moral imagination leads man into the soul world, moral intuition into the lower Devachan, and moral technique (which as spiritual impulse can rule and transform the earthly world with all its material and socially given facts) leads up into upper Devachan.

In the middle of this development stands man's 'I' which unfolds freedom out of its thinking, and seeks to actualize this freedom in its deeds based on love. One can also say that the development of the 'I' consists in the very fact that it first grasps the concept of the free human being based on its cognition in order then, through work on itself, to add the new perception to this concept. For 'only he [the human being] can turn *himself* into a *free* being' (GA 4; emphasis by Rudolf Steiner). This constant work on the self which ultimately turns the human being into a free entity has decisive consequences for man's after-death life. For the human being's free deeds contain what is absolutely required by the spiritual world so that it can progress in its own development. What was described in the second half of this chapter can also be summarized in Diagram 25 on the next page.

At the heights of Cosmic Midnight, love and intuition are identical. This is why cognition represents a cosmic deed arising out of the direct impregnation through the Holy Spirit. On the earth this highest spiritual condition is reflected in the attainment on the part of the human 'I' of true freedom that springs from thought-produced intuitions, and takes on life in creative deeds of love. Thus the path of *The Philosophy of Freedom* leads in its continuation through modern initiation directly into the spiritual world even to the conscious experience of the Cosmic Midnight Hour. There, moreover, lies the key to cognition of the secret of resurrection, and with that to the ideal of love and freedom—an ideal that ultimately must be actualized on the earth. Rudolf Steiner could only lift the veil from this secret in anthroposophy because he had risen on his path of initiation, as we have seen, all the way to the conscious experience of the Cosmic Midnight Hour in intuition.

What is more, it is only because Rudolf Steiner in intuition was able to bridge over the whole path of the human soul between two incarnations out of the resurrection forces effective in his 'I' that he attained to the objectives and true insights about reincarnation and karma. The result of this spiritual research was the knowledge that 'the living Christ is the living teacher of reincarnation out of the spiritual worlds today,[176] and likewise the fact that starting from our time He begins to be active among humankind as Lord of Karma.

In this chapter we have shown how the first idea, that of reincarnation of the human 'I' which can truly be established only by tracing the *whole path* of the soul between two incarnations, is grounded seedlike in *The Philosophy of Freedom*. In the following chapter it will have to be shown

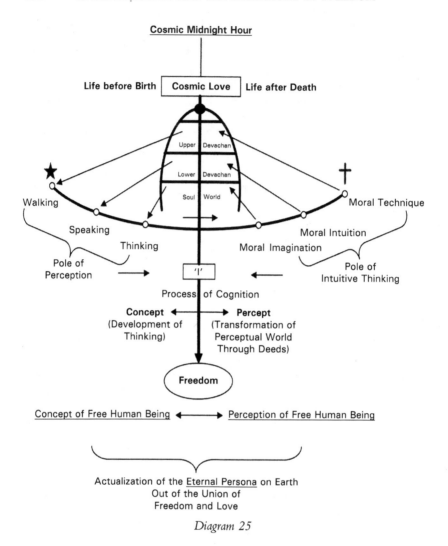

Diagram 25

how the second idea, the modern idea of karma, is likewise present in this book.

Both together represent Rudolf Steiner's essential task in the twentieth century which he above all began to actualize to the full extent *after* the Christmas Conference.[177]

What was only as if obscurely begun in *The Philosophy of Freedom*—and even with the founding of anthroposophy at the beginning of the last century could not immediately and fully make its appearance[178]—now reached its real breakthrough and highest unfolding out of the esoteric impulse of the Christmas Conference.

With this we have yet another affirmation of what was demonstrated elsewhere in detail[179], namely that the Christmas Conference and the subsequent karma lectures were the actual fulfilment of this Mystery book in Rudolf Steiner's life.

13. The Impulse of Freedom and the Christian Mysteries of Karma

In a spiritual-scientific deliberation of anthroposophy, it is notable that on the one hand Rudolf Steiner decidedly traces its roots back to *The Philosophy of Freedom*, and on the other concludes its whole development on earth with the mighty karma-revelation of the year 1924. The fact that right at the beginning of his anthroposophical activity in 1902 Rudolf Steiner wanted to start with the above revelations in connection with the establishment of the German Section of the Theosophical Society points moreover to the central significance of this theme in his life's work. At that time, however, on account of the opposition by the leading groups of that society, he could not carry on with this theme. As a result, according to his own words, 'actual esotericism had to wait for 21 years while the whole of anthroposophy 'drifted into a more theoretical direction' (GA 240, 24 August 1924). Only due to the spiritual impulse of the Christmas Conference did it become possible for Rudolf Steiner unreservedly to approach that part of his main task, which consisted in the research and presentation of reincarnation and karma.[180]

As mentioned already at the end of the last chapter, the fulfilment of this task was directly connected with the current activity of the Christ. This action by Rudolf Steiner therefore belonged to the decisive building stones of future Christianity, an action that he carried out in the pure service to Christ.

In the centre of all of Rudolf Steiner's karma deliberations—as a further result of the Mystery of Golgotha (fulfilled by him at the Turning Point of Time) and like a radiant background to the whole theme of his spirit-research—stands the essential fact that Christ assumes a new office in the cosmos, a function beginning in our time. He becomes Lord of humanity's karma.

This new activity of the Christ, described in detail on many different occasions, first had to be introduced to humanity as a cognitive fact so as to bring it about that at least a small portion of humanity (namely anthroposophists) can consciously participate in this Mystery that will unfold until the end of Earth evolution. 'In truth this is something that begins in the twentieth century and will continue on until the end of the Earth. The judgement begins starting in our twentieth century, meaning the ordering of karma.' (GA 130, 2 December 1911.) And in the fulfilment of this task, the Christ will increasingly count on the free and conscious cooperation of human beings.

At this point an important question arises: How do the starting point of freedom introduced in *The Philosophy of Freedom* and the law of karma relate to one another? On the whole, Rudolf Steiner pointed out and explained in many passages of his work that the ideas of human freedom and karma do not contradict each other inasmuch as both originate from the sources of Christian esotericism.[181] One aspect, but in a certain regard a decisive one in this linkage, must here be mentioned because the above-posed question can be answered from it, not just generally but quite concretely by determining a direct relationship between *The Philosophy of Freedom* and the activity of karma when it is understood and carried out in the light of the Christ Impulse.

In the lecture of 15 September 1922 (GA 215), Rudolf Steiner describes how, during man's earthly life concerning his own moral fibre and actions, an unvarnished judgement is continually formed in the half-conscious depths of feelings and particularly in the unconscious regions of the will. Out of this evaluation of man that takes its course unconsciously and contains the whole moral content of his life, a sort of spiritual being arises directly following death. Rudolf Steiner calls it 'a moral-spiritual value-being [German: *Wertwesenheit*]'. (GA 25, Chap. X.) This newly originating being (which at the same time bears within itself man's 'destiny-seed') has a natural affinity to the Moon-sphere, out of which the first connection of the earthly karma with the spiritual world is formed after death.[182]

Following the time in Kamaloka, the human being must ascend into the purely spiritual world, and hence depart from the Moon-sphere. For it is only in the spiritual regions that, ascending beyond the Sun-sphere, one can prepare one's karma and specifically form a cosmic seed for the future physical body on earth. In order to rise into these higher regions of the spiritual world, first the separation from the above-depicted karma-being has to take place. Not until liberation from moral burden does the further journey between two incarnations become possible in the first place for the human being. Only at the end of one's cosmic path, directly prior to birth on the earth, one must once again unite anew with this moral-spiritual destiny-being, and thus with all the consequences of one's earlier earth-karma.

The afore-mentioned separation from this moral 'value-being' could never be carried out on one's own since time immemorial. In order to accomplish this, one was in need of higher assistance at this point of one's journey after death. In pre-Christian times, such help came out of the

Sun-region from that entity that later appeared on earth at the Turning Point of Time as the Christ. With this help, the separation from the 'destiny-being' was possible, but only in a way where the exalted Sun-impulse did not yet extend to the next incarnation. As a result, the reunion with the 'destiny-being' occurred as an iron necessity to which the soul was pushed prior to being born on earth, as if due to a cosmic sense of duty. This is why the soul experienced the destiny (karma) that burdened it in earthly life as a misfortune that could not be changed with human powers. In ancient Greece this was artistically presented in an especially descriptive form (in the Orient one experienced this even more strongly). In Oedipus we have a classic example of the desperate attempt by human beings to struggle against their fate, something that ultimately ended in defeat. And likewise in the two non-Christian monotheistic religions Judaism and Islam, one can for this reason find to this day the predominance of the Mosaic law and inexorable divine will over man. The connection of these two religions with the Moon impulse points also to that direction.

In the above-mentioned lecture, Rudolf Steiner furthermore points out how, with the appearance of the Christ on earth (and above all through his union with mankind through the Mystery of Golgotha), a decisive change had taken place in this cosmic-earthly process. It consists of the fact that a human being, who in his former incarnation has acquired a deeper relationship to the Christ Impulse and the Mystery of Golgotha, thereby now receives the strength to separate himself in the Moon-sphere in a quite different form from his moral-spiritual 'value-being' than was the case in pre-Christian times. For connected to the Christ-power, such a human soul can shape its after-death passage through the spheres of the planets and fixed stars in such a manner that, at the end of this journey during its second sojourn in the Moon-sphere, the union with the 'destiny-being' can be carried out in a new and completely *free* way.

Rudolf Steiner says that, with the Christ-power in the soul, 'the [human being] breaks away from the Moon-sphere by such means that he can now work in the starry spheres in a way that allows him [upon his return to the Moon-sphere where his destiny-seed meets him in a *free* manner] to integrate himself in a *free* spirit-action with this destiny-seed' (GA 215, 15 September 1922). The deeper and more intense a man's relationship to the Christ Impulse becomes with the aid of spiritual science, the freer and more consciously will he unite each time with his 'destiny-seed' or the moral-spiritual 'destiny being' in order, therewith, to develop more and more on earth into a co-worker of the Christ in the field of karma. A person who carries the Christ Impulse in the soul can feel certain even before being born here on earth: 'World evolution can only take its course in the right way if we humans integrate this, our destiny-seed and take what we have prepared as our destiny and straighten it out once again in the compensating future earth life' (ibid.).

More still, only two months later Rudolf Steiner describes in an additional lecture how in our age we encounter two beings in the spiritual world directly prior to birth: the presently leading Time Spirit Michael, and the Christ Himself. A comparison of the two lectures shows that this encounter can only be comprehended as a consequence of one's *free* connection with one's own destiny-seed. Above all, in the last moment when the etheric body is already fully developed but its linkage with the physical genome has not yet taken place, the human being experiences this encounter which Rudolf Steiner describes as follows: 'Michael carries the light of spiritual cognition up front, as it were. At the rear, the Christ bears the requirements of general love for humanity.' (GA 218, 19 November 1922.) Through this encounter man becomes willing not only to unite freely with his destiny-being, and therewith to accept and carry out his own karma on earth, but he will moreover be willing to shoulder the karma of other human beings, something that in the future perspective will lead even to the sacrifice of one's own body, prepared as it had been out of the cosmos. Rudolf Steiner describes how a person will then voluntarily give up his body to his fellow human being directly prior to the birth of the latter (ibid.). It follows from this that we have here the fount for the development of a new karmic direction that links up directly with Michael-Christ and later on will bring about a new and quite *free* development of karma.

The above-described possibility 'to unite one's own destiny or karma with one's evolving being in an independent manner' (GA 215, 15 September 1922), which means not as a duty imposed by higher powers, still has a further decisive consequence for the following earthly life. According to Rudolf Steiner, the consequence of this 'free spiritual deed' that was carried out prior to birth in the light of the Christ is the most intensively experienced freedom in the coming earth life. 'And the earthly replica of this deed, carried out as it was in the supersensible realm, becomes *human freedom* in the subsequent earthy existence' (ibid.). Having expressed these significant words, Rudolf Steiner then makes a direct reference to his *Philosophy of Freedom*: 'A proper comprehension of the idea of destiny and tracing it all the way into the spiritual worlds does not establish a philosophy of determination but a true philosophy of freedom as I had to put forward in the nineties of the last century in my book *The Philosophy of Freedom*' (ibid.). These words refer to the esoteric foundations of this book that consist in the connection of the freedom-experiences (depicted in the book) with the Christ Impulse, as well as the free spiritual deed (carried out by the soul) directly prior to its incarnation on earth in the spiritual world.

What has been said throws quite a new light on the dispute Rudolf Steiner conducts at the end of Chapter IX with Immanuel Kant. To the homage of duty by Kant from the first part of *Critique of Practical Reason*, Rudolf Steiner holds up his own homage of freedom: 'Freedom! Thou kindly and human name, thou that dost comprise all that is morally most lovable, all that my manhood most prizes ...' (GA 4.). Then Rudolf Steiner defines the difference between his position and the Kantian one as follows: 'This is the contrast between a morality based on mere law and one based on free morality' (ibid.).

The deeper reasons for this polarity follow from what was said above. Kant belonged among those human beings who, from their earlier incarnation, brought along the Christ Impulse into after-death existence least of all. Therefore, prior to their next life on earth, they experienced the union with the 'destiny-seed' purely as a compelling necessity. After the fact, Kant experienced this union, which had remained unconscious to him, as a most arduous duty and tried with all means available to him to exalt it on earth. From this, the dualistic character of Kant's philosophy likewise becomes understandable. For his union with the 'destiny-seed' occurred involuntarily and therefore remained largely foreign to him. This is why he tried unconsciously to repress this seed of his being to an unattainable world beyond where, as 'the thing in itself', it remains eternally separated from the cognitive forces of man. In this way, Kant bore his own 'destiny-seed' within himself as an alien being, and while he remained connected to it against his will he constantly had to consider it to be lying beyond the limitations of cognition.[183]

In contrast to Kant, Rudolf Steiner could engage in the union with his 'destiny-seed' in full freedom based on the deepest unity with the Christ Impulse prior to his last incarnation. He was therefore able to attain on earth to the most powerful experience of freedom on the basis of which *The Philosophy of Freedom* originated as the most Christian philosophy of the modern age. 'It went ... without saying that on the one side I tried to write the *Philosophy of Freedom* ... On the other side, however, it was primarily the Mystery of Golgotha that had to be revealed ... These two matters simply belong together.' (GA 212, 7 May 1922.) In this way, Rudolf Steiner can be the greatest example for us of such a union with one's own 'destiny-seed'. Due to the fact that he had carried out this union in the prenatal realm in the light of the Christ freely and in full awareness, he was prepared thereby to fulfil his main task in his life on earth: he could pass on to humanity the mighty revelations of karma that are designated to form the foundation for the activity of the Christ as Lord of Karma.

In this manner, the philosophy of freedom that Rudolf Steiner conceived in his youth and the knowledge of karma he proclaimed at the end of his life are inseparably linked with each other.[184] For they stem from the same source in the supersensible out of which flow those forces into the human soul that make possible for it a conscious encounter with Michael and the Christ prior to earthly incarnation.

In the previous chapter it was pointed out how, at the summit of its after-death journey, the human soul is illuminated by the Holy Spirit during the Midnight Hour. And when the soul moreover brings along a deepened relationship to the Christ Impulse out of the last incarnation, this impulse strengthens the soul's connection with the Holy Spirit to such a degree that it can take its effectiveness along to earthly birth, and moreover into the life on earth. This strengthened presence of the Holy Spirit in the human soul brings about a completely free union with one's own 'destiny-seed', and as a result the conscious encounter with the 'light of Michael and the love of the Christ'. (GA 218, 19 November 1922.) These two prenatal experiences bring it about that the human being can arrive on the one hand at the experience of freedom in the sense of the Michael age[185] and on the other to perception of the Christ in the etheric realm.[186]

This is why we discover in the earthly life of Rudolf Steiner—who probably participated in these two prenatal experiences the most strongly (and therefore could report about them[187])—their two main effects: the establishment of human freedom entirely in the Michaelic sense in his early work, and the proclamation of the etheric Second Coming of the Christ as the central message of anthroposophy. Both tasks are intimately linked with one another and are a direct result of the activity of the Holy Spirit in the human being. Strengthened by the Christ Impulse in the spiritual world, the Holy Spirit can thereby cross over the threshold of birth so as to continue being active in man even on earth as the true Spirit of Freedom. Then such a person can say: 'On the one side I can therefore take my stand totally on the basis of freedom but on the other side upon the foundation of the Christ-fact.' (GA 212, 7 May 1922.) For freedom and the Christ Impulse form an inseparable unity through the illumination with the Holy Spirit.

Moreover, this statement affirms that Rudolf Steiner experienced the above-described encounter with Michael and Christ prior to his birth in a particularly intense and conscious manner in order to establish human freedom subsequently on this basis in such a way that the forces of 'Michael-Christ'[188] can be directly active in it. For pure thinking (as written about in the first part of *The Philosophy of Freedom*) leads in its continuation and further amplification into the spiritual world so that 'the light of spiritual cognition', which Michael brings to man in the prenatal sphere, can radiate forth anew. In the earthly deeds, which in accordance with the second part of *The Philosophy of Freedom* are enacted purely out of 'love for the object', 'the general love of humanity' newly lights up, the love that human beings are called up to practise by the Christ in prenatal existence. (GA 218, 19 November 1922.)

Only on his own and in full freedom can man work his way up to pure thinking and deeds of love. This is why, as a result of having lived *The Philosophy of Freedom* and as the crowning point of this book's spirit-path, a *free* encounter with Michael and Christ takes place, now no longer in the prenatal sphere but on the earth itself—even though in supersensible form. This is moreover the reason why what in the first and second part of *The Philosophy of Freedom* was initially contained only in concealed form became a manifest fact in Rudolf Steiner's life in his spiritual biography.[189]

In the earlier quoted lecture of 15 September 1922, Rudolf Steiner describes yet another consequence of the free union on the part of the human soul with its 'destiny-seed'. By means of this union, the soul can furthermore remember its passage through the additional starry worlds in the accompaniment of the Christ in its coming earth life as an all-encompassing feeling of connectedness with God. Rudolf Steiner describes this consequence in the following words: 'By experiencing the Christ in himself, modern man can sense the freedom and, in connection with that freedom, likewise the feeling of permeation with God ... something that can be a reflection of what is experienced during the passage through the starry world to the Moon-sphere and in this sphere.' (GA 215, 15 September 1922.)

During their passage through the starry world, all human beings can only grasp a portion of that world with their consciousness.[190] When we undergo this journey with the Christ Impulse in our soul, however, we constantly live with the feeling of complete God-permeation, hence in the constant union with the whole. And if one tries subsequently to recall this lofty spiritual condition on earth, one can hardly formulate it any better than in the following words from the concluding part of *The Philosophy of Freedom*: 'Every man embraces in his thinking only a part of the total world of ideas, and to that extent individuals differ even in the actual content of their thinking. But all these contents are within a self-contained whole, which embraces the thought contents of all men. Hence in thinking, every person lays hold of the *universal primordial Being* which pervades all humans. To live in reality, filled with the content of thought, is at the same time to *live in God*.' (GA 4, third part.)

Based on this fundamental experience that on earth *all* human beings partake of the same world of ideas (the world that is revealed outwardly as the starry sky), the heavens that human beings traverse in the time between death and a new birth and where they directly experience the 'universal primordial Being which pervades all men', on this is founded the community-building impulse of *The Philosophy of Freedom*.

Considered from the esoteric viewpoint, the 'community of free spirits' described in this book is moreover the one in which, based on complete freedom, human beings can work on their common karma in the sense of the Christ Impulse. In his anthroposophical lectures, Rudolf Steiner calls such a community 'the foundation [Ger.: *Stiftung*] structured on the "I"-nature of the humanity of the future' (GA 123, 11 September 1910), and describes it as follows: 'Due to the fact that the threads of individuals are woven into the karma of the whole community, a net is woven. Through what the Christ has brought down from the heights, this net in its characteristic is intended to be a replica of the order in the heavens. This means that, according to the order of the spiritual world, the karma of the individual is to be united with overall karma, not in an arbitrary sense but in such a way that the community-organism is meant to become a replica of the order in the heavens.' (Ibid.) This new faculty to shape the karmic relationships between human beings as a replica of the order in the heavens is the direct consequence of the soul's passage through the starry world in the accompaniment of the Christ as well, as the freely entered-into union with the 'destiny-seed' immediately prior to earthly birth. For, as has already been shown, both human freedom and the possibility to work on earth freely on one's karma originate out of the same spiritual fount.

Here lies the basis for a new community of human beings ('the humanity of the future'), who based on complete freedom and insight into their karmic connections can secure the work on their common karma in accordance with the Christ as Lord of Karma, for karma works only among humans. This is the reason why work on such karma demands a specific community of human beings, not merely in general but in a concrete earthly form. For this reason Rudolf Steiner speaks in the karma lectures not only about the karma of the anthroposophical movement but above all quite decidedly about the karma of the *Anthroposophical Society* that in fact actually exists here on earth.

To become co-worker of the Christ in this area, such a community primarily needs two faculties that Rudolf Steiner refers to in connection with his *Philosophy of Freedom*: the development of *intuitive thinking* as guarantee of individual freedom, and *trust* in the interhuman relationships (see GA 335, 15 June 1920). In *The Philosophy of Freedom* Rudolf Steiner expresses himself in regard to trust in the following words: 'A free man lives with the trust that the other free man belongs (together with him) to a spiritual world, and in his intentions will harmonize with him.' From the esoteric standpoint it is indeed so. In the Midnight Hour, all souls are illuminated by *one* Holy Spirit and then experience together the starry world (which is enfilled out of the power of the Christ Impulse by the creative thoughts of the hierarchies) as a unity.[191] Out of this experience springs the wondrous inner certainty on earth that Rudolf Steiner addresses when he writes that in *his intentions* the free person will always encounter the other free person. What such free intentions are here on earth is the awareness in the starry world of one's own karma and how it is woven together by the higher hierarchies with the karma of other human beings, and the free decision to continue to work further on this karma (the voluntary connection with one's own 'destiny-seed'). Because of this decision spiritual strength streams on earth towards the individual, strength that enables him in the future to take upon himself in full freedom the karma of other people and to help in bearing it.[192]

In the Gospel of John, Christ Himself offers the greatest example. He states in the farewell discourse: 'No man can have greater love than this, that he offer up his life for his friends.' (John 15:13; JM.) In the Russian translation of this passage, instead of the word 'life' it says 'soul', something that points even more accurately to the secret of taking karma upon oneself. For this is only possible through offering up one's own soul forces. But what signifies the full realization of these words was shown by Christ Himself in the Mystery of Golgotha and His subsequent union with the karma of all of humanity.

What Christ accomplished on the divine level was realized by Rudolf Steiner on the human level through his complete union (all the way to his own karma) with the Anthroposophical Society at the Christmas Conference.[193] With this sacrifice that he decided on, based on full *freedom* of his intuitive thinking and out of boundless *trust* in the members, he could set the highest example of the realization of his *Philosophy of Freedom*.[194]

Concurrently with the Christmas Conference, Rudolf Steiner took the first step for forming the above-described new community. For that purpose he gave this new community the mighty karma-insights as well as the supersensible Foundation Stone that originates out of the same spiritual world adjacent to the earth where, prior to birth, man's union with his or her 'destiny-seed' takes place, as well as the encounter following from the one with Michael and Christ. On this Foundation Stone of Love as the spiritual fount of the community-building forces of the General Anthroposophical Society, this new community is to stand without faltering. Only then will it remain true to its Christian–Michaelic karma in order to continue working on this karma in full freedom in accordance with the Christ as Lord of Karma.

14. *The Philosophy of Freedom* and the Modern Science of the Grail

Rudolf Steiner characterizes the content of his main anthroposophical book *Occult Science, an Outline* as the 'science of the Grail'. Here, based on what has already been depicted in this work, the question comes up concerning the relationship of such a science of the Grail to *The Philosophy of Freedom*.

So as to answer this question, one first has to call to mind that the true Mysteries of the Grail are to be found today only in the spiritual world adjacent to the earth and Rudolf Steiner points this out in the following words: 'Now, one who wanted to find the way ... to the Holy Grail had to know how to tread spiritual paths' (GA 233, 31 December 1923). In another passage, Rudolf Steiner designates the temple of the Grail as a 'spiritual temple' that cannot be found on earth. For this reason, an individual who approaches the Grail Mysteries today with modern faculties of cognition has to liberate them above all from any influence coming from an individual's corporeal organization. Otherwise these Mysteries cannot be approached at all.

Here, the same thing applies that was stated already in Chapter 11 about the relationship of the true Rosicrucians to Michael. It is not without reason that Rudolf Steiner also points out that they had become the spiritual heirs to the Grail Mysteries during the transition to the modern age.[195] Even as a Grail seeker in the early Middle Ages had to ennoble his soul forces, which meant freeing them from all earthly-bodily impressions and dependencies, so in the epoch of the consciousness soul the forces of cognition must be spiritualized and liberated in a similar way from the bodily organization and sense impressions. This is precisely the path to pure or sense-free thinking that is described in the first part of *The Philosophy of Freedom*. This is why the path to intuitive thinking outlined in it is at the same time the beginning of the modern path to the Grail Mysteries. The exceptional state here represents the portal through which one can enter into the world of imaginations fully conscious and freely in order, there, to find and go into the Grail temple.

The second part of *The Philosophy of Freedom* describes the deeds which man as a free being can carry out based on his cognizing 'I', deeds in which love for the action appears as the main motif. In the further development of the faculty of moral intuition, such deeds can lead a person to become capable of working on earth based on his or her own initiative out of the Grail's nature in full freedom. For the content of the Grail chalice is the substance of love out of which one tries to act in accordance with *The Philosophy of Freedom*. And because the all-embracing law holds sway in the spiritual world that like always strives for like, one who acts on earth purely out of love for the object sooner or later comes into contact with the Grail Mysteries. Then, one's matured moral intuition can glean the impulses towards action in the spiritual world directly out of the Grail chalice. Such an individual will subsequently be active on earth as a messenger of the Grail temple without consciously (meaning clairvoyantly) having to be present in it.

One could likewise say: The *sense-free thinking* (as characterized by Rudolf Steiner in *The Philosophy of Freedom*) is at the same time the path to the supersensible Grail temple, and the subsequently following deeds of *love* lead to the realization of the Grail impulse on earth. For only a person with pure thinking, who at the same time acts out of unselfish love which fills his heart, can become a true knight of the Grail—however not in the ancient sense but solely in the way it corresponds to the consciousness soul, meaning out of fully experienced freedom. This is why the actualization of the content of *The Philosophy of Freedom* flows directly into the science of the Grail.

This connection can be even more accurately traced by means of *The Philosophy of Freedom*. As we have seen, in its ninth chapter the two paths are described that attain their culmination correspondingly in 'pure thinking' and 'conceptual intuition' and then unite in an inseparable union. These two attributes are the most important prerequisites for drawing closer to the reality of the Grail on the modern path of cognition (or knowledge).

In the Grail legends, particularly by Chrestien de Troyes, the sacred chalice is always borne by a young maiden (Ger.: *Jungfrau*] during the Grail service.[196] Rudolf Steiner confirms this fact based on his spirit-research. 'Then a young maiden entered with a golden chalice. Out of it radiated such a light that it outshone all the lights of the hall' (GA 148, 6 January 1914). Here in this event, the young maiden represents the forces of the Sophia or Cosmic Wisdom. She possesses above all two characteristics: inner purity and the direct relationship to the spiritual world's content of wisdom that come to expression in the main colours of the Sophia, *white* and *gold*. This is why in the case of the 'gesture of cognition' of the eurythmy-figure Rudolf Steiner assigns these two Sophia-colours: the white garment and the golden veil.

In pursuing the path of *The Philosophy of Freedom*, we can develop these

two Sophia-qualities in a quite modern form: the first quality through the
purification of our cognitive forces, that is through attaining their full
independence from the physical body and its sensory influences. This
corresponds to the level of *pure thinking* with which we can then delve
into the spiritual world's content of wisdom through *conceptual intuition* so
as to fetch from that wisdom-content the moral impulses for our actions.
In the imagination of the Grail, these two qualities that pass over into each
other are like the two hands with which the young maiden carries the
sacred chalice.

In accordance with Diagram 25, on p. 158, what has been said can be
depicted as follows:

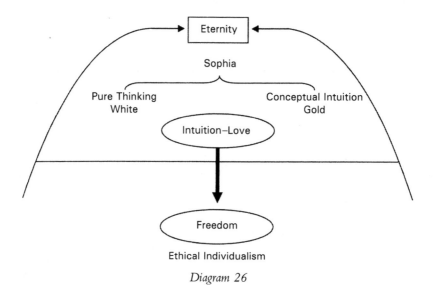

Diagram 26

After this preparatory stage has been reached, there comes the actual
connection with the Grail. One can discover this in *The Philosophy of
Freedom* if one meticulously seeks in it for the application of the term
'love'. For spiritual love, the only kind of love referred to in this book,
always has an essential living relationship to the content of the sacred
vessel—the chalice that bears in itself the eternal 'I' of man that can only
be recognized and grasped in intuition which in turn consists of love.

The word 'love' occurs in the book in three passages. (The following
passages are not quoted in chronological sequence but traced according to
their inner reference.) First, in defining the good deeds of man, mention is
made of the 'intuition immersed in *love*'. With this, a spiritual process is
referred to in which the thought-intuition of man consciously immerses

itself into the pure substance of love and by doing so rises to the *moral* intuition. For love is the main source of every kind of morality in the spiritual world. As a result man can experience his 'active thinking' as consisting of pure spiritual love; this thinking is now fully pervaded by the 'force of *love* in a spiritual way'. This is the second reference to love that occurs in one of the additions of 1918. This word occurs a third time when mention is made of how man, having absolved this inner process, continues on to his actions in the outer world. But these can only be designated as free when they have been carried out based on 'love for the object', meaning out of 'love for the deed'.

Altogether we have three stages, one following upon the other:

immersion of intuition into love;
experiencing thinking as consisting of love;
acting out of love for the deed.

Although not expressed exactly in these words, modern man's Grail initiation occurs in this way, but this initiation likewise consists of three stages. On the first stage, the love-immersed intuition finds the sacred chalice in the spiritual world adjacent to the earth. For 'in intuitively experienced thinking, man is placed into a spiritual world also as a cognizing being' (GA 4). The Grail is accessible to such spiritual cognition as well. On the second stage, this experiencing of the inner nature of thinking as consisting of pure love leads to spiritual communion. This can be comprehended as follows. As early as seven years prior to the publication of the *Philosophy of Freedom,* in his introductions to Goethe's natural-scientific Writings, Rudolf Steiner clearly brought this direction of his thinking to expression in the epochal sentence: '*Becoming aware of the idea in reality is the true communion of man.*' Commenting on these words he continued on: 'In regard to ideas, thinking has the same significance as the eye has to light ... *It is an organ of conception* (GA 1; emphasis by Rudolf Steiner). It is hardly necessary here to mention that 'idea' does not refer to the shadowy dead thoughts of the human brain (with which of course no communion is possible) but the idea-beings of the spiritual world, which are to be grasped in a body-free state.

The second step consists of immersing oneself into love with an intuition attained in accordance with *The Philosophy of Freedom,* thus experiencing the inner nature of thinking as consisting of pure spiritual love, and at the same time utilizing it as a supersensible organ of cognition. Then this *organ, consisting* as it does *of love,* will in the objective spiritual world cognize only those objects which are akin to it, meaning those like it consist of love, that is to say bear the love-substance within themselves.

Such an 'object' is the Grail in the spiritual world, which is filled with the love-substance of the Christ Being's Cosmic 'I'! And with the Grail, in a new fully conscious, free manner, the purely spiritual communion now takes place.

From what has been said it likewise becomes understandable why Rudolf Steiner could arrive at the contents of *The Philosophy of Freedom* by means of his work on Goethe's natural-scientific works. Especially in Goethe there lived—although for him largely in an unconscious manner—a genuine Grail mood, an attitude which for all this penetrated his creative work from within that much more intensely. 'Goethe dwelled in this Grail mood, even though in the dimmest forces of his awareness. Try to discover this Grail mood; you will find it everywhere [in his work].' (GA 185, 3 November 1918.) This Grail mood is characterized by Rudolf Steiner in the same lecture as follows: 'This whole Grail mood is one of bringing about a connection between the most intimate nature of the human soul, where the consciousness soul awakens, and the spiritual worlds. If I may say so, it is the striving to lift up the sense-perceptible world into the spiritual world in a man-made manner.' (Ibid.)

This awakening of the consciousness soul in Goethe's case is connected with the elaboration of his natural science (GA 26, 14 December 1924). This is why this Grail mood lives above all in his natural-scientific writings in which a decisive step was undertaken towards the new connection of nature with the spiritual. On this basis Rudolf Steiner could elaborate further at the end of the nineteenth century. This was something that led to the establishment of the Goetheanum in which the sense-perceptible world was newly linked to the spiritual world in the full light of the consciousness soul.

A further aspect of the Grail search belongs to the next step, a step that directly links up to the preceding process. It consists of 'causing this Grail striving ... everywhere to tend towards the individual element, both in the ethical domain and the scientific field. This is a striving that above all wishes to focus on individual persons and their development.' (GA 185, 3 November 1918.) Immediately following this utterance, Rudolf Steiner outlines how this individualism already penetrates the natural-scientific writings of Goethe and subsequently 'can culminate only in a philosophy of freedom' (ibid.). With this statement, Rudolf Steiner personally connects the modern Grail search with the whole character of his *Philosophy of Freedom*. And this is why he can later say about this book: 'This is why my *Philosophy of Freedom* has been called the philosophy of individualism in the most extreme sense. It indeed had to be because on the other side it is *the most Christian of the philosophies*.' (GA 212, 7 May 1922.)

It must also be noted here that the words by Rudolf Steiner quoted above regarding the 'Grail mood' or 'Grail striving' are contained in a lecture cycle in which, just a week earlier on the occasion of the new edition of *The Philosophy of Freedom*, he had dedicated a whole lecture to this book (27 October 1918). In this new edition, he moreover had added to the original text the decisive important addendums, which in their way once again document the relationship of the Grail theme to his book.

We thus have in these depictions a quite special path to the Grail. It begins with Goethe's natural-scientific writings and continues in Goetheanism in order then to find in the end its higher elaboration in *The Philosophy of Freedom*. One can also say: What remained in Goethe still in the unconscious or lowest forces of his consciousness was placed through Rudolf Steiner into the full light of cognition and therefore grasped by the higher forces of the consciousness soul. From a later comment by Rudolf Steiner one can conclude that the impulse that guided him to this path was at the same time the inner call by humanity which, with the beginning of the Michaelic age, could be heard increasingly. 'For when we understand the true innermost call of humanity; we are still seekers after the Holy Grail and ought to be such seekers after the Holy Grail.' (GA 204, 16 April 1921.)

This call was heard by the young Rudolf Steiner in his soul, and from then on he became a modern Grail seeker. He first searched where the paths might be in contemporary culture for the fulfilment of this call. Thus he came upon Goethe and his natural-scientific writings and then, following the establishment of Goetheanism, to *The Philosophy of Freedom* in which his inner Grail striving became expressed most clearly. The consistent and unceasing pursuit of this path brought him around the turn of the century to his Grail experience as the crowning point of this whole development. With that, what had been laid out more philosophically in *The Philosophy of Freedom* thus found complete fulfilment in life. This happened because Rudolf Steiner did not find access to Christianity through some sort of association with outward traditions, beliefs or denominations, but directly in the spiritual world itself. For what was of significance to him 'was not what human beings did or said [in regard to Christ] but what the soul experiences if it just surrendered devotedly to what occurred supersensibly in the continuing effects of the Christ Impulse' (GA 148, 1 June 1914). These words correspond exactly to the following autobiographical account in *The Course of My Life*: 'Nowhere in the denominations could I find the Christianity I had to search for [the Grail Christianity]. I had to ... immerse myself on my own in Christianity, that is to say in that world in which the spiritual speaks about it.'

(GA 28, Chap. XXVI.) The fact that the 'spiritually having stood before the Mystery of Golgotha' (ibid.) that followed from this also signified that the fully valid Grail initiation was already depicted elsewhere in detail.[197]

The path of the Grail search in the life of Rudolf Steiner can be summed up as follows:

Goethe's natural science	→	Goetheanism	→	*The Philosophy Freedom*	→	Grail initiation around the turn of the century	→	Establishment of the science of the Grail or anthroposophy

Diagram 27

★

Our depiction would remain incomplete if at this point a certain danger would not also be indicated that proceeds from an occult stream which consciously works in opposition to the above-described Grail search. As was mentioned before, in Goetheanism (and particularly in the Grail science that builds on it) the spiritualization of the sensory that is being lifted up into the spiritual world is striven for as the highest goal of humanity's evolution. Against it, the aforementioned occult stream attempts to chain the spiritual, alienating it from its true nature, to matter. This stream is Jesuitism. 'This is the reason'—says Rudolf Steiner—'for the eternal enmity that Jesuitism has sworn and will ever more swear against Goetheanism.' (GA 185, 2 November 1918.) Yet a still greater enmity is being raised from this direction against *The Philosophy of Freedom*, for in it the modern Grail impulse is linked inseparably with the nature of freedom. This freedom, originating as it does in the Christ Light, is loathed the most by this occult order, because this freedom's victory in mankind will signify the end of Jesuitism's power over human souls.

In two instances Rudolf Steiner expressed himself in more detail concerning the ominous elements contained in the occult exercises of the Jesuits, exercises that are directed against any kind of freedom: in the first lecture of the cycle *From Jesus to Christ*, in which he communicates the most significant results of his spirit-research concerning the nature of the resurrection of Christ; and in the lecture cycle *From Symptom to Reality in Modern History* (2 November 1918) given on the occasion of the new edition of *The Philosophy of Freedom*, where he deals with the relationship of the Grail impulse to Goetheanism and therefore to this book.[198] In both cases Rudolf Steiner felt inwardly obligated to refer to the opposite stream out of which one fought and fights the most powerfully against anthroposophy as the science of the Grail and resurrection.[199] For in the spiritual life of modern humanity there exists no greater polarity than the blind obedience of the Jesuits and the ethical individualism of *The Philosophy of Freedom*.[200]

★

It follows from the overall presentation of this work that the Christ Impulse will work today (and increasingly in the future) through the direction that proceeds from *The Philosophy of Freedom* and continues on in anthroposophy. This is why the actual future of Christianity on earth is rooted in *ethical individualism*. For it relies on the direct presence of the Christ Impulse in every human soul, which for this reason no longer requires any outward 'mediation' in its relationship with that impulse. Instead, the soul can unite on its own with the content of the Grail vessel on the path of the new Christian Mysteries in full freedom.

In this sense the following words by Rudolf Steiner can be understood as a direct reference to the spiritual seeds of the Grail science in *The Philosophy of Freedom*: 'There appears what is depicted in the second part of my *Philosophy of Freedom*, namely ethical individualism which now actually builds on the Christ Impulse in man—even though this is not expressed [in such words] in my *Philosophy of Freedom*' (GA 74, 24 May 1920). When *this* ethical individualism rises up to actual freedom—for 'freedom in human actions is only possible from the standpoint of ethical individualism' (GA 4)—it then becomes the wellspring of spiritual love in human life. Then there originate in the soul of man all the 'moral ideals' out of the 'power of spiritual love'. (GA 74, 24 May 1920.) In the spiritual world, the highest wellspring of spiritual love—and with that all moral ideals—is the Holy Grail out of which man can gain the individual moral ideals by virtue of his moral imagination, in order then to actualize them in his deeds of love on earth.

★

Two further motifs link *The Philosophy of Freedom* with the science of the Grail: the motif of the 'I' and the motif of immortality. Concerning the Grail Mystery, Rudolf Steiner himself says in this regard: 'In the beginning was the Mystery of the higher human "I"; in the Grail it was preserved; with the Grail it remained connected, and in the Grail lives the "I" that is connected with the eternal and immortal just as the lower "I" is with the temporary and mortal' (GA 112, 24 June 1909). In accord with *The Philosophy of Freedom,* this transition from the lower to the higher 'I' can be described as follows.

The 'I' of man which in thinking 'touches world affairs at one corner' arrives through observation of them at the path that leads to the conscious grasp of its eternal and immortal essence. At the same time, this signifies the step from the ordinary (lower) 'I' to the higher one that Rudolf Steiner designates in *The Philosophy of Freedom* as the real 'I' of man. 'The real "I" is positioned within thinking's very own nature, but "I"-consciousness is not.' The ' "I" ... is therefore to be found [only] within thinking'. This is why the thinking that in the exceptional state can observe itself—something that contains a genuine meditative process—is in a position to discover the higher 'I' that stands in the midst of world affairs.

The following words by Rudolf Steiner from his lecture, 'Philosophy and Anthroposophy', affirm that we are in fact dealing with the higher 'I', which can only be grasped by man in *pure thinking*: 'Thinking does not verify the reality of the "I". But it is equally certain that the true "I" cannot be experienced through anything else except pure thinking. Indeed, the *actual "I"* extends into pure thinking, and for ordinary human consciousness only into this.'[201] (GA 35, 17 August 1908.) Based on the direct contrast brought up between the real 'I' and 'I'-consciousness, it also follows from the context of the above-quoted passage in the book that it is not the lower 'I' (which is dependent on the physical body) that is referred to here, and that we normally identify with the 'I'-consciousness that comes into being through the corporeal organization, but the higher 'I', which lives independently of the body and therefore can only be grasped in pure (sense-free) thinking through the conceptual intuition.[202]

Rudolf Steiner himself made the first contact with his higher 'I' at the age of 19. In a letter to a friend, he describes this experience in the following moving words: 'It was the night from 10 to 11 January in which I did not sleep even one wink. I had occupied myself with several philosophical problems until about 12.30 a.m. when I finally stretched out on my bed. My intention was to explore the previous year and whether there was truth in what Schelling says: "In every one of us dwells a mysterious wondrous ability to withdraw from all the vicissitudes of time into our innermost self, denuded of all that was added from outside, and there, under the sway of the immutable, to behold the eternal in us." I believed, and believe even now, to have quite clearly discovered that innermost ability in me ... what does a sleepless night amount to as compared to such a discovery!' (GA 38, 13 January 1881.)

In this description, which ties in with the just quoted sentence by Schelling, the reference to the self ('I') that lives in man's innermost depths denuded of all that comes from outside is significant. In no way can this refer to the ordinary 'I' of the human being. This is moreover confirmed by the fact that that the comprehension of man's eternal source of being is connected with this self. For it is not the ordinary human 'I', entangled as it is in the most diverse relations with the outer world, but the higher 'I' which, independent of all sense impressions, transmits to us the experience of immortality through the revelation of our eternal being. This new capability to approach his higher 'I' was what the young Rudolf Steiner had discovered that night in himself. With it began his path as a Grail seeker. And this path led him twelve years later to the *Philosophy of Freedom*.

The above-mentioned experience was described in detail much later once more by Rudolf Steiner in his book *Occult Science, an Outline* (GA 13) in quite objective form. 'This is the first purely spiritual experience: The observation of a soul-spiritual "I"-being. This being has lifted itself as a new self out of the [ordinary] self that is only tied to the physical senses and physical reason.' In *The Philosophy of Freedom*, to grasp the spiritual reality of the actual 'I' in intuitive thinking corresponds to this experience.

Subsequent to such a birth of the actual or higher 'I' in the human being, there follows as the second task the bringing about of the right relationship between it and the ordinary (lower) 'I'. For that, a corresponding soul development is necessary. This takes its course mainly in two directions—the further improvement of thinking and the unfolding of the moral will. 'Just as it is the ruler in the thought-world, so the soul is moreover to become ruler in the region of the will' (GA 13). 'For the higher schooling, we human beings have to become accustomed sternly to obey *our own* commands' (ibid.), meaning only what we truly will to do based on the acquired insights.

In *The Philosophy of Freedom*, this working on one's self corresponds to the schooling of thinking to which the whole content of the book is dedicated, but particularly its first part. Then follows the overcoming of any dependence on the characterological predisposition and egoism, which on both paths are overcome based on Chapter IX of the second part, which likewise offers the direction for free deeds. And when, at the end, the two paths unite on the level of moral intuition, the basis is created to attain that condition which Rudolf Steiner characterizes in *Occult Science, an Outline* as follows: 'What he [the spirit disciple] is in his ordinary self . . . he must lead and guide by means of the new-born self.' This 'leading and guiding' of the ordinary 'I' on the part of one's higher 'I' is possible only through moral intuition.

On this path of awakening and inner unfolding of the higher 'I', the bringing about of its relationship to the objective spiritual world is considered to be the third stage. 'The second newly born "I" can now be led to perception in the spiritual world' (GA 13). This concluding stage already leads beyond the boundary that Rudolf Steiner intentionally set for his book, but all its contents point in this direction. This is why he could write in 1918: 'From the living comprehension of what is meant in this book by intuitive thinking, the subsequent entrance into the world of spiritual perception will quite naturally result' (GA 4). This only becomes possible because, already in exercising intuitive thinking, the first activity of the higher 'I' takes place in man. Otherwise intuitive thinking could never lead into the spiritual world, for in that world it is not the body-bound ordinary 'I' but only the higher 'I' that can live and work. This is why Rudolf Steiner writes: 'The spiritual world of perception, once experienced by man, cannot appear unfamiliar to him, because in intuitive thinking he already has an experience which is purely spiritual in character' (ibid.). Only those experiences are 'purely spiritual in character', however, which can be attained from the standpoint of the higher 'I'.

If the thought that is here expressed appears too unusual for the reader, namely that in his *Philosophy of Freedom* Rudolf Steiner has pointed out a spiritual path to the higher 'I' (even if still in a purely philosophical form), the following can be called to mind. In the lecture of 4 June 1906 (GA 35), Rudolf Steiner pointed out that Schiller in his 'Aesthetic Letters' had traced out this path from the lower to the higher 'I': 'A dogmatist of occultism may perhaps find nothing more in these "Letters" than the high-spirited speculations of a bright artistic mind. In reality, however, the attempt is being made in them to offer direction for a state of consciousness differing from the ordinary one. A stage on the path to the "higher self" is supposed to be described.' A still higher state of consciousness that is a more advanced stage on the way to the higher self than in Schiller's 'Aesthetic Letters' is depicted in *The Philosophy of Freedom*. One can even say that in a certain respect Rudolf Steiner later on picked up on this philosophical starting point by Schiller and brought it to a kind of 'culmination' in his book.[203]

It is moreover significant in this regard that in his lectures on the Philosophy of Thomas Aquinas, where he also refers to his debate over Kant, Rudolf Steiner likewise mentions Schiller at this point as his precursor to this conflict, and then states the following: 'Over against this philistine principle [of Kant's "duty"] that Schiller had already opposed— over against it one had to place the *philosophy of freedom*; the *transformed* *"I"* that has evolved upward into the sphere of spirituality, and up there in that sphere the *transformed "I"* begins to love virtue and therefore practises virtue because it loves virtue based on its own individuality.' (GA 74, 24 May 1920.)

Rudolf Steiner designates this 'transformed I' in *The Philosophy of Freedom* as man's 'actual I', probably in contrast to the ordinary (philistine) 'I' that is still fully body-bound, meaning dependent on its characterological predisposition and entangled in all its egoisms. Even though Rudolf Steiner (like Schiller in his *Letters*) does not make use of anthroposophical terminology in his book, it is clear from the expositions that one obviously deals here with the path to the higher 'I' that alone is able to endure '*up* in the sphere of spirituality'.

As quoted earlier (Chapter 2, p. 33), the existence of the spiritual world and the innermost 'I' of man that belongs to this spiritual world are designated by Rudolf Steiner as two 'fundamental points' that are made in his book. Following this, he says of these two basic facts of *The Philosophy of Freedom* that they are 'a sort of message from the spiritual world to more recent humanity' (GA 258, 11 June 1923). This is at the same time the message from man's 'eternal and immortal "I"' that stands in a connection with the spiritual world and is the only one that can carry out truly free deeds on earth. For only the higher 'I' of man possesses eternal character from the beginning. It passes through all the earth-incarnations and is immortal in this sense. This is why Rudolf Steiner states: 'In so far as human beings instinctively carry out deeds that are accomplished by their immortal human being, they perform free deeds.'[204] The word 'instinctive' in this regard points out that man can perform free deeds on earth (meaning already out of his higher 'I') even before he has himself fully awakened in it (The latter is then possible on the path of modern initiation.)

Rudolf Steiner additionally sums up this connection of freedom and immortality in regard to his *Philosophy of Freedom* as follows: 'The immortal man is a free man; the willing that derives out of immortality is a free one ... Man with his ordinary actions approaches these free actions. Mortal man is on the way to freedom.' With this, the true way to freedom is at the same time the way to the experience of the immortality of one's own 'I', which signifies the encounter with the higher 'I' which is capable of the conscious communion with the Grail.

What was mentioned here throws new light on the earlier quoted key words in *The Philosophy of Freedom*: 'We cannot, however, think out the concept of man to its conclusion without coming upon the *free spirit* as the purest expression of human nature' (GA 4, Chap. IX; emphasis by Rudolf Steiner). In this sentence, it is not without good reason that Rudolf Steiner emphasizes the words 'free spirit' which he uses here instead of 'free man'. For the spiritual in the human being is his higher 'I' (the 'immortal man' in the earthly man) which alone can act freely. This is why Rudolf Steiner says that mortal man (the ordinary 'I') can only be 'on the way to freedom'.

This path to freedom takes shape as follows. To the concept 'free spirit' man has to create the corresponding perception on his own through inner work on himself in order then to connect it with his own concept and thereby to become a free being in all reality. This path of self-transformation, which leads man to the conscious grasping of his inner-most and eternal essence of being out of which alone he can perform free actions in the world so as to fulfil his spiritual destiny on earth, is at the same time the modern path to the Grail that culminates in the spiritual communion with it.

Creating the perception of the free spirit signifies for man to take conscious hold of himself in his higher 'I' as a purely spiritual entity that is free and immortal—something that is possible only in connection with the Grail.

According to *Occult Science, an Outline*, the most important message of the science of the Grail consists in the reference to the future transfor-mation of the ancient Cosmos of Wisdom into the future Cosmos of Love (along with the gradual spiritualization of that cosmos). This only becomes possible because man's 'I' learns more and more to ray out love from itself as the highest creative force of the universe. Thus Rudolf Steiner writes: 'Everything that the 'I' can unfold within is supposed to turn into *love*' (GA 13; emphasis by Rudolf Steiner). Man attains to this love when, on the cognitive path, he takes the wisdom of the outer world into his 'I', which has become free so as to give birth anew to that wisdom as love.

Precisely this path is described in the two parts of *The Philosophy of Freedom*. In the first part, it is a matter of the living connection with the general thought-content of the world, meaning with the whole world-wisdom in intuitive thinking. This is why mention is made of the 'common primal being that penetrates all human beings' and which man can only 'grasp in his thinking'. In the second part, we deal with man's participation in the gradual coming about of the future cosmos through his free deeds of love, hence with the actualization of the 'highest ideal of human development' that proceeds out of the modern 'cognition of the Grail': the 'spiritualization that man attains *through his own work*' (GA 13). Rudolf Steiner laid the foundations for man's 'own work' in his *Philosophy of Freedom*.

★

In conclusion, still another aspect of *The Philosophy of Freedom* must be pointed out which links this book particularly with the main issue of our epoch, which in turn has a direct connection to Parzival's initiation. According to Rudolf Steiner, Parzival's initiation—the one of the consciousness soul—is exemplary for the entire post-Atlantean cultural epoch (GA 144, 7 February 1913). As is known, the ability to ask questions played a decisive role during Parzival's Grail search. 'Learning to ask questions implies advancement in humanity's evolution' (GA 148, 6 January 1914). Moreover, this faculty fully retains its significance in anthroposophy as well. 'In the spiritual stream we must learn to ask questions,' emphasizes Rudolf Steiner (ibid.).

In the light of this task, the cognitive process of *The Philosophy of Freedom* is especially topical and once again reveals itself as the Grail search of modern man. According to this book, cognition consists of the union of the perception that comes from outside with the specific concept that arises out of the inner being of the human soul. It is only when these two elements are fitted together in thinking through the activity of the human 'I' that man reaches the experience of complete reality. In this sense, any perception that draws close to man can be experienced as a question that addresses the human soul to which man adds the corresponding concept as an answer. Moreover in this sense the cognitive process can be understood as an incessant asking and answering in which man, however, remains continually passive. Such passivity is endemic today for all of natural science which for this reason cannot advance to the reality of the world.

The path of *The Philosophy of Freedom* that continues on in anthroposophy's schooling of the spirit is completely different. From the very beginning, the human being has to unfold the activity of thinking that leads to the point of producing the exceptional state. In the latter, thinking confronts man as the being in which percept and concept merge, hence question and answer flow into one. In the further pursuit of this path, which leads to truly meditating, question and answer change places. For during the transition from man's pure thinking into the world of imaginations, man's meditative thought activity turns increasingly into constant questions that call forth the corresponding imaginations as a reply out of the spiritual world. Man thereby becomes inwardly an active person inasmuch as he directs questions in his meditative life to the spiritual world so as to receive the answers in the form of objective spiritual perceptions.

Here on the path of inner discipline, there occurs what normally happens only after death as a complete inversion of the whole human being. The outer now changes to the inner and the inner to the outer, or in other words the questions that previously were posed only from outside to the human soul (so that it could still remain passive) originate now from within the soul as its own essential questions. The soul's whole subsequent life depends existentially on the answers to these questions.

One can moreover find this transition from inner passivity to spiritual activity in Parzival's path of destiny. During his first arrival in the Grail castle, he is questioned in detail by Gurnemanz, something that corresponds to the general way matters proceed in today's natural science. There in the castle, meaning already in the spiritual world, Parzival must himself pose questions based on his inner activity (meditation), but he fails. In so doing he revealed the fundamental weakness of today's humanity and pointed to the posing of questions as the necessary basic precondition of modern spiritual cognition.

Friedrich Rittelmeyer once wrote of Rudolf Steiner that his investigations in the spiritual world were like pleas that were not always fulfilled. Here in place of the word 'plea', 'question' could be used as well.[205]

★

Another important aspect of *The Philosophy of Freedom* that in a manner of speaking represents the background to its whole presentation is the correlation between the two cosmic forces, wisdom and love, predisposed in it. Thus in the first part of the book the path of modern cognition is described on which science today gathers its knowledge, the knowledge out of which wisdom shapes itself. For wisdom originates in every true process of cognition. In a similar way we deal in the second part of the book with the development of selfless love, which makes its appearance as pure love for the object or as love of the deed. Both these paths have their basis in the body-free intuition which in the first part of the book appears as 'conceptual intuition' and in the second part as 'moral intuition'. With that, human freedom is fully guaranteed in both cases.

One can also say: The highest fruit of the first part of *The Philosophy of Freedom* is the new *wisdom* that originates out of the science of freedom; the highest fruit of the second part is the new creative *love* that is born out of the reality of freedom. The union of the two occurs as follows. After wisdom in cognition and love of the deed have made their appearance, the cognitive intuition merges directly into love. And in the light of this 'intuition, bathed as it is in love', appears 'in the very activation of thinking itself' the 'power of love in spiritual form'. Consequently there originates in the human soul what can be designated as love-instilled wisdom.

From the later spiritual-scientific researches accomplished by Rudolf Steiner, such a joining of wisdom and love in humanity's evolution has become possible only through the appearance of the Christ on earth and the Mystery of Golgotha. For 'the Christ who has stepped out of the spiritual worlds has connected wisdom with love' (GA 143, 17 December 1912). What actually occurred there was characterized by Rudolf Steiner like this: 'First [there was] wisdom, then love, then wisdom aglow with love' (GA 102, 24 March 1908). As depicted above, these three stages can likewise be discovered in *The Philosophy of Freedom*, something that can be taken as further proof of the deeply Christian substance of this book.

Following the events at the Turning Point of Time, the secret knowledge of this union of wisdom and love lived primarily in the Grail Mysteries. They had as their earthly-cosmic symbol the sickle of the moon that bears the disc of the sun.

Here, the sickle of the moon refers to the wisdom that has received into itself love as the spiritual Sun. This is yet another aspect that points to the union of *The Philosophy of Freedom* with the Grail Mysteries.

Behind the described union of wisdom and love, another process is concealed in the spiritual world itself. In the lecture of 20 December 1918 (GA 186), Rudolf Steiner speaks about the fact that behind all the earthly events a mighty struggle exists in the esoteric sense between wisdom and love in the very kingdom of the hierarchies: 'There stands the Spirit of Wisdom over against the Spirit of Love, and the Spirit of Love over against the Spirit of Wisdom.' And this battle that earlier only found its replica in human unconsciousness must now be grasped by man's consciousness in the epoch of the consciousness soul and gradually be settled.

The inner force that man requires for victory in this struggle is already germinally contained in *The Philosophy of Freedom* and will later be brought to full development on the inner path of anthroposophical schooling. 'What is written in the book *Knowledge of the Higher Worlds and Its Attainment* is supposed to lead man to where he can conclude this inner struggle victoriously' (ibid.). If one therefore searches in accordance with this utterance by Rudolf Steiner for the union of wisdom and love in that book, one does indeed find it in the two last chapters, where both the encounter with the Lesser and then with the Greater Guardian of the Threshold is described.

Thus in the chapter before the last one, wisdom originating out of cognition is mentioned as the most important fruit on the path of schooling. In this sense the Lesser Guardian says to the spirit disciple: 'Your own *wisdom* must now . . . be so great that it can assume the task of that hidden wisdom which has left you' (GA 10). Here we therefore deal with a new wisdom to which the first part of *The Philosophy of Freedom* does indeed lead. In the last chapter the new love is mentioned as the most important fruit of the encounter with the Greater Guardian: 'What man will receive in the higher regions of the supersensible [where he can be admitted only after the successful encounter with the Greater Guardian] is not anything that approaches him, merely something that proceeds from him: the *love* for the world around him.' This love is then expressed above all in the free decision 'to offer up one's gifts . . . on the sacrificial altar of humanity'. In accordance with *The Philosophy of Freedom*, this means that man begins to act only out of love for the object (on this stage of development the object being the whole of mankind). Rudolf Steiner calls what derives out of this union of wisdom and love 'the sensation of the new freedom' that a human being, as a fully conscious inhabitant of both worlds, attains through initiation.

According to Rudolf Steiner, the encounters with the two guardians follow one upon the other without much delay; *soon after* the first encounter the second one follows (GA 10; GA 13). In accordance with the depictions in the seventh chapter, it can be said that man experiences in the figure of the Lesser Guardian how far he himself has progressed in work on his *image* [Ger.: *Gleichnis* in the sense of *allegory* or *simile*]. Above all else, this guardian shows him how far away he still is from his primordial (original) god-likeness. By contrast, in the encounter with the Greater Guardian of the Threshold, the goal of the entire evolution of man is revealed to him through the *likeness* that is preserved in the spiritual world. For man attains to the *image* step by step through perfecting the Lesser Guardian. With his likeness he will unite in the future all at once. This is proclaimed by the Greater Guardian of the Threshold to the spirit disciple as the union with the Guardian himself.

All this has a further relation to wisdom and love. For wisdom contains in itself the various degrees of perfection, and can only be developed gradually and step by step. Love on the other hand can be attained fully by man only as a whole. Correspondingly he therefore works level by level on the transformation of the Lesser Guardian, and then unites all at once with the Greater Guardian as the highest ideal and goal of Earth development. Here too wisdom and love are linked together.

This union of wisdom and love (which we—although in different forms—find in *The Philosophy of Freedom* as well as on the modern path of schooling that is based on this book) leads on the intuitive stage of initiation to the actual encounter with Sophia and Christ as spiritual beings. In the spiritual world, Sophia is not only the representative of wisdom but likewise of beauty. This is why it is always emphasized in regard to the Lesser Guardian of the Threshold that his being must be 'transformed into radiant beauty' by man (GA 10). The prototype for this work is exemplified in the spiritual world by the heavenly Sophia because it is a matter here of the acquisition by the human being of her two main characteristics, wisdom (gold) and beauty (white). In this regard, the Greater Guardian of the Threshold is not primarily the prototype of wisdom but of love, out of which arise 'selfless devotion and willingness to sacrifice' (ibid.). In the fourth part of the Foundation Stone Meditation, this blend of wisdom and love are depicted in the form of the cooperation of head and heart in the human being in contrast to their separate appearance at the Turning Point of Time in the Mystery streams of the Kings and Shepherds.

In *The Philosophy of Freedom,* this blend of the two streams occurs as if still in a hidden germinal state. Its first part deals above all with philosophy as an art and philosophers as '*conceptual artists*' [Ger.: *Begriffskünstler*] (GA 4; emphasis by Rudolf Steiner).[206] And the second part deals with deeds of love that arise out of human freedom, and through their moral substance begin to resemble the cosmic-earthly deeds of the Christ more and more. For in the earthly life of the Christ we have the highest example for man, a human being who was active purely based on love for the action and the object (humanity) in utter selflessness, and in so doing brought the nature of true manhood to full expression.

This path of 'man's becoming human' (Novalis) is established in the second part of *The Philosophy of Freedom,* where it is pointed out that only man himself through inner discipline can turn himself into a *free* being. In this way, thinking the concept 'man' through to its own practical conclusion, man who is then recognized as free spirit brings about the connection with the Sophia; and its realization in life through man's self-transformation leads to the union with Christ. Both processes together form the transition from *The Philosophy of Freedom* to anthroposophy. Here, the Christ as the highest primal archetype of the Anthropos—Representative of Man—and His wisdom—Sophia—are jointly present.

This is why in the Grail Mysteries, as was said earlier, a virgin as the earthly representative of the Sophia or Cosmic Wisdom bears the chalice with the Christ substance, which is the substance of love. This is the earthly replica of the cosmic Grail imagination: the sun borne by the moon sickle. Similarly, in *The Philosophy of Freedom*, the *wisdom* of the conceptual intuitions turns into pure *love* of the object in the free deeds of the human being through the mediation of moral imagination.

15. The Creation of the Foundation Stone Out of the Substance of the Grail

Among the most important tasks that have to be accomplished in our time is the imbuement of intellectuality and freedom with the Christ Impulse. So as to be able to carry this out, we must first of all attain to pure (that is sense-free) thinking in accordance with *The Philosophy of Freedom*. Only in this way, on the path of intellectuality, can we take hold of and experience true freedom. With this, moreover, that stage of the inner development of thinking is now reached on which thinking's permeation with the Christ Impulse is possible. For today in the consciousness soul epoch, the conscious association with the Christ is only assured based on full human freedom. This, however, signifies that one first has to acquire this freedom. 'The Christ Being is placed in humanity's evolution in such a way that the relationship of man to Christ can only be a *free* one' (GA 201, 16 May 1920).

Such a relationship then has two consequences, one on the level of consciousness, the other on that of existence. The first consequence was mentioned earlier (see Chapter 2). It consists in our being able to discover a new connection to 'the Spirit of the Cosmos', meaning to the spiritual world as a whole, that we absolutely need for our further development on earth.

Since the second consequence relates not only to our consciousness but likewise to our existence, it has much further extending consequences that even reach beyond the limits of Earth evolution because they already prepare the next embodiment of Earth, the Jupiter Cosmos. Rudolf Steiner describes this unique process that takes place here as follows: 'In turn, this sense-free thinking requires the connection with the world. It does not find it if it does not relate with what has moved as an actually *new substance* into World evolution through the Mystery of Golgotha' (ibid.).

What in fact does take place here is the same process that Rudolf Steiner designates elsewhere and from a different viewpoint as 'something mighty' (see Chapter 2). In the lecture of 16 May 1920, he places this event not only into a human but into a still greater cosmic perspective. There he describes how through the activity of thinking the material substance of the body is constantly destroyed in the human being. With that, man is distinguished in the most decisive manner possible from the whole remaining universe. For in the latter the substances are subject only to the process of transformation, while in earthly man they are *completely annihilated*.

According to Rudolf Steiner, this world process was arranged by the Father God in such wise that from the moment humans had ascended to individual thinking they turned into permanent destroyers of their corporeal organism. The process indicated here is of decisive significance for the whole planet Earth: 'When, ultimately, all substances of the earth will have passed through the human organization so that it will be utilized for thinking in the human organizations, earth will cease to exist as a cosmic body' (ibid.). What will then remain of it? Only what has passed through the thinking of man. And the way thinking is constituted today, it is merely pure images, pictures that on their own possess no reality and as such are nothing but semblance. For man to be a free being, his thinking as wellspring of his freedom had to become void of being, a mere picture. As a result, at the end of Earth evolution, 'of all that was before ... there will only remain behind the images, the painting of the world, as it were' (ibid.). This 'painting' would then be filled with infinite wisdom but without any reality whatever, and therefore without a future.

In this situation, humanity could attain its freedom, the goal of Earth evolution, but without the possibility of utilizing it anywhere in the world all. Moreover, in this way the transition from Earth to (New) Jupiter would not be assured and as a result there would be no cosmic future for Earth and humankind. Nevertheless, that it does not appear that way today is solely due to the Mystery of Golgotha. For into the old withering cosmos, the Father placed the spirit-seeds of the new cosmos of the Son out of which human beings who consciously unite with the Christ will create a new reality.

In other words, what became pictures void of living being in the thinking of man for the sake of human freedom can be transformed by Christ from mere semblance [Ger.: *Schein*] into existence [Ger.: *Sein*]. These absolutely *lifeless images* can be *resurrected* in the soul of man to *new life* by being filled with the new 'Christian substantiality' (ibid.), that is with the 'new substance' deriving from Christ and thus elevated to a higher reality. 'These images do acquire a reality for the future inasmuch as *new substantiality* penetrates them, the substance that is given through the Mystery of Golgotha' (ibid.). And this enlivening substance that bestows a new cosmic existence to the mere images is the resurrection substance from the Phantom Body of the Christ.

Through this act of inner resurrection in pure or sense-free thinking, which is possible through a direct connection with the powers of the Christ's Resurrection-body, a bridge can be created between the moral order, newly originating in man out of the kingdom of the Son, and the withering (dying) natural order of the Father. Rudolf Steiner elucidates this transition with a case in point that is exemplary of the whole indicated path. What exists in the physical world as the element of warmth, which can gradually lead the earth to none other than natural death (heat death), turns in human thinking—as do all other natural phenomena—into mere image, an abstraction of modern science devoid of living being. With this we have on the side of nature the process of an unstoppable external destruction and on the side of humans merely the insubstantial content of their thinking. A way out of this otherwise unsolvable situation is only possible through man's conscious connection with the Christ through which our thinking can evolve into a new human-cosmic reality. According to Rudolf Steiner, in this lies the most essential mission of Christianity. 'Christianity will not be understood until we tell ourselves that, specifically here in the region of warmth, there is transformation of such a kind taking place in man through which matter is destroyed; that mere imagery-existence draws forth out of matter; that this picture-existence will, however, be made into a new reality through the connection of the human soul with the Christ substance' (ibid.). This new reality that originates out of warmth is the substance of 'human-cosmic love' [Ger.: *Menschen-Welten-Liebe*]. The whole of the future Jupiter-existence will consist of this substance. And that something like this can even happen eventually in the future was designated by Rudolf Steiner in the same lecture as 'the cosmic significance of the Mystery of Golgotha' (ibid.).

In this description it is striking that to begin with Rudolf Steiner only speaks of the world of the Father and the Son and does not explicitly mention the third entity of the Trinity, the Holy Spirit. In a thorough study of the lecture, however, it is noted that he prefaces the above-described transformation of human thinking through the Christ substance with a reference to the Parzival saga and the fundamental transformation that the Grail Mysteries have undergone through Parzival as the first representative of initiation out of the forces of the consciousness soul. 'Whereas the Grail saga still shows the raying in from outside, over against this the figure of Parzival is placed who is supposed to ray out of the centre into the pictures what will once again give them reality' (ibid.). Applied to the Grail, this signifies that the latter is no longer illuminated from outside, meaning out of the spiritual world, but is becoming radiant itself because, for the first time, an initiate confronts it who attained to initiation in his 'I'. Such a new king of the Grail can take the Christ-substance of the Grail so intensely into his 'I' that it is then capable of radiating out of this centre of his being into the surrounding spiritual world, thus making that world accessible to the free cognition of man.

Viewed from the spiritual-scientific standpoint, this process can also be understood as follows. As Rudolf Steiner conveys in the lecture on 21 September 1909 (GA 114), during the Fall only two forms of ether were thrust into this event: light-ether and warmth-ether. The two higher forms of ether, the sound- and life-ether, were preserved in the spiritual world.[207] Through the Mystery of Golgotha the first two were saved. And from then on we find the secret of their salvation in the Mystery of the Grail, which possesses a supersensible (imaginative) form that is filled from within with warmth-ether and enveloped from outside with light-ether as if with a luminous aura. Viewed against this background, Parzival was the first Grail king who was in a position to link up the essence of the Grail in such a way with his individual 'I' that the two redeemed forms of ether could radiate out of his inner being into the world like the light of purified cognition and the warmth of spiritual love.

A similar deed, namely to make the Mysteries of the Grail accessible in our age for the first time to *all* human beings of good will, was brought about by Rudolf Steiner during the creation of the supersensible Foundation Stone at the Christmas Conference. For since then anyone can plant this imaginative Foundation Stone, with its content of warmth of love and its aura of light-thoughts, freely into the ground of his or her heart. During the Foundation Stone laying, Rudolf Steiner pointed this out in the following words: 'Dear friends, let us take this deeply into our souls. With it [the nature of the Foundation Stone] let us warm our souls, and with it let us enlighten our souls. Let us preserve this *warmth of soul* and this *light of soul* which, out of good will, we have planted in our hearts today.' (GA 260, 25 December 1923.) And then Rudolf Steiner links this light and this warmth of the Foundation Stone directly with the light and warmth of the Christ which, at the Turning Point of Time in the 'cosmic darkness' of Earth evolution, He brought as the redeemed forms of ether to the point of radiating and warming. With this, the light and the warmth of the Foundation Stone were 'energized' to such an extent that they could begin to shine forth and send out warmth into the world from man's inner being, meaning out of the depths of the human heart (as had been the case long ago with Parzival) and in so doing to manifest effectively out into the external world as the forces of cognition and spiritual love (ibid.).[208]

As is well known from all Grail traditions, in the centre of the Grail revelation stands the appearance of the Holy Spirit who initially approaches from the spiritual heights and descends onto the radiant chalice. With Parzival's elevation to the Grail's new king, a significant metamorphosis occurred at just this point of the Grail ceremony. Here for the first time in the whole Grail history up to then, he as the first initiate of the consciousness soul could so intensely fill the content of the Grail with his individual 'I' that the Holy Spirit penetrated the chalice not only from outside but also in the human heart so as to have an effect on the world from this new abode.[209]

Something like this but now already within the New Mysteries, which in principle are accessible to all human beings, occurs at the Christmas Conference during the Foundation Stone laying which Rudolf Steiner concludes (turning to all the anthroposophists present) with the reference: 'Then will you ... carry the Spirit that reigns in the shining light of thoughts around the dodecahedral Stone of Love [when one is willing to implant it in the ground of one's heart] out into the world where it should radiate *light* and *warmth* for the progress of human souls, for the progress of the world (ibid.).' With this—as a result of the laying of the Foundation Stone—we have in the New Mysteries a similar situation as to what happened in the case of the closed circle of the Grail servants in the ninth century after Parzival had become king of the Grail, the first to do so due purely to the strength of his 'I'-force. From then on as was said earlier, the Grail impulse could work out of the 'I' of man. With it, Parzival attained a certain stage of Spirit Self development.[210]

In his book *Theosophy* (GA 9), Rudolf Steiner characterizes the relationship of the human 'I' to the Spirit Self in a manner that quite accurately describes the renewed nature of the Grail initiation as inaugurated through Parzival: 'The Spirit rays into the "I" and lives in it as in its "sheath" ... The Spirit shapes the "I" from within to outside ... The Spirit shaping [the "I"] and living as an "I" may be called "Spirit Self" because it manifests as the "I" or "self" of the human being ... The Spirit Self is a manifestation [revelation] of the spiritual world within the "I".' This Spirit which is effectively working in and as the 'I', which emanates out of the spiritual world, is the Holy Spirit of the Grail Mysteries who, beginning with Parzival, can work not only from outside but directly out of the inner human being; out of the centre of his 'I'.

Present in this new way in man, the Holy Spirit can guide us to fully conscious activity within the Grail Mysteries. For the Holy Spirit is present in us so that we can attain cognition of the spiritual world so as to find in it the creative Christ substance as it was conserved in the Grail. For 'inasmuch as the Christ sent humanity the Holy Spirit [at Whitsuntide], He enabled them to rise on their own out of the intellectual sphere to comprehension of the spiritual ... so that man, through the spirit indwelling him (if he but inclines to the Christ), can comprehend the supersensible' (GA 214, 30 July 1922). With this, the initiate of the Grail can moreover recognize how the holy vessel is continually united with the forces of the Trinity.[211] Rudolf Steiner asserts this at the end of the above-quoted lecture by saying: 'One who beholds the cross on Golgotha must at the same time behold the Trinity, for in reality the Christ reveals the Trinity through His whole involvement with earthly humanity's evolution' (ibid.). And when we are mindful that the spiritual essence of what occurred on the Cross (and since then connects the Christ with all human beings until the end of earthly days) was retained in the sacred Grail chalice for the future, it follows from this that in its content, which consists of pure Christ substance, all three forces of the Trinity continue to live and work, but now in a new way because they are *within* humanity's evolution. Ever since Parzival, every Christian initiate who comes to the Grail based on the fully developed consciousness soul can (through the spiritual communion with the Grail and based on its trinitarian forces) thereby act within the world, indeed even become independently creative.

Through the special connection of the Grail Mysteries (renewed in their form through Parzival) with the Christ substance (the substance that can infuse the pictorial content of thinking since the Mystery of Golgotha), Rudolf Steiner has not only referred to the cooperation of the Trinity in this process but above all to the fact that *this* spiritual *Christ substance* represents the essential content of the sacred vessel. It follows from this that the whole process of infusion of the thought-pictures with reality is a Grail process through and through, a process belonging fully to the New Mysteries which can therefore be denoted as the modern Grail Mysteries.[212]

What has been stated can help us understand more accurately how, during the Christmas Conference, Rudolf Steiner created the Foundation Stone of Love in its human-cosmic dual form. First, with the creative forces of his free 'I', he formed the future Foundation Stone in his sense-free thinking out of the spiritual-scientific cognition of the threefold human being. As Rudolf Steiner himself reports, he spiritually cognized threefold man already for decades, but it was only in 1917 that he could 'bring it to maturity' so far (GA 260, 25 December 1923) that he could fully take hold of it with his pure thinking and as a result could then present it in generally comprehensible thought-forms.[213]

Then on the second stage this idea was permeated by the Christ Impulse, which gave it a substantial content or 'a form-giving substance', of which Rudolf Steiner speaks about at the laying of the Foundation

Stone and which from this moment onwards represents the spiritual nature of the Foundation Stone (ibid.).

It follows from what was stated before that viewed esoterically this spiritual substance, permeated as it is by the Christ Impulse, is none other than the substance of the Grail. Even though it was collected initially at the Turning Point of Time in its physical form as blood from the wounds of the Redeemer in a chalice of jasper, soon afterwards it passed through the process of etherization and turned into a purely etheric-spiritual substance (GA 130, 1 October 1911) that was capable on its own of creating a new form in the spiritual world, a supersensible chalice in which it was then preserved by angels and chosen souls of departed human beings. (GA 214, 23 July 1922.) This is why this Grail substance, which is permeated by the Christ Impulse, can moreover be designated as a *'form-giving* substance', for it is able to reproduce this impulse's supersensible (imaginative) form or structure by itself again and again. As to its nature, it belongs to the macrocosm since the Turning Point of Time. Its special characteristic, however, is that it can also be received by human beings (the communion with the Grail), opening up conscious access for them to the highest spiritual forces of the macrocosm, above all to the forces of the Trinity as described above, because they have been connected with the activity of the Grail from the very beginning.

Now we can correctly comprehend the next stage in the process of the creation of the Foundation Stone. For only through its direct connection with the content of the Grail could this 'formative substance' receive into itself the forces of the divine Trinity. Rudolf Steiner describes this process in the following words: 'When now, at this moment, we unite these three forces, the forces of the heights, the forces of the circumference, the forces of the depths [that earlier had been described as the forces of the Father, the Son and the Holy Spirit] in a substance that gives form, then in our soul's comprehension we can bring the universal dodecahedron opposite the human dodecahedron' (ibid.). With this, the creation of the Foundation Stone reaches its cosmic dimension. For the here-described confrontation of human and divine creation contains the actual beginning of the new Cosmos of Love of which Rudolf Steiner speaks at the end of his book *Occult Science, an Outline.* This is why the Foundation Stone of the Christmas Conference could only be generated out of the *substance of love.* Subsequently, as the start of the new creation that had not emerged through the gods (hierarchies) but for the first time through a free human 'I', it was supposed to be shown to, that is to say placed over against, the hierarchies.

At the end of the New Testament, this future cosmos is pointed out in the mighty imagination of the Heavenly Jerusalem (Rev. 21), which according to Rudolf Steiner's spirit-research will eventually be built out of white magic, meaning out of the magic of love by free human beings as the Jupiter-condition of our cosmos (GA 104, 29 June 1908). Merely the reference to the 'city' in this imagination affirms that it will be a matter here of a free creation by human beings.

Among the Rosicrucians, the imagination of the temple of humanity existed as a preparatory stage for this cosmic future of humankind. The building of that temple in the spiritual-social sense was viewed by them as their central esoteric mission (see GA 93, 22 May 1905).

In such a spiritual building of the temple or city, we have a lofty but purely human ideal that can only be realized by earthly mankind. For the angels (hierarchies), even the most exalted ones, cannot build a 'city'. On the other hand, what the higher beings bestowed on human beings without their having had any involvement in it was the original paradisaical condition that is recounted at the beginning of the Bible in the imagination of a 'garden' with its non-human, divine nature. Notwithstanding its entanglement in the Fall of Man, this nature that surrounds us to this day remains pervaded by the substance of wisdom, just as eventually the above type of nature on New Jupiter will be pervaded with the substance of love that humanity—as a nascent hierarchy of freedom and love—will produce out of the individual 'I'.

The thus described creation-process of the Foundation Stone corresponds exactly to the great rhythm of the Foundation Stone Meditation; with it Rudolf Steiner accompanied the whole proceedings of the Foundation Stone laying on 25 December 1923.[214] This rhythm also consists of three parts and shows the path that was established through the Christ's appearance on earth. This path guides man (microcosm) into the totality of the spiritual world (macrocosm), the totality that encompasses all the spheres from the Divine Trinity through the three-times-three groups of the hierarchical beings all the way to the world of elemental spirits and human beings.

Now, the main prerequisite for creating the supersensible Foundation Stone is the metamorphosis that we must first undertake on our own 'I'. This, however, is possible today only on the modern path of initiation. Under ordinary circumstances, man is familiar only with ordinary 'I'-consciousness, which depends on the body and appears to us as our earth consciousness; but this 'I' possesses no reality. This is why Rudolf Steiner points out again and again: 'In order to recognize the "I" as the one through which the submersion of the human soul into full reality can be discerned, we must carefully guard against considering the real "I" to be the ordinary "I" of which we have common awareness' (GA 35, 17 August 1908). If on the other hand we grasp this earthly 'I' in the sense of *The Philosophy of Freedom* in our pure thinking, we can enter upon the path that guides us to the experience of the reality of our own 'I'.

Rudolf Steiner moreover characterizes in the same lecture how by degrees one can draw near the real 'I': 'Thinking does not affirm the reality of the "I" but it is just as certain that the true "I"[215] cannot be experienced through anything other than pure thinking. For the real "I" does indeed extend into pure thinking, and for ordinary human consciousness *only* into this. A person who merely thinks arrives only at the thought of the "I"; one who *experiences* what can be *experienced in pure thinking* causes ... something real to be the content of his consciousness inasmuch as he experiences the "I" through [pure] thinking.' (Ibid.; emphasis by Rudolf Steiner.)

When the 'I' of the human being is thus taken hold of as spiritual reality in pure thinking, it can be permeated on the next level by the Christ Impulse. In the second part of the Foundation Stone Meditation, the words 'Do thine own I / Unite / Unto the I of the World' point this out. As a consequence of this, a new connection with the macrocosm, or the whole objective spiritual world, opens up for the real 'I' into which it can now submerge in full consciousness. Rudolf Steiner describes this in the same lecture as follows: 'For inasmuch as in pure thinking one comes to know the true "I" as an [actual] experience, one learns to know what full reality really is. And from this experience one can penetrate further into other domains of true reality.' These are the various regions of the macrocosm or the objective spiritual world. To penetrate into them cognitively is the task of anthroposophy. This is why Rudolf Steiner continues: 'This is what anthroposophy tries [to do]. It does not stop at the experiences of ordinary consciousness. It strives for a research of reality that works with a transformed consciousness. *For the purposes of its research, ordinary consciousness cuts off such research of reality, with the exception of the "I" experienced in pure thinking.*' (Ibid.)

Even though Rudolf Steiner does not explicitly mention the permeation of the 'I' with the Christ Impulse in this passage, one can still unmistakeably conclude (particularly based on the above-quoted lecture of 16 March 1920 and also his own biography) that the transition from *The Philosophy of Freedom* to anthroposophy became possible only through the conscious encounter of the human 'I' with the cosmic 'I' of the Christ in the domain of intuition.

Expressed in the later spiritual-scientific terminology, it can be said that (through the portal of the exceptional state in pure thinking)

Rudolf Steiner carried out the step from earthly 'I'-consciousness (ordinary 'I') to his higher 'I' that dwells in the spiritual world as spirit among spirits. For him already in his youth, this was a direct supersensible experience as confirmed in the earlier cited letter from the beginning of the year 1881 (see Chapter 14). In his autobiography, Rudolf Steiner also describes how as a 20-year old he could behold the 'I' as a spirit being in the supersensible world among other spiritual entities (see Chapter 2), which implies that to a far-reaching extent he was already then in possession of his higher 'I'. For the purpose of inaugurating anthroposophy, however, he had to take a further step, namely the transition to what he later termed as the *true* 'I' of man.[216] This step was only possible as a result of the conscious encounter with Christ in Intuition. In order to make sure of this, it was necessary to attain what he later described in a completely impersonal way: 'Now it must be possible to fashion the 'I' into a Christ-receptive organ once the 'I' has learned thinking for a while through Christianity and has applied its thoughts to the outside world' (GA 109, 15 February 1909). In these words the acquisition of thinking through Christianity relates to the whole development of occidental philosophy beginning with central Scholasticism and lasting until its last flowering through Fichte, Schelling and Hegel; and in the application of thoughts to the outer world, we deal with the unfolding of modern natural science. Rudolf Steiner occupied himself with both philosophy and natural science in the most intensive way during the time of his academic studies in Vienna as well as in the following years that he spent in Weimar and Berlin. This is why these words exhibit biographical character in a personal as well as spiritual-scientific sense.

Only by being able to develop his 'I' on the path of initiation into a Christ-receptive organ could Rudolf Steiner be in a position to carry out the inner step from the higher 'I' to the true 'I'. With that he reached the level that allowed him fully consciously not only to research the higher worlds all the way to their highest regions, but moreover to bring down the results of this research through the portal of pure thinking and to present them in clear and generally comprehensible concepts. This was possible for him because the only thing he could take with him during his spirit-researches into higher worlds was the 'I' that had been 'experienced in pure thinking' and was infused with the Christ-substance, or that of the Grail. Thereby his relationship to earth consciousness (and the earthly world in general) was constantly guaranteed on all levels of being in supersensible existence.

In archetypal form we rediscover this path in the afore-described threefold rhythm of the Foundation Stone Meditation as well as in the three stages of the process of the Foundation Stone's creation.

The following can throw light on the kind of spiritual dimension that this deed by Rudolf Steiner had (and has). At the end of the depiction of his philosophical treatise of 1899, 'Der Individualismus in der Philosophie' [Individualism in Philosophy], the following words appear: 'It seems almost superfluous after these considerations to state that "I" refers only to the bodily, real "I" of the individual, not to a general "I" stripped off from the former' (GA 30). This clearly brings to expression that at the point of departure of his whole path into the spiritual world and back again Rudolf Steiner always took along the earthly 'I' (meaning the 'I' that is given to all human beings in direct inner experience), that is to say the human *personality* that can only be experienced on earth in the concrete physical body. He then took hold of this earthly personality in his pure thinking and lifted it up to the spiritual world where it assumed actuality of character through the connection with the higher 'I' and following that, penetrated by the Christ-substance of the true 'I', it became the *eternal persona*.

16. The Foundation Stone and
The Philosophy of Freedom

In the book *Occult Science, an Outline*, which represents an overview of the whole of anthroposophy, Rudolf Steiner designates this outline as the science of the Grail. In that way, this theme pervades the ongoing development of anthroposophy and reaches its culmination at the Christmas Conference through the creation of the supersensible Foundation Stone on 25 December 1923.

As has been defined in detail elsewhere, this creation by Rudolf Steiner is deeply connected to the innermost nature of the Grail Mysteries.[217] At the same time, the whole event of the Christmas Conference can be understood in Rudolf Steiner's life as the fulfilment of *The Philosophy of Freedom*.[218] This book's relationship to the Grail Mysteries was mentioned in more general terms in the previous chapter. That gives rise as well, however, to the question of its relationship to the innermost nature of the Christmas Conference itself, or rather to what represents the innermost centre of this conference, namely the Foundation Stone.

In order to answer this question, one must call to mind something that belongs among the most important determinations of *The Philosophy of Freedom*. This is that in the process of cognition man's 'I' not only reproduces outer reality but creates it anew. In this sense 'cognition itself becomes a process of reality' in which, 'through hard work, the "I" obtains reality'. (GA 74, 24 May 1920.) If one takes this discovery by Rudolf Steiner not in an abstract philosophical sense but in a quite literal and actual one, then the path outlined in *The Philosophy of Freedom*— provided *it is* continued into the spiritual world—leads to creation of a new reality, that is to a new creation. And this new creation is the Foundation Stone of the Christmas Conference.

The relationship between *The Philosophy of Freedom* and the Foundation Stone is, however, much more far-reaching. In order to decipher this relationship it becomes necessary to place the following words by Rudolf Steiner into the centre, words in which he summarizes the whole content of his book in precise and brief form. In so doing it must be taken into account that this quote is found in the lecture cycle on the Philosophy of Thomas Aquinas (GA 74), which has a karmic-biographical relation to Rudolf Steiner's life. For it is pointed out in this cycle how the world-historical question with which Thomas Aquinas died in the thirteenth century was conclusively answered later in *The Philosophy of Freedom* and in spiritual science that was based on the latter book.

Here it is a matter of the text already partly quoted in the last chapter in connection with the modern Grail Mysteries: 'There originates what was described in the second part of my *Philosophy of Freedom*, namely *ethical individualism* which in actual fact *builds on the Christ Impulse in the human being,* even though this is not expressly stated in my *Philosophy of Freedom.* It builds on what the human being struggles to attain in the way of freedom by transforming ordinary thinking into what is called in my *Philosophy of Freedom pure thinking,* which rises into the spiritual world and out of that world gives birth to the incentives for moral actions. It gives birth to them by means of something that otherwise is tied to the human corporeality—the impulse of love—which in rising upwards becomes spiritualized. And inasmuch as the moral ideals are gleaned out of the spiritual world through *moral imagination,* they express themselves in its [moral imagination's] power, the power of *spiritual love.*' (GA 74, 24 May 1920.)

If one grasps the content of this quote following the italicized key words, one can make a most important discovery. Ethical individualism, as the central concept of the book and as the goal of humanity's evolution in the fifth post-Atlantean cultural period, takes on form accordingly based on the Christ Impulse and consists of three main elements or faculties:

1. pure thinking,
2. moral imagination,
3. spiritual love,

which in working together form a kind of cross. Pure thinking 'rises upward into the spiritual world', hence works from below to above. Moral imagination on the other hand, which draws on ideals from the spiritual world, is directed more from above to below. Finally, the force of spiritual love that guides the human being to free deeds out of love for the object represents the horizontal line and thereby shapes the social life of human beings.

Now we look more closely at the three essential parts of ethical individualism. According to *The Philosophy of Freedom,* pure thinking is attainable only through the separation of man's faculties of cognition from any dependence on the corporeal physical organization, and is therefore also depicted by Rudolf Steiner as 'sense-free thinking'. As a consequence of its separation from the physical body, it can enter into the spiritual world. There it unfolds itself as an entity that is quite alive. Rudolf Steiner denotes this as the resurrection out of the tomb of the human brain. Such thinking becomes radiant in the spiritual world. Moreover, if it is further developed by means of the schooling methods of the book *Knowledge of the Higher Worlds and Its Attainment*, it can in time illuminate the beings and processes of the higher worlds, and by doing so make them visible. Once this stage is reached, the human being can become capable of the following. Rudolf Steiner describes that in the lecture of 13 January 1924 (GA 233a). Man has to receive the facts of materialistic science into his thinking (which has become sense-free), for instance the teachings of Haeckel and Darwin, and lift them up by way of modern spiritual discipleship into the spiritual world and there take them to the gods. From them, he then receives back what is described in *Occult Science, an Outline* as our cosmic evolution. The mediator, however, in this process is pure thinking, because only through such thinking is it possible to bring scientific knowledge towards the entities of the spiritual world.

Now in addition, Rudolf Steiner recounts the following in *The Philosophy of Freedom*: 'Ethical individualism is . . . the crowning of the edifice that *Darwin* and *Haeckel* have striven for in natural science. It [ethical individualism] is the spiritualized teaching of evolution transferred to the moral life.' (GA 4; emphasis by Rudolf Steiner.) Here the question arises: What happens if—on the same path that Rudolf Steiner sketches in the above-mentioned lecture—one not only lifts into the spiritual world the teachings by Haeckel and Darwin but likewise (through the mediation of pure thinking as an idea) their 'crowning', namely 'ethical individualism' itself? Then one does not merely encounter the gods in general but the Time Spirit Michael. What one then receives back from him as Sun-countenance of the Christ is that which corresponds in the spiritual world to ethical individualism of earthly man. And that is the secret of the *spiritual Sun* in its connection with the Christ Being, the Sun that stands in the centre of the spirit-cosmos, as well as the cosmic-earthly significance of the Mystery of Golgotha which is the spiritual axis of the entire World evolution as described in *Occult Science*.

Based on this, the sun's additional secret and its connection with human freedom can become manifest. Rudolf Steiner points this out by saying: 'When we . . . rightly acquire a feeling for the condition of the sun [Ger.: *Sonnensein*], not by merely numerically calculating it nor viewing it through instruments, we feel that it is related to everything that dwells in us as freedom, as what can happen through us ourselves in the future' (GA 240, 25 January 1924). But what a person who is sensitive to spiritual matters can thus feel, an initiate can *know* quite accurately through encountering the Archangel Michael, namely that in the cosmos the spiritual nature of the sun corresponds to 'ethical individualism', concerning which Rudolf Steiner states that it is only on this basis that human freedom is even possible.[219] This is why the 'hymn of freedom' that Rudolf Steiner places over against the Kantian homage of duty (GA 4) can be continued with the further words that relate to the spiritual Sun in his lecture: 'Oh, thou Cosmic Son of Freedom, I feel thee to be akin to all in me that bestows on my own being the freedom and faculty of decision for the future!' (GA 240, ibid.)

If we add to these words concerning the sun's relationship to freedom those dealing with its relationship to intellectuality, 'The sun is the wellspring of all that is intellectual', as stated by Rudolf Steiner (GA 240, 21 August 1924), we have an answer to the question that could have arisen in reading the previous chapter. From where did freedom and intellectuality descend to human beings on earth? They originate from Michael's Sun-kingdom, where the cosmic wellspring of earthly freedom is to be found.

Now, out of this Sun-kingdom at the Turning Point of Time, the Christ-entity (the Cosmic Sun itself) likewise descended to the earth so that, once gifted with intellectuality and freedom, the human being can find new and fully conscious access to the whole cosmos, meaning to its spirit. Today we have advanced so far in this development that what had taken place objectively in the world at the Turning Point of Time must now, beginning in our time in the New Christian Mysteries (which have originated through anthroposophy on the basis of *The Philosophy of Freedom*), move more and more into general human awareness. 'What takes place in the world is that out of spiritual heights the Christ, the *Spirit Sun*, has moved down into the earthly worlds so that what humanly moved out of the supersensible into the sensible [intellectuality and freedom] might meet up with what cosmically has moved out of the supersensible into the sensible. This came to pass so that man might come together in the right way with the spirit of the cosmos. For man can take his stand in the world only when the spirit within him finds the spirit outside him in the right way.' (GA 257, 30 January 1923.)

It is exactly this new connection of the spirit in man (who has attained his freedom through cognition) with the spirit of the cosmos (which only became possible through the lighting up of the Christ Sun on the earth) that was proclaimed by Rudolf Steiner during the first reading of the Foundation Stone Meditation (during the esoteric laying of the Foundation Stone of the General Anthroposophical Society on 25 December 1923) as the starting point of the New Mysteries. In this special, unique rhythm that gave the Christmas Conference its archetypically Christian definition, Rudolf Steiner on this day first read the microcosmic parts of the first three segments of the meditation which deal with the spirit in man (his 'I'), the person who through exercise in cognition ascends to true inner freedom; then the fourth segment of the meditation was read, in the centre of which stands the appearance of the Christ Sun on earth. Then the microcosmic segments were read once more, but now linked in each case with the macrocosmic parts that deal with the spirit in the cosmos, the spirit that now connects with the spirit of man which has become free, meaning with his 'I'. In the esoteric sense, this mighty archetypal rhythm of the Christmas Conference can be designated as the rhythm of the Mystery of Golgotha and consequently as the mantric foundation of the New Mysteries as such.[220]

For this, too, one can find in *The Philosophy of Freedom* an almost prophetic first indication. From the words by Rudolf Steiner mentioned more than once already in this work, it becomes obvious that *The Philosophy of Freedom* rests on two 'fundamental points': there exists a spiritual world, and man's 'I' as a spiritual being finds that it has a connection with that world. One can moreover comprehend these words in the sense of the above expressed context: the spirit of the cosmos exists and the spirit in man (his 'I') is in a constant connection with it. Thus, *The Philosophy of Freedom* is the unique and inalienable foundation of the new Michael-Christ Mysteries, which were later on established out of anthroposophy by Rudolf Steiner.

In the above-quoted lecture of 13 January 1924, it is furthermore reported how at the dawn of the modern age the Rosicrucians consistently practised the occult bearing up into the spiritual world of natural-scientific insights (for example, the Copernican world system). In so doing, however, they could encounter Michael only in a half-unconscious, dreamlike condition of soul. Only with the beginning of Michael's present epoch of leadership could an encounter with him in full consciousness become possible. If one considers at this point that Rudolf Steiner conceived *The Philosophy of Freedom* in a completely Michaelic state of mind, one can well imagine that in the spiritual world its content (summed up in the idea of ethical individualism as in a focal point) could become the portal for the conscious encounter with Michael and later for receiving the Christ Mysteries from him, Mysteries that after the turn of the century Rudolf Steiner brought out in pure thought-form as anthroposophy.

The second fundamental element of ethical individualism is moral imagination (Ger.: *moralische Phantasie* or 'fantasy'). This concept has its place at the very centre of the whole book and in this form was newly coined by Rudolf Steiner, even including its formulation in words. He himself speaks about this as follows: 'In my *Philosophy of Freedom*, published in 1894, I called one chapter "Moral Imagination" [*Phantasie*]. In the spiritual-scientific sense, one could also say "*Imaginative Moral Impulses*". I wished to point out that the domain that otherwise is grasped artistically only in imagination [*Phantasie*] must now by necessity be grasped in earnest by humanity, the reason being that this is the level we must attain *in order to take into ourselves the spiritual* [element] which is not grasped by the brain.'(GA 193, 12 June 1919.) In these words likewise, the effect of moral imagination [*Phantasie*] from above to below is indicated: it brings the supersensible down into the human being in the form of moral imaginations. In another passage Rudolf Steiner moreover states that such mental activity by the human being already contains a sort of 'clairvoyance', but one of which the latter is as yet unaware.[221]

Of the three main human fields of activity—science, art and religion—it is above all art that is linked with the essence of imagination [*Phantasie*]. As is well known, imagination has at all times been disdained in science, and even in religion it is not particularly welcome. By contrast, this characteristic of art (particularly in the form of *exact imagination* [*Phantasie*], which can build up all the way to the 'imaginative faculty', can moreover be transferred to other domains of human spiritual activity. This is why, in his *Philosophy of Freedom,* Rudolf Steiner describes philosophy as an 'art' and terms 'all true philosophers'—and in this sense himself too—'*artists of concepts*'. Then he goes so far as to describe the essential question in his book which must be answered therein like this: 'How does philosophy as an art [relate] to the freedom of man?' (GA 4; emphasis by Rudolf Steiner.)

Here Rudolf Steiner had only one actual predecessor, who had advanced in this direction to the extent it was possible in his lifetime. Equally great as a poet *and* philosopher, this was Friedrich Schiller, who in his main philosophical work, *Briefe über die ästhetische Erziehung des Menschen* (Letters on the aesthetic education of man), had come closest to a comprehension of the essential nature of moral imagination [*Phantasie*]. He describes in this work how man must struggle to attain his freedom within himself between the two poles devoid of freedom, namely the duress of logical laws and moral commands on the part of the spirit, and the compulsion of his instincts and urges originating from his corporeality. Only flanked by these two as it were in the mid-region, the actual human being exists as a free artistic nature who out of the kingdom of his imagination [*Phantasie*] finds freedom in his soul and learns to utilize it properly. Although Schiller characterizes this faculty merely as being 'aesthetic', even so it essentially has an obviously ennobling and therefore moral effect. Schiller wishes to establish a new aestheticism that can have a moral effect on a person; however, since his starting point remains pure art (with the faculty of imagination in its centre), *such* a moral effect upon someone always leaves that individual free. In this way Schiller came very close to the reality of moral imagination. And according to Rudolf Steiner, it is through moral imagination alone that moral ideals can be brought out of the spiritual world.

Schiller, who possessed a special faculty for bringing moral ideals out of the spiritual world and to present them through his art in a manner leaving anybody completely free, practised the faculty of moral imagination himself to an unusually large degree. The only problem in his case was that he could not bring this process to full awareness in himself. Therefore, the idea of freedom remained for him—as it did in a different manner also for Goethe—an emotional experience, finding its way neither into the region of cognition nor the will. Rudolf Steiner refers to this peculiarity in the relationship to freedom of both poet-friends with the following words: 'The element contained as the first impetus in Schiller's letters about *The Aesthetic Education of Man* and in all of Goethe's artistic creations—and that is the realization of human freedom through inner struggle and striving—can actually be attained only when it is acknowledged that to what we have in artistic experience as free beings we can add free experience in the domain of thinking and free experience in the domain of will.'[222] This lack of exercising thinking and willing on the part of Schiller and Goethe was made up for in *The Philosophy of Freedom* in the first part for the domain of thinking, and in the second part for that of willing. Moral imagination, however, remained also in Rudolf Steiner's case at the very centre as that human faculty which alone can connect the two poles (above and below) and with that can become the basis for man's complete freedom as expression of his *total* nature. And this development extends even further in anthroposophy. This is why Rudolf Steiner states: 'This we first had to struggle to attain through the introduction of anthroposophical spiritual science, namely that freedom could be acknowledged in the domains of thinking and willing. Schiller and Goethe after all recognized it only in the domain of feeling.' (Ibid.)

In other words, what was begun early on in *The Philosophy of Freedom* for fathoming freedom in the human being had to be continued further through spiritual science. When one pictures this continuation not only 'philosophically' but in a quite real consequential sense proceeding further on the basis of *The Philosophy of Freedom*, the following path is possible.

If the central faculty that this book refers to (namely moral imagination) is developed further in accordance with the book *Knowledge of the Higher Worlds and Its Attainment* to its highest potential, not only can the imaginations of the spiritual world be perceived (this can already be accomplished through fully developed pure thinking), but new imaginations can likewise be *created* within the spiritual world, imaginations that will then exist independently as free form-creations of the human being. And similar to how a person begins to create through moral imagination a new reality out of nothing on earth, the initiate who has progressed much further on this path can do this also in the spiritual world. For there exists a close kinship between the Creation out of Nothing and the way moral imagination works. In both cases, we deal with free action on the part of the human being out of conditions or relationships.

Activation of moral imagination consists, for instance, in the following. Someone comes across a certain situation in life consisting of a sum of pre-existing perceptions. Out of their inherent conditions and relationships, this person lets something quite *new* come about in a free way. In the same sense, Rudolf Steiner also describes the nature of the Creation out of Nothing by saying 'that the human being can create new things out of [existing] conditions; that relationships into which we have been placed can be turned into the basis for new things that man himself creates' (GA 107, 17 June 1909). 'That is why,' continues Rudolf Steiner, 'every true theory of evolution will never be able to set aside the thought of the Creation out of Nothing.'(Ibid.) This means that just as ethical individualism represents the crowning point of natural evolution, so the faculty connected with the former, namely not only to become creative on earth but also from the spiritual world as well, represents the goal of its further evolution. Thus, every human being will in the future likewise appear as a free creator in the higher worlds.

The main element and third part of ethical individualism is the power of spiritual love. It originates in accordance with *The Philosophy of Freedom* from the actions that a human being carries out based on pure love for the object. If on the path of inner schooling (as described in the book *Knowledge of the Higher Worlds*) such love is borne upward into the spiritual world, then it is effective there not only in producing forms, i.e. imaginations, but moreover in shaping a new substance out of which in future time the Cosmos of Love can originate (see GA 13). Already on this level, man begins to be freely creative in the cosmic sense. And with that he increasingly fulfils his true destiny in the universe.

From what has been presented one can conclude that when ethical individualism becomes fully conscious of its relationship to the Christ, meaning when it actually relies on the Christ Impulse in the human being, it can take its three inborn *human* faculties—pure thinking, moral imagination and spiritual love—and transform them on the modern path of inner schooling into *cosmic* or *universal* faculties.

This occurs by means of the fact that pure thinking is borne into the spiritual world and there acquires a radiant and thereby perceptive trait. Moral imagination receives the power to create forms, or imaginations, in the supersensible world out of nothing. And spiritual love becomes the creator of the new spirit-substance in the higher worlds.

If we now consider these three qualities in a twofold cosmic-human significance as thought-light, imaginative form, and love-substance, we arrive at the essential nature of the Foundation Stone which Rudolf Steiner created at the Christmas Conference out of cosmic-human forces as his freest deed. Along with that, what was still pictured in *The Philosophy of Freedom* from the human aspect received its cosmic dimension that consists of the fact that the human being as free creator can work for the first time in the spiritual world as well, meaning in the sense of the Tenth Hierarchy.

On this basis, the twofold cosmic-human nature of the Foundation Stone can be comprehended in a quite new way in its dual form, above all in its profound connection with the content of *The Philosophy of Freedom* with its culmination in ethical individualism. For at its creation during the Christmas Conference, the spiritual Foundation Stone received its truly human-cosmic perspective. Immediately afterwards, Rudolf Steiner brings it to the point of spiritual luminescence, and with that to inner visibility. Then he describes its appearance as follows: 'Then shall we carry away with us from here what we need. Then shall the Foundation Stone shine forth before the eyes of our soul, that Foundation Stone which has received its substance from cosmic-human love, its picture image (its form) from cosmic-human imagination, and its brilliant radiance from cosmic-human thoughts—its brilliant radiance that can shine towards us with warm light whenever we recollect this moment, with light that spurs on our deeds, our thinking, our feeling and our willing.' (GA 260, 25 December 1923.)

As was described in detail elsewhere, out of these three forces of the Foundation Stone, Rudolf Steiner had earlier consistently developed the whole of anthroposophy in its 21 years of growth. In the first seven years he established it as the modern science of the spirit by bearing the spiritualized human thoughts up to the hierarchies so as to receive from them the cosmic thoughts which he then summarized in his book *Occult Science, an Outline*. In the second seven-year period, he raised human imaginations into the spiritual world in order then to be given the cosmic imaginations from the gods, imaginations that found their actualization above all in the colours and forms of the First Goetheanum. And in the third seven-year period, Rudolf Steiner carried his pure love for action into the spiritual world and received from it the creative forces in order to inaugurate all the daughter-movements on earth.[223] Finally during the Christmas Conference, he created the Foundation Stone out of these three forces, the Foundation Stone which as we have seen has its origin in the three faculties of ethical individualism: pure thinking, moral imagination and spiritual love.

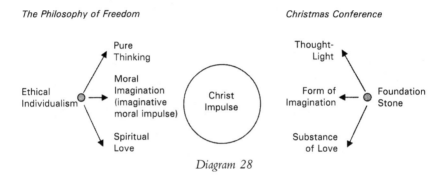

Diagram 28

In summation it can be said that if true ethical individualism 'builds on the Christ Impulse in man', the human being, who really has actualized this impulse within himself, can find the Christ Impulse in his 'I' in the sense of the words 'Not I but Christ in me' and thereby carry out the decisive step from unconditional cognition to unconditional action, or pure Creation out of Nothing. Rudolf Steiner carried out this step archetypically with the creation of the Foundation Stone. With that the three human qualities of ethical individualism take on a new human-cosmic dimension that finds its realization in the threefold nature of the Foundation Stone.

The above-ascertained connection between the threefold nature of ethical individualism and the three elements of the Foundation Stone throws new light on the relationship of the two with the two spiritual streams that will eventually bring anthroposophy to its culmination, namely the Platonic and Aristotelian ones. As has already been shown elsewhere,[224] the union of these streams was pre-established by Rudolf Steiner in the essence of the Foundation Stone—in the advancement of thinking all the way to radiant power which demonstrates above all the characteristic of the Aristotelians. On the other hand, the form-producing power of imaginations is more akin to the Platonists. Both streams then unite in the joint work of attaining the substance of the Foundation Stone, which consists of pure love.

The same can be said of the nature of ethical individualism and its three fundamental characteristics. Thus attainment of pure thinking tends more towards Aristotelian traits, whereas in moral imagination the Platonic element is more prevalent. In the free deeds out of spiritual love, both streams ultimately unite in a higher unity. This indeed has to be so, because ethical individualism represents the ideal of every human being as to its inner nature and origin.

This moreover relates also to the whole content of *The Philosophy of Freedom*, which according to its form appears to be more Aristotelian but at the same time contains a strong Platonic element. It is with good reason that Rudolf Steiner in the first introduction of this book designates philosophers as 'artists in the realm of concepts'. (Among such philosophers, Plato was no doubt one of the greatest, whereas Aristotle was much more the first scientist and researcher.) Likewise, the text of the *Credo*, which Rudolf Steiner authored around 1888 (meaning during the time when in his mind he was already occupied with working out the basic ideas of his *Philosophy of Freedom*), has a strong Platonic character (see GA 40).

Another indication by Rudolf Steiner can help us furthermore to understand the creating of the Foundation Stone as a *cosmic-human creation* out of both the forces of the Holy Trinity and the threefold essence of ethical individualism in a still deeper sense. In an earlier lecture, Rudolf Steiner thus links the main characteristics of ethical individualism with the higher members of man's being. He states that what he characterized in *The Philosophy of Freedom* as 'pure thinking' is called Manas or Spirit Self in spiritual-scientific terminology. What he described in the book as 'moral imagination' corresponds in spiritual science to Buddhi or Life Spirit. Viewed practically, this signifies the following. If ethical individualism truly builds on the Christ Impulse in the way this impulse is active in the human soul only after the Mystery of Golgotha, then the further development of pure thinking leads to the experience of the Spirit Self and the corresponding development of moral imagination to taking hold of the Life Spirit. From the entire context it therefore follows unmistakably in the same way that the third and highest characteristic of ethical individualism, spiritual love, can be considered in connection with Atma or Spirit Man, that is to say, it leads there in its further development.

In his early lectures, Rudolf Steiner frequently describes how the spiritual threefoldness in the human being (Manas–Buddhi–Atma) represents a microcosmic replica of the Divine Trinity in the macrocosm (for example GA 94, 28 October 1906). It follows from this that an individual who, like Rudolf Steiner, has developed in himself this higher threefoldness on the path of modern initiation[225] reaches the point of creatively handling the Trinitarian forces in our cosmos. Then the forces of the Holy Spirit can enlighten his pure thinking that has arisen to the level of Manas. Out of the encircling round of the earth Christ can penetrate the free activity of his moral imagination that has reached the Buddhi level. And working out of the cosmic depths, the creative forces of the Father can unite with his spiritual love that bears within itself the seeds of Atma. In this way on the basis of the ongoing evolution of ethical individualism, such an initiate can freely bring about completely new *relationships* to the Holy Trinity in order to undertake, subsequently based on them, the Creation out of Nothing.[226]

Here, the relation between the Buddhi principle and moral imagination is of particular significance. For Rudolf Steiner brings this second spiritual principle into a direct connection with the Christ's activity in the human soul, something that in earlier lectures he even had designated as the divine Buddhi. (GA 93, 4 November 1904.)

As was mentioned before, the faculty of moral imagination stands in the centre of *The Philosophy of Freedom* and demonstrates exactly where ethical individualism counts most directly on the Christ Impulse in the human being. It causes a process of constant becoming in him or her and has its human reflection above all in the full unfolding of moral imagination. In it a person begins to create on the level of 'I'-*consciousness* as freely and independently as otherwise only the Word of Worlds—who originates from the Holy Trinity—did on the level of *existence* during the creation of the world. If moreover the faculty of spiritual love is added, then human beings themselves can begin to be creative in the spiritual world. Then they are in a position to establish the new creation consisting of pure love-substance.

It was out of this primal fount of genuine creation in which the whole unconditionality of Rudolf Steiner's theory of knowledge is furthermore rooted that he created the Foundation Stone of Love at the Christmas Conference. He describes this process of creation that he performed out of the cosmic forces of the Holy Trinity (meaning out of its forces as they work in the macrocosm) in the following words: 'Out of these three forces, out of the Spirit of the heights, out of the force of Christ in the encircling round, out of the working of the Father, the creative activity of the Father that streams out of the depths, let us at this moment give form in our souls to the dodecahedral Foundation Stone ...' (GA 260, 25 December 1923.) This deed is verily the beginning of a new creation that proceeds from the free human being and inherently has its cognitive roots already in Rudolf Steiner's early work.

With the help of what was stated above, we can now better understand the connection of the three faculties of ethical individualism with the Trinitarian character of the Foundation Stone. The Foundation Stone itself consists of three main segments. Each one of them on its part is put together in every case from three elements, a cosmic (Trinitarian) one, a human one, and that element which brings to expression man's own threefold being.

1 Cosmic-human Thinking

The thinking referred to here is in no way the ordinary body-bound one but the *pure thinking* of *The Philosophy of Freedom*, which during man's further evolution unites with the whole human being and in so doing attains Manas quality. Through this, the power of the Holy Spirit out of the heights of the cosmos can now illuminate this thinking and lead man to higher insights.

Cosmic		Human		Thinking
Holy Spirit	←	Manas	←	Pure Thinking

It is similar in the case of the second main segment of the Foundation Stone:

2 Cosmic-human Imagination

Here the singular form of the word 'imagination' refers above all to the faculty of *moral imagination*,[227] which in its further development (and when it takes hold on its part of the whole human being) acquires Buddhi quality. Through it, the Christ Force can now work in man:

Cosmic		Human		Imagination
Christ	←	Buddhi	←	Moral Imagination

Thirdly, *spiritual love* can likewise imbue the whole human being whereby his actions—even though in the very early rudimentary state—can exhibit an Atma quality:

3 Cosmic-human Love

Here, the human being can unite with the creative Father Forces that arise out of the cosmic depths.

Cosmic		Human		Love
Father	←	Atma	←	Spiritual Love

Thus, the further development of ethical individualism, which becomes aware of its being rooted in the Christ Impulse with the help of anthroposophy, attains to its highest fulfilment. Out of the newly acquired relationship to the forces of the Trinity, the human being rises to free creating out of nothing, hence to man's cosmic destiny as the Tenth Hierarchy of freedom and love.

In this way, pure thinking represents the pole of freedom of *ethical individualism* upon which man takes complete hold of the essence of his 'I' through the portal of the exceptional state and with that of his human *individuality*. Spiritual love represents the actual *ethical* pole of his being, out of which emerge all moral impulses—impulses that, once grasped by pure thinking, become conscious in man's 'I'. Both qualities meet in the central realm, that of moral imagination, which represents the central force of ethical individualism. For in moral imagination the two qualities (freedom out of pure thinking and morality out of spiritual love) are harmoniously united and in their combined activity can begin to nurture the new faculty in man which, as was demonstrated before, stands nearest to the creative Word of Worlds.

★

The here depicted relation between the three essential components of ethical individualism and the Foundation Stone can furthermore be comprehended in the following way. As previously shown elsewhere, the lecture of 13 January 1924, given precisely twelve days after the conclusion of the Christmas Conference, offers an esoteric key for its events.[228] Rudolf Steiner describes here among other topics how an initiate today can approach Michael in the spiritual world. First, he has to develop the faculty of being able to read in the astral light of the cosmos where the 'secrets of existence' are recorded. Then, based on the insights thereby acquired and out of his freedom, he has to do something in the world so as to be able to appear before Michael with the consequences of his deeds and have them judged by the archangel. In the event that Michael senses such free human deeds to be 'justified before the reign of the cosmos' (GA 233a, 13 January 1924), the following can then happen: 'When, based on freedom and stimulated by the reading of the astral light, a human being does this or that consciously or unconsciously, then Michael carries that which is an earthly deed out into the cosmos so it becomes a cosmic deed' (ibid.).

An important question arises at this point: Is the here described process only feasible for an initiate, that is for one who can read in the astral light, or does the possibility exist for all human beings today to draw near to

Michael on such a path? The latter is actually the case. When we study anthroposophy not in the ordinary abstract sense but in the studying itself ascend to pure thinking so that it becomes for us the first stage of modern initiation (see GA 13), then through our purified thinking we have taken in the same insights that an initiate generally can read only in the astral light. For in a certain respect all results of anthroposophical research are acquired this way; they are all supersensible facts read in the astral light. Now if a person takes them in through his thinking, he resembles an initiate who has to carry these spiritual contents in his thinking for the purpose of communicating them to others in the same way as one who subsequently studies these supersensible facts. And although such a person cannot research these contents in the spiritual world (that is, read in the astral light), once he has understood them rightly with his thinking he can act, based upon them, as freely as can an initiate. So as to transform the insights that are based on the study of spiritual science into truly *free* deeds, however, their implementation must initially be left up to moral imagination so that they can subsequently be carried out based on pure love of the action. Thus on this modern path of the human being to Michael, we have the activation of all three characteristics of ethical individualism.

One can therefore say that today only this path really leads to Michael, but only under the condition that prior to that a person has come to terms with anthroposophical insights and has thoroughly made them his own. In so doing the main characteristic of such appropriation of higher knowledge consists of the following. When we bring the study of spiritual knowledge to the point of pure thinking, we thereby do not receive anything foreign into ourselves, only something that has lived in us from the very beginning since we ourselves descended as spirit beings out of the supersensible world onto the earth. This distinguishes the study of anthroposophy fundamentally from any other study. Rudolf Steiner points this out in the following words: 'Although the thoughts [of spiritual science] are already present when one surrenders oneself [as a student] to them, one cannot think them unless in each case one *recreates them anew* in one's soul' (GA 13). It is through this very 'recreating them anew' (something that is only possible in pure thinking) that the spiritual-scientific thoughts become the property of the human soul as if the soul itself had discovered them in the astral light. And more: 'What is important is that the spirit-researcher awakens thoughts in his listeners and readers which they must first produce *out* of themselves, whereas one who describes matters of sensory reality refers to something that can be observed by listeners and readers in the sense world' (ibid.; emphasis by Rudolf Steiner).[229] When human beings do things in the world that are brought out of their own thoughts in accordance with ethical individualism, meaning that they accept them into their moral imagination and then work based on it, then these are deeds that can be affirmed by Michael and then continue being effective in the spiritual world as *cosmic deeds* of man. In this way ethical individualism acquires its cosmic dimension.

Rudolf Steiner archetypically demonstrated what this actually implies by creating the supersensible Foundation Stone at the Christmas Conference. Now if one compares more incipient deeds that are based on ethical individualism with this highest creator-deed by Rudolf Steiner, one can say of the first that in doing them human beings gradually learn to find the spirit in their 'I' so that, as spirit beings, they become able to work freely in the world. During the creation of the Foundation Stone on the other hand the opposite occurred. The free 'I' of a human being ascended fully consciously into the spiritual world in order there to become creative, something that corresponds to the condition of the ' "I" in the Spirit'. We have with this the whole development of ethical individualism before us, beginning with its earthly-human origin in 'Spirit in the "I" ' and concluding with its cosmic dimension in the ' "I" in the Spirit'.

The above-said moreover has a direct connection to what Rudolf Steiner characterized in the karma lectures of 1924 as the supersensible preparation of anthroposophy. It passed through two preparatory cosmic stages before it descended to earth. On both stages, the Michael entity played a central role, first in the Michael School, then in the Imaginative cultus. This is why Rudolf Steiner could describe the whole of anthroposophy in the way he established it in the twentieth century as 'the gift by Michael'. (GA 152, 2 May 1913.)

Thus we have all together three stages:

1. The supersensible Michael School
2. The Imaginative Cultus
3. Anthroposophy's founding on earth.

The three constituent parts of ethical individualism are linked as well with these three stages in so far as man develops and practises ethical individualism on the foundation of anthroposophical insights. First, out of one's 'I'-consciousness, one sets out with the strength of pure thinking on an intense study of anthroposophy (something, as we have seen, that in a certain regard is equal to reading in the astral light). If one then desires on such a basis to be active in the world, one has to attain to the unfolding of one's own moral imagination in the sense of ethical individualism. If the activation of this imagination is then truly nurtured out of anthroposophy, the 'moral imaginative impulses originating from anthroposophy will bear in themselves what lives in the soul of an anthroposophist in the way of moral creative impulses based on his or her participation in the super-sensible Imaginative Cultus. Ultimately, if such an individual goes on to carry out deeds in the world and is successful in performing them really unselfishly based on pure love for the spirit (which is recognized in the object), then the inspirations out of the lofty Michael School will work their way into such deeds (for in this supersensible school Michael's teachings were themselves spiritual deeds of love) so that the human being can work as the inspirations' direct emissary in the world.

The path to Michael, the stages which were revealed here in the light of ethical individualism, thus leads up from the study of anthroposophy to the Imaginative Cultus and simultaneously to the supersensible Michael School.

What was said so far can be summed up as follows:

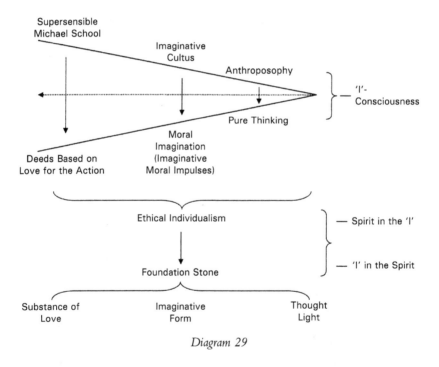

Diagram 29

Likewise, the three elements of the Foundation Stone correspond to the three stages of anthroposophy's heavenly-earthly development. Accordingly, the whole thought-content of anthroposophy radiates in the light of the Foundation Stone; in its imaginative form lives a direct connection with the essence of the Imaginative Cultus, and in its love-substance works the same Sun-power out of which Michael led his supersensible school in the Sun-region, the world-encompassing sphere of love. Anyone can unite with this evolutionary path of anthroposophy if, based on personal freedom, there is the willingness to implant the Foundation Stone into his or her heart. In so doing, one inwardly not only unites with this threefold happening but likewise with the other souls who, together with him or her experienced this supersensible evolution of anthroposophy in the past. A person then seeks out such souls on earth again in order to unite with them in a new human community. In this way, the Foundation Stone in one's heart turns into something that Rudolf Steiner referred to already at its inception. It becomes the supersensible foundation for the Anthroposophical Society as an association of the actual Michael-disciples on earth. For this purpose, he bestowed on this society the Foundation Stone immediately after he had created it. This is why he continued with the above-mentioned words concerning the Foundation Stone's creation out of the forces of the Trinity as follows: '... [the Foundation Stone] which we lower into the soil of our souls so that it may remain a powerful sign there in the strong grounds of our soul existence, and so that in the future working of the Anthroposophical Society we may stand on this firm Foundation Stone' (GA 260, 25 December 1923). This means that the Foundation Stone, which could only originate through Rudolf Steiner's free individual deed, was then offered up by him personally so that it could continue to live on in the hearts of the anthroposophists as the spiritual foundation of the Anthroposophical Society. In this form, the transition from the individual element to the social element occurred during the cultic act of the laying of the Foundation Stone.

With this, the whole above-described path that leads from the three qualities of ethical individualism to the spiritual Foundation Stone of the Anthroposophical Society acquires yet another decisive characteristic, which is traceable on all the earlier depicted stages, namely a *social* one.

As early as in Friedrich Schiller's case, in a sense one can discover (in his state of mind) a quite germinal prophetic presentiment of this future. Having in detail dealt with and established the state of the aesthetic free human being in his 'Letters', at the end of his work he poses the question concerning a community of aesthetic human beings. He then tries to answer this in the form of an aesthetic state or kingdom (naturally, Schiller uses terminology corresponding to his age).

Thus he writes in the last, the twenty-seventh letter, *'To give freedom through freedom,* that is the basic law of this kingdom.' And he continues: 'Only the aesthetic state can actualize it [the society of free human beings] because such a state carries out the will of the whole [population] through the nature of the individual.'[230] With this Schiller points to the transition from the individual element to the social element necessary for the future.

This motif moreover plays a central role during the Christmas Conference, for its Foundation Stone can be implanted in the human heart's ground only through a purely individual deed by one who acts based on spiritual insight and complete freedom. Now if this has been done correctly, then the Foundation Stone lives and works in the human heart as the Foundation Stone of a new human community, which was given the name 'General (meaning general human) Anthroposophical Society' by Rudolf Steiner at the Christmas Conference.

The transformation of the Foundation Stone's individual effect into its social effectiveness that unites human beings occurs at the Christmas Conference through the appearance of the Spirit in the radiant thought-aura around the Foundation Stone. This Spirit is none other than the new Pentecost Spirit who works in every human being individually and yet always remains the same, and in that way unites all human beings in a free community.[231] This is why this Spirit is the actual founder of a free community of individuals (or a community of free spirits), for in it dwells the perfect synthesis of individuality and community from the very beginning, hence the harmonious relationship between freedom (as the highest individual accomplishment of man) and love (as man's highest social accomplishment).

This spirit of the new Pentecost community that freely stands on the supersensible (ideal) Foundation Stone represents its fourth and highest element. One finds this Spirit referred to already in the *Philosophy of Freedom.* For as Schiller did in his manner, so Rudolf Steiner too poses the decisive question in his *Philosophy of Freedom* concerning the transition from the description of man as an individual free being to the next level that forms a community of morally free individuals. And precisely in the book's passage where Rudolf Steiner deals with this question as we have already seen, there appears the reference to the communal spirit who alone can guarantee the unity of free human beings: 'Only because human individuals are of *one spirit* can they likewise live their lives side by side' (GA 4, Chap. IX).

We thus have a correspondence between the *Philosophy of Freedom* and the Foundation Stone in all its four elements:

The Philosophy of Freedom		Christmas Conference
Ethical Individualism		*Foundation Stone*:
1. Pure Thinking	—	Cosmic-human Thought
2. Moral Imagination	—	Cosmic-human Imagination
3. Moral Love	—	Cosmic-human Love
4. *Communal Spirit*	—	*Spirit of the Foundation Stone*[232]

The joining together of the individual and social elements appears at the Christmas Conference not only in the relationship of man to the Foundation Stone and the Anthroposophical Society, but likewise in the Foundation Stone Meditation as has been shown already in the ninth chapter. This meditation begins with the mighty beckoning call of the human soul to itself and concludes in the fourth segment with the great 'We'-chord.

Likewise, the relationship of anthroposophists to Michael is shaped in this domain of tensions between individuality and community. For the starting point of the modern path to Michael is initially located quite individually in the attainment of pure thinking, with the force of which a person (beginning from our age onward) can carry the Michaelic intelligence (which has fallen to earth) back up to Michael. On the other hand, Michael himself has preordained the joint activity of all his disciples on earth in his supersensible school. This is why it is only on the basis of the recognized Sun-karma that unites them that, as true Michaelites and guardians of the spiritual Foundation Stone, they can find the means to come together in the Anthroposophical Society so as to actualize the mighty Michaelic tasks of our time.[233]

In regard to anthroposophy (the being), we have a similar transition through the Christmas Conference from the individual to the social element. This being is directly addressed twice during the laying of the Foundation Stone on 25 December and called by its name 'Anthroposophia'. The connection with her can only be established through an individual deed by the human being, inasmuch as 'we allow our hearts to be imbued with life [through her]'. This implies uniting one's own soul so intensely with the thoughts of anthroposophy that they find their way from the head to the heart, appearing there so filled with life and spiritual substance that the entry of the being Anthroposophia into the heart and the heart's resulting imbuement with life becomes possible through her. Only when this has taken place can the next step occur as a direct consequence. Then out of this heart-impulse, the Anthroposophical Society can be transformed into 'a true union of human beings *for Anthroposophia*'. (GA 260, 25 December 1923.)

In the ninth chapter of the *Philosophy of Freedom*, one can likewise discover the reference to these two aspects of the individual and social element. As was already quoted earlier, Rudolf Steiner writes in his book of the one common or the '*one spirit*' that penetrates all free human beings every time in a completely individual manner with the original Whitsun effect. 'Even though egoism can grow stronger all the time, *every 'I''* will have the communal spirit if it shares in the Spirit of Truth' (GA 97, 8 March 1907). And immediately in the next sentence of the same chapter, Rudolf Steiner speaks of the common or '*one* spiritual world' to which belong all other free human beings. This then is the reason why they can harmonize with each other in their intentions.

As was already shown in Chapter 10, this 'common world of ideas' is moreover that of the Heavenly Sophia, whose revelation on earth is anthroposophy in modern scientific thought-form. In the spiritual world she is a uniform being uniting humanity, a being that here on earth in her thought-imbued form of appearance as an object of study especially promotes the individualization of the human being in accordance with the development of the consciousness soul.[234]

All these stages and forms of the union by the individual element with that of the social one have their origin in the appearance of the Christ on earth. For in this fact, we have at the same time the complete revelation of the 'I' of all mankind as well as the archetype of the higher 'I' of each individual earthly human being (see GA 112, 24 June 1909). Thus He works simultaneously in the individual human 'I', yet also where two or more human beings voluntarily unite 'in His Name' (Matt. 18:20), which means in His Spirit, the Spirit which then works in them as the Whitsun Spirit or 'the Spirit of Truth'.[235]

One can therefore say that the individualizing effect of the Spirit begins to work in a socially developing way in accordance with the renewed Whitsun spirit and establishes a new community which is mentioned in *The Philosophy of Freedom* as the community of free human beings. And working through the being Anthroposophia, the Heavenly Sophia makes available to the consciousness soul of the human being a common (generally comprehensible) world of ideas, a world out of which everybody in full freedom can obtain individually differing thought-inspirations.

The process described here is likewise connected with the working of the Holy Spirit, for 'the Spirit that will make man free is the Holy Spirit' (GA 87, 17 March 1907). It follows from this that the nature of freedom cannot be comprehended at all without the Holy Spirit. Yet in every epoch, its activity is linked with the corresponding Time Spirit, a fact that makes it clear that in our age it works in humanity particularly through Michael. As was depicted in Chapter 4, Rudolf Steiner calls the Holy Spirit likewise the 'Spirit of Truth' who reveals Himself individually but at the same time always has a community-building effect. This is why, in *The Philosophy of Freedom*, Rudolf Steiner does not stop at the comprehension of freedom in the individual domain but in a quite self-evident way continues on to write about the emergence of a community of free human minds.

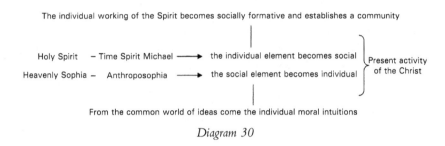

Diagram 30

These two paths, from the individual to the social element and from the social to the individual one, find their harmonious union and their highest archetype in the *present-day* activity of the Christ. As Lord of Karma, He above all brings about the connection of the individual element with the social one. For according to Rudolf Steiner, the consequence of this karmic activity of the Christ is that the equalization of man's individual karma can serve the greatest possible benefit of the community and (as seen from the perspective of the future) all of mankind. (GA 130, 2 December 1911.) At the same time, in the light of the Christ, a community can help bear the karma of the individual human member and in so doing gradually becomes a replica of conformity to heavenly laws. Rudolf Steiner calls this the 'establishment, built on the nature of the "I", of future humanity' (GA 123, 11 September 1910). Today to enter upon these two paths is one of the central tasks of the Anthroposophical Society. Due to the fact that Rudolf Steiner communicated to the society's members their karma, this society received its spiritual mission to develop towards a new karma-community in order subsequently to be capable of working in accord with the Christ Impulse in the field of karma.

Likewise, the supersensible Foundation Stone of the Christmas Conference forms the unshakeable base for such new karma-work. For the possibility to connect the individual and social elements at any time harmoniously in accordance with the Christ Impulse is immanently present in the nature of the supersensible Foundation Stone. In order better to comprehend all this, we must consider this connection more from the cosmic standpoint.

Rudolf Steiner developed this aspect of the theme above all in the lecture of 25 January 1924. In it he first points out that in pre-Christian times the individualization of humanity took place only through the influence of the Moon forces. These forces are, however, linked with the past of World evolution and therefore always have a hardening, mineralizing effect on the human being and with that an effect that separates and closes one off in one's self. Conversely, the forces of the Sun, which lead into the future, have an effect only on humanity as a whole—not on the solitary individual. This polarity between past and future (the original Sun-Moon polarity) or individuality and community was resolved in a unique manner by Christ for all times. This was done on the one hand inasmuch as He bore within Himself as representative of the Sun-kingdom the element of community that encompasses all mankind; on the other hand, through connecting his heavenly destiny with the earth, He created the possibility henceforth to engage Himself with each individuality, meaning the personal 'I' of every human being.

This is why Rudolf Steiner concludes this theme with the following words: 'Due to the fact that Christ changed from a Sun-being into an Earth-being, He has gained access to the single human individualities. The other Sun-beings, who have remained in the Sun, did not gain access to single human individualities, only to the general element of humanity' (GA 240, 25 January 1924). After Rudolf Steiner had summarized the new situation created through the Christ, he made a decisive reference that connects the above-mentioned new situation directly with all the events of the laying of the Foundation Stone. 'In the above-described way, the Christ Impulse has access to the *individuality of man* and must work in particular in his or her innermost depths if it is to become effective at all in the human being. It is not the forces of the intellect but the deepest soul and heart forces that must receive (or accept) the Christ Impulse. *But once this impulse is received it does not become effective in the sense of the individually human element but wholly in that of the overall human one.* This overall human working lends itself to the Christ because He is a Sun-being.' (Ibid.)

It is the same in the case of the Foundation Stone of the Christmas Conference which therefore cannot be received by the intellect, but only by the *heart* or *soul* of the human being (both above words were used by Rudolf Steiner during the laying of the Foundation Stone) into his or her inner state of mind. In this way what had to be grasped by the 'individually human' element became something that went on being effective in the soul in an 'overall human' way, meaning in this actual case as the 'spiritual foundation stone' for the *true* Anthroposophical Society. Therefore, not only does it follow from the content of this chapter that the Christmas Conference became the esoteric and at the same time world-historical fulfilment of the *Philosophy of Freedom*, but also that in the faculties that develop ethical individualism in the human being (on the basis of which the community of free human spirits can originate), the threefold essence of the Foundation Stone is already contained in a concealed way as if in a seed.

It was, however, only because Rudolf Steiner had elevated these three faculties of ethical individualism to the threefold spirit in man that he was in a position to guide this spirit in man to the threefold spirit in the universe in order, out of the union of both, to actualize the first human cosmic creation as a free product [Ger.: *Erzeugnis*] by a human being and foundation of the new Christian Mysteries.

With this it became manifest for the first time what it means when a human being 'in the true sense of the word changes from creature to creator'.[236]

Epilogue

'One who would want to have an
overview of *all* my work would see
accord, whereas another finds only
contradiction because he does not
have that overview.'[237]

> *Rudolf Steiner in a letter to*
> *Johanna Mücke on 22 September 1903*

The reader who has had the patience to read this book to its very end will
note that one is dealing here with a quite different approach to *The
Philosophy of Freedom* than is otherwise the case in the rather copious
literature that deals with this theme.

The reason is that most works about *The Philosophy of Freedom* attempt
to comprehend this book based on the general context of Rudolf
Steiner's early works, in order then to form a bridge to the later communications built on his research results in the spiritual world. That it is
not such an easy matter to build such a bridge is borne out by the fact that
many of the works of this sort remain standing at *The Philosophy of Freedom*
and do not dare take even one step across into anthroposophy; or they
attempt this crossing in quite a vague form in order to avoid the danger of
having to speak about a 'break' in Rudolf Steiner's development.[238]

In the present work, on the other hand, another path was chosen from
the very beginning. The somewhat bold attempt was made to follow the
opposite stream of time, namely to look back as it were from what Rudolf
Steiner established later as anthroposophy (and developed during three
seven-year periods) to his main early work (*The Philosophy of Freedom*) so as
to look at this book from this visual direction in a completely new light.

Here we must above all pay heed to the words by Rudolf Steiner that
are placed at the head of this epilogue as a motto. For in order not to be
constantly held up on these new paths by so-called contradictions (which
in actual fact are not contradictions), one has to try at the outset to acquire
'an overview' of 'everything', meaning to include the whole of anthroposophy in one's considerations. Obviously it is never possible to allow
for *everything* or even to take it into consideration approximately. On the
other hand, it is always possible to start out from the main directions of the
entirety of anthroposophy in order thereby to arrive at the firm conviction that in Rudolf Steiner's case, even in the transition from his philo-

sophical early work to the later anthroposophical one, we consistently deal only with a further development, not with 'contradictions' attributed to him out of misconceptions. Considering this matter more deeply, this is why we can experience Rudolf Steiner's own testimony as entirely corresponding with the facts and, based on this insight, can have full faith in him. 'I do not move forward in contradictions as many believe. If that were the case, I would gladly admit it. It would, however, not reflect the reality of my spiritual progress. I moved forward by finding [and adding] new areas to what lived in my soul.' (GA 28, Chap. XXX.)

So may this present book contribute further proof of the accuracy of these words so that this self-testimony by Rudolf Steiner can be experienced by the unprejudiced reader as being in full accord with his inner development and course of life. Most of all, the above-quoted words by Rudolf Steiner had to be verified through the already demonstrated accord between *The Philosophy of Freedom*, as culmination of the philosophical early work (the subtitle of which is 'Some Results of Introspective Observation Following the Methods of Natural Science'), and *Occult Science, an Outline*, which like a quintessence contains in itself the whole of anthroposophy.

It can be assumed that the considerations of *The Philosophy of Freedom* undertaken here will not immediately please all those who have thoroughly studied the above book. I can well understand this. I am also aware that the present work only represents a first beginning. Nevertheless, aside from many other already existing attempts to comprehend more deeply this fundamental work by Rudolf Steiner, this somewhat unusual approach has its justification. For it is hoped that people who initially came in contact with anthroposophy and only later became acquainted with *The Philosophy of Freedom* might find the contents of my book helpful in a completely new way for learning to value and love this special work by Rudolf Steiner. I know many anthroposophists who have lived for decades with anthroposophy and still have difficulties with this book. Above all, for people such as these, I would like to help make access to this book easier and more profound.

At this point it may be permissible to make a more personal remark. For me, a bit of destiny is connected with the origin of the present work. It was not my good fortune to become acquainted from the very start with *The Philosophy of Freedom* either. When at the end of the Sixties while still in Russia I encountered anthroposophy, only those works by Rudolf Steiner were available to me that had been published prior to the Revolution through the Russian Anthroposophical Society. For reasons unknown to me even to this day, of all books the translation and publication of *The Philosophy of Freedom* had been delayed for so long that ultimately no book by Rudolf Steiner could be published any more. Thus, the first Russian edition of this book came about as a typescript in a small circle of anthroposophical emigrants in Paris. As a result, I could not read this book until after I had for many years thoroughly studied all the basic anthroposophical books and many lectures by Rudolf Steiner. Thus it was part of my destiny as an anthroposophist to journey on the path from Rudolf Steiner's later works back to his early work, in a manner of speaking in the sequence from anthroposophy to *The Philosophy of Free-dom*. And the reader finds the result of this path in this present work.

From what has been said it likewise becomes clear that one is dealing here with the attempt to read *The Philosophy of Freedom* not only as a philosophical book but to comprehend it in the deepest sense as an *esoteric* work in which all the seeds for the later anthroposophy are already contained.

Just as in the nineteenth century there still were people in Europe who knew that the texts by Aristotle were no 'philosophy' in the customary sense but meditation books, which despite their thought-imbued form contain the knowledge of the Mysteries, so it is in the case of *The Philosophy of Freedom*, even if in a slightly different way. It too, although expressed in strictly scientific forms of thought that are suited to the age of the consciousness soul, already bears—as if in the background—the essence of the New Mysteries, and with that the whole 'new esotericism'.[239]

Even as in its own time the hidden content of the works by Aristotle could only be deciphered correctly with the help of Mystery knowledge and meditation, so it is today with the esoteric foundations of *The Philosophy of Freedom*, which can only be discovered and opened up in reconstructible form by means of anthroposophy and, above all, through intense meditative work.

In no way does this signify, however, that the first encounter with this book did not make a profound and enduring impression on me. I can still remember quite clearly how I attempted to explain the essence of *The Philosophy of Freedom* to a friend during several hours of a fairly long train ride. Yet this theme had to remain to begin with as if in the background of my life so that it could grow to maturity undisturbed and quietly. In particular, occupying myself with the Christmas Conference advanced my understanding of this book and its importance for the development of anthroposophy very much.

To start with, its direct relationship to the present-day activity of the Michael impulse arose clearly in my mind. This is why I wrote already in my first book, *Rudolf Steiner and the Founding of the New Mysteries*, 'This inner nature of Michael's battle with the dragon came to expression at the beginning of the new Michael Age in *The Philosophy of Freedom*. It is not possible here to go into closer detail on this great work of the human spirit in our time, but suffice it to say that, properly understood, this book will be a great weapon in the future with which Michael can battle against Ahriman in the souls and spirits of human beings.'[240]

These words were written exactly a quarter of a century ago. What was not possible for me then, however, namely to go into closer detail of *The Philosophy of Freedom*, is now in the present work supposed to happen as a sort of summation of the anthroposophical work undertaken since then.

The view presented here of *The Philosophy of Freedom* was initially offered in Chapter 7 of my *May Human Beings Hear It!* where the theme was considered above all from the standpoint of Rudolf Steiner's biography and the development of the Anthroposophical Movement. Into the centre of the above considerations, the two most important deeds (or accomplishments) were placed by Rudolf Steiner, deeds that like two columns of strength bear the whole edifice of anthroposophy: *The Philosophy of Freedom* and the Christmas Conference of 1923/1924.[241]

In order to bring out the connection between these two deeds, accomplishments that in a certain regard constitute the beginning and end of his earthly activity, this grand metamorphosis was indicated in the above-mentioned seventh chapter that pervades the unfolding of anthroposophy on earth and consists of four stages: *The Philosophy of Freedom*—*Occult Science, an Outline*—the First Goetheanum—the Christmas Conference.

This fourfold metamorphosis can be characterized briefly as follows. In *The Philosophy of Freedom*, Rudolf Steiner laid the foundation for the scientific path of cognition (which is equally applicable for exploration of physical/sensory nature as well as for the spiritual world). Consequently, pursuing this path of cognition led to the establishment of anthroposophy as the modern *spiritual science*. Rudolf Steiner introduced this science in all its dimensions particularly in his book *Occult Science, an Outline* in purely scientific modes of thought. Subsequently, he brought it to expression in visible imaginations of artistic forms and colours in the First Goetheanum. Later after this structure had gone through the fiery transformation, he received the imaginations anew out of the cosmos as a wholly spiritual impulse, and out of this wellspring carried out the complete Christmas Conference and shaped it as the highest fulfilment of *The Philosophy of Freedom* on earth. (See more details about this in my above-mentioned book *May Human Beings Hear It!*)

During the description of the four stages of this metamorphosis, the first—and in a certain sense most difficult to establish—transition from the book *The Philosophy of Freedom* to *Occult Science, an Outline* seemed to have eluded me somewhat, and so the question remained for me: How are these two main works by Rudolf Steiner connected to each other? Here his sparse indications barely helped for he mostly referred to this connection in a fleeting manner without linking it with a detailed explanation. One could gain the impression that in this way he meant to induce his disciples to solve this task on their own.

With the present book, *one* such attempt is meant to be undertaken. In so doing, I was guided in particular by those comments by Rudolf Steiner in which he indicates that the totality of anthroposophy—albeit in hidden form (like a huge tree in a small seed)—can be found in *The Philosophy of Freedom*. In one lecture there is even the indication that this book not only culminates in anthroposophy in line with the path of knowledge described there but also as to its contents: 'Fundamentally speaking, the deliberations of anthroposophically based writings of subsequent years are but a sum of everything that originally was pointed out in my *Philosophy of Freedom*' (GA 335, 15 June 1920).

As if in sketches, the entire content of anthroposophy is found in just one work by Rudolf Steiner as mentioned earlier, namely in *Occult Science an Outline*. In the last epilogue to this book, which Rudolf Steiner wrote two-and-a-half months prior to his death, one can read: 'The book does contain the outlines of anthroposophy as a whole … Everything I have since been able to state—if fitted into the right passage of this book—appears like a further deliberation of the original sketch.' And if one considers the sum total content of this book, one does indeed discover in it *all* the most important themes of anthroposophy:

1. The scientific nature of anthroposophy
2. The spiritual structure of man (spiritual-scientific anthropology)
3. Life between death and new birth
4. Karma as law of human life
5. Evolution of the world
6. Activity of hierarchies
7. The central significance of the Christ Impulse and the Mystery of Golgotha
8. Modern initiation
9. Future development of man and the world
10. Anthroposophy as modern spiritual science.

It was the main concern of this my work to show that all these basic themes of anthroposophy all the way to the Foundation Stone of the Christmas Conference were already contained as if in a concealed germinal condition in *The Philosophy of Freedom*.

With that the bridge was created between Rudolf Steiner's two most important books, and likewise the connection between his later work and the earlier one. After all, this (for some readers) somewhat unusual connection was supposed to help him integrate *The Philosophy of Freedom* even more firmly into the whole anthroposophical body of work so as to deepen and more consciously shape one's own relationship to both the earlier and later works. Then, the task that I posed to myself with these deliberations will be fulfilled.

It moreover becomes discernible from both works that the nature of freedom is much more complicated, and the inner path to its actual fulfilment is a much deeper mystery than is perchance assumed. This is why one should not be surprised that it requires the whole of anthroposophy to understand *The Philosophy of Freedom*. Thus the cognitive work on this book is still very much at its beginning, and its practical realization will yet last to the end of Earth evolution. The unshakeable foundation stone for this was placed by Rudolf Steiner with his life's work into humanity.

Sergei O. Prokofieff
Dornach, Michaelmas 2005

About the Inner Being of the Human 'I'

Every human being who begins to study anthroposophy will soon realize that the Mystery of the human 'I' stands in its very centre. It belongs among the most important questions of anthroposophical Christology and at the same time the most difficult ones of anthroposophy as a whole.

From the standpoint of esoteric Christianity, the word 'I-am' of the seven 'I-am' words of the Gospel of John is no grammatical formulation but the Mystery-name of the Christ Himself. For in Christ we have the God of the 'I'-principle, who is the actual Cosmic 'I'. Rudolf Steiner on one occasion brought this to expression in quite drastic words: 'The true and only name of the Christ is "I-am"; anyone who does not know this, who does not understand it and calls Him by a different name, knows absolutely nothing about Him. "I-am" is His only name.' (GA 266/1, 27 May 1909.) The often-mentioned fact by Rudolf Steiner that the German word *ICH* or 'I' contains the initials of 'Jesus Christ' points in the same direction. And in the lecture of 11 October 1911, he states that through the Mystery of Golgotha the human 'I' was saved for all future time of World evolution (GA 131). It follows from this that the question concerning the nature of the human 'I' can only be answered by means of its deepest connection with the Christ Impulse.

When in Great Britain, according to a report by Carl Unger, Rudolf Steiner wrote in English (following an appeal to define the nature of anthroposophy), 'Anthroposophy is a knowledge produced by the higher self in man' (*Gesammelte Werke*, Vol. I, Stuttgart 1964, p. 305).

When reference is made in this connection to a higher 'I' (or ego), the existence of a lower 'I' (or self) follows from this. Indeed one discovers it in nearly all the basic works by Rudolf Steiner that deal with modern man's path of inner discipline. In *Occult Science, an Outline* alone, he makes use of quite diverse depictions concerning the 'I': earth-'I', earthly [terrestrial] 'I', lower 'I', ordinary 'I', first 'I'. Likewise in his lectures, still other designations can be found, for example, mortal 'I' (GA 112, 24 June 1909), the first self (GA 147, 29 August, 1913), and even physical 'I' (GA 119, 29 March 1910) or physical self (GA 10). This 'I' (ego or self) is connected from the beginning with the nature of the physical body through which its mortality or transience comes about. It goes without saying that Rudolf Steiner does not connect any valuation with all these designations. He merely indicates the relationship of the 'I', only accessible to our supersensible organs of perception, with the spiritual (higher) world, and the other 'I' with the physical (lower) world which opens to our corporeal perception.

Likewise for the higher 'I', Rudolf Steiner makes use of various terms, most frequently higher 'I' (GA 13), then second 'I' (ibid.), or new 'I' (ibid.), real 'I' (GA 4, GA 35, GA 187, 27 December 1918) as well as other self (GA 17), spiritual 'I' (GA 10), superordinate 'I' (GA 16), newborn 'I' or newborn self (GA 13). Rudolf Steiner also uses the words 'I' and 'self' as synonyms (see GA 10 and 13). All this demonstrates how freely he deals in his works with this terminology.

The relationship of the lower to the higher 'I', as well as the transition from one to the other, has a central significance for the modern path of inner discipline and is described in *Occult Science, an Outline* and *Knowledge of the Higher Worlds and Its Attainment* in detail. Particularly in the latter book this process is specifically compared with the birth of a child. Also in the lecture of 24 June 1909, Rudolf Steiner speaks of how 'within this [transitory] "I" another, higher "I" is born as the child is born from the mother' (GA 112).

Now it is part of the nature of modern initiation that following the birth of this second 'I' the ordinary or first 'I' of the human being retains its earthly consciousness to the fullest extent, so that during the split of the personality the inner life of man suffers no harm, only an increasing spiritual enrichment. 'The here characterized split is carried out in full presence of mind [Ger.: *Besonnenheit*] *only* in the realm of soul. It is so fully perceived that a clearly conscious standing within the ordinary "I" is not in any way diminished. In so doing, *this* "I" loses nothing of its inner firmness and collectedness.' (GA 113, 24 August, 1909; emphasis by Rudolf Steiner.)

In 1913 Rudolf Steiner published his book *The Threshold of the Spiritual World* (GA 17), in which he introduces for the first time a third 'I' that he denotes as the true 'I'. If the higher 'I' or other self originates from the spiritual world, which means the upper one of the three worlds as described in *Theosophy*, then the true 'I' belongs to a 'supra-spiritual world'.

Despite the clearly established definition and distinction between the two egos (see above, higher 'I', true 'I'), in the cycle *The Secrets of the Threshold* given the same year Rudolf Steiner applied these two designations frequently as synonyms. This can be explained because in certain situations the true 'I' works through the other 'I' so that both can be viewed in a given case as a unity. 'We have called attention to the fact that human beings can also emerge out of their astral body and can be in their true "I". Their environment is then the supra-spiritual world. Inasmuch as we enter that world, we ultimately attain to what human beings always possess in the depths of their soul, their true "I", whereas—already in the spiritual world—we there attain to the form in which the true "I", the other self, manifests, namely ensheathed by the living being of thoughts [Ger.: *Gedankenlebewesenheit*] ... This is we ourselves, this other self, this true "I".' (GA 147, 31 August 1913.) And in another passage of the same cycle, Rudolf Steiner points out that only when one encounters the true 'I' in the supra-spiritual world, one moreover discovers how it was earlier 'still ensheathed ... in the other self' (30 August 1913).

In earlier lectures, Rudolf Steiner likewise used the two designations synonymously: 'What we commonly experience as our "I" [ego], our self within the physical world, is as yet not our true self; it is not yet what we call our higher self' (GA 113, 25 August 1909). In view of the 'I'-being's intricateness, Rudolf Steiner in his later lectures often uses the collective designation, 'I-organization'.

An attempt to track down the nature and origin of these three 'I'-forms was undertaken in my book *May Human Beings Hear It!* This is why the corresponding passages can be recounted here along with a few supplementations. As to the inner structure of the human 'I' as depicted in the book *The Threshold of the Spiritual World* by Rudolf Steiner, one must distinguish between three issues. First there is our earthly 'I'-consciousness that is connected with the normal or lower 'I' which we attain as a result of our incarnation in the physical body. 'This "I"-experience can at first occur for the human being only in the sense world when he or she is enclosed by the physical-sensory body' (GA 17). Then follows the so-called 'other self' that in other writings by Rudolf Steiner is also called the higher 'I' and 'brings itself to expression in repeated earth-lives' (elsewhere). Man's spiritual centre, on the other hand, is his true 'I' or the divine spark in him or her. Only in our true 'I' can we experience ourselves to the full extent as a spiritual being among other spiritual beings (the hierarchies).

Now if we consider this process from the standpoint of World evolution, one can say: The first or lower 'I' is merely an imperfect replica within the corporeal sheath of the other 'I' that works through the lesser one. This other 'I' consists of the 'I'-substance that the Spirits of Form— or put more accurately, the seven Elohim sojourning on the Sun— sacrificed at the beginning of the Earth aeon to humanity. This occurred during the Lemurian period and represented the beginning of the actual *human* evolution on our planet. In the ordinary person who is no initiate, this 'other self' or 'I' does not enter his or her earthly sheath at all but stays behind at birth in the spiritual world. In the course of the incarnation it sends merely its replica into the earthly sheaths, which is experienced as one's individual 'I'-consciousness. Rudolf Steiner points this out in the following words: 'You will say: Does this now mean that the human being today is not supposed to find his "I"? No, indeed he does not find it, for the *actual* [real] "I" remains at a standstill, as we are being born. What we experience as our "I" is merely a mirror image of the *actual* "I". This is only something that reflects the prenatal "I" in us. We in fact only experience a mirror image of the "I"; only quite indirectly do we experience something of the actual "I".' (GA 187, 27 December 1918.)[242] It follows unmistakably from other remarks by Rudolf Steiner (see further below) that in the case of this 'I' that remains behind in the spiritual world, it can only be the higher 'I'.

As to the higher 'I' one can at least find an indication concerning its origin in one place of Rudolf Steiner's work. In the cycle dealing with the biblical story of Creation (GA 122), he describes how, when the seven Sun Elohim determined to endow the human being with the 'I'-substance, their own 'I'-substance which they originally bore within them appeared insufficient to them for their intention. This is why they united with each other and thereby created a new being in the Sun's region that Rudolf Steiner designated with the term 'Elohim-ness' (Germ: *Elohim-heit*). In this manner they could rise to a higher stage of their development and receive an impulse out of the highest sphere situated beyond the Seraphim, meaning beyond the hierarchical cosmos. For in order to pervade the human being with the 'I' as the central principle of Earth evolution, they had to receive the impulse for this from the *Word of Worlds* itself, the mediator between the divine Trinity and the world of the hierarchies.

Not only does a primordial kinship exist between the true 'I' of man and the Word of Worlds, but above all a direct linkage of this highest aspect of the 'I' with the Christ. For in him the Word of Worlds itself became flesh on the earth and opened up the possibility to humanity not only of experiencing that other 'I' *in the physical body* (something that had been possible already in pre-Christian initiation to a degree)[243] but likewise the true 'I'.

This threefold structure of the human 'I' has its macrocosmic archetype in the Mysteries of the threefold Sun which contains the secret of the union of the Word of Worlds with it, or, put differently, the transformation of the Word of Worlds into the Word of the Sun which earthly humans later called the Christ. In his esoteric lessons, Rudolf Steiner described this threefold Sun as the 'physical, spiritual and Christ Sun' (GA 266/3, 18 May 1913). Thanks to the first sun that sends light and warmth to the earth, human beings can develop 'I'-consciousness in their physical body. Through the twofold working of the sunlight on the human being, the natural (external) and etheric (inner) effects originate. Above all the second etheric working of the sun is expressed in the more intimate processes connected with the activity of the sense organs in man. Their impressions of the world surrounding us make possible the awakening of our 'I'-consciousness.

Rudolf Steiner called the second or 'Spiritual Sun' the one 'that has bestowed on us the "I"-consciousness' (ibid.). This refers to the working of the seven Sun Elohim, the true creators of the human 'I', the other 'I'. That is the reason Rudolf Steiner also called this second Sun the ' "I"-producing Sun'. (GA 266/3, 1 June 1913.) Finally, the third Sun is Christ Himself or the Word of Worlds, which on the sun became to begin with the Sun Word or Sun Logos and then the God-Man on earth. 'This third Sun has united since the Mystery of Golgotha with the earth.[244] The knowledge of this has been preserved by Rosicrucianism.' (GA 266/3, 18 May 1913.) Even into our present age, the Rosicrucians safeguard the secret in their Mysteries that 'this Spiritual (third) Sun is the Christ Principle, which [since the Mystery of Golgotha] can be experienced by human beings when they grasp Paul's statement, '"Not I but the Christ in me".' (Ibid.) For only the Christ as God of the human 'I' can endow us with the forces of the true 'I'. We can thereby not only become aware of the fact that we are beings who progress from one incarnation to the next (this experience can already be conveyed to us by experiencing the other 'I'), but moreover that we become conscious that we are entities who partake of eternity. Thus it is 'the Christ who with His grace-filled Sun-forces bestows on us the higher "I" ' (ibid.)[245] and makes it possible for us 'to attain to eternal life' (ibid.). In Rosicrucian terminology this implies discovering the divine personality (persona) in one's self.

It becomes clear from all this that the union with the true 'I' is the ultimate goal of any actual 'I'-development in accordance with Paul's saying, 'Not I but Christ in me.' But one must realize here that the 'I' which like a chalice is capable of receiving the true 'I', which in turn is related to the nature of the Christ, is not our ordinary, everyday 'I' but the other 'I' which has to be born first in man by way of the modern Christian-Rosicrucian initiation. This is why Rudolf Steiner stated at the conclusion of the esoteric lesson quoted above, 'More and more to grasp this Spiritual Sun, the Christ in one's self, to awaken it more and more powerfully, that must be the task of every esotericist of the Rose Cross.'

The approach to this *Spiritual Sun* that united at the Turning Point of Time as the 'Christ Sun' with Earth evolution stands at the centre of the fourth, concluding segment of the Foundation Stone Meditation. And in its first three parts the three levels of 'I'-development are characterized that lead to this goal. Thus in the first microcosmic part of the meditation we have the words:

> Thine own I
> Comes to being
> Within the I of God.

That is at the same time a spiritual mirror image of the 'I'-condition one experiences in our age in ordinary 'I' (or ego) consciousness. For on earth this has no direct relationship to the higher human 'I', which during one's incarnation does not descend into the physical body. That higher 'I' on its part remains in the spiritual world from which it originated in the very beginning as in the womb of those divine-spiritual beings who created it.

If, on the other hand, man takes hold of his earthly 'I' in pure thinking and leads it on the path of modern initiation to the reality of the higher 'I', the possibility arises for such a person to pervade it with the Christ substance. This process is characterized in the second microcosmic part:

> [Where the surging
> Deeds of the World's Becoming]
> Do thine own I
> Unite
> Unto the I of the World.

Through this 'I'-resembling connection with the Christ, a human being can then rise to the experience of the true 'I' and thereby enter into a conscious relationship to the whole macrocosm, meaning to the essential groupings of the spiritual hierarchies or entities of gods who are inhabiting the macrocosm. Now this occurs precisely the way it is described in the three macrocosmic parts except in the opposite direction. It moves from man and the world of the elemental spirits surrounding him through the three times three groupings of the nine hierarchies all the way to the spirit-sphere of the Trinity itself.

Along with this experience of the true 'I', the experience of highest freedom is moreover connected from which alone a human being can consciously enter into new and free relationships with the gods. The result of this is that they send towards him the light of their 'eternal aims', aims which in turn represent the highest archetype of man as the religion of the gods (see Chapters 9 and 12).

The words from the third microcosmic part of the meditation correspond to this:

> Where the eternal aims of Gods
> World-Being's Light
> On thine own I
> Bestow
> For thy free Willing.

What has been stated can be deepened even more if we consider that the
first part begins with the reference to 'the world of space' in which man
develops his ego-consciousness (ordinary 'I'). The second part refers to
the 'rhythmic tides of time'. If this line in the meditation is furthermore
taken as a reference to the esoteric stream of time,[246] or rather to that
living time which Christ brought to mankind from the Sun (see GA 236,
4 June 1924), then this is moreover the stream of time in which the higher
'I' of the human being dwells in the spiritual world. And in the third part
we deal with the 'grounds of the eternal' with which the true 'I' of man is
connected above all else.

The relationship of the three egos can be elucidated through the
drawing below:

The chalice corresponds here to the higher or other 'I' which is destined
to bear and harbour the true 'I' in it very centre. This 'I'-chalice is surrounded by a radiance which is reflected in the physical sheath and
produces the earthly 'I'-consciousness or the ordinary 'I' of man.[247]

What was said above allows us better to comprehend the role played by
the two Guardians of the Threshold in the unfolding process of man's
threefold 'I'-nature. Thus, viewed from the threshold to the spiritual
world, the human double corresponds to the ordinary 'I'. When a person
continues on the modern path of inner schooling from the earthly 'I' to
the higher 'I', he or she then encounters the Lesser Guardian of the
Threshold. In the further pursuit of this path from the higher to the true

'I', the spirit disciple encounters the Greater Guardian and, along with taking hold of the true 'I' in Intuition, man stands before the Cosmic Christ as the Word of Worlds, the Logos with which, as to its substance, the true 'I' is identical.

Extremely dramatic experiences or trials precede this decisive encounter. Rudolf Steiner mentions them from a more external aspect in Chapter XXVI of his autobiography. He describes there how he had to enter with his consciousness into the region of the ahrimanic spirits, meaning the kingdom of death or nothingness, in order there to find the connection to the Mystery of Golgotha and subsequently the resurrection forces of the Christ.

Rudolf Steiner describes this dramatic happening from the inner aspect in the cycle *The Secrets of the Threshold*. There he first illustrates how at a certain stage of inner development the human being (in order to attain experience of his or her true 'I' at the threshold) has to overcome, indeed eradicate at this threshold of existence everything from within the self that is linked with the earthly ego (the ego that primarily consists of the memories of earth life) without losing him- or herself, that is to say his or her 'I'-consciousness. This eradication of all memories that still connect man with the earthly past can be carried out only based on a *free* decision of will. 'This "free deed" occurs only through free inner willing, through an energetic deed of will' (GA 147, 30 August 1813). It alone can be compared to an actual jump across the World Abyss. In unconscious form, this takes place in every human being at the moment of falling asleep. 'It is, however, something quite different to abandon one's memory-filled "I" to eradication, to forgetfulness, to the Abyss in full consciousness! Actually for a while to stand in the spiritual world at the Abyss of Existence opposite the Nothingness as a nothing! It is the most shattering experience that one can have and it has to be approached with great confidence. So as to go as a nothing to the Abyss, it is necessary to have the confidence that the true "I" will be brought towards one out of the [supra-spiritual] world. And that does occur . . . Thus, an inner experience of ascending to the supra-spiritual world signifies experiencing a completely new world at the Abyss of Existence and the receiving of the true "I" out of this supra-spiritual world at the Abyss of Existence.' (Ibid.)

The only earthly memory man can take along from this abyss into the spiritual world is that of the Mystery of Golgotha, for it is the single earthly event that simultaneously possesses supersensible nature. ('It is the only deed on the earth that is completely supersensible' GA 143, 17 December 1912). If a person arrives with such a memory of the Mystery of Golgotha at the threshold to the spiritual world, then the entity—who here before the Abyss meets the one about to be initiated and 'brings towards' him or her the true 'I'—is Christ Himself. Due to this, the initiate who in this way has grasped the true 'I' can now bring about a conscious connection to the supra-spiritual world which represents the environs for the true 'I'. (See GA 17.)

Here we must now take into consideration that the memory of the Mystery of Golgotha, which is brought all the way to the threshold of the spiritual world, is something quite different from ordinary earthly memory. Here it is a matter of the actual search for the very essence of Christianity in the spiritual world itself, the essence that consists in the Resurrection of Christ. This is why Rudolf Steiner wrote in his auto-biography that at this particular time he had to immerse himself in Christianity, 'namely in that world in which the spiritual speaks about it'. (GA 28, Chap. XXVI.)

In Rudolf Steiner's life, this discovery of the innermost essence of Christianity led to the crowning of his whole initiation which he described as 'spiritually having stood before the Mystery of Golgotha' (ibid.). As a direct result of this, he could from then on join his earthly and heavenly 'I' at any time in full consciousness and presence of mind. From this originated his special faculty to activate spiritual research on all levels of cosmic existence and present the results of it in clear, generally com-prehensible forms of thought in his work.

As has already been demonstrated in Chapter 8, the path for attaining this faculty led through an inner experience that in its dramatic impact is only comparable to the brief time in the life of Jesus of Nazareth when, forsaken by the ego of Zarathustra and as yet not having received the Christ into himself, he went down to the Jordan. For along with Zar-athustra's leaving his soul, all the inner forces that had led Jesus during the 18 years of the former's presence departed from him at the same time as well. The whole treasure of memories that in this way had been in his soul's possession, and to a large extent made up the content of his 'I', had suddenly vanished. Now, as if standing at the Abyss of Nothing, through the final effort of his whole being, Jesus had to find his way to the baptism in the Jordan out of that strength which, prior to his twelfth year of life, had been available to him when the Zarathustra-'I' had as yet not joined his being. Filled by limitless confidence that the union itself with the descending Christ would become possible, he went to the Jordan.

What came to pass here, like a world-historical archetype, corresponds in modern initiation to the above-described 'shattering experience' that a human being on the verge of initiation is able to endure in the spiritual world only out of the forces of 'utter confidence' with which he or she steps up 'as a Nothing to the Abyss'. This primal trust, which at the Turning Point of Time was exhibited by Jesus of Nazareth on his way to the Jordan, must be summoned up since then by every person about to be initiated at the Abyss of Existence in order to carry out the transition from the Jesus-consciousness to the Christ-consciousness, something that corresponds in modern initiation to the step from the higher to the true 'I'. Around the turn of the last century, Rudolf Steiner carried out this step. And out of the Christ-consciousness attained in the 'true I', he could then establish anthroposophy on the earth as the modern science of the spirit.

The 'supra-spiritual world', out of which the true 'I' originates in the very beginning, lies as such above the three worlds with which the human being is ordinarily connected: the physical, soul, and spiritual world. From it follows that the 'supra-spiritual world' is identical with the still higher sphere that Rudolf Steiner designates as the Buddhi plane or World of Predestination.[248] From there comes the mighty imagination of the circle of the twelve Bodhisattvas who, like twelve stars surrounding the sun, are gathered around the Cosmic Christ. This imagination belongs among the central results of the research by anthroposophical Christology (see GA 113, 25 October 1909) and points to the direction that in future time will lead to the ultimate reconciliation between East and West.

Based on what was said above, this imagination can be understood to mean that the twelve Bodhisattvas, who as initiates have already attained the stage of the higher 'I', now behold in the Buddhi sphere the fount of the true 'I' so as to receive from it the forces for their earthly missions.[249] This moreover corresponds to the indication given by Rudolf Steiner that six of these Bodhisattvas who serve the Christ had the task to prepare his appearance on the earth, and the six others will bear the consequences of the Mystery of Golgotha into humanity (ibid.).[250]

The archetypal imagination from the Buddhi sphere reveals at the same time the inner relationship of the true 'I' to the higher 'I'. This relationship is likewise mirrored on the two lower levels, those of higher and earthly 'I'. In point of fact, wherever it is a matter of 'I'-development, there directly originates the image of a centre surrounded by twelve groupings or the imagination of the sun in the middle of the twelve constellations.

On the level of the earthly 'I', Rudolf Steiner characterizes the latter's environs as consisting of the twelve world-views.[251] Starting out from his earthly ego-consciousness, man is capable in the course of human development to grasp an ever-growing number of these world-views. When, after a series of incarnations, he will have passed through all twelve viewpoints, he will—at least on the level of thinking—consciously have grasped the fundamental characteristics of his earthly ego. One can even say that every human ego participates in this process today if it just shares in the general cultural development of humanity thoroughly enough.

A genuine spirit-disciple (Chela) attains to the next higher stage if he or she has essentially arrived at the birth of the higher 'I' in the soul on the path of discipleship. By so doing one can step out of one's earthly nature completely and is then in a position to view one's ego from outside. As a result it appears to such an individual as if replicated into a twelvefold structure. Now, occupying the standpoint of the higher 'I', one experiences one's self as if in a centre surrounded by twelve different images of one's ego. And just as a human being on earth—who could pass through all twelve world-views—has fully grasped the nature of his or her earthly 'I', it is similar in the case of the higher 'I'. One who in the spiritual world could penetrate all twelve forms (images) of the 'I' with his/her super-sensible cognitive power has in so doing comprehended to a large degree the nature of his/her higher 'I'. In other words, just as the summation of the twelve world-views reveals the nature (or being) of the earthly ego in its constant process of evolving, so in the spiritual world the twelve images making their appearance there reveal the nature of the human being's higher 'I' in the same way.

Likewise this is the case with the true 'I'. Its nature is in fact revealed only when it is reflected back from the surrounding circle of the twelve higher 'I'-forms, something that actually happens in the supra-spiritual or Buddhi sphere. Now, because everything can only consist of being at this spiritual height, the twelve higher egos are represented by the circle of the twelve Bodhisattvas. This means, here appear the twelve Masters who in their 'twelve-hood' have developed the higher 'I' to such an extent that as a twelve-hood they can jointly reveal something of the nature (or being) of the true 'I' and are thereby in a position to behold the cosmic primal source and highest fount of the twelve Masters in their midst as the Christ or Spiritual Sun.

Even as the human being has only 'grasped'[252] his complete 'I' when he comprehends all twelve forms of its appearance in the spiritual world, so the cosmic nature of the Christ can only be understood when one encompasses the whole circle of the twelve Bodhisattvas, that is to say when one has risen up to the Primal Being that penetrates them all and which Christian esotericism designates as the Holy Spirit (see GA 113, 31 August 1909). Only when an initiate embraces this twelve-hood has he in reality recognized the being (nature) of the true 'I'. Such a master is then enfilled with the Holy Spirit. As a result he can behold the Cosmic Christ in the midst of the twelve Bodhisattvas with his spiritual eyes—and thus the origin of his true 'I'.

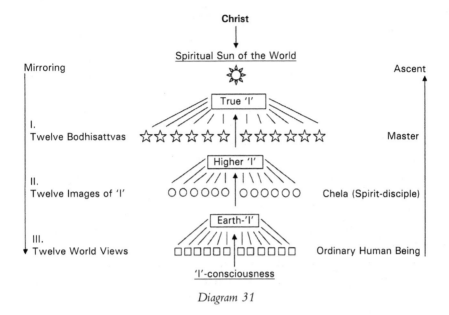

Diagram 31

It is striking in the case of these three levels of 'I'-unfolding that for all of them Rudolf Steiner utilizes the image of the sun in the circle of twelve constellations. This affirms the fact of the mirroring that was mentioned earlier within these various spheres. (On the lowest level on the other hand in connection with the earthly 'I', the sun does not only appear in the centre of the twelve world views but still stands in the midst of the seven planets. (See GA 151, 22 January 1914.) On the mid-level that relates to the higher 'I', man's 'I' does begin to work out of the solar force but as yet it cannot penetrate upwards to the sun's essential being. This is why Rudolf Steiner still utilizes the image of the sun as a comparison. (See GA 119, 29 March 1910.) Only on the highest level, which is linked with the true 'I', the 'Christ Sun' itself appears so as to imbue the twelve Bodhisattvas with divine *life* that turns to Cosmic Wisdom in them. This is why human beings will truly be able to recognize the Christ in His full cosmic significance only after the last of the twelve has fulfilled his mission on earth.

Because we are dealing in the case of the twelve Bodhisattvas with an archetype that is reflected on the two lower levels in the twelve images of the 'I' and the twelve world-views, Rudolf Steiner's description will be quoted word for word here in this regard: 'With this we have risen up into the sphere of the Bodhisattvas and have entered into a circle of twelve stars—and in their midst the sun that illuminates and enwarms them, the sun from which they derive that fount of life which they must then bear down again onto the earth.' (GA 116, 25 October 1909.) From this and other similar descriptions by Rudolf Steiner, it becomes clear that he himself had attained the corresponding level in modern initiation so that he could subsequently communicate such results of his spirit-research to human beings.

As has been demonstrated earlier, these three egos of man correspond in their cosmic aspect to the secret of the threefold Sun and in their human aspect to the three stages of man's spiritual development. Rudolf Steiner characterizes these stages in particular in earlier lectures as follows: first one who has attained the highest standard of the general civilization in his or her age (or is even a genius); second there is the stage of a genuine chela or spirit-disciple; and finally the stage of a true Master (see GA 94, 28 October 1906). Of these three, the first works to acquire and connect all twelve world-views, the harmony of which encompasses the whole of humanity's civilization. The second seeks to bring about the spiritual synthesis of all the images of his or her 'I' encountered in the spiritual world. And the Master rises up to the point of taking hold of his/her true 'I' so as to experience the Christ in the Buddhi sphere with its forces.[253]

★

The working together of the three forms of the 'I' can likewise be illustrated in the figure of a cross. In it the horizontal line corresponds to the development of the higher 'I' or the human *individuality* which passes through all the earthly incarnations. It starts at **A** (the first earthly incarnation) and reaches its goal at Ω (the final earthly incarnation). It is this development that Christ means when he says: 'I am the **A** and the Ω, the beginning and the end' (Rev. 1:8).

The vertical line shows the genesis of the human *personality*, which forms a kind of axis or column that is destined to connect heaven and earth in a new inseparable unity.[254] Concerning this column, its foundation corresponds to the earthly 'I' or personality of the human being. It is only in this personality where, on the basis of the physical body, full self-awareness and, as a result, genuine freedom can be attained. On the other hand, the uppermost part of the column corresponds to man's true 'I', which in the heights of the spiritual world reveals the 'eternal persona'. Rudolf Steiner states: 'An experience of self in the true 'I' is present approximately in the middle between death and a new birth' (GA 147, 31 August 1913). And that means, it only occurs in the spiritual heights of the Cosmic Midnight Hour, where out of the forces of the true 'I' the human being encounters the future goal of his or her development by experiencing the eternal persona.

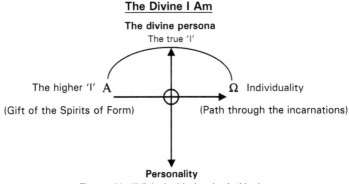

Diagram 32

As follows from the above-described drawing, the conscious relationship between the true 'I', that is, man's eternal persona, and his/her earthly 'I' was brought about for the first time through the appearance of the Christ on the earth. And through the Mystery of Golgotha the possibility to unite earthly consciousness as bearer of human autonomy and freedom with the true 'I' was given to every human being who consciously unites with the Christ Impulse. Here, this path that leads the earthly 'I' to the true 'I' runs solely through the earlier union of man with his/her higher 'I' (see the crossing-point in Diagram 32). On the path of the Christ from His spiritual heights to the earth, this point corresponds to his union with the Sun.

In the pre-Christian initiation path it was Krishna in particular who led his disciples to the experience of the higher 'I'. This is why Rudolf Steiner states: 'Thus, when man looks up to Krishna, he looks at the same time up to his own higher self' (GA 142, 30 December 1912). Since the Mystery of Golgotha in which the decisive step from the individuality to the personality was preordained, this path has changed thoroughly. What is valid from then on is described by Rudolf Steiner in the following words: ' "I" is the Krishna-word; "Not I but the Christ in me" is the word of the Christian impulse' (GA 146, 5 June 1913). For only in the sense of this second saying does the union of man with the true 'I' take place, and consequently with the eternal persona, the goal of his/her whole evolution.

Moreover, these accounts were meant to show that the question concerning the nature of the human 'I' does not only belong among the most important but the most complicated questions in anthroposophy.

For the secret of the 'I' penetrates through all the worlds and can never be ultimately figured out. In *Theosophy* (GA 9), the following mysterious words refer to this: 'A "seeing one" can behold the effect of the "I" on the aura. The "I" itself is invisible even to him; it is indeed within the "veiled holiest of holies" of the human being.'

★

Another secret is the relationship of the 'I' to the three spiritual members of man's being, chiefly to Manas or Spirit Self. The best-known is Rudolf Steiner's definition in this regard, according to which the Spirit Self represents the astral body that has been completely spiritualized by the 'I'. (Correspondingly the Life Spirit and Spirit Man are the etheric and physical bodies transformed by the 'I'.)

Another description of the Spirit Self that is also found in *Theosophy* is less taken into consideration. It goes like this: 'The spirit radiates into the "I" and dwells in it as in its "sheath", just as the "I" lives in body and soul as in its "sheaths". The spirit forms the "I" from within outward and the mineral world from without inward. The "I-shaping" spirit, living as it does as spirit, may be termed "Spirit Self", because it appears as "I" or "self" of man.' (GA 9.)

What is remarkable in these words is that the term 'I' obviously refers to both the earthly 'I' and the higher 'I'. For the mineral world forms the earthly 'I' from the outside inward. The spirit on the other hand forms the higher 'I' from within outward. This characterizes the situation in man's evolution which, following the birth of the higher 'I', arises in the earthly 'I' and thus forms a bridge for taking hold of the Spirit Self.

The process in which the spirit, coming from the higher worlds, forms the 'I' of man from within and shapes it further can only be experienced by the awakened higher 'I'.[255] This process can take place, however, only when the astral body has been purified and spiritualized to a certain degree by man himself. Otherwise this work of the spirit on man's ego cannot occur in the right way. If these two activities are viewed together, one has outlined the nature of the Spirit Self. In its actuality it is both the transforming work of the ego on the astral body and, as its consequence, the presence and working of the spirit within the 'I'. Through his higher 'I' man can consciously participate in this twofold unfolding of the Spirit Self in his being.

In this regard, the following passage from the cycle on the Gospel of John attains special significance. It is the passage in which Rudolf Steiner comes to speak of the wedding at Cana in connection with the Sixth Period, and in so doing characterizes the relationship between the higher self and Manas. 'It will be a very important Cultural Period, this Sixth one . . . [It will be the time in which], for that segment of human beings who are undergoing a normal development, the higher self will descend into them, *to begin with in its lower form as Spirit Self or Manas*. A coming together of the human ego, the way it has evolved gradually, with the higher "I", with the unifying "I", will then come to pass. We can call that a spiritual marriage—and this is what one always called the union of the human "I" with Manas, or the Spirit Self in Christian esotericism.' (GA 103, 30 May 1908–I.) And in an earlier lecture, Rudolf Steiner links the secret of this inner work of the awakened higher 'I' on the forming of man's three spiritual members of his being with the most intimate and holiest tasks of the genuine Rosicrucians. 'Atma-Buddhi-Manas, the higher self, is the secret that will become manifest when the sixth sub-race will have matured to that. Then Christian Rosenkreutz will no longer have to stand there as the one who gives warning; rather everything that signifies conflict on the external plane will find peace through the Brazen Sea, through the sacred Golden Triangle.' (GA 93, 4 November 1904.) Here the Golden Triangle points to the threefoldness of Manas-Buddhi-Atman and to the Brazen Sea which, generated in the inner human being, leads to the awakening of the higher 'I' as indicated in the fire-trial of Hiram.[256]

In this manner Rudolf Steiner links the substance of John's Gospel with the Mystery-experience of Hiram and consequently with the esoteric stream of Christian Rosenkreutz, who through his initiation in the thirteenth century attained the stage of the true 'I'.

From the two previous quotes, it follows unmistakably that the spiritual members of man's being correspond to the three upward-moving stages of ego-development and that in the sixth cultural period the accurate connection with the Spirit Self may take place only on the basis of the awakened higher 'I', or else the connection with it will in the most eminent sense have luciferic character, a danger that Rudolf Steiner explicitly pointed out.[257]

While in regard to receiving the higher spiritual members of being in the coming cultural periods, the higher 'I' has more the task of a conscious supervision of this process, and only a modest possibility of partaking in it. This higher 'I' will play an active and creative role in the full unfolding of the higher spiritual members of being in the future planetary stages of our cosmos. For the ultimate transformation of the astral body into the Spirit Self on the coming (New) Jupiter can only occur based on the forces of the fully developed higher 'I'. And for such a form of creative activity it will have had to attain, already during the Earth aeon, a conscious connection with Christ on the stage of the true 'I'. The same holds true for the transformation of the ether body into Life Spirit on Venus, and even more so for the transformation of the physical body into Spirit Man on Vulcan.

This whole evolution in which the ego-development forms an upward moving axis can best be illustrated by a kind of caduceus-sign (staff of Mercury):

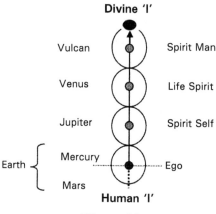

Diagram 33

Here special emphasis must be placed on the fact that the connection with the Manas-forces in the sixth cultural epoch will have a completely different character from the one on future Jupiter. In the first case it is a matter of the pouring out of Manas into the human being out of spiritual heights as a kind of higher revelation; in the second case it is the taking hold of this connection by individual humans out of the full power of their 'I'. This is why Rudolf Steiner says: 'On [New] Jupiter man will relate to the Spirit Self approximately the way he relates to the "I" on earth' (GA 130, 9 January 1912). When we now bring what was said above into connection with the earlier mentioned definition of the Spirit Self (namely the astral body that has been completely transformed by the 'I'), we can also characterize the whole process as follows. On the future Jupiter, the astral body as Manas will be permeated to the smallest particle of its substance with the power of the individual 'I' and in this way have become an accurate astral replica of the same individual 'I'. The same will occur on the future Venus with the ether body. In its transformed shape as Life Spirit, it will be permeated to the smallest particle with the power of the 'I'-force. And on Vulcan the same metamorphosis will take hold of the physical body. Its supersensible form will then bear a conscious ego-stamp even into all its most delicate branches, whereby the 'I' itself will have attained the highest stage of its evolution. 'Our ego is the baby among the human members; it is the youngest. This "I" will be formed, as now is the physical body, only on Vulcan [meaning, it will also reach the fourth level which the physical body has attained in its development from Ancient Saturn until now] . . . This "I", however, rests at the same time in the womb of the spiritual world.' (GA 157a, 20 November 1915.) That we are obviously dealing here with the higher ego is affirmed by words from another lecture where this 'I', which remains in the spiritual world without descending to earthly incarnations, is described as coming from the Spirits of Form. 'The "I" remains; the "I" basically remains in the form in which it is bestowed on us, as we know, by the Spirits of Form. This "I" is preserved (held) in the spiritual world.' (GA 165, 19 December 1915.)

In other places too, Rudolf Steiner affirms that the 'I' of man will reach its ultimate perfection on Vulcan: 'On the final incorporation on Vulcan, the 'I' will have achieved its highest development.' (GA 99, 31 May 1907.) This will happen when the 'I' will in a manner of speaking have fashioned the whole physical body into something ego-like down to its smallest particle. What this actually means was made evident in the spiritual-historical sense in the Resurrection of the Christ, where for the first time an earthly body originated that in absolute perfection mirrored the 'I' of the Christ and therefore could simultaneously exist in the physical as well as in the spiritual world. This is why Rudolf Steiner says: 'We have there [in the Mystery of Golgotha] the entity as God that man as the human being will be at the end of the Vulcan development.' (GA 346, 7 September 1924.) It is for this reason that the seventh spiritual member of man is called *Spirit Man*. For this is a being which as man has become spirit all the way to the physical body. And the path for the attainment of this goal has been opened up through the Resurrection of the Christ for all human beings on earth.

From the very beginning, this transformation process was understood in Rosicrucian esotericism as the building of the inner temple. Rudolf Steiner likewise refers to this when he states: 'What is just now starting out, the "baby" in the human being, is the "I". This is fourfold man who contains the ego within as the temple contains the statue of a god.' (GA 93a, 7 October 1905.) Out of the fourfold human being, the crowning point of whom is the earthly ego as bearer of freedom, the temple is built for the higher 'I' which subsequently moves into this temple as the divine statue. This higher 'I', on the other hand, is then in a position—as is the magic lamp from Goethe's Fairy Tale—to transform the temple from within: the astral body into the Spirit Self, the ether body into the Life Spirit, and the physical body into Spirit Man. Earthly man thereby gradually changes into Cosmic Man. From the viewpoint of the higher ego's own development, these three transformations correspond to the cognitive stages of Imagination, Inspiration and Intuition.

This process can only be started and carried out by the human being on the earth out of its earth-ego. For only in this 'I' can human freedom as a decisive condition of the whole path be experienced and ultimately taken along into the further unfolding of the higher self. 'This is the person who has developed his/her higher self. Here in the physical world is the location for its cultivation' (GA 94, 5 March 1906). The attainment of the final goal is only possible, however, through the conscious relation to the true 'I' (see Diagram 33). Only this relation allows the I-forces to reach their full unfolding and enables them to work even into the physical body.

As was already depicted, the first stage of this process is the work of the 'I' on the astral body out of which emerges Manas. If this work has sufficiently advanced in the human being inasmuch as his or her 'I' has to a large degree united with Manas, Rudolf Steiner uses the two terms as synonyms. Above all in the early lectures he utilizes the two designations in this manner: 'Manas is the fifth principle, the spiritual principle in man that is to arise, to which a temple should be erected' (GA 93, 22 May 1905). And in a somewhat later lecture he says: 'When we picture the Cosmic Intelligence as the world of thoughts that are accessible to the higher "I" (Manas) . . .' or further on: 'Picture in the following the power of the higher "I" in man, of Manas . . .' (GA 94, 9 June 1906; the word 'Manas' in the original in parenthesis).[258] Likewise the connection with the higher self is frequently described by Rudolf Steiner in words that almost precisely recount man's union with the Spirit Self in the sixth cultural epoch. In both cases it is a matter of the pouring out of the higher spiritual forces from above into the human entity. 'The inner being [of man] must be made receptive for the absorption of the higher self. When it is receptive, there man's higher self streams out of the spiritual world into the human being.' (GA 103, 31 May 1908.) Man must become prepared for this soul-receptivity through conscious purification of his/her astral body out of the forces of the earthly 'I'.

The most remarkable example of such an equation of the concepts 'Manas' and 'higher self' comes into play when it is considered from the standpoint of the activity of the angels. Thus, Rudolf Steiner states in regard to the nocturnal encounter of the human being with his/her angel: 'And whether it is said that man looks up to his higher self that he is supposed to resemble more and more or looks up to his angel as his great model, both are fundamentally one and the same on the spiritual level' (GA 105, 6 August 1908). Already early on in the book *Knowledge of the Higher Worlds and Its Attainment*, Rudolf Steiner refers to such a relationship of the human being's higher 'I' with entities of the spiritual world, even though this is formulated more generally in that book which is intended for the general public. 'And he [the spirit disciple] learns to recognize that this higher self is linked with spiritual entities of a higher sort and *forms a unity with them*. It is significant that in a later lecture, of 20 February 1917, Rudolf Steiner asserts almost the same in regard to the relationship of man's Spirit Self to his angel.

To this view out of the angelic sphere, Rudolf Steiner moreover adds a human aspect. Becoming aware of the higher 'I' is brought into connection here with the being and activity of the leading initiates in humanity's development: 'What will be our self in a few thousand years, is presently our higher self. In order truly to become acquainted with the higher self, we have to seek it where it is even today, namely in the higher individualities. This is the interaction of the student with the Masters.' (GA 93a, 18 October 1905.) The time-frame 'in a few thousand years' refers to begin with to the sixth cultural epoch, during which time humanity will receive the forces of the Spirit Self out of the spiritual world. And when an individual prepares himself properly for this future already in our age, he will also be able to experience his 'I'-being during the epoch of the Spirit Self in a new form. 'It is due to the very fact that man is made ready during our fifth post-Atlantean age to experience the "I" in the sixth age in *a new form* that through the fifth age he experiences this "I" only as a mirror-image in a manner of speaking. This is the characteristic of the age of the consciousness soul where man receives his "I" merely as a mirror image so that he lives into the age of the Spirit Self and can experience the "I" which is shaped differently *in a new form* once again.' (GA 187, 27 December 1918.)

It is only through the mirroring experience of the 'I' in the fifth post-Atlantean cultural period that we can bring our 'I'-consciousness to full unfolding, thereby attaining inner freedom. We can then take this 'I'-conscious freedom into the higher 'I' and unite it in the sixth epoch with the Spirit Self that streams down from above. By these means the human being will attain to a conscious access of the forces of the spirit in the way that it corresponds to the second definition of the Spirit Self in *Theosophy* (see above). This signifies that the spirit which comes out of the spiritual worlds and shapes the 'I' from within will make more and more of an appearance along with the descending of the Spirit Self forces and shall lead the 'I' to ever higher stages of its state of consciousness in the spiritual world. This is why Rudolf Steiner says that the sixth cultural epoch will be a clairvoyant epoch, in which all human beings who then stand on the highest level of the general evolution of humanity will possess the ability to look into the spiritual world fully consciously (see GA 13).

What will be poured out in the sixth cultural epoch as a general faculty over all mankind, can be attained already today on the anthroposophical path of inner schooling. In order to understand this path of schooling better, it must also be born in mind that in our time, parallel to the individual 'I'-development, the present culture of humanity likewise constantly works on the purification of the astral body out of the 'I'-impulse, hence on its gradual transformation into the Spirit Self. 'In general we can say of today's human beings: They use occurrences and experiences for the purpose of reshaping their astral bodies ... Now, what is quite consciously worked into the astral body by the "I" is called the Spirit Self or Manas.' (GA 94, 28 October 1906.)[259]

What in this way presently takes place through general humanity's civilization cannot yet be extended on the same level of development to the two higher members (Buddhi and Atma). For 'today's human beings live in the Manas condition. This means that we can indeed work on our astral body but as yet cannot change essential aspects of our ether body and least of all on our physical body' (ibid.), for the inner work on their spiritual transformation is only possible with the forces of the awakened higher 'I'. This is why Rudolf Steiner says: 'Through the work of *our higher "I"* we restructure the transitory bodies given to us by the gods and create eternal bodies for ourselves' (GA 93a, 24 October 1905). And in regard to the Spirit Self, such esoteric work must already begin today. For the general cultural development of humanity no longer suffices for the future. The transformation of the astral body into the Spirit Self must for that reason take place even now in our time on two different levels: on the one hand out of the forces of the earth-ego for all human beings within the general cultural evolution, and on the other hand out of the forces of the higher 'I' in the case of those people who on the modern path of schooling wish to prepare for the sixth cultural epoch. One can designate this inner work as a path that leads towards the Spirit Self. By these means, the fifth and sixth epochs have a common task and this is why Rudolf Steiner emphasizes in *Occult Science* that the fifth and sixth ages 'are in a manner of speaking the decisive ones'. In *Theosophy* this is indicated in the following words: 'Consciousness soul and Spirit Self form a unity.' Now this unity comes about because, based on his 'I', man unites his consciousness soul with the spirit so that it turns into the 'spirit-enfilled' consciousness soul (ibid.). For their spiritualization begins already with the first stage of the modern path of schooling, a stage that Rudolf Steiner designates as the study of spiritual-scientific communications (see GA 13).

In the sixth cultural epoch, the Manas in those human beings (who through their esoteric development have already prepared themselves in the fifth epoch) will be in a position to receive the outpouring of the Buddhi forces. 'In the sixth age the Spirit Self [evolved in the fifth epoch out of the consciousness soul] will link up with the Life Spirit ... In the sixth age, the lofty wedding of humanity will be celebrated where the Spirit Self unites with the Life Spirit' (GA 100, 25 November 1907). In the Gospel of John, prophetic reference is made to this in the wedding at Cana (ibid.). There the wedding of the forces of Christ and Sophia occur that corresponds to the union of Buddhi and Manas in the human being, a union that in the sixth cultural epoch will find its culmination and will penetrate through humanity's whole cultural evolution in the way Novalis had preconceived it.[260]

The outpouring of Buddhi will then occur for human beings not in the way the preceding lighting up of natural clairvoyance takes place, but like a kind of spontaneous initiation, which as a result will bring along a deeper and more conscious connection with the spiritual world. For 'the moment of the engendering of Buddhi is called in all Mysteries the second birth, new birth or awakening' (GA 94, 28 October 1906).[261] This 'new birth' in the spirit will then bring the 'I'-consciousness in the human being to proper flowering, something that will indeed occur in the sixth epoch. When we call to mind here once more that Christ first and foremost brought the forces of the Buddhi to earth, we will understand the following words correctly: 'Christ appears to bestow forces on humanity so that in the sixth age the highest "I"-consciousness can be attained' (GA 100, 25 November 1907).

The awakening of Lazarus at the Turning Point of Time and Christian Rosenkreutz in the middle of the thirteenth century will stand as a kind of archetype for such 'new births'. That is why the Rose Cross 'will be the symbol of the new Christianity of the sixth sub-race' (GA 93, 4 November 1904), the Christianity of Christ and Sophia that is already being prepared today in anthroposophy. 'Those who prepare themselves today for the development of the Spirit Self in their inner being will in the next age make this deeper, more spiritual Christianity [based on the Buddhi] ever more accessible to humanity' (GA 100, 21 November 1907).

Today, only a highly evolved spirit disciple can attain this stage within an actual initiation. For, 'the Chela directly approaches the point of purifying everything even into his etheric body. "Chela-hood" is completed when he has allowed the Buddhi to stream fully into his life-body so that the life-body he ennobles from out of his [higher] "I" has turned into the Life Spirit' (GA 94, 28 October 1906). Still higher is the stage of a 'Master' who, already within Earth evolution (based on the higher 'I'), has begun to transform his physical body into Spirit Man up to a degree. With that he has reached the ideal of the seventh cultural epoch. A Master like this 'stands above karma' (GA 93a, 24 October 1905). Out of this lofty height he is capable of assuming the karma of other human beings, something which then affects him even into his physical body.

This is what Rudolf Steiner carried out at the Christmas Conference during the new founding of the Anthroposophical Society, when voluntarily he united himself even including his karma with this society, and with that embarked on the sacrificial path in the sense of the Imitation of Christ befitting our age. And the spiritual world that fully affirmed his deed then endowed him with the mightiest karma-revelations, as well as with the establishment of the Michael School on the earth.[262]

Addendum II
Three Streams in the Evolution of the Earth

During Earth evolution it is possible to distinguish between different spiritual streams that simultaneously permeate humanity's history. The main stream is connected with the development of the ego (the 'I'). To make this clear, Rudolf Steiner brings the sevenfold condition of the human being into connection with the whole cosmic evolution from Ancient Saturn all the way to future Vulcan. The unfolding of the fourth or 'I'-principle in the human being results from this as our earth's central task. What is more, Rudolf Steiner calls this main stream a macrocosmic one, a stream which the Christ as Cosmic (or World) 'I' is connected to, and out of the forces of which He is constantly active. All the other streams that develop the spiritual members of the human being (Manas, Buddhi and Atma) within Earth evolution are of a microcosmic nature (see GA 130, 9 January 1912).

Among such microcosmic streams belongs one that above all the others penetrates the entire post-Atlantean epoch. As is known, Rudolf Steiner in this context links the seven post-Atlantean cultural periods with the fashioning of the following members of man's being: the Ancient Indian period with the ether body, the Ancient Persian period with the astral body, the Egyptian-Chaldaean one with the sentient soul, the Graeco-Roman one with the intellectual soul, and the present period with the consciousness soul. The two future ones, the sixth and the seventh periods, are correspondingly linked with the Spirit Self and Life Spirit. It follows from this that our time is principally given the task to develop the consciousness soul, that member of the human being in which the individual and autonomous 'I' can attain to its greatest unfolding.

This is first and foremost the microcosmic 'I'-stream connected with our present age that works like a replica of the great macrocosmic 'I'-stream which encompasses the whole Earth aeon. Still less known among anthroposophists is a third stream that spreads out in the historical development of humanity between the above-mentioned macrocosmic and the microcosmic 'I'-stream and therefore can be designated as a micro-macrocosmic stream. Rudolf Steiner describes these streams in detail only once, in the lecture of 31 October 1906. Here he initially considers the seven large epochs of Earth evolution, which in the old, still theosophical terminology were denoted as main or root races. Rudolf

Steiner again brings these into connection with the development of the human members of being: the Polaric epoch with the physical body, the Hyperborean with the ether body, and the Lemurian with the astral body.[263] Then the Atlantean epoch comes about which represents the absolute middle of the Earth-aeon. There, as the essential goal of Earth evolution, the ego-principle began to affect humanity—still working out of the cosmos. Rudolf Steiner states in this regard that the Christ Being, who at that time was linked with the Sun, carried out this first effect of the 'I'-principle, meaning out of the central macrocosmic 'I'-stream.[264]

Correspondingly, out of this stream, the post-Atlantean epoch with its seven cultural periods was as a whole permeated by the Manas impulse. And this took place once more through the various members of man's being: in the Ancient Indian period the Manas came into the sentient body of man; in the Ancient Persian period into the sentient soul; in the Egyptian into the rational (or intellectual) soul; and in the Graeco-Roman into the consciousness soul. Due to this, the fourth period was predestined for the flashing up of the first experience of the individual 'I' in Greek philosophy. Moreover, the Christ appeared on earth in this period so that, corresponding to this stream, He principally brought into mankind's evolution His 'I' and His Spirit Self which then continued to work in esoteric Christianity (see GA 240, 27 August 1924).

Now we come to our fifth post-Atlantean cultural period. Here something special results in this micro-macrocosmic stream. This is why Rudolf Steiner characterizes this age in the following words: 'This fifth sub-race is our Anglo-Germanic race which is to bring to expression the Spirit Self in the Spirit Self, Manas in Manas. This means, the human being shall learn to comprehend what the Spirit Self actually is; the human being will stand within Manas. Manas will at last work in itself.' (GA 94, 31 October 1906.) What this actually implies for man's earthly consciousness is then characterized as follows by Rudolf Steiner: 'To grasp thinking with thinking, to catch hold of thinking in thinking, to finish rounding out the serpent of eternity—this is the task of the fifth sub-race' (ibid.). The serpent that bites its own tail is the ancient symbol for the higher 'I'. And the modern scientific path that leads to the higher 'I' passes, as was already shown in this book, through the exceptional state in which thinking thinks about itself and at the same time cognizes its own activity, or in other words, takes hold of itself as if at one corner. For 'thinking is that organ where human nature catches hold of itself as if at one corner' (ibid.), meaning, at the tip, or corner, of its eternal existence, something that signifies its rise to the higher or real 'I'. This is why Rudolf Steiner concludes this description of our present period with the words,

'To stimulate this in man—that is the purpose of the book *The Philosophy of Freedom.*' (Ibid.)[265]

From what is stated above, the unique signature of our age emerges. On the one hand, we have the blossoming forth of the individual 'I' in the consciousness soul in which the whole macrocosmic 'I'-stream as chief stream of the Earth aeon is microcosmically mirrored. At the same time this ego-development occurs in the background of the weaving of 'Manas in Manas', something which opens up the possibility to the human being not to perish in materialism due to the ego's bond with the physical body, but instead (as if secretly supporting itself on the Manas-forces) step by step to ascent with a matured 'I'-consciousness (out of full freedom) into the spiritual world. This becomes possible today through anthroposophy for all human beings who are of good will. In anthroposophy the microcosmic stream flows by way of *The Philosophy of Freedom* into the macrocosmic stream and thereby allows human beings to go and meet their cosmic-earthly destiny.

This working together of the three streams has special Christological significance for our age. For it reveals a direct relationship to the present activity of the Christ in humanity's evolution. Thus, Rudolf Steiner speaks of His appearance in etheric-imaginative form as the most important event of our time, an event that begins in the twentieth century and will become more and more frequent in humankind during the next three thousand years

Then Rudolf Steiner brings this etheric return (Second Coming) of the Christ into connection with the middle micro-macrocosmic stream of Manas. Based on the forces of the Spirit Self, dawning already in our time in humanity, the Christ can be perceived in this new imaginative form. 'But we must clearly understand that we ... *now* gradually work our way out of the life in the consciousness soul to the life in the Spirit Self. *I have often indicated how entering into the Spirit Self occurs.* I pointed out that those people who will experience a manifestation of the Christ Impulse will become more numerous in the next three thousand years; that human beings become gradually capable of experiencing the Christ Impulse in the spiritual worlds.' (GA 133, 20 May 1912.) It follows from this that particularly the weaving of 'Manas into Manas' existing in the fifth post-Atlantean cultural period brings about the Christ Impulse's dawning in the consciousness soul and thereby calls forth the new clairvoyant faculties in the human being, forces which then lead to the beholding of the Christ in the etheric.[266]

Yet a second field of activity on the part of the Christ is connected with today's age, which in comparison to His etheric return will encompass not three thousand years but rather *the remaining Earth evolution*. That is His new activity as Lord of Karma (see more detail in Chapter 13). Rudolf Steiner describes His 'entering' upon this new 'office' in the following words: 'We have pointed out that the Christ in a manner of speaking appears on the earth in His office as judge—in contrast to the suffering Christ of Golgotha as the triumphant Christ, as the Lord of Karma ... In truth it is something that begins in the twentieth century and goes on to the end of the Earth. The Judgment begins in our twentieth century, meaning the ordering or karma.' (GA 130, 2 December 1911.)

From the fact that this second activity of the Christ will extend 'to the end of the Earth', there results its connection with the macrocosmic 'I'-stream which in a sense encompasses the whole of Earth evolution. Likewise, any change on the level of karma can only be carried out based on the 'I'-force, and to the extent that this deals with the destiny of all of mankind on earth can only be brought about out of the macrocosmic 'I'-stream.

The increasingly conscious perception (and in the future even cooperation) of human beings in both contemporary directions of activity by the Christ must today be carefully prepared. Such a preparation occurs particularly through the in-depth study of anthroposophy as the first stage on the modern path of initiation, a path which as a matter of fact can only be entered upon out of the first microcosmic 'I'-stream. Part of this is that through the independent and conscious efforts of the individual 'I' in studying spiritual science, aside from becoming acquainted with the various activities of the Christ in our time, the very quality of thinking itself with which one approaches such contents will change fundamentally. What is attainable otherwise only through occupying oneself with *The Philosophy of Freedom* and other epistemological writings by Rudolf Steiner is reached here also in a somewhat different manner through the study of anthroposophy, namely sense-free or pure thinking. For this is the most important pre-condition and guarantee that the encounter with the Etheric Christ, as well as the working together with Him in the field of karma, does not occur in a luciferic manner, meaning in an uncontrolled form, but rather with the full inclusion of human thinking and therefore also wide-awake 'I'-consciousness.

That such a sense-free thinking, that is to say pure thinking, becomes possible also by means of the study of anthroposophy is emphasized by Rudolf Steiner again and again, for example in the words: 'Study in the Rosicrucian sense is not what is called "study" in ordinary life. In the Rosicrucian sense one would actually have to call this "living in pure thoughts".' (GA 284, 19 May 1907.) He furthermore points this out in his main anthroposophical work *Occult Science, an Outline*.

Thus we have the three described streams that are connected with the present activity of the Christ as well as with the nature of anthroposophy as follows. The first is the microcosmic ego-stream. From its forces, the contemporary human being reaches the point of experiencing freedom. Only on the basis of this experience does the study of spiritual science become even possible. Here in the realm of sense-free thinking, the very first contact with the resurrection-forces of the Christ takes place (as mentioned already earlier in this book) in the way they can work today in human consciousness. Above this first stream lies the second or Manas-stream which bears within itself the forces of the new clairvoyance that will gradually unfold in humankind without any specific spiritual schooling and will lead to the experience of the Etheric Christ. This Manas-stream can therefore be designated likewise as micro-macrocosmic, because in it the encounter of the human being with the cosmic being of the Christ takes place. Finally, still higher there lies the third or macrocosmic stream, the stream out of which the Christ shall work until the end of the Earth aeon on the karma of mankind.

Yet another special task is connected with the study of anthroposophy, based as it is on the first stream. This task consists of the direct preparation of the human being for the encounter with the Etheric Christ. Thus, spiritual science is none other than a spiritual language that human beings can learn in order to speak with the Etheric Christ, pose questions to Him about the most important concerns of life and to receive His answers on them. Yet in order to become really fluent in this new language one must bring the contents of spiritual science to the point of grasping them in sense-free thinking, which alone possesses the purity of cognitive forces that make it possible for the human being *consciously* to draw near the Etheric Christ in the spiritual world adjacent to the earth.[267]

When this occurs then there can occur something in actual fact which Rudolf Steiner depicts in the following words: 'Why do we occupy ourselves with spiritual science? It is as if we were supposed to learn the vocabulary of that language through which we draw close to the [Etheric] Christ ... We are to learn His language ... Let us therefore not merely seek spiritual science as a teaching but as a language for acquiring, and then let us wait until we find the questions in this language that we are allowed to pose to the Christ. He will answer; yes, He *will* answer!' (GA 175, 6 February 1917; emphasis by Rudolf Steiner.)

From what has been said here we come upon a twofold movement that links the microcosmic 'I'-stream and the Manas-stream. In the first the

human being can learn to acquire the spiritual language of the Etheric
Christ in complete freedom; from the second there enter into the first the
forces of the new clairvoyance with which the Etheric Christ can be
perceived. A similar working together becomes evident likewise in the
case of the third macrocosmic 'I'-stream. In it the Christ works today as
Lord of Karma. Now when His karma-ordering activity takes hold of the
second Manas-stream with its inherent clairvoyant powers, then this
activity of the Christ becomes visible for such a person in a special
manner. In many of his lectures, Rudolf Steiner describes how, already
beginning in our time and increasingly in the future, a human being
engaging in some act will in a sort of imagination be able to see the karmic
consequences which this act will have for him or her in the future, and
likewise a picture of what will eventually have to be done so as to kar-
mically offset one's deed. 'One will tell oneself: Here, I have done this.
Now, I am being shown *what I must do as compensation for it* [this deed] that
would always hold me back in [my quest for] perfection if I would not
carry out the compensation.' (GA 116, 8 May 1910.)

The inner emergence of such imaginations will be a consequence of
the effect of the macrocosmic 'I'-stream upon that of Manas and their
further working together will lead the human being to the direct
experiencing of the Lord of Karma, as well as to the possibility gradually
to become His co-worker in the domain of karma.

But even this combination of the two streams must in a manner of
speaking be readied from below consciously and freely, meaning out of
the forces of the third microcosmic ego-stream through occupying
oneself with anthroposophy. For if this does not happen, the individual
will not comprehend the encounter with Christ as Lord of Karma and
then 'the Lord of Karma will appear to him or her like a frightful
punishment' (GA 131, 14 October 1911). And directly following this
admonition, Rudolf Steiner continues: 'Now, this is why the propagation
of the anthroposophical world-view occurs in our time so that the human
being can be prepared on the physical plane ... to become cognizant of
the Christ event' (ibid.). In particular the all-encompassing communications about the working of karma that Rudolf Steiner offered in an inner
continuance of the Christmas Conference in the cycle of 82 karma lectures represent the basis for an encounter with Christ as Lord of Karma as
well as the conscious work alongside Him on His activity of putting
karma into order.

When we refrain from taking the study of anthroposophy as something
theoretical or abstract, but (as Rudolf Steiner did indeed intend it) in the
sense of the first stage of modern initiation, then out of this study the

corresponding actions in our life must follow. For it is inherent in the karma of every anthroposophist to be a person of initiative (see GA 237, 4 August 1924). Mention has already been made in Chapter 16 of this book concerning the actions referred to here. There it was pointed out that they can have a spiritual quality and effect, as is otherwise true only of actions by an initiate who carries them out directly based on reading in the astral light.

As we have already seen, the starting point for such actions must be sought in pure thinking that has been attained from the study of anthroposophy. For in order to discover the path to free deeds (or actions) the human being will require the full force of his/her moral imagination, or expressed more in spiritual-scientific terminology, the 'imaginative moral impulses'. (GA 193, 12 June 1919.) These can then come from Christ Himself, if we take the study to mean learning a new spiritual language with which we can pose our questions to the Etheric Christ and then in fact actually pose them to Him. Then the answers by Christ will not only appear in an 'audible' form, but likewise as germinating imaginative pictures of the new clairvoyance that can be grasped by moral imagination in a completely free manner. The moral imagination of human beings will thus be filled with the answers that come from Christ, meaning with the substance of the Cosmic Word that 'speaks' in imaginations. Christ Himself will then be present in the moral imagination of man.

As the next step, the earthly action will then follow. Now, since the moral imagination leading to this action is pervaded by the Christ-substance, it will have a very special attribute. It will be in full accord with the karma of the individual human being and moreover, through collaboration by the Christ, in accord with the positive karma of the whole of mankind. In other words, during such actions moral imagination will on its own guide the human being to such deeds that can contribute to the most effective balance between the individual's and humanity's karma. Then moral imagination will gradually pass over into the new karma-beholding. Man will thereby learn to carry out actions on earth that are performed out of purest spiritual love of his karma. With that, the third ingredient of ethical individualism, the acting out of love for the object but now on the level of karma, will come to be developed. Thus, human beings will work moreover on the level of karma in accordance with *The Philosophy of Freedom*, which means that men and women are free here too. We shall be able to work out of love for karma.

This will be possible beginning in our age only because this faculty to love one's karma was preordained already at the Turning Point of Time by Christ in humanity's evolution. Today, since the Christ has assumed His 'office' as Lord of Karma in the guidance of mankind, not only must the teaching of karma in the Christian sense be received into the general awareness of humanity, it must above all be realized that out of this awareness one can act *freely* in the domain of karma, meaning out of love for karma. Rudolf Steiner says in this regard: 'Thus one learns to love karma and then this is the impulse to cognize the Christ [as Lord of Karma]. To love their karma was something human beings only learned through the Mystery of Golgotha.' (GA 143, 17 April 1912.) Still, it is only after the beginning of the Christ's activity as Lord of Karma that this possibility can be grasped by human beings consciously and freely. And *The Philosophy of Freedom* with its ideal of ethical individualism leads to the fulfilment of this goal. For this book demonstrates how a human being today can begin to act out of love for the object, and the object in this case is karma itself.

On this path that leads from a more concentrated study of anthroposophy to moral imagination, which is fructified by Christ, and from there to the free deeds based on love for karma, man will gradually become a co-worker of the Christ as Lord of Karma. At the same time this is the path that is the purest consequence of ethical individualism that has really been lived and concretely practised in earth life.

As was already depicted in Chapter 16, the three main steps of this path correspond to the threefold nature of the Foundation Stone. In this manner the beginning and end of the evolution of anthroposophy on earth come together in the light of the present activity by the Christ as Lord of Karma. And the Christmas Conference appears in the life of its founder as the most perfect fulfilment of *The Philosophy of Freedom*, or as the truly lived ethical individualism that 'now actually builds on the Christ Impulse'. (GA 74, 24 May 1920.)

Based on what has been stated, the connection of ethical individualism and its three component parts with the Christ Impulse can be depicted as on Diagram 34 (opposite).

As was stated already at the beginning of Chapter 10, the free sacrificial deed by Rudolf Steiner that culminated in his absolute union with the karma of the Anthroposophical Society forms the archetype of a human action that was carried out based on pure love for karma, and hence occurred in complete and direct accord with the Lord of Karma. When we comprehend this, we can learn from Rudolf Steiner's life what it actually means to be a co-worker of the Christ in the realm of karma. Then ethical individualism will not remain for us as only a pleasant theory but become a higher reality that is totally rooted in the Christ Impulse. At

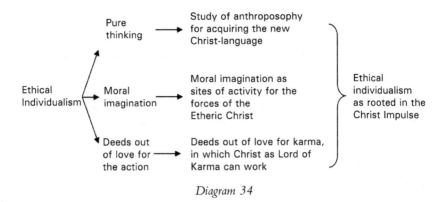

Diagram 34

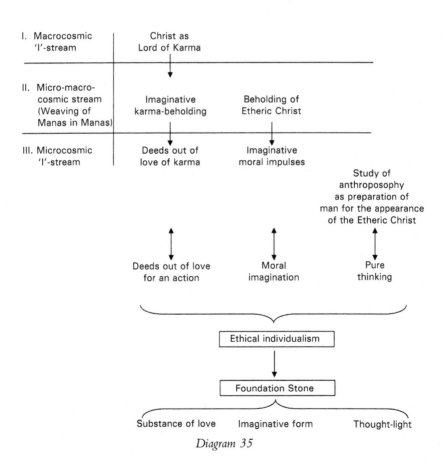

Diagram 35

the same time we will recognize the central significance of the Foundation Stone as well as the whole impact of the fact that since its creation every human being can implant it in the ground of his or her heart as an inner basis and at the same time a new community-building-impulse for the Anthroposophical Society as a modern karma-community, in which human beings can practise ethical individualism in accordance with the Christ as Lord of Karma in order, thereby, to become His co-workers in the domain of karma.

The summation of the working of the three streams results in the outline in Diagram 35 on previous page.

Notes

If not otherwise noted, all emphases are by S. O. Prokofieff even in quotes.

1. Quoted following Rudolf Steiner, 'Goethe als Vater einer neuen Ästhetik (Goethe as father of a new aestheticism) in GA 30.
2. 'Pure thinking', for which Rudolf Steiner also uses the term 'sense-free [thinking]' as a synonym, is called this because it is indeed free of all that is sensory, hence pure. The process of purification of thinking unfolds through the inner efforts of the human 'I' in the direction from below to above. From above to below in reverse of this process from the other side, 'conceptual' or 'thought intuition' works and comprises 'intuitive thinking'. The purer and less sense-bound thinking is (more independent from the brain and sense impressions), the more capable it becomes of grasping genuine intuitions. One can say that pure thinking and intuitive thinking strive towards each other and are the designations that characterize the same process from two different sides. When human beings consciously carry out this twofold development, they make use of or activate what Rudolf Steiner described as 'living thinking'. (Since he often deals rather freely with these designations, the terms referred to here can occur in various contexts of his work in place of one another.)
3. In the works by Rudolf Steiner, as well as in secondary anthroposophical literature, many practical references can be found for the development of such attention.
4. See Chapter 14, '*The Philosophy of Freedom* and the Science of the Grail', also Chapters 15 and 16. The two images, those of the spear and the chalice, also play a most important role in the Grail Mysteries.
5. In the ground-plan of the First Goetheanum one can clearly experience the presence of the Rose Cross, the centre of which coincides with the speaker's podium; the three 'upper' roses are connected with the smaller cupola (macrocosm), the four 'lower' with the large cupola (microcosm).
6. In Luke's Gospel the angels say directly: 'Why do you seek the Living One among the dead? He is not here, he has risen' (24:5–6 JM).
7. In the fourth post-Atlantean period, Mary Magdalene still needed an external inducement to attain to a vision of the Christ (He calls her by name). This was moreover tied to the fact that she was mainly prompted by feeling (moved by powerful emotion, she wept at the tomb). In feeling the human being is in general only half-conscious, that is why one needs an impulse from outside to awaken fully. Today in the period of the consciousness soul, we have to arouse this impulse by ourselves so as to come to an experience of the Etheric Christ. This is possible for us because we no longer proceed from feeling but from thinking, for it is only in thinking that we are fully awake. (In the explanations to the first rhythm of the Foundation Stone Meditation, Rudolf Steiner therefore speaks of the human soul that calls upon itself.) Likewise the seeing of the angels *within* the tomb shows that in those times thinking had not yet died

completely as is the case today in our period of freedom. For a completion of the picture, one could add that in the scene of Emmaus the will of the human being was also addressed. Now in will humans are completely asleep. Therefore, in order to awaken them to the reality of the Resurrection, Christ must carry out an action. (The call alone is not enough.) This takes place through the breaking of the bread. Yet at the moment of their cognition, Christ becomes invisible for humans (Luke 24:30 f.), for they are not yet mature enough to experience Him in their will. We find a reference to today's situation in the story of Thomas who wishes to see and touch everything *himself.*

8. In Greek it says in the first part, ἐστράφη ὀπίσω ('turned oneself back' or 'turned backwards' (20:14), and in the second case, στραφεῖσα ('turned oneself around') (20:16). In addition, the two verb forms are in the passive case, which indicates that in those days human beings still required an impulse from outside for their inner transformation.

9. See more on this in Carl Unger: *Was ist Anthroposophie?* (What is Anthroposophy?), Dornach 1996.

10. In this connection Rudolf Steiner speaks moreover of the three supersensible Christ-revelations that will occur as a consequence of the Mystery of Golgotha: His etheric return (Second Coming), which is beginning in the present time, then His astral appearance, and finally His highest, the 'I'-revelation. (GA 130, 4 November 1911.)

11. See more about this in S. O. Prokofieff's *May Human Beings Hear It!*, Chapter 'The Foundation Stone Meditation. Karma and Resurrection' and Supplement VIII, 'The Spiritual and the Sacramental Communion'.

12. Moreover, in comparison to the bodies of remaining humanity, the body of the Christ was prepared for this purpose in a completely unique way throughout the whole of mankind's evolution. The loftiest initiates on earth as well as the beings of the spiritual world worked on it. Rudolf Steiner describes the preparation of this special body fully in many lectures, particularly in GA 114 and GA 118.

13. What has been said here gives us a better understanding for Rudolf Steiner's critical attitude during his work on the 'pre-anthroposophical' writings in regard to official Christianity (see GA 28, Chap. XXVI). For the latter always proceeded from the separation of the world into the purely material (recognizable) world existence and purely spiritual (unrecognizable) existence beyond. This dualism that refers back spiritually and historically to Plato and was intensified particularly by Kant can never allow for a proper understanding of the connection of the Christ with Jesus, and therefore of His Resurrection. Over against this, with all his inner strength, young Rudolf Steiner had to place his spiritual monism rooted as it was in true Aristotelianism. It is a monism that everywhere in matter beholds the presence and effectiveness of the spirit. In this way it forms the only appropriate basis through which the Mystery of Golgotha can truly be comprehended. In it for all future time, the Christ inseparably united the world on this side with the world beyond

14. It would be most advisable for the reader to study the lecture of 8 May 1910 in its entirety since it offers an important key to the understanding of *The Philo-*

sophy of Freedom. See also Friedwart Husemann, *Rudolf Steiners Entwicklung* (Rudolf Steiner's development), Chapter 'Der Quellort der Liebe in der Erkenntnis' (The source of love in cognition), Stuttgart 1999. What has been said does not contradict the unconditionality of its path of cognition. It merely indicates that this book could only be written *after* the Mystery of Golgotha. For in that way the world-sphere was created in which a philosophy of freedom is possible in the first place.

14a. What is more, at the time of Plato and Aristotle—and really until the eighth Christian century AD—when they were thinking, human beings had the clear feeling that the thoughts were flowing to them out of the spiritual world. Only after the Cosmic Intelligence (which had originally been managed by Michael) had finally reached the earth—as a result of the Mystery of Golgotha—human beings came to the experience that they themselves produce their thoughts. (GA 240, 19 July 1924.) Only this way, cognition later on became possible in the modern sense and also made possible its high point in the epistemology of *Truth and Science* and *The Philosophy of Freedom* by Rudolf Steiner.

14b. Only as a consequence of this distance from the spirit could Aristotle explore the laws of thinking and establish logic.

15. In the lecture of 28 August 1924 (GA 243), Rudolf Steiner describes these two paths (directions) as that of the Moon and Saturn.

16. See details as well in Addendum I.

17. See GA 10 and GA 13. The designation lower 'I' is used by Rudolf Steiner only to characterize the objective fact that, with reference to his earthly 'I', man possesses still another 'I' that is on a higher level but of which he is unaware to begin with. No value judgement is pronounced here on man's earthly 'I', for, as will be shown later on in the book, it is *this* 'I' that forms the point of departure for man's ascent to fulfilment of his/her spiritual destiny, which consists in becoming aware and taking hold of one's eternal personality.

18. See for instance in GA 165, 19 December 1915.

19. See above all *Knowledge of the Higher Worlds and Its Attainment* (GA 10), Chapter, 'Some Results of Initiation', *Occult Science, an Outline* (GA 13), Chapter 'Knowledge of Higher Worlds', as well as Addendum I in this book.

20. In this higher sphere manifests the glorious imagination of the Christ as Spiritual Sun of the World surrounded by the circle of the twelve Bodhisattvas (see GA 116, 25 October 1909). In anthroposophical Christology, this imagination belongs among the most important results of Rudolf Steiner's spiritual research. See Addendum I concerning this sphere's connection to the nature and origin of man's true 'I'.

21. See Addendum I.

22. In *Occult Science an Outline* (GA 13) Rudolf Steiner points out that only such an encounter with the Christ in Intuition (which represents a higher stage of modern initiation) reveals the whole cosmic significance of the Mystery of Golgotha, meaning the Resurrection of the Christ, to the spirit disciple based on his or her own experience.

23. To this realm belong above all the insights of the nature and activity of human

karma of which Rudolf Steiner spoke after the Christmas Conference in the karma lectures.

24. The transition from the lower to the higher 'I' takes place beginning from point 3 through point 4 to point 5.

25. This is why Rudolf Steiner in his autobiography writes about 'spiritually having stood *before the Mystery of Golgotha*'. See in more detail further on in this book.

26. In *The Philosophy of Freedom* Rudolf Steiner writes: 'The intermediate point between concept and percept is the *mental picture*' (emphasis by Rudolf Steiner).

26a. This sequence is also pointed out in *The Philosophy of Freedom*: 'He [the human being] will strive for moral ideals when his moral imagination is active enough to arouse intuitions in him . . . ' (GA 4, Chap. XIII). These words make it clear that one must first develop moral imagination strongly enough within ones self in order then to attain to the level of intuition.

27. Lecture of 1 May 1918: 'Der übersinnliche Mensch und die Fragen der Willensfreiheit' (Supersensible man and the questions of freedom of will) in *Was in der anthroposophischen Gesellschaft vorgeht* (What is happening in the Anthroposophical Society), seventeenth annual set, 1940, No. 14 ff.

28. Modern physiology likewise is familiar with the outward side of this process, namely that every action of human consciousness is accompanied by the dying down and disintegration of cells in the brain and nervous system. See on this also S. O. Prokofieff, *What is Anthroposophy?*, Chapter 2, Temple Lodge Publishing, 2006.

29. Concerning this relationship between the attainment of freedom and the effect of the death-forces in the human organism, see more in *What is Anthroposophy?*

30. See more about this in *What is Anthroposophy?*

31. In the same lecture Rudolf Steiner mentions more concrete numbers. Even if 'in the millions upon millions of human beings' this condition of moral degeneracy will come to pass, even 'a mere dozen human beings' will through their moral enthusiasm be able to bring the earth to shine in the cosmos.

32. This is why Rudolf Steiner so resolutely emphasizes in his early article, 'Der Egoismus in der Philosophie' (Egoism in philosophy) (1899) that his only concern is the 'tangible [*leibhaftige*] "I" of individual man' (in GA 30).

33. See more about this in *What is Anthroposophy?*

34. Here Rudolf Steiner refers back to the ancient Rosicrucian tradition, according to which something essentially new originated in the universe besides the Holy Trinity of Father, Son and Holy Spirit through the bodily incarnation of the Christ in Jesus of Nazareth, namely the 'Son of Man' or the 'eternal persona'. It bears spiritual forces in itself that in time can bestow immortality, and along with that eternal life, to the 'I'-consciousness of every human personality who seeks a conscious relationship to this 'persona'. (See *Geheime Figuren der Rosenkreuzer aus dem 16. und 17. Jahrhundert* (Secret figures of the Rosicrucians from the sixteenth and seventeenth century), booklet I, pp. 29, 31, 33, Altona 1785; and booklet II, pp. 52, 53, 56, Altona 1785.

35. This world of spiritual perceptions is then presented by him in his book *Theosophy*. See in more detail in Friedwart Husemann, *Die Theosophie im Spiegel*

der Philosophie der Freiheit (*Theosophy* in the mirror of *The Philosophy of Freedom*) in the weekly magazine, *Das Goetheanum*, Newsletter No. 25, 20 June 2004.

36. The participation of pure thinking in this process is necessary because in ordinary thinking the process is moved into the domain of memories. A mere memory of what was once thought, however, leads in no way to the exceptional state that one is trying to reach.

37. Above all, the differentiation that he makes at the beginning of Chapter IX between 'I'-consciousness and the actual 'I' (in preparing for the second edition) points unmistakably in this direction.

38. See more about this stage of initiation in Rudolf Steiner's life in S. O. Prokofieff, *Rudolf Steiner and the Founding of the New Mysteries*, Chapter 'The Great Sun Period' and Chapter 'The Path of the Teacher of Humanity'.

39. Concerning the spiritual communion, see in more detail in S. O. Prokofieff, *May Human Beings Hear It!*, Chapter 'The Foundation Stone Meditation. Karma and Reincarnation' and Supplement VIII, 'The Spiritual and the Sacramental Communion'; also *The Foundation Stone Meditation, A Key to the New Christian Mysteries*, Addendum: 'The Three Forms of Communion and the Foundation Stone Meditation'.

40. See more about this in *May Human Beings Hear It!* Chapter 'Rudolf Steiner's Life in the Light of the Christmas Conference'.

41. See also *What is Anthroposophy?*

42. This motif of man's inner enslavement in regard to his body and with that to the whole world of sense perceptions, as well as the necessity to liberate oneself from this, is a subject that occurs repeatedly in the Gospels.

43. In *The Philosophy of Freedom*, this Pentecostal motif is pointed out in Chapter IX, which deals with the *common spirit* that alone makes it possible for free human beings to live side by side and with each other. See more about it in this book.

44. The 'Hague Conversation' with W. J. Stein, published in the book by W. J. Stein/Rudolf Steiner, *Dokumentation eines wegweisenden Zusammenwirkens* (Documentation of a trail-blazing cooperation), Dornach 1985.

45. Concerning anthroposophy as a 'resurrection-science', see more in *What is Anthroposophy?*

46. In *The Philosophy of Freedom,* Rudolf Steiner summarizes these three main elements of human cognition in the following words: 'If our personality expressed itself merely in a cognizant way, the sum of all that is objective would be given in seeing, concept (thinking), and mental picture' (GA 4). For man consists of these three as a cognizing being, something in which chiefly the Cherubim in their cosmic activity show the greatest interest.

47. Concerning the three forms of man's 'I'—ordinary 'I', higher 'I' (self), and true 'I'—see in Rudolf Steiner's *The Threshold to the Spiritual World* (GA 17) as well as in S. O. Prokofieff, *May Human Beings Hear It!*, Chapter 'The Foundation Stone Meditation in Eurythmy'.

48. See GA 110, 14 April 1909–II.

49. See GA 110, 14 April 1909–II and GA 346, 7 September 1924.

50. This difference between the seven lower hierarchies (from the Angels all the way to the Thrones), and the two highest, the Cherubim and Seraphim, can

also be discovered in *Geheime Figuren der Rosenkreuzer aus dem 16. und 17. Jahrhundert* (Secret figures of the Rosicrucians from the sixteenth and seventeenth century), Booklet I, p. 33, Altona 1785. An understanding of this difference can, however, only be attained through anthroposophy. It shows that it is the above-mentioned seven hierarchies that up to now are principally involved in the whole evolution of our cosmos. The two highest hierarchies remain as if in the background.

51. In the lecture of 7 April 1912 (GA 136) Rudolf Steiner recounts the impression that a clairvoyant can have of these exalted beings: 'Wisdom that has been gathered ... for millions of years of world evolution stream towards us with exalted power from the beings whom we call Cherubim. They are thus the 'Spirits of highest wisdom.' (GA 110, 14 April, 1909–II.)

52. See GA 110, 14 April 1909–II.

53. See also Diagram 8.

54. Concerning this whole cosmic evolution see more details in S. O. Prokofieff, *The Foundation Stone Meditation. A Key to the New Christian Mysteries*, Chapter 'The Foundation Stone Meditation and the Cosmic Working of the Hierarchies'. In connection with what was said and the content of Diagram 8, the following must be noted. In order to assure the transition from the Earth to Jupiter, or in accordance with St John, to build the New Jerusalem, human beings must ascend to the stage of the 'micro-logos' (transition from 4 to 5). This is only possible, however, through the realization of the words by Paul, 'Not I, but the Christ in me'. At the end of the Vulcan-age on the other hand, human beings will rise to the stage of cosmic creators, the stage on which they will work in the universe as 'Macro-Logos beings' (transition from 7 to 8). This will not signify, however, that human beings will become identical to the World Logos (Christ), for they will even then remain merely hierarchical beings (notwithstanding the fact that they will represent a completely new kind of hierarchy in the cosmic totality. Christ, on the other hand, does not belong to the hierarchical but to the purely divine world lying above the former one. He will therefore also remain the highest archetype for this whole new evolution.

55. See GA 222, 16 and 18 March 1923.

56. This is why in the Foundation Stone Meditation the former are called 'Spirits of Light' and the latter 'Spirits of Soul' (GA 260a).

57. The 'Conversation in The Hague' with W. J. Stein is published in the book by W. J. Stein/Rudolf Steiner, *Dokumentation eines wegweisenden Zusammenwirkes* (Documentation of a trail-blazing cooperation), Dornach 1985.

58. See more details in *May Human Beings Hear It!*, Chapter 'The Foundation Stone Meditation. Karma and Resurrection'.

59. In the second sentence the words 'is and was and comes' correspond to points 4; 1 (2, 3); 7 (6, 5) in Diagram 9.

60. See more about this in Chapter 6.

61. See Note 58.

62. See Note 61.

63. It was already shown in Chapter 1 how these two paths relate to each other and how they form a unity on the higher levels of initiation.

64. In modern initiation, the so-called 'Path of the Moon' leads to the first experience; the 'Path of Saturn' to the second one (GA 243, 21 August 1924).

65. Not merely the cognition (the study) of *The Philosophy of Freedom* is meant by this but its full actualization in human life, as was the case with Rudolf Steiner.

66. In the light of these considerations, the lecture by Rudolf Steiner 'Neues Denken und neues Wollen (New thinking and new willing) (GA 257, 6 February 1923), in which he directly connects with the two parts of *The Philosophy of Freedom*, appears in its full Christian and esoteric depth.

67. 'And there appeared to them tongues as of fire, distributed and resting on each one of them' (Acts 2:3).

68. John 14:17. This refers in a deeper esoteric sense to the title of the book *Truth and Science* in which as if in seed-form the phrase 'spiritual science' is present, for the Spirit working in the latter is the Spirit of Truth.

69. Rudolf Steiner speaks for the first time about creating an 'epistemology ... in the sense of Paul' in the lecture of 8 May 1910 (GA 116).

70. These three sciences can in their essence be related to the nature of the three great Christian festivals:

Natural science (Goetheanism)	—	Christmas
Science of freedom	—	Easter
Spiritual science	—	Whitsun

    It is also striking that all three sciences had outstanding forerunners at the time of German Idealism. For Goetheanism it was of course Goethe; the genuine starting points of a science of freedom is found in Schiller, above all in his work *Über die ästhetische Erziehung des Menschen in einer Reihe von Briefen* (About the aesthetic education of man in a series of letters), and the beginnings of spiritual science in Novalis (see GA 126, 1 January 1911).

71. In a certain regard, the transition from the second to the third science is represented in Goethe's *Fairy Tale* in whose imaginations the impulse of freedom is permeated by the Christ Impulse.

72. Rudolf Steiner describes this process in the lecture of 30 July 1922 (GA 214).

73. See F. W. Schelling, *Die Philosophie der Offenbarung* (The philosophy of revelation), Lecture 36. In this regard today's science in its materialistic form resembles Peter in the condition of his darkened state of mind and threefold denial of the Christ.

74. See on this also in S.O. Prokofieff, *The Mystery of John the Baptist and John the Evangelist*, Temple Lodge Publishing, 2005.

75. This is why the seven I-AM words by the Christ are found only in his Gospel.

76. See GA 103 and GA 104.

77. The subtitle of *The Philosophy of Freedom* reads: 'Some results of *introspective* observation following the methods of natural science'. In the preface to the new edition of 1918, Rudolf Steiner writes that his book makes reference 'to a domain of *soul* experience' (GA 4), where the most important questions of life mentioned in the earlier preface can be solved. Here one can call attention also to Schiller's *Ästhetische Briefe* (Aesthetical letters) in which he ascribed the experience of freedom especially to man's soul that finds itself between the compulsion of the body and the compulsion of the intellect (spirit).

78. See in more detail in S. O. Prokofieff, *What is Anthroposophy?*

79. See more details about the will in thinking and thinking in the will, and also their cosmic consequences in the lecture 'New Thinking and New Willing' (GA 257, 6 February 1923). The correlation of the will with the Tree of Life becomes evident because the human being sojourns in the spiritual world in will as if in its very life-element. This is why in the first part of the Foundation Stone Meditation the verb 'live' stands in the place of 'to will' ('And thou shalt truly *live*').

80. See concerning Rudolf Steiner's direct relationship to the Time Spirit Michael during his work on *The Philosophy of Freedom* in Weimar in S. O. Prokofieff, *May Human Beings Hear It!*, Chapter 'Rudolf Steiner's Course of Life in the Light of the Christmas Conference', and Chapter '*The Philosophy of Freedom* and the Christmas Conference'.

81. Rudolf Steiner says concerning this: 'The one true name of the Christ is "I Am"; one who does not know this does not understand it and calls him by a different name, does not know anything at all about him.' (GA 266–I, 27 May 1909.)

Tr. 1 The German simply says *gelebt* or lived. What is meant is: 'inwardly lived and experienced'. (Translator's Note.)

82. See more about this in GA 131, 14 October 1911.

83. See GA 103, 22 May 1908.

84. This is why in Christian tradition it is first and foremost the Spirits of Universal Love, the Seraphim, who are depicted as cosmic beings aglow in the fire of love.

85. See GA 194, 22 November 1919. Concerning the two Michael-revelations see also S. O. Prokofieff, *May Human Beings Hear It!*, Chapter '*The Philosophy of Freedom* and the Christmas Conference', and Chapter 'The Foundation Stone Meditation. Karma and Resurrection'.

86. In accordance with the two parts of *The Philosophy of Freedom*, this baptism with fire and spirit can be understood as follows. Through the practice of the first part, a person arrives at the penetration of thinking with the will. In that way one can grasp oneself as a spiritual being. And through the practice of the second part one brings the light of one's thinking into the realm of the will which causes this light to turn into fire, a fire that is akin to the cosmic fire (see more about it in this chapter).

87. While Rudolf Steiner worked in Weimar on *The Philosophy of Freedom*, he experienced his first encounter with Michael in the spiritual world. See *May Human Beings Hear It!*, Chapter 'Rudolf Steiner's Course of Life in the Light of the Christmas Conference', and Chapter '*The Philosophy of Freedom* and the Christmas Conference'.

88. See GA 240, 19 July 1924, as well as the essay 'Cosmic Thoughts in Michael's and in Ahriman's Working' (GA 26, 16 November 1924).

89. See more about this in *May Human Beings Hear it!*, Chapter 'Rudolf Steiner's Course of Life in the Light of the Christmas Conference', and Chapter '*The Philosophy of Freedom* and the Christmas Conference'.

90. That we are dealing here only with a part is made evident in the lecture of 8

August 1924 (GA237), which described how, during the descent of the Cosmic Intelligence, not all but only a part of the Angels who were linked to Michael left his kingdom.

91. See about this in *May Human Beings Hear it!,* Chapter 'The Mystery Act of the Foundation Stone Laying on 25 December 1923'.

92. Translated from the Russian Bible. Martin Luther has: 'Let us make man, an image that is like us'. The Standard Revised Edition has: 'Let us make man in our image, after our likeness'.

93. See for example in the work *The Ascetic Words* by the Holy Diadoch, Bishop of Photika (fifth century), 'Word 89' containing the text: 'Through the baptism there arises in us the Grace of the Image of God. The Likeness of God, on the other hand, is drawn [painted] by it [by Grace] afterwards along with man's efforts to acquire the virtues, above all of which stands love—the highest attribute of God-likeness.' (*Philokaly,* Vol. 3, Moscow 1900.)

94. That this theme belongs to the content of the Fifth Gospel is made evident by the lecture of 27 May 1914 (GA 152), where the stages preceeding the Mystery of Golgotha are brought into direct connection with the communications concerning the earthly life of Christ Jesus.

95. The thus united image and likeness also correspond to the two so-called biblical stories of Creation. (See more details on this in M. Debus, *Maria-Sophia,* Stuttgart 2000.) The image is connected with the first *perfect* Creation through the Elohim (gods) and can therefore not fall into sin. By contrast the likeness reflects the second *imperfect* Creation through a god (Yahweh) which consequently leads into the earthly evolution.

96. Even the polarity of 'darkness' and 'light' as well as the transformation of the first into the second, something that was the main motif of Zarathustra's teachings and his activity during the founding of the second post-Atlantean cultural period, is found in the quoted words.

97. The whole subject of the Academy of Gondishapur in the seventh century and its continuation in western civilization belongs here. (See GA 182, 16 October 1918, and GA 184, 11 and 12 October 1918.)

98. See also *May Human Beings Hear it!,* Chapter 'The Rhythms of the Christmas Conference'.

99. This connection of *The Philosophy of Freedom* and the teachings of Paul is moreover founded on the content of the Fifth Gospel. For as stated earlier, the communications from the Fifth Gospel begin with the lifting of the secret of the two Jesus boys, meaning with the reference to Adam's celestial sister-soul. Among all the Apostles of Christ Jesus it was most of all Paul who through his Damascus experience was particularly capable of penetrating into the secret of this special entity. (GA 142, 1 January 1913.) Thus, like no other, he was initiated into the Mystery of the Old and the New Adam, and with that into the Mystery of Jesus of Nazareth (GA 131, 10 October 1911), and likewise into the nature of the Fifth Gospel. From this source Paul could develop the initial stages for a new epistemology that found full elaboration in Rudolf Steiner's early work. Even according to general Christian tradition,

Luke was a student of the apostle Paul. This means that the content of the Third Gospel, the only one in which a few facts concerning the biography of the Luke-Jesus are related, date back to Paul. Concerning the special relationship of Paul to the nature of the Luke-Jesus, see the outstanding work by Mathilde Scholl, 'Der Weg nach Damascus' ('The path to Damascus'), published as a postscript in the book by E. Meffert, *Mathilde Scholl,* Dornach 1991.

100. Concerning Paul's teachings about the First and Second Adam, see also GA 131, 10 October 1911.

101. In philosophy, this medieval doctrine of the Church has been solidly positioned through Kant's 'thing in itself' on the one hand, and on the other through his 'moral imperative'. This is why Rudolf Steiner first had to thoroughly refute this error by Kant in order then to establish his philosophy on freedom in the space thus freed. Furthermore, no subjugation under an outer authority or an ethical system of laws was possibel for the ethical individualism of *The Philosophy of Freedom.*

102. See GA 6, Chapter: 'The Consequences of the Platonic World View'. In the only way possible for his time, Aristotle early on tried to overcome this Platonic dualism of two worlds, the one of ideas and the other of the physical objects. With that, at the height of Greek antiquity, he prepared the future comprehension of the secret of resurrection.

103. In overwhelming desperation, already in a state of mental derangement, he signed the last letters that he wrote shortly before his death with 'The Crucified One'. The tragic earthly destiny of Nietzsche can be compared on the microcosmic level with the destiny of Jesus of Nazareth, had Jesus not been able at the Baptism in the Jordan to receive the Christ into his being. It must be taken into consideration here that Nietzsche lived at the end of the Kali Yuga, meaning (still) at the age when conscious access to the spiritual world was extraordinarily difficult.

104. In the Foundation Stone Meditation Rudolf Steiner speaks of the 'simple [or "humble"—in German *arme,* literally "poor"] Shepherds' hearts' (GA 260), but in the sense of the First Beatitude, 'Blessed are the beggars for spirit, for within themselves they find the realm of the heavens.' (Matt. 5:3 JM.) Here the term 'realm of heaven' points to what, in humans, belongs to that realm, namely their likeness.

105. See S. O. Prokofieff, 'The Mysteries of the Shepherds and the Kings in the light of Anthroposophy' in *The Encounter with Evil,* Temple Lodge Publishing, 1999.

106. The difference with the original image is above all that in the former the freedom of man, fully and conclusively attainable to him only today in the epoch of the consciousness soul, was not given. In paradise man was still completely dependent on the hierarchies.

107. Already in the plant kingdom even—due to the fact that plants possess an etheric body—the hierarchies are present and that much more in the higher kingdoms. Rudolf Steiner speaks about the fact that human beings can experience the nature of freedom only within the mineral kingdom in the

lecture of 17 February 1924: 'Only in the kingdom of the mineral world does man move about freely. There is the domain of his freedom.' (GA 235.) That is the kingdom, however, in which only those forces hold sway that are destructive, death-dealing ones for humankind. 'It is no wonder that man is free in this domain, for it is the realm that has no other claim on him than to destroy him if it takes hold of him' (ibid.).

108. See S. O. Prokofieff *What is Anthroposophy?*, Chapter 'Rudolf Steiner's Path of Development.'

109. Beginning with the primal sacrifice of the Thrones on Ancient Saturn and on to that of the Spirits of Form (the Elohim), who bestowed the substance of the 'I' on human beings, the whole of evolution is based on the principle of sacrifice. In humanity's evolution, this creative principle appears in its highest form in the Mystery of Golgotha. From then on it can be made fully real by every human being who has attained to the corresponding evolutionary stage, but now based on the new forces of freedom and love. This development, which begins on earth, will reach its culmination and initial conclusion on Vulcan, where mankind on its own will form a new zodiac in order to begin the creation of the new solar system through a cosmic deed of sacrifice. Rudolf Steiner calls this stage the 'great cosmic offering-service'. (GA 110, 14 April 1909–II.) For the same reason Rudolf Steiner writes at the end of his main book of inner schooling, *Knowledge of the Higher Worlds*, that the true Christian initiates (among whom he himself belongs) value 'selfless devotion and willingness to sacrifice' the most in a spirit disciple, meaning the inner qualities that are the most important for the imitation of Christ (GA 10).

110. Nothing of their symptomatic significance is changed because these three encounters occurred chronologically in opposite sequence.

111. What was said does not contradict the fact that Rudolf Steiner considered many of Haeckel's as well as Nietzsche's ideas to be very significant. For these ideas, if only placed on a different basis, can have most spiritual consequences.

112. Rudolf Steiner's connection with the Theosophical Society was also similarly motivated; he wished to move this society out of its pre-Christian, oriental cultural background to its original Christian-Rosicrucian sources.

113. See more detail in *Rudolf Steiner and the Founding of the New Mysteries*, Chapter 'The Path of the Teacher of Humanity'.

114. See more in S. O. Prokofieff, *Rudolf Steiner and the Founding of the New Mysteries*, Chapter 'The Path of the Teacher of Humanity', and in *May Human Beings Hear It!*, Chapter 'Rudolf Steiner's Course of Life in the Light of the Christmas Conference'.

115. See S. O. Prokofieff, *The Foundation Stone Meditation. A Key to the New Christian Mysteries*, Chapter 'The Foundation Stone Meditation in Eurythmy and the Mystery of the Two Jesus Boys'.

116. As is known, Rudolf Steiner spoke about the secret of the two Jesus boys (a mystery that represents the very heart of the Fifth Gospel) for the first time in 1909 in the cycle about the Gospel of Luke. In accordance with the Saturn-rhythm the following configuration becomes apparent:

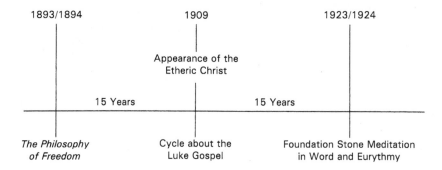

See also about the connection of *The Philosophy of Freedom* and the Christmas Conference in *May Human Beings Hear It!*, Chapter '*The Philosophy of Freedom and the Christmas Conference*'.

117. See GA 112, 6 July 1909.

118. This is, for example, how Andrei Belyi experienced it in 1913, in Christiania (Oslo). See *Reminiscences of Rudolf Steiner*, Chapter 'Rudolf Steiner and the Theme of the Christus'.

119. What has been said only concerns a human 'I' that has passed through a number of incarnations on earth, as was the case with Zarathustra. It was completely different in the case of the Luke-Jesus, who at the Turning Point of Time had come to earth for the first time and whose 'I' was 'like an empty sphere' (GA 131, 12 October 1911) in regard to all earthly experiences that represent the actual content of the 'I'. It thus differed fundamentally from all other human egos. (See more details on this in *The Foundation Stone Meditation. A Key to the Christian Mysteries*, Chapter, 'The Foundation Stone Meditation in Eurythmy and the Mystery of the Two Jesus Boys'.)

120. This can be seen especially clearly in the unusual spiritual faculties that arose in Rudolf Steiner after this experience. (See on this S. O. Prokofieff, *What is Anthroposophy?*, Chapter Rudolf Steiner's Path of Development.)

121. Moreover, through these 'dead mineral substances' the ahrimanic 'thorn' works of which Rudolf Steiner speaks in connection with the apostle Paul in the above-quoted lecture.

122. In this passing through the abyss of powerlessness, a human being on the path of modern initiation experiences something resembling what the spirit-disciples experienced in the ancient Mysteries. Rudolf Steiner characterizes these experiences as follows: 'A possibility exists here that can be terrible, namely that man loses his reactions and feelings for actual reality and no new one opens up to him. He then floats as if in emptiness. He feels as if he had withered away. The former values are gone and no new ones have arisen for him.' (This is also the desperate situation in which Nietzsche found himself, which cast him into the abyss.) Now come the crucial words: 'Man reaches the point where, for him, the spirit declares all life to be death. He is then no longer in the world. He is under the world—in the netherworld ... Fortunate is he who does not go under.' (GA 8, Chapter 'Mysteries and Mystery Wisdom'.) This experience, but

now on the path of modern initiation, corresponds exactly to what Rudolf Steiner describes in *The Story of My Life* as his passage through the domain of the ahrimanic beings or spirits of death (see GA 28, Chap. XXVI). Now the difference with the ancient Mysteries is that in Christian initiation human 'I'-consciousness remains fully intact on all levels. One therefore cannot speak of a fundamental alteration or even an exchange of personality. This is why it is so important for Rudolf Steiner to show in his autobiographical presentation that in his inner development no break occurred anywhere.

123. Through her cosmic portal, Christ came out of His spiritual heights down to the sun. See more on this in S. O. Prokofieff, *The Heavenly Sophia and the Being Anthroposophia*, Part II, Chapter 'The Heavenly Sophia and the Cosmic Mysteries of the Christ'.

124. In the essay of 25 October 1924 (GA 26) Rudolf Steiner describes the step-by-step withdrawal of the divine-spiritual forces of the hierarchies out of the cosmos, which represents one condition for the attainment of man's individual freedom. This withdrawal can likewise be linked with the cosmic development. On Old Saturn the hierarchies themselves were still present in their creation with their very being; on the Old Sun they were only effective through their revelations, and on the Old Moon merely through their effects. On earth, along with the creation of the mineral kingdom, they withdrew completely from the latter. With that, they left the world, the 'work-world', abandoned by them, to humankind as a site where we can attain our absolute freedom.

125. This does not mean that man will stand in the absolute sense above all the hierarchies but that he will have qualities that none of the hierarchies possess, hence that he will only be placed above them in *this* sense.

126. In this regard it is of significance that already in his youth, when searching for the unconditional cognition from which the nature of freedom can be fathomed, Rudolf Steiner comes to speak of the absolute. As a 20-year-old, he writes to his friend: 'The essential concept and nature of man consists of the longing for the absolute, the eternal and immortal. To undertake to prove this is nonsense. Rather, it demonstrates that one is caught up in utter nonsense to ever demand proof in this regard.' For anything that can be proven is in no way the very first, and therefore no longer unconditional. So Rudolf Steiner continues in his writing: 'Highest reality can only be attributed to the absolute ... The striving for the absolute—this longing of man is *freedom*. Any other goal produces error, deception and illusion; it owes its origin not to freedom but to *arbitrariness*.' This means, no genuine unconditional theory of cognition can be developed from it, one that can establish the true freedom in man. And that absolutely has to happen, for: 'Illusion must be destroyed, the veil has to be lifted. And [then] truth, the Deity, stands before us.' (GA 38, letter from 16 August 1881; emphasis by Rudolf Steiner.) This is why the path Rudolf Steiner embarks on here leads to his *Philosophy of Freedom* and from it to the personal encounter with the one who alone could say of Himself, 'I am the truth' (John 14:6).

127. In this context the reference concerning the Christ's path to the Father signifies that the faculty of working as the micro-logos is passed on through the Mystery of Golgotha into the full possession of the human being.

128. Many passages in Rudolf Steiner's early work clearly demonstrate how strongly he sensed this secret of man's evolution even in his youth; for example, when he speaks in his article from the year 1886, 'Die Natur und unsere Ideale' (Nature and our ideals) (GA 30) of 'divine freedom', meaning, of the freedom that was given to us by God Himself (p. 238), or when he points out that 'we ... have received into ourselves the highest potential of existence' (p. 239).

129. See more on this in S. O. Prokofieff, *The Cycle of the Year as a Path of Initiation*, Part II, 'The Mystery of Advent as the Mystery of the Nathan-soul'.

130. The unspoken question of freedom stands in the centre of Goethe's *Fairy Tale*, for it was written by Goethe as a reply to Schiller's 'Aesthetic Letters' in which the figuring out of human freedom plays a major role.

131. See more details in *May Human Beings Hear It!*, Chapter 'The Mystery Act of the Foundation Stone Laying on 25 December 1923'.

132. See more details in *May Human Beings Hear It!*, Chapter 'The Philosophy of Freedom and the Christmas Conference'.

133. See lecture of 25 October 1918 (GA 185) and also S. O. Prokofieff, *The Encounter with Evil and Its Overcoming Through Spiritual Science*.

134. Rudolf Steiner speaks about the connection of love with the sixth cultural period in the lecture of 3 December 1911 (GA 130).

135. See S. O. Prokofieff, *The Heavenly Sophia and the Being Anthroposophia*.

136. See *The Foundation Stone, A Key to the New Christian Mysteries*, Chapter 'The Merging of the Rosicrucian and the Michaelic Stream in the Foundation Stone Meditation'.

137. See for instance GA 121, 17 June 1910.

138. Here, another parallel is striking. In their alchemistic experiments the Rosicrucians searched for the experience of the 'prima materia' or the 'essence of the world' which lies between the boundary of the physical-sensory and spiritual world, hence guaranteeing the connection between both and at the same time the transition from one to the other (see GA 130, 27 September 1911). What had to be attained by the ancient Rosicrucians still with the aid of external means is to be realized today on the purely inner path through the metamorphosis of human thinking. For what corresponds today to the search for the 'prima materia' is what in *The Philosophy of Freedom* is depicted as the 'exceptional state', one through which the human being can find the passage out of the physical into the spiritual world (see Chapter 1).

139. How this actually occurs can be studied in the lecture of 13 January 1924 (GA 233a).

140. See *The Foundation Stone. A Key to the New Christian Mysteries*, Chapter 'The Merging of the Rosicrucian and the Michaelic Stream in the Foundation Stone Meditation'.

141. From what has been said one can understand how the Sophia-impulse and the Michael-impulse are connected with each other in Rudolf Steiner's life. As we have seen in Chapter 10, during the creation of his early work the being of the Sophia passed through his consciousness soul; at the same time he encountered Michael in the spiritual world adjacent to the earth. After the turn of the century, during the founding of Anthroposophy, the Sophia who had turned

into Anthroposophia was experienced by him as an objective being of the spiritual world (see lecture of 3 February 1913), whereas the power of Michael worked in his inner being. In *The Anthroposophical Leading Thoughts* (the 'Michael Letters'), Rudolf Steiner writes in this regard: 'Michael, who has spoken from "on high", can be heard from within where he will assume his new abode' (GA 26). And the first human being in whom Michael found his 'new abode' was Rudolf Steiner as the founder of anthroposophy after the turn of the century.

Earlier Writings: Sophia within—Michael without.

Later Writings: Michael within—Sophia without.

142. See more details about these three encounters in Rudolf Steiner's life in *May Human Beings Hear It!*, Chapter 'Rudolf Steiner's Course of Life in the Light of the Christmas Conference'.

143. In his autobiographical lecture of 4 February 1913 (published in *Das Wesen der Anthroposophie*), Rudolf Steiner describes how, beginning from the age of seven, he could perceive the elemental spirits in nature in a spiritually direct way. This faculty of natural clairvoyance developed in him long before he encountered the Rosicrucian Master.

144. This rhythm consists of the three microcosmic segments of the first part of the Foundation Stone Meditation, then out of the fourth part, and in the end once more out of the three microcosmic segments of the first three parts, but now connected with the corresponding macrocosmic segments. See more on this in *May Human Beings Hear It!*, Chapter 'The Rhythms of the Christmas Conference'.

145. See in more detail in *What is Anthroposophy?*

146. As was mentioned before in this book, when a person is born on earth this eternal individuality (the higher 'I') does not descend at all into his or her body. It remains throughout the earthly incarnation in the spiritual world.

147. In many lectures Rudolf Steiner characterizes the Mystery of Golgotha as a sort of 'heavenly window' through which humanity could look upon the affairs of the gods and with that into the spiritual stream of time in which they live and work. (See for instance GA 148, 18 December 1913.)

148. From the viewpoint of the two directions, one can consider the symbolic form of the cross as the connection of the two time-streams: the exoteric one unfolds in the horizontal direction, the esoteric stream comes down from above. From the standpoint of the three dimensions of time to which to begin with earthly time is tied, one requires the blossoming of the seven roses on the cross for the transition to spiritual time.

149. In this sense, the black dead cross of the rose-cross meditation (see GA 13) is the necessary condition for man's freedom, which can only come about on earth in the mineral world.

150. Following a certain Rosicrucian tradition that summed up the three types of (nine) hierarchical beings in each case in one category, Rudolf Steiner speaks here of humanity not as the Tenth but as the Fourth Hierarchy.

151. What is said here does not contradict the fact that freedom must still be attained by every person in the sense of *The Philosophy of Freedom* on his/her own. For

what Rudolf Steiner communicates here based on his spiritual research in regard to the Michael-mission merely represents the *cosmic* side of the very complicated process through which the conditions must be created on earth, conditions based on which we can bring about our spiritual destiny through our own faculties.

152. See *May Human Beings Hear It!*, Chapter 'The Mystery Act of the Foundation Stone Laying on 25 December 1923', and *The Foundation Stone. A Key to the New Christian Mysteries*, Chapter 'The Merging of the Rosicrucian and Michaelic Stream in the Foundation Stone Meditation'.

153. See on this GA 131, 6 October 1911. That knowledge of reincarnation and karma existed in the Rosicrucian stream from the very beginning is borne out by the fact that during the initiation of Christian Rosenkreutz in the thirteenth century the circle of the twelve hierophants was aware of his earlier incarnation as a contemporary of the Mystery of Golgotha. (See GA 130, 27 September 1911.)

154. See more on this in S. O. Prokofieff, *The Cycle of the Year as a Path of Initiation*, Part XII, 'The Vidar Mystery'.

155. See on this, for instance, GA 131, 14 October 1911.

156. Many contemporary symptoms indicate by now that the struggle with the Fenris Wolf will be particularly hard in the domain of karma-viewing and karma research.

157. This does not contradict the words by Rudolf Steiner referred to in the fourth chapter that one is dealing here with *two* paths. For these words are contained in the book *Spiritual Science, an Outline* which was written for the general public. In the circle of his close students, on the other hand, Rudolf Steiner definitely wanted to see his early work taken up in the process of spirit-schooling.

158. In the autobiographical lecture of 4 February 1913 (published in *The Nature of Anthroposophy*), Rudolf Steiner mentions his first supersensible experience in connection with the world of those who have died when he was a seven-year-old boy. Continuing on, in the third chapter of the book *The Course of my Life*, it says that as an 18-year-old, he could follow the dead on their path into the spiritual world. 'A world of spiritual beings existed for me. It was a direct perception for me that the 'I', which itself is spirit, lives in a world of spirits.' (GA 28.) This faculty had developed in him even more concretely when he turned 20. 'I followed the human being who had died further on his path into the spiritual world' (ibid.). And as a 27-year-old, he could speak about repeated earth lives of a human being based on 'concrete perceptions' of the spiritual world (ibid., Chapter VII).

159. When here and in other passages the reference was always to the *heights* of the Midnight Hour, one must clearly understand that in this domain the spatial directions no longer have significance. This is why one can just as well speak about the *depths* of the Midnight Hour in the sense that Rudolf Steiner described it for instance in the lecture of 25 May 1924 (GA 239). There he says that, unlike on our earth, during the Midnight Hour our 'heaven' is to be found not above but below in the depths of the world (universe), where the highest—the First Hierarchy—works into matter.

160. It goes without saying that the preconditions for such a relationship of a human being with the lowest regions of the soul world lie in his or her earlier incarnations.

161. The difference with the practice of tact on the first stage consists of the following. In the first case the tactful actions are brought about through repeated external doings and therefore, to a large extent, still have an unconscious quality. By contrast, the actions on this third stage are determined through thinking and mental pictures, hence through conscious inner activity of man himself. Due to this, they can thereby be designated as *his* actions to a large extent.

162. The complete liberation from all terrestrial inclinations on this level of after-life existence results consequently in the encounter and permeation with the Holy Spirit, which will be discussed later on in this chapter.

163. Through the key words used by Rudolf Steiner for these two paths (the *urge* or driving force on the one side and on the other the *motive*), the unconscious component of action is placed in the foreground in the first case (hence the one that comes from the prenatal realm). In the second, the intention-linked and thus much more conscious component is emphasized, which for that reason determines man's life after death in particular. Obviously, actions carried out based on urges will likewise have consequences for the life after death; tendencies to certain motives of action can also originate from the life before birth. Still, Rudolf Steiner himself makes a clear distinction between both paths.

164. Here, the difference becomes evident between both paths that were mentioned in Chapter 1, paths that both lead to the same goal. In *The Philosophy of Freedom* the path of the conceptual intuition advances to action based on love. On the path of schooling in the sense of *Occult Science, an Outline*, the spirit-disciple arrives at Intuition as the highest stage of modern initiation only through spiritualization and conscious development of his or her faculty of love.

165. See concerning this activity of the hierarchies for example in the lectures of 25 May and 9 June 1924 (GA 239).

166. See more on this kind of karma in S. O. Prokofieff, *The Foundation Stone. A Key to the Christian Mysteries*, Chapter, 'The Foundation Stone Meditation and the Forming of Human Karma'.

167. Lecture of 1 May 1918 in Munich, 'Der übersinnliche Mensch und die Fragen der Willensfreiheit und Seelenunsterblichkeit nach Ergebnissen der Geisteswissenschaft' (Supersensible man and the questions of freedom of will and soul-immortality according to results from spiritual science), published in *Was in the Anthroposophischen Gesellschaft vorgeht* (What goes on in the Anthroposophical Society), in the seventeenth annual set 1940, No. 14 ff. (not yet published in the complete works [GA]).

168. See more in *May Human Beings Hear It!*, Chapter 'The Foundation Stone Meditation. Karma and Resurrection'.

169. In this regard Rudolf Steiner writes that 'in ideal intuition nothing but its own self-reliant being is active' (GA 4). For intuition itself he gives the following definition: '*Intuition* is the conscious experience of a purely spiritual content that takes its course in the purely spiritual' (emphasis by Rudolf Steiner). From this

follows that in *true* intuition nothing of human egoism can be contained any more. For any sort of egoism unavoidably bears within itself unspiritual elements that stem from the as yet not overcome dependency of the soul on the physical body.

170. In *Occult Science, an Outline,* Rudolf Steiner writes that on this highest stage of Intuition the Greater Guardian of the Threshold manifests today to the initiate as the Christ.

171. Rudolf Steiner often stresses the point that one requires the faculty of pure, that is to say, sense-free thinking for actual comprehension of spiritual-scientific contents.

172. In order to characterize this feature of love, Rudolf Steiner makes use of a metaphor in the lecture of 5 April 1912 (GA 136), namely a glass of water that becomes fuller the more a person pours out the water.

173. In the lecture 'Love and Its Meaning in the World' (GA 142, 17 December 1912), Rudolf Steiner therefore states: 'Spiritual science and true activities of love and deeds of love should be one and the same.' And such '*true* activities of love and deeds of love', meaning those that do not contain any element of egoism because they emerge out of pure moral intuition, are described in *The Philosophy of Freedom.*

174. From the inserted Diagram 23 on p. 147, one can moreover better understand an essential aspect of the Whitsun event at the Turning Point of Time in which the future union of *cosmic* love and *earthly* freedom were for the first time instilled (like a tendency) among human beings (the vertical arrows). For this reason Rudolf Steiner describes this event as the penetration of the disciples with the overall reigning power of cosmic love (GA 148, 2 October 1913) and at the same time calls Pentecost 'the festival of the free individuality'. (GA 118, 15 May 1910.) With that the humanity of the future, which has its beginning in our own time, is established as the coming Hierarchy of Freedom and Love.

175. The actual birth of the 'I' occurs around age 21. On the other hand, the first 'I'-manifestation appears as early as age three.

176. GA 118, 15 May 1910. These words are found in the lecture that Rudolf Steiner gave on a Whitsun Sunday under the title, 'Whitsun, the Festival of the Free Individuality'. In doing this, he brought together the pentecostal idea of freedom with the Christian teaching of reincarnation.

177. To the question posed in 1922 by Walter Johannes Stein in The Hague about what constituted Rudolf Steiner's main task, the latter tersely replied with the two words 'Reincarnation and karma'. (W. J. Stein/Rudolf Steiner, *Dokumentation eines wegweisenden Zusammenwirkens* (Documentation of a trail-blazing cooperation), Dornach 1985.

178. See Chapter 13.

179. See more detail in *May Human Beings Hear It!,* Chapter '*The Philosophy of Freedom* and the Christmas Conference'.

180. Looking back on the Christmas Conference, Rudolf Steiner reported in this regard that because of this conference 'the demons must be silent who earlier prevented one from expressing these matters [the truths of karma]'. (GA 240, 12 August 1924.)

181. Rudolf Steiner pointed out in many passages that there is no contradiction here. See for example GA 95, 8 August 1906; GA 99, 5 June 1907; GA 167, 16 May 1916; GA 235, 23 February 1924; and above all the cycle *Necessity and Freedom* (GA 166).

182. According to Rudolf Steiner, this takes place through the cooperation of the so-called Moon Teachers of Wisdom who participate in the further development of human karma in the Moon-sphere (see more on this in GA 236, 11 May 1924).

183. As Kant's young contemporary from the eighteenth to the nineteenth century, the individual who bore this inner impulse of freedom most strongly in his being was Friedrich Schiller. Following his initial enthusiasm for Kant, that is why he tried to refute him in this decisive point. He placed his 'free inclination' over against the Kantian imperative of duty. Schiller moreover recognized that in this free inclination lies the chief characteristic of Christianity that distinguishes it from both the other monotheistic religions. Schiller sums this up in the following words: 'If one studies the peculiar trait of Christianity that distinguishes it from all other monotheistic religions, this trait is found in none other than the abolishment of the Law or Kant's imperative, in the place of which Christianity wishes to place a free tendency.' (Letter to Goethe, 17 August 1795.) From this it follows that Schiller, who in his earlier incarnation absorbed the Christ Impulse in an especially intense manner into his being (see GA 239, 10 June 1924), then carried out the connection with his 'destiny-seed' consciously and freely.

184. The first reference to his philosophy of freedom is found in the letter of 22 July 1881 (GA 38).

185. See on this GA 26.

186. See the lecture of 14 April 1914 (GA 153).

187. See the lectures of 15 September 1922 (GA 215) and 19 November 1922 (GA 218).

188. Rudolf Steiner uses such a combination of the two names in the article 'The Michael-Christ experience of man' (GA 26, 2 November 1924).

189. See more in *May Human Beings Hear It!*, Chapter 'Rudolf Steiner's Course of Life in the Light of the Christmas Conference'.

190. Not until the end of his development—as descibed in this book in Chapter 9— will man be able to encompass the whole spiritual world with his higher consciousness.

191. Here, the Christ Impulse sees to it that the human being feels the starry world spiritually to be a *unity*; the Holy Spirit sees to it that man is allowed to experience that world in community with other human souls.

192. See more in S. O. Prokofieff, *The Occult Significance of Forgiveness*.

193. See more in *May Human Beings Hear It!*, Chapter 'Rudolf Steiner and the Karma of the Anthroposophical Society'.

194. See more in *May Human Beings Hear It!*, Chapter '*The Philosophy of Freedom* and the Christmas Conference'.

195. That the Rosicrucians became the guardians of the Holy Chalice is mentioned among other things by Rudolf Steiner in the lecture of 24 June 1909 (GA 112).

196. Rudolf Steiner mentions that the report by Chrestien de Troys about the Grail Mysteries is particularly accurate.

197. *May Human Beings Hear It!*, Chapter 'Rudolf Steiner's Course of Life in the Light of the Christmas Conference'.

198. Concerning the exercises given by Ignatius of Loyola, there are references in the first cycle, in the lecture of 5 October 1911 (GA 131), and in the second cycle in the lecture of 2 November 1918 (GA 185).

199. See on this in Prokofieff's *Valentin Tomberg and Anthroposophy*, Temple Lodge Publishing, 2005.

200. See more on Jesuitism in S. O. Prokofieff, *The Case of Valentin Tomberg. Anthroposophy or Jesuitism?*, Temple Lodge Publishing, 1997.

201. Rudolf Steiner had this lecture published in a second, rewritten version the same year as the second, supplemented edition of *The Philosophy of Freedom* (1918). In this new edition of his book, at the beginning of Chapter IX, he introduced the concept of the 'I' into the main text. That he refers here to the higher 'I' of man becomes obvious from the lecture given by him at the end of the same year. There he contrasts real 'I' with our earthly 'I' and designates the latter merely as the 'mirror image of the "I" ' (GA 187, 27 December 1918). Although in this lecture Rudolf Steiner uses the term true 'I' rather than the designation higher 'I', in other writings he likewise employs both designations synonymously (see for instance GA 113, 25 August 1909), something that attests to the inner working of the true 'I' through the higher 'I'. This is why such free usage of the concepts does not contradict their exacting and accurate differentiation and definition in the book *The Threshold of the Spiritual World* (GA 17).

202. Likewise, the twofold path that is depicted in Chapter IX can be understood as referring to the path from the lower to the higher 'I'. For it runs from the lower urges and pure egoism to pure thinking and conceptual intuitions.

203. Concerning the relationship between Schiller's 'Aesthetic Letters' to *The Philosophy of Freedom,* see further below in Chapter 16. Rudolf Steiner himself affirms his connecting to Schiller in regard to the idea of freedom as well as his continuing of Schiller's own thoughts about it in the following words: 'What it was that the German spiritual life strove for in Schiller, when he placed himself over against Kant and had some inkling of a concept of freedom [as was worked out later in *The Philosophy of Freedom*], makes it fitting for us further to develop it in the present time.' (GA 333, 19 December 1919.)

204. Lecture of 1 May 1918 in Munich, 'Der übersinnliche Mensch und die Fragen der Willensfreiheit und Seelenunsterblichkeit nach Ergebnissen der Geistes-wissenschaft' (Supersensible man and questions concerning freedom of will and immortality of the soul according to results of spiritual science) in *Was in der Anthroposophischen Gesellschaft vorgeht*, seventeenth annual edition, 1940, No. 14 ff. (not yet published in the GA (the collected works). The next quote is likewise from this lecture.

205. Friedrich Rittelmeyer, *Rudolf Steiner Enters My Life*, Floris Books, 1982.

206. In the Russian translation of the Bible, Sophia is designated as 'artist' (feminine noun-form) by God' (Prov. 8:30). And as the being of wisdom her artistry is above all to be viewed as the creative unfolding of the being of thought.

207. In this passage of the same lecture, Rudolf Steiner refers to the secret of the two paradisaical trees, the Tree of Knowledge and that of Life, and with that to the two Jesus figures.

208. As was presented in detail elsewhere, the first and second part of *The Philosophy of Freedom* led to this thought-light and love-substance of the Foundation Stone. See more in *May Human Beings Hear It!*, Chapter, '*The Philosophy of Freedom* and the Christmas Conference'.

209. In the lecture of 16 May 1920 (GA 201), Rudolf Steiner adds an impressive drawing to the corresponding passage in his explanations.

210. This corresponds to Rudolf Steiner's indication in the lecture of 27 August 1924 (GA 240), namely that the 'I' and Spirit Self of Christ were experienced most of all in the Grail-stream.

211. In this regard it is of vital significance that Parzival is the first who, in the sense of the modern initiation of the consciousness soul (see GA 144, 7 February 1913), entered the Grail castle the second time freely based on his own 'I'-initiative. This means he did so in accord with the saying of the Christ: 'From the days of John the Baptist, and even more now, the kingdom of heaven is found through the will; those who exert their will can freely grasp it.' (Matt. 11:12; JM.) In the epic by Wolfram von Eschenbach, the words that Trevrizent speaks to Parzival, after the latter has found the Grail for the second time, point to this: 'A greater miracle has hardly ever happened than this—that by sheer boldness you have obtained from God that his endless Trinity has made allowance to your will.'

212. Already in the eighth and ninth century, the spiritualization of the Michaelic Intelligence, which can begin in our Michaelic epoch, was prepared in the Grail Mysteries on earth. Rudolf Steiner refers to this in the following words: 'The Grail principle contained the aspiration to reckon with the fact that in the future intelligence would have to be found on the earth and that it no longer streams down from the heavens' (GA 240, 21 August 1924). Both descriptions (in the text and this note) shed light on the same process, but from different sides. For to lead the Michaelic Intelligence [which has become earthly and with that merely image-like] back to the Time Spirit, the human being must first raise this intelligence up into his pure thinking and there pervade it with the Christ-substance that alone can bestow on it the nature of reality. Only in this way can the now earthly earlier Michaelic Intelligence become such that Michael can take it back into his cosmic kingdom as a new foundation of conscious cooperative activity between human beings and the gods.

213. The discovery of the threefoldness of the human body belongs among the most remarkable results of Rudolf Steiner's research. He mentions it for the first time in the addendum of the book *Von Seelenrätseln* (Riddles of the soul) (GA 21). This threefoldness represents the archetype of the physical body that one needs in order to comprehend the nature of the Resurrection of the Christ in a spiritual-scientific sense. See *May Human Beings Hear It!*, Chapter 'The Foundation Stone Meditation. Karma and Resurrection'.

214. *May Human Beings Hear It!*, Chapter 'The Rhythms of the Christmas Conference'.

215. As was noted earlier elsewhere, here Rudolf Steiner uses the designation true 'I' merely as a synonym for the real 'I' and not in the sense it is used later in the book *The Threshold of the Spiritual World* (GA 17). See more above in Chapter 2.

216. See about the three egos of man in Chapter 1 and Addendum I.

217. S. O. Prokofieff, *Rudolf Steiner and the Founding of the New Mysteries*, Chapter 'The Michael Age and the New Grail Event'.

218. *May Human Beings Hear It!*, Chapter 'Rudolf Steiner's Course of Life in the Light of the Christmas Conference' and '*The Philosophy of Freedom* and the Christmas Conference'.

219. See GA 4, Chapter IX.

220. See in more detail in *May Human Beings Hear It!*, Chapter 'The Rhythms of the Christmas Conference'.

221. Lecture of 19 December 1919 (GA 333). Here, Rudolf Steiner speaks about the rudimentary stages of clairvoyance only in regard to moral intuition, but based on his other descriptions we can assume that this clairvoyance begins already with the exercise of moral imagination.

222. GA 210, 10 March 1922. Although in this passage Rudolf Steiner points to a similar relationship of the two poets regarding freedom, his other statements make it abundantly clear that in respect to *this* question Schiller was not only far ahead of Goethe but likewise ahead of his own and the entire following time. Rudolf Steiner points this out in the lecture entitled 'Schiller und die Gegenwart' (Schiller and the present age), with the words: 'The question of freedom likely arises in Schiller's soul as profoundly as it has never been posed and pondered in all of German cultural life' (GA 53, 4 May 1905).

223. See *May Human Beings Hear It!*, Chapter 'The Anthroposophical Society as the Temple of the New Mysteries'.

224. See S. O. Prokofieff: *Die Anthroposophische Gesellschaft und das Wesen Anthroposophia. Das Jahrhundertende und die Aufgaben der Anthroposophischen Gesellschaft* (The Anthroposophical Society and the being Anthroposophia. The turn of the century and the tasks of the Anthroposophical Society), Chapter II.

225. See more details in regard to Rudolf Steiner's life in S. O. Prokofieff, *Rudolf Steiner and the Founding of the New Mysteries*, Chapter: 'The Path of the Teacher of Humanity'.

226. The fact that the Foundation Stone was created out of the forces of the Trinity by no means contradicts the statement that at the same time it represents an absolute Creation out of Nothing. Precisely the above-mentioned characteristic of such a 'creation out of nothing' makes it evident that in so doing one always works creatively out of conditions or relationships (as is likewise true of moral imagination). As a modern initiate, Rudolf Steiner could arrive at such a relationship, such a connection with the Holy Trinity so that based on it the new creation became possible.

227. Here it may be called to mind once more that Rudolf Steiner designates 'moral imagination' in spiritual-scientific terminology also as 'imaginative moral impulses'. (See GA 193, 12 June 1919.)

228. *May Human Beings Hear It!*, Chapter '*The Philosophy of Freedom* and the Christmas Conference', and *The Foundation Stone. A Key to the Christian Mys-*

teries, Chapter 'The Merging of the Rosicrucian and the Michaelic Stream in the Foundation Stone Meditation'.

229. It is also significant that, immediately following these words, Rudolf Steiner points to the importance of his *Philosophy of Freedom* and in this context mentions 'pure thinking'.

230. Friedrich Schiller, *Sämtliche Werke*, in 5 Bänden (Complete works, in five volumes), Band V, p. 667, Carl Hansen Verlag, München 1989.

231. Concerning the Christmas Conference as the modern Whitsun event, see *Rudolf Steiner and The Founding of the New Mysteries*, Part III, 'Anthroposophy: The Proclamation of World Pentecost'.

232. These four elements also correspond to the four segments of the Foundation Stone Meditation in which the concluding fourth segment begins with the reference to the Light of the World Spirit.

233. For this reason, Rudolf Steiner indicates as the main condition for the Michael School on earth *the trust* (in each other) and (spirit of) unity among all true Michael-disciples. (See lecture of 30 January 1924 as well as Letter Four 'To the Members' in GA 260a.)

234. Concerning the nature of the Heavenly Sophia and her relationship to the being Anthroposophia, see S. O. Prokofieff, *The Heavenly Sophia and the Being Anthroposophia*.

235. See Chapter Four in this book. In esoteric Christianity, 'name' is linked with the Manas principle, thus likewise with the Holy Spirit.

236. GA 107, 17 June 1909.

237. Emphasis by Rudolf Steiner.

238. There are also publications in which the authors succeeded in building such a bridge. Among them are first of all the contributions by Karen Swassjan in *Urphenomene* (Archetypal Phenomena), Dornach 1995, and the book by Friedrich Husemann, *Rudolf Steiners Entwicklung* (Rudolf Steiner's Development), Dornach 1999.

239. See GA 15, Chapter III.

240. See *Rudolf Steiner and the Founding of the New Mysteries*, Chapter 'The Great Sun Period'.

241. During the Christmas Conference, Rudolf Steiner himself pointed out that spiritual science should not only be traced back to its beginning at the start of the twentieth century but furthermore to the publication of *The Philosophy of Freedom* (GA 260, 27 December 1923). This once again documents the direct relationship of this book with the essence of the Christmas Conference.

242. It is significant that Rudolf Steiner uses the term actual 'I' here, for the now quoted lecture was given the same year in which the second edition of *The Philosophy of Freedom* had been published in which, aside from many single supplements, he had moreover rewritten the whole beginning of the ninth chapter and had fitted in the expression 'actual "I"' into the new text. The fact that man's higher 'I' does not descend into his or her incarnation is also mentioned by Rudolf Steiner in the lectures of 19 December 1915 (GA 165) and 1 March 1917 (GA 66).

243. Many of the initiations in pre-Christian times were founded on such a con-

scious union with the higher or other 'I'. The figure of Krishna stands above all others like an archetype for what such a form of initiation is (see GA 146).

244. This third Sun was also called the 'Spiritual Sun' by Rudolf Steiner. It is 'the mediator of the highest spiritual forces that link the forces beyond the sun with those within the sun' (GA 266/3, 18 May 1913).

245. In the quoted esoteric lesson, Rudolf Steiner used a somewhat different terminology from the one in the book *The Threshold of the Spiritual World*, where for the first time he introduced the term 'true I' and accurately defined it in detail.

246. Rudolf Steiner speaks of the fact that the recognition of this esoteric stream of time 'is the condition for spiritual vision' (GA 262), something that is possible in modern initiation only through the awakening of the higher 'I'.

247. *May Human Beings Hear It!*, Chapter 'The Foundation Stone Meditation in Eurythmy. An Esoteric Contemplation'.

248. In the lecture of 28 March 1910 (GA 119), Rudolf Steiner also calls this spiritual domain 'world of archetypal images'.

249. Thus, following the union with his true 'I', Rudolf Steiner could in the same way raise his consciousness into the Buddhi sphere in order to assume the Bodhisattva-task from there. See on this *Rudolf Steiner and the Founding of the New Mysteries*, Chapter 'The Path of the Teacher of Humanity'.

250. To what was said it must be added here that in contrast to the Bodhisattvas who between their incarnations rise each time from earth into the Buddhi sphere, Christ himself descends from the opposite direction, meaning out of still highher spirit worlds into the Buddhi sphere (see GA 116, 25 October 1909). It follows from this that the actual origin of the true 'I' must be sought not in the Buddhi sphere but in yet higher worlds.

251. Rudolf Steiner speaks about the twelve world-views exhaustively in the cycle *Human and Cosmic Thought* (GA 151).

252. Rudolf Steiner speaks about the twelve images of the 'I' constituting 'a complete "I"' of the human being in the spiritual world in GA 119, 29 March 1910.

253. See a further aspect of these three developmental stages of man at the end of this Addendum.

254. See the motif of the columns on the northern green glass window of the First Goetheanum.

255. Instead of the higher 'I', one can therefore also speak of the 'I' here, because the shining forth of the higher 'I' in man's consciousness indicates that one's ordinary 'I' is being penetrated by the spiritual power of the higher 'I', whereby one can attain to the conscious experience of the Spirit.

256. See ibid. After Hiram had plunged into the Brazen Sea and had reached the centre of the earth, he received from Cain himself the golden triangle and the hammer for the future evolution of humanity. The latter symbolizes the creative force of the higher 'I'. For this reason, the god of the 'I'-force, Thor in Germanic mythology, possesses a hammer as his instrument and weapon. (See GA 121.)

257. See above all the lecture of 9 January 1912 (GA 130) as well as S. O. Prokofieff's *Die geistigen Aufgaben Mittel- und Osteuropas* (The spiritual tasks of Central and Eastern Europe), Dornach 1993.

258. Since Rudolf Steiner repeats the same thought twice in this paragraph, the possibility of an error in hearing, even in the case of somewhat abbreviated notes, is slight.

259. This is why Rudolf Steiner so often mentions that one important task of anthroposophy consists of the preparation of the sixth post-Atlantean cultural period. See for example GA 93, 4 November 1904; GA 93a, 5 November 1904; GA 94, 8 July 1906; GA 130, 3 December 1911; GA 159/160, 15 June 1915.

260. See S. O. Prokofieff, *Eternal Individuality. Towards a Karmic Biography of Novalis*, Chapter 'Christ and Sophia—the Mysteries of the Sixth Cultural Eoch'.

261. In many passages of his work Rudolf Steiner employs almost the same words for describing the birth of the higher 'I' in man.

262. *May Human Beings Hear It!*, Chapter 'Rudolf Steiner and the Karma of the Anthroposophical Society', and *The Occult Significance of Forgiveness*, Chapter 'The Manichaean Impulse in Rudolf Steiner's Life'.

263. This is why the luciferic beings became involved in humanity's evolution and caused the Fall. For the goal of their attack was man's astral body.

264. This process which Rudolf Steiner entitles the cosmic or sun-birth of the human 'I' is described by him in the lecture of 16 September 1924 (GA 346).

265. At the end of the same lecture, Rudolf Steiner mentions that in the sixth cultural epoch the Manas in man will receive the Buddhi principle into itself, the shining in of what can be characterized as the Christian concept of 'grace'.

266. Based on his spiritual research, Rudolf Steiner moreover reports on two still loftier Christ-revelations that will take place in the future (see GA 130, 17 September 1911). It follows from what was said here that they will be linked in the same sense with the dawning of the forces of Life Spirit and Spirit Man in the human soul as are the revelations of the Etheric Christ with the forces of the Spirit Self today.

267. This is why Rudolf Steiner characterizes the new clairvoyance through which human beings will behold the Etheric Christ as 'intellectual clairvoyance', which can be attained based on the transformation of thinking. (See GA 130, 18 November 1911 as well as Chapter 1 in this book.)

Works by Rudolf Steiner referred to

English titles of works by Rudolf Steiner are given only in cases where a similar (though not always identical) volume to the original German edition from the collected works—the *Gesamtausgabe* (abbreviated as 'GA')—has been published in English translation. In many cases lectures are available in typescript or in print as single lectures or compilations from the collected works. For information on these, contact Rudolf Steiner House Library, 35 Park Road, London NW1 6XT, or similar anthroposophical libraries around the world.

Publishers:

AP:	Anthroposophic Press/SteinerBooks (USA)
APC:	Anthroposophical Publishing Company (London)
RSP:	Rudolf Steiner Press (England)
SBC	Steiner Book Centre
TL:	Temple Lodge Publishing

Books

GA 1	*Goethe the Scientist* (AP); also published as *Nature's Open Secret* (AP)
GA 2	*The Theory of Knowledge Implicit in Goethe's World-Conception* (AP and RSP)
GA 3	*Truth and Science* (Mercury Press)
GA 4	*The Philosophy of Freedom* (RSP and AP)
GA 6	*Goethe's Conception of the World* (APC and AP)
GA 7	*Mystics After Modernism* (AP)
GA 8	*Christianity as Mystical Fact and the Mysteries of Antiquity* (RSP)
GA 9	*Theosophy* (RSP)
GA 10	*Knowledge of the Higher Worlds* (RSP; AP: *How to Know Higher Worlds*)
GA 12	*The Stages of Higher Knowledge* (AP)
GA 13	*Occult Science* (RSP; AP: *An Outline of Esoteric Science*)
GA 15	*The Spiritual Guidance of Humanity* (AP)
GA 16/17	*A Road to Self-Knowledge*, and *The Threshold of the Spiritual World* (RSP)
GA 21	*Von Seelenrätseln*. Extracts appear in *The Case for Anthroposophy* (RSP)
GA 25	*Philosophy, Cosmology and Religion* (AP)
GA 26	*Anthroposophical Leading Thoughts* (RSP)
GA 28	*The Course of My Life* (AP); *Autobiography*
GA 30	*Methodische Grundlagen der Anthroposophie. Gesammelte Aufsätze zur Philosophie, Naturwissenschaft, Ästhetik und Seelenkunde (1884–1901)*
GA 32	*Gesammelte Aufsätze zur Literatur (1884–1902)*
GA 35	*Philosophie und Anthroposophie* (Collected articles 1904–23)

Posthumous Publications

GA 39	*Briefe*, Vol. I, 1881–90
GA 40	*Wahrspruchworte (c. 1886–1925)*

Public Lectures

GA 53	*Ursprung und Ziel des Menschen. Grundbegriff der Geisteswissenschaft* (1904–05)
GA 66	*Geist und Stoff, Leben und Tod* (1917)
GA 74	*The Redemption of Thinking* (AP, 1961)
GA 78	*Anthroposophie, ihre Erkenntniswurzeln und Lebensfrüchte*

Lectures to Members of the Anthroposophical Society

GA 93	*The Temple Legend and the Golden Legend* (RSP)
GA 93a	*Foundations of Esotericism* (RSP)
GA 94	*Kosmogonie*
GA 95	*Founding a Science of the Spirit* (RSP)
GA 96	*Ursprungsimpulse der Geisteswissenschaft*
GA 97	*The Christian Mystery* (Completion Press)
GA 99	*Rosicrucian Wisdom* (RSP)
GA 100	*Menschheitsentwicklung und Christus-Erkenntnis*
GA 102	*The Influence of Spiritual Beings Upon Man* (AP)
GA 103	*The Gospel of John* (AP)
GA 104	*The Apocalypse of St John*
GA 105	*Universe, Earth and Man* (RSP)
GA 107	*Being of Man and His Future Evolution* (RSP)
GA 109	*The Principle of Spiritual Economy* (RSP and AP)
GA 110	*The Spiritual Hierarchies and their Reflection in the Physical World* (AP)
GA 112	*The Gospel of St John in Relation to the Other Three Gospels* (RSP and AP)
GA 113	*The East in the Light of the West* (RSP and AP)
GA 114	*Gospel of St Luke* (RSP)
GA 116	*The Christ-Impulse and the Development of Ego-Consciousness* (AP)
GA 118	*True Nature of the Second Coming* (RSP)
GA 123	*The Gospel of St Matthew* (RSP)
GA 126	*Occult History* (APC)
GA 130	*Esoteric Christianity and the Mission of Christian Rosenkreutz* (RSP)
GA 131	*From Jesus to Christ* (RSP)
GA 132	*The Inner Realities of Evolution* (RSP)
GA 133	*Earthly and Cosmic Man* (RSP)
GA 136	*The Spiritual Beings in the Heavenly Bodies and in the Kingdom of Nature* (RSP)
GA 142	*The Bhagavad Gita and the Epistles of Paul* (AP)
GA 143	*Erfahrungen des Übersinnlichen. Die drei Wege der Seele zu Christus*
GA 144	*The Mysteries of the East and of Christianity* (RSP)

GA 146   *The Occult Significance of the Bhagavad Gita* (AP)
GA 147   *The Secrets of the Threshold* (AP)
GA 148   *The Fifth Gospel* (RSP)
GA 151   *Human and Cosmic Thought* (RSP)
GA 152   *Vorstufen zum Mysterium von Golgatha*
GA 153   *Inner Nature of Man and the Life Between Death and a New Birth* (APC)
GA 155   *Christ and the Human Soul* (RSP)
GA 156   *Occult Reading and Occult Hearing* (RSP)
GA 157a   *The Forming of Destiny and Life after Death* (APC)
GA 159   *Das Geheimnis des Todes*
GA 165   *Die geistige Vereinigung der Menschheit durch den Christus-Impuls*
GA 166   *Notwendigkeit und Freiheit im Weltengeschehen und im menschlichen Handeln*
GA 167   *Gegenwärtiges und Vergangenes im Menschengeiste*
GA 175   *Bausteine zu einer Erkenntnis des Mysteriums von Golgatha*
GA 176   *Menschliche und menschheitliche Entwicklungswahrheiten. Das Karma des Materialismus*
GA 182   *Der Tod als Lebenswandlung*
GA 183   *Die Wissenschaft vom Werden des Menschen*
GA 184   *Die Polarität von Dauer und Entwicklung im Menschenleben*
GA 186   *Die soziale Grundforderung unserer Zeit—In geänderter Zietlage*
GA 187   *Wie kann die Menschheit den Christus wiederfinden? Das dreifache Schattendasein unserer Zeit und das neue Christus-Licht*
GA 188   *Der Goetheanismus, ein Umwandlungsimpuls und Auferstehungsgedanke. Menschenwissenschaft und Sozialwissenschaft*
GA 193   *The Inner Aspect of the Social Question* (RSP)
GA 194   *The Mission of the Archangel Michael* (AP)
GA 201   *Mystery of the Universe* (RSP)
GA 202   *Die Brücke zwischen der Weltgeistigkeit und dem Physischen des Menschen,* which includes four lectures available in English: *The Search for the New Isis*
GA 204   *Materialism and the Task of Anthroposophy* (AP)
GA 210   *Old and New Methods of Initiation* (RSP)
GA 211   *The Sun Mystery and the Mystery of Death and Resurrection* (AP)
GA 212   *The Human Soul in Relation to World Evolution*
GA 214   *The Mystery of the Trinity* (AP)
GA 215   *Philosophy, Cosmology and Religion* (AP)
GA 218   *Geistige Zusammenhänge in der Gestaltung des menschlichen Organismus*
GA 222   *The Driving Force of Spiritual Powers in World History* (AP)
GA 227   *The Evolution of Consciousness* (RSP)
GA 233   *World History in the Light of Anthroposophy* (RSP)
GA 233a   *Rosicrucianism and Modern Initiation and The Easter Festival* (RSP)
GA 235   *Karmic Relationships*—Vol. I (RSP)
GA 236   *Karmic Relationships*—Vol. II (RSP)
GA 237   *Karmic Relationships*—Vol. III (RSP)
GA 239   *Karmic Relationships*—Vol. V (RSP) and *Karmic Relationships*—Vol. VII (RSP)

GA 240   *Karmic Relationships*—Vol. VI (RSP) and *Karmic Relationships*—Vol. VIII (RSP)

GA 243   *True and False Paths in Spiritual Investigation* (RSP)

GA 257   *Awakening to Community* (AP)

GA 258   *The Anthroposophic Movement* (H. Collison)

GA 260   *The Christmas Conference for the Founding of the General Anthroposophical Society 1923/1924* (AP)

GA 260a   *Die Konstitution der Allgemeinen Anthroposophischen Gesellschaft imd der Freien Hochschule für Geisteswissenschaft. Der Wiederaufbau des Goetheanums*

GA 262   *Correspondences and Documents 1901–1925. Rudolf Steiner and Marie Steiner von Sievers* (RSP and AP)

GA 264   *From the History and Contents of the First Section of the Esoteric School 1904–1914* (AP)

GA 266/1   *Esoteric Lessons 1904–1914* (AP)

GA 266/3   *Aus den Inhalten der esoterischen Stunden*, Vol. III

GA 284   *Occult Signs and Symbols* (AP)

GA 333   *Gedankenfreiheit und soziale Kräfte. Die sozialen Forderungen der Gegenwart und ihre praktische Verwirklichung*

GA 335   *Die Krisis der Gegenwart und der Weg zum gesunden Denken*

GA 346   *The Book of Revelation and the Work of the Priest* (RSP)